DAVID SARNOFF

Books by Eugene Lyons

❧

DAVID SARNOFF: A Biography

HERBERT HOOVER: A Biography

OUR SECRET ALLIES: The Peoples of Russia

OUR UNKNOWN EX-PRESIDENT: A Portrait of Herbert Hoover

THE RED DECADE

STALIN, CZAR OF ALL THE RUSSIAS

ASSIGNMENT IN UTOPIA

WE COVER THE WORLD (editor)

MOSCOW CAROUSEL

SIX SOVIET PLAYS (editor)

LIFE AND DEATH OF SACCO AND VANZETTI

DAVID SARNOFF

A BIOGRAPHY BY

EUGENE LYONS

HARPER & ROW, PUBLISHERS

NEW YORK

LIBRARY OF CONGRESS CATALOG CARD NUMBER: 66–10632

D-Q

To my grandchildren

JULIE ANN AND DAVID LYONS HAIMES

CONTENTS

ℐ

ILLUSTRATIONS

அ

The following are grouped in a separate section after page 180.

David Sarnoff

Abraham and Leah Sarnoff, David's parents

David Sarnoff, aged 5, with his mother, in Uzlian, Russia

When he was delivering newspapers and working as a messenger boy

Sarnoff in 1907, when he was an office boy for the Marconi Wireless Telegraph Company of America

As wireless operator at the Marconi station at Siasconset

On the S.S. *Beothic,* in 1911

On duty at the radio station atop the Wanamaker store in New York, 1912

Sarnoff demonstrating RCA transoceanic station at New Brunswick, New Jersey, 1921

Guglielmo Marconi and Sarnoff in 1933

Sarnoff announcing the start of television broadcasting, at the New York World's Fair, 1939

President Roosevelt with the original members of the Fair Employment Practices Committee in 1941

David Sarnoff and Maestro Arturo Toscanini

A birthday greeting from Toscanini

Jo Davidson and his bust of David Sarnoff

Vice-President Lyndon B. Johnson and Senator Jacob Javits with Sarnoff in Washington, 1961

Lizette Sarnoff and the three sons, Robert, Thomas and Edward

Sarnoff in uniform

In a rare casual moment

DAVID SARNOFF

1

Success Story

The life of David Sarnoff has been cited times without number as a great—and typical—American success story. It has emerged, one might say, as the rags-to-riches classic of this period. Not because it is of greater magnitude than others of its kind but because it relates to the quintessential stuffs of our twentieth-century world—radio, television, communication satellites, the gadgetry of the electronic age.

These are among the things that have given the last sixty years their special character and Sarnoff, more than any other one man, has nourished and directed their unfolding. Thus he has probably affected the patterns of the daily lives of more Americans than anyone since Thomas Edison.

He has helped to shape and has been shaped by the technological age. This is true of hundreds, of course. But in Sarnoff's case the fact is invested with drama approaching melodrama by reason of his background. This authentic son of the twentieth century came to it from an almost medieval world. The man who for over half a century set the pace in the most modern reaches of science and technology came from a primitive soil and brought to his labors a mind suckled on the Old Testament and the Prophets.

David Sarnoff's career, said Dr. Karl T. Compton, then president of the Massachusetts Institute of Technology, "is material for one of the stories which, put together, constitutes the epic of America. It is a career which illustrates what can be accomplished when native ability, ambition, and character find scope in private enterprise in a land of opportunity." Myriad other such judgments could be quoted, all implying that Sarnoff represents a prototype, a conspicuous example of a familiar species.

1

But this seems to me a simplification that obscures and reduces the actuality. His success story is great, but it decidedly is not typical. Sarnoff—as an individual, not as a symbol of achievement against overwhelming odds—bears little resemblance to the conventional self-made industrialist, in either American literature or American life.

His origins, his personality, his deepest interests, the color of his mind would have baffled Sinclair Lewis's Babbitt, and they have, in fact, baffled many a standardized man of affairs who dealt with him through the decades. He doesn't conform to the pattern, in that he is not an extrovert, is not especially gregarious, and decidedly has not limited his companionship to men of business. In his circle of close friends there have been through the years a good many prominent financiers, industrialists and top executives, not only in electronics and communications but in unrelated fields. Their common bonds, however, have not been finance and business but shared enthusiasm for ideas, science, world affairs and, especially, a broadly philosophic approach to life.

Few of the scores who have written about David Sarnoff, or eulogized him on set occasions, have resisted the temptation of fitting him into the American folklore summed up by Horatio Alger. The analogy with an Alger hero is inescapable and it is true as far as it goes. Yet it falls short of the whole truth. For Sarnoff's is the kind of career Horatio Alger would have hesitated to dream up—it would have seemed too much even for *his* readers. Nor, for that matter, could he have conceived a hero so complex in character and motivation.

David was not only a slumland newsboy but an immigrant child, without a word of English at the outset. At a tender age he found himself suddenly in the immigrant ghetto of New York's Lower East Side, an enclave so far removed from the mainstream of American life that escaping it amounted to a second migration. The office boy who ends up as president of the company is standard American biographical fare. But Sarnoff became a lot more than that. He became, in a genuine sense, the president of a whole new industry that revolutionized the nation's quotidian life: the "administrative genius" of the electronic age, as one magazine writer put it, its architect and its prophet.

Moreover, his accomplishments would be measured least of all in wealth, which was the only yardstick Alger knew, first of all in impact on his times. The "rags" part of the legend is accurate, the "riches" part is not—unless we extend the word to compass the intangibles of prestige and power and inner satisfactions that do not appear on bank statements.

The dominant figure in a multibillion-dollar economic complex, Sarnoff did not remotely become a "tycoon" or "mogul" financially. Dozens of men—manufacturers, distributors, broadcasters, promoters—made vast fortunes in radio, television, and electronics, but Sarnoff was not among them. He has been simply a well-paid employee of a corporation who did not share in its profits—a manager, not an owner. The modest amounts of RCA stock he acquired during most of his life he bought out of savings, like any other small investor. As of 1942—when he was already the outstanding man in the industry—he owned only $25,000 in RCA stock, purchased at market prices.

In the prime of his career, Sarnoff continually had flattering offers from competitors and from other areas of the business world. He never even considered them seriously—with one exception. In the middle thirties the head of one of the country's most successful advertising agencies proposed that he give up the presidency of the Radio Corporation and become president of this firm—with a guarantee of at least a million dollars a year for five years. That did touch off a search of conscience and long discussions with Lizette, his wife. He was then drawing a relatively modest salary. Five million dollars in five years, as a minimum, was clearly more than Sarnoff at that juncture could hope to earn in a lifetime where he was. But in the end he turned down the invitation, and Lizette Sarnoff joined him in the decision.

He had, in one of his own favorite phrases, "hitched his wagon to the electron" and could not be diverted from its exciting course. His energies and emotions were too deeply committed, his mind too polarized, by a vision of the emerging electronic age, and he was convinced that the Radio Corporation was the best instrument for its realization—he himself its destined leader.

This is not to suggest that the man's acquisitive instincts were feeble, for they were robust enough. No one with his memory of extreme poverty could fail to have a healthy respect for money. But at critical junctures in his progress the prospect of wealth was invariably overshadowed by his creative drives. Money was among the motivations that fueled his career, but it was decidedly secondary. Far stronger, I believe, was the urge to achieve status as an American, a conscious determination to identify himself with his new environment.

Above all, however, he was impelled by the drama of a new industry aborning, the goad of new forces waiting to be unleashed, his acute awareness of things to come—things so much more clearly visible to him than to others in his milieu that it had some of the quality of revelation.

As I studied the data of his biography, the feeling grew that I was dealing not merely with an exceptionally able entrepreneur but with a dedicated creative craftsman, molding the raw stuffs of the electronic age in the way a sculptor molds his clay. Others before me, I found, had had this feeling. Dr. Gleason L. Archer, president of Suffolk University in Massachusetts, for instance. In a history of the radio industry he published in 1939, Dr. Archer recounted how Sarnoff, having recorded his prevision of network broadcasting in 1922, kept returning to the idea—"adding each time a bit of detail, even as an artist might return from time to time to an unfinished picture to sketch in some new feature, adding a light here, a shadow there, until the entire artistic conception could stand forth in completeness."

Sarnoff himself was conscious of this inner process. "I do not think that a man, any man, begins to reach for the stars or the moon," he said once, "simply because he makes up his mind to do so. He cannot do otherwise. In a real sense, he cannot stop himself." Obviously this was subjective, an allusion to the creative ferments and urges governing his decisions.

With a man like Sarnoff what looks from the outside like naked ambition, the pursuit of personal success, is incidental to the pursuit of perfection. "You can get happiness and serenity," he explained on another occasion, even "at the lower end of the ladder." But "you cannot enjoy the ecstasy of achievement." Ecstasy—an emotion that seems out of place in the stereotyped success story and surely would have embarrassed Mr. Babbitt.

2

Every industry has its hardheaded businessmen and its dreamers, the pragmatic and the imaginative, for a balance between prudent policies and "visionary" impulses. Electronics has had both types in a single leader. "David," Owen D. Young once declared, "has that rare combination of permitting his head to be in the clouds and keeping his feet on the ground." It is the continuous interplay of the two Sarnoffs in one package that has given his life some of its unique quality.

Millionaires who got that way by capitalizing on some existing product or need—steel, rails, oil, aviation, radio itself for that matter—are familiar in the American economy. What sets Sarnoff aside from the clan of self-made industrialists is that he has helped create the things and the needs he worked with, and that he has been more fascinated by the creative than the money-making aspects of his dual role.

In 1963, addressing the personnel at the David Sarnoff Research Center in Princeton, New Jersey, he alluded to a businessman who had fought long and passionately to block the advent of television and who, upon his death, left "only about twenty or thirty million dollars—most of which he made in television." This was not the first time Sarnoff, quite understandably, had spoken with some asperity of individuals who made fortunes in a field to which they contributed little and the progress of which, in some instances, they had even impeded. His private pantheon of industrial heroes includes the great pioneers in oil, rails, steel, telegraphy, and other basic industries. But it has no niches for those who followed the pioneers, stayed long enough to accumulate millions, then walked out. He has drawn a clear line between the creators and the manipulators.

In his refusal to accept money as the primary test of achievement and in many other respects, all related to his personality and character, Sarnoff repudiated the clichés of our national folklore. He could never be described as a "typical businessman." Always he was more at home among intellectuals, musicians, political thinkers than, let us say, at a Rotary or Lions' Club meeting. He has never played golf or poker or developed other of the common stigmata of the typical American executive. One cannot even imagine him in a convivial elbow-lifting group.

His obsessive concerns have been technological and sociological. Often his board of directors, gathered to discuss dollars-and-cents problems, has been treated by Sarnoff to an unscheduled dissertation on the state of the world, the plight of mankind, the course of the cold war, or some other large theme far removed from the workaday interests of his audience. Many of these men also served on other business boards but only at RCA did they run the risk of extracurricular political discussion and philosophic digressions.

Stockholders convened at annual meetings, too, were likely to be given, along with statistics on RCA business, previews of tomorrow. They have been treated to impromptu estimates of the equation of war and peace, the social and economic revolutions implicit in computers, or the effects of orbited communication satellites on the future of network broadcasting.

Whether those in the captive audiences enjoyed the display or not, they could not reasonably complain of its quality. For Sarnoff, when the mood is upon him, is remarkably lucid and eloquent. He brings to his subject, besides, that fillip of passion some men reserve for disquisitions on baseball or heavyweight prizefights.

Those who know him best are familiar with his zest for talk and debate. In a small company the conversation might begin with the weather or the current movie, but usually Sarnoff manages to steer it into serious discussion of our military posture, the East-West conflict, or some other matter that happens to be on his mind. The more opposition his views provoke the more he seems to relish the ensuing argument.

At best, his conversation is so articulate, so logically organized, that it could be put into print with little editing. A prolific public speaker, his prepared, formal speeches have been models of clarity. In later years, as his schedule grew too heavy for the luxury of purely personal composition, he has had the help of a staff in researching and preparing the more important addresses. But the end product, usually after he has worked over a dozen or more drafts, always bears the stamp of his mind and style.

Some of his most effective speeches have been extemporaneous. During the week of his seventy-fourth birthday, Sarnoff was the "Special Guest," as the printed program put it, at a dinner in Hollywood, Florida, given by the Jewish Theological Seminary. A thousand or more guests filled the Diplomat Hotel ballroom. He had expected only to say a few polite words in acknowledgment of the honor. The postprandial oratory, however, developed in such a way that he was prompted to make a fairly long address. Through entirely off the cuff, it had as much substance and a lot more wit than his carefully prefabricated speeches.

Fortunately, given his makeup, fate propelled Sarnoff into an art and industry with tentacles and feelers in all of life and all the world's affairs. In most callings time operates to limit and confine men; they are likely to become ever more expert in their specialized fields and alienated from other things. But radio and television are coextensive with the whole of science, education, the arts; sensitive to national and international events; in continuous communication with the whole world. Being at once instruments of entertainment and news, culture and education, and the leading advertising medium as well, there is literally no department of life on which they do not impinge.

Its variety of impact, indeed, is a crucial part of the fascination that "the electron" has exercised on Sarnoff. It has given him scope for the expression of a many-sided personality and a universal curiosity. *Fortune,* a magazine of business, was alluding to this when it wrote that the head of RCA "is a whole cast of characters—the *dramatis personae* of a long play about business." The cast, it suggested, included a philosopher and a prophet. His bulging collection of academic degrees (as of late 1965 the score stands at twenty-four), awards, medals, official citations reflects the multiplicity of his interests, since in the main they came to him from organizations and institutions not directly related to his business.

The range of his activities, however, does not diminish the fact that Sarnoff's principal handiwork has been the Radio Corporation of America. With the possible exception of the Ford Motor Company, no gigantic American corporation is to a comparable degree the creation of one man. He visualized the organization as it was to become—strong, integrated, independent of outside control—from the beginning, when others saw it only as a limited accessory to the electric industry. Then he went on systematically to make his vision come true. There are extremely few top-rank American corporations which have been under the active control of the same man for such a long period.

The extraordinary fact, as we shall see, is that he was engaged in molding and guiding the company—and through it the entire new industry—even in years before he became president, which is to say long before he held any mandate or explicit authority for these purposes.

Sarnoff steers clear of the word "empire" as applied to RCA. It has overtones of monopoly and he has had too much grief from antitrust suits to encourage the concept. But an empire, nonetheless, is what he rules. At this writing, in his seventy-fifth year, he directs the greatest electronics complex in the world. Owned by some 240,000 stockholders, it does close to two billion dollars of business a year and employs close to one hundred thousand men and women. It holds primacy or is an important factor not only in radio and television but in phonograph records, sound films, automation, computers, the proliferating hardware of the new space age: rockets, missiles, earth-orbiting satellites. And most important from Sarnoff's own vantage point, numberless wonders of electronics yet unborn are incubating in RCA laboratories.

The Radio Corporation manufactures products ranging from tiny transistors to rocket-launching apparatus. This productivity is centered in some thirty American and thirteen foreign plants. RCA Communications, with over eighty radio-telegraph circuits, covers the whole world and carries an estimated two hundred million words—the equivalent of two thousand full-sized books—annually. The corporation controls an array of subsidiaries ranging from the National Broadcasting Company to RCA Institutes.

From his deceptively hushed and relaxed offices on the fifty-third floor of the RCA Building in Rockefeller Center, David Sarnoff can look out upon the sprawling metropolis to which he came as a bewildered little foreigner in 1900. As he sits at his immaculate desk, with instruments at his fingertips for immediate communication with the whole world, his mind is on other things than his own career. But sometimes he must pause to marvel at the incredible distance he has covered in the intervening years.

3

In the symphony of Sarnoff's life the dominant motif, an insistent drumbeat even under its most lyrical passages, has been struggle. Nothing came to him easily or uncontested. Almost always he faced opposition, skepticism, road-blocks, sometimes the guerrilla warfare of garden-variety racial prejudice. Victory in one engagement was usually the prelude to another, without a breathing space. Often he was fighting many battles simultaneously.

In the beginning there was the grim struggle for bread and a roof for himself and his family. A small boy, a "greenhorn," a bit undersized even for his ten or eleven years, he was up against tough-as-nails newsboys on Manhattan's Lower East Side. Then, in the Hell's Kitchen district on the West Side, running a newsstand as if he were a grown man, he was a natural target for the mischief of the toughest breed of juveniles in the city in those days.

In both the Marconi Company and its successor, the Radio Corporation, the bright-eyed David seemed at first an outsider, almost an interloper. His extreme youth and irrepressible dynamism at times went against the grain of mature, conservative men who were his bosses and associates. He must have appeared too eager, too confident, too intrusive for his years and station. He could have been under no illusions that he was liked by everyone around him.

Of course, he soon made strong friends among them, but he was also the object of envy, malice, and even plots to get him out. Especially was this true in the initial RCA years. He had been taken over from Marconi along with its files and furniture. As his stature grew he was resented by some of the older, more seasoned officials who had regarded his presence as temporary.

The memoranda with which he pelted his superiors eventually made a legend of perspicacity. But at the time, however meekly he might couch his suggestions, they implied criticism, and this frequently in technical and business matters outside his prescribed field of operation. Again and again he took positions contrary to accepted opinions in the shop. Had he been proved outrageously wrong he might have been forgiven, but when he was repeatedly proved right, it was too much of a strain on normal human tolerance. To make matters worse, he could not always take No for an answer but kept returning to his pet ideas at intervals after they had been rejected. He had little capacity for compromise on those things that truly mattered to him.

Even after he was too entrenched to fear for his job, struggle remained his portion, now in a larger arena for larger stakes. He fought against pervasive indifference to his intuitive certainty that short-wave radio was the answer to transoceanic telegraphy and telephony; then to his concept of coast-to-coast network broadcasting, eventually embodied in the National Broadcasting Company. In both instances his planning ran years ahead of the current capabilities of science and invention; perhaps those in authority cannot be blamed for being a bit annoyed by the overimaginative and persistent mind in their midst.

At the same time, throughout the 1920's and into the thirties, Sarnoff conducted his patient but relentless war to win for the Radio Corporation the full scope of manufacture and research without which, he was convinced, the company would remain a secondary and hamstrung entity. In this he was challenging the built-in contractual prerogatives of the electric titans, General Electric and Westinghouse—though they had the power, through their control of RCA, to fire him without notice.

Far from being ended when he became president, struggle was merely raised to higher, more demanding levels. In this again the folklore of success went awry. The Alger hero, once at the top of the ladder, lives in opulence and ease ever after. But Sarnoff's most trying and momentous battles were still to come. They made headlines and headaches and history. Few envied him his new job, since its acquisition coincided with the collapse of the American and world economy in unprecedented depression. As if this were not enough, the government, within months after Sarnoff assumed the presidency, filed an all-out antitrust suit against RCA and its electric associates. More than two years of nerve-racking struggle went into averting this threat to the survival of the company he had so recently unified.

Despite these piled-up troubles, Sarnoff took on what was perhaps the greatest fight of his career, long, bitter, costly, and conducted against the overwhelming opposition of his own industry. In seeming contempt of the depression and the obvious need for retrenchment, he chose to push the development and commercial introduction of television, at an ultimate cost to RCA of some $50 million! It was mostly a lonely war he fought. The hostility churned up by his subsequent fight for color television was almost as intense. At Sarnoff's insistence RCA was to spend $130 million on color before it saw any cash returns. Eventually he won this war too.

These are only highlights in a story of continuous struggle. It became for him almost a way of life. In the process he gained a reputation as a prophet, but like prophets through the ages he was obstructed and ridiculed by those whom he would lead—or drive—to his promised land.

During the larger part of his business life Sarnoff found himself committed to objectives which others considered "impossible," though in time each item in turn became commonplace. Repeatedly he staked immense sums as well as his career on the emerging future as he conceived it, dim and unconvincing as it might look to others. And there were few, particularly in the earlier battles, to whom he could turn for counsel. For he was in a field so new, so lacking in experience and precedent, that counsel was hard to come by. Whether it was a "harebrained" Music Box or the gamble that science would produce all-electronic color, he had to rely in the final analysis on his own judgment.

4

Every biography, it has been said, is also an autobiography, in that it reveals a lot about the author. In the present case this is to some extent *literally* true. The writer and his subject are first cousins. David Sarnoff's mother was the eldest of eight sisters, mine the second eldest. I was still a schoolboy when David was already cutting a swath in the mysterious world of wireless telegraphy, his name ever more often in the newspapers and his face in the newsreels. His growing importance naturally impressed our multitudinous family long before it registered on the national mind. We were proud and awed and we basked in his reflected glory.

The blood tie has given me some obvious advantages. Having followed the Sarnoff career, in its larger outlines, all my life, I started with direct knowledge of many things that another biographer could have learned, if at all, only by the sweat of research. On the other hand, it imposes the serious disadvantage that it may open the book to the suspicion of nepotic bias. A conscientious writer, in undertaking a biography of someone he admires, needs to guard himself against making the portrait too bright, too eulogistic. In the present instance, because of the family relationship, this is especially necessary.

Therefore, I have searched diligently for "shadows" that would help make Sarnoff more human and credible. I found a good many, of course, and will try to weave them into the narrative. Yet the quest has not been too productive. If there are in Sarnoff's life any great scandals and blunders, I was not successful in turning them up. I could not, alas, discover a single spectacular failure to match the many spectacular successes. He had his share of defeats but they were never big or significant enough to match his victories. There was no dearth of "negative" facts and opinions but somehow they seemed trivial in the sum-total of the man's life. Even the most hostile critics stopped short of impugning his essential probity and integrity.

David Sarnoff is neither a superman nor a paragon of virtue. Although the word in its devalued journalistic usage has been applied to him innumerable times, he is not in the stricter dictionary sense a "genius." Suffice that he has a first-rate mind, is supernally able and energetic, and is endowed with imagination and moral courage of a high order. These qualities he has brought to bear for sixty years not only in his specialized field but in the service of his country in peace and in war. Beyond most men in business and industry, he has been immersed in the larger problems of his times and under inner pressures to help solve them.

Like all men, he has his quota of flaws in character and personality. In a long lifetime he has accumulated enemies as well as friends. He has been accused, on the one hand, of being "tough" and "hard-boiled" in driving to his goals and dealing with people; and, on the other, of being blind to the weaknesses of those whom he likes and admires. Such judgments, of course, are highly subjective. His exceptional self-confidence, for instance, is regarded as one of his strongest characteristics by admirers and as plain vanity by others. Similarly his faith in his own judgments, often against prevailing opinion, has been hailed as intellectual power by some, as intellectual arrogance by others. Certainly Sarnoff has never underrated his own abilities. Speaking of the electronics industry he once said: "In a big ship sailing an uncharted sea one fellow needs to be on the bridge. I happen to be that fellow."

For the rest, the strictures I collected were variations on the theme that he has been less astute in business than is generally supposed. RCA was not the first to broadcast nor the first to sell radio sets. In both manufacturing and broadcasting, at various times, it made less money than its nearest competitors.

This kind of criticism was summed up by a writer in *Fortune* in 1948. He gave RCA full marks for pioneering and frontier-breaking, "but when it comes to the marketplace to peddle its wares it has often been outscored by its rivals. As any common shareholder can testify, RCA sows better than it reaps." By way of accounting for the long intervals when the corporation's earnings were being devoured by research, he added: "There is nothing spurious about Mr. Sarnoff's somewhat missionary approach to the science of electronics. His chief pride is that RCA has been a creative and constructive force. He waits to follow the light of electronics wherever it may lead."

To an outsider, concerned with Sarnoff's total influence on his times, his rating as a businessman, one way or the other, seems somewhat irrelevant if not carping. His place in the economic-technological history of this century assuredly will not be sought or found on a dividends graph. The imputation that money-making held a secondary place in his personal priorities of interests may, indeed, enhance his stature.

Probably no industrial leader in our times has been as extensively reported upon in the press. For one American who could name the head of, let us say, the American Telephone Company or General Electric, a hundred are likely to know the head of RCA. In the electronics world there is not one practitioner with even a remotely valid claim to equality in leadership with Sarnoff. Recently a columnist who once specialized in writing about radio referred to him as "the great maharajah of communications." Though the accent was ironical, the phrase does reflect the public image of the man.

For decades, to be sure, an efficient public relations department, such as every big corporation has, has been busy extolling both the company and its boss. But few image builders have had a subject so congenial to their skills, such magnificent materials to work with. Sarnoff's life, as one of them put it to me, "has been pure theatre. We don't have to invent a thing, but just play up the true drama of his career." After all discounts are made for exaggeration and myth-making, therefore, there still remain an extraordinary human being and an extraordinary life.

This is the man, this is the decidedly untypical success story, I propose to deal with in the pages that follow.

2

Twin of the Electron

It is all but impossible to fix the precise time of the birth of any invention in the scientific realm. Wireless communication is no exception in this respect. Any significant date selected—the announcement of some key discovery, the filing of a basic patent, transmission of signals over a notable distance—is necessarily arbitrary.

Centuries of experiments with the mysterious phenomena of magnetism and electricity prepared the ground. The immediate progenitors of the electron, to quote Dr. Karl T. Compton, "were the electromagnetic theory of light, spectroscopy and the leakage of electricity through gases. First cousins were X-rays and radioactivity and the quantum theory."

The long road to modern radio is marked, to mention a few at random, by names like Sir Roger Bacon in the early seventeenth century; Benjamin Franklin and the Italian Alessandro Volta in the eighteenth; Joseph Henry, Michael Faraday, Sir Oliver Lodge in the nineteenth.

In 1719 a Dutch scientist "bottled" electricity in his Leyden jar, precursor of today's condenser. In 1774 Volta immortalized his name in the word "volts" by devising the first crude battery producing a continuous flow of electricity in one direction. Faraday, an Englishman, discovered the principles of electrical induction in 1831. In the later 1880's a Scottish savant, James Clerk Maxwell, proved by mathematical analysis that electromagnetic waves should exist and that they should travel at the speed of light.

Actually, when we stop to think about it, the transmission of sound *without* wires predates the wired variety. What else is the beating out of messages on drums in the jungle or, for that matter, ordinary face-to-face conversation? The problem that fascinated generations of experimenters was how to extend the distance of transmission far beyond the reach of voice or tom-tom or gunshot, and the solution, many of them were convinced, lay in somehow harnessing electricity to carry the signals through space.

Many attempts were made in the United States, as in other countries, in the middle years of the nineteenth century to transmit electric-spark signals between widely separated points. In 1842 Samuel Morse, the inventor of wire telegraphy, succeeded in sending intelligible wireless signals across broad rivers, and others later performed the same feat. Ever since the advent of telegraphy it has been known that the presence of electric current magnetizes metallic objects at some distance. An American scientist, Dr. Joseph Henry, was able in 1843 to magnetize needles placed 220 feet from current-carrying wires.

Here were tantalizing portents of electrical effects across "empty space." In 1882 a Professor Dolbear of Harvard was granted a patent on an apparatus for communicating electrically without wires. But his method, like all these experiments, was based on electrical induction rather than the electric (more precisely, electromagnetic) waves which in due course yielded the true answers.

More and more devices for producing and detecting those waves raised hopes and encouraged research. Myriad insights and techniques, some of them not obviously relevant to the radio arts aborning, provided the essential ingredients. Then came the time of ripeness, the years when many gifted men in all parts of the civilized world began to put together the bits and pieces, the flashes of intuition and lucky accidents, to make the first patterns of practical operation. The climactic period, when it is fair to say that modern wireless telegraphy finally came into being, was the last decade of the nineteenth century.

And it was in the first year of that decade, on February 27, 1891, that David Sarnoff was born. On the basis of this coincidence someone wrote, in the years of his growing fame, when his name was fast becoming a synonym for radio and electronic progress, that David Sarnoff and the electron were "twins." The rhetorical fancy caught on and became a favorite with his biographers and eulogists ever after.

February of 1891:

Only four years before, in Germany, a young scientist named Heinrich Hertz had finally devised crude apparatus for producing and detecting electromagnetic waves, thereafter called Hertzian waves. They became the object of eager experimenting the world over. The dream of projecting sound through space seemed at last within grasp and those obsessed with it, in formal and makeshift laboratories, stepped up the pace of their eager tinkering.

In France, about the time of Sarnoff's birth, Professor Édouard Branly had just perfected an appliance for picking up wireless impulses, soon renowned as the Branly Coherer. In England, in 1892, Sir William Crookes proved the theoretical feasibility of "telegraphy through space" in an article in the *Fortnightly Review,* adding impetus to the search for the missing links that would turn the theory into practice. Sir Oliver Lodge, active in many fields of scientific inquiry, was also caught up by the surge of interest in wireless, concentrating on tuning devices for specific wave lengths. In the United States, Thomas Edison in 1895 patented a system of induction telegraphy which embodied elements later useful to wireless communication.

Most importantly, in the light of history, was the research being carried on—in the year and presumably on the very day Sarnoff was born—by a seventeen-year-old Irish-Italian lad named Guglielmo Marconi. In his father's vegetable garden outside Bologna he was busily experimenting with the freshly discovered potentials of electromagnetic waves. Strange plants grew in that garden to intrigue neighbors and perhaps to alarm the youngster's family. These were tall poles, with wire strung along them, the lower end connected with the ground; dangling from arms atop the pole, like the fringes of a lampshade, were hundreds of short wires.

Marconi's search bore fruit, in 1895, in his confirmation of the principle of the antenna, or "aerial," and the importance of a ground connection to complete a transmitting and receiving system. A year later he betook himself to London, where the British Post Office provided him with facilities for further testing. In 1896 the twenty-two-year-old inventor was granted the first patent ever issued for wireless telegraphy by electromagnetic waves.

To exploit this and related patents commercially, the Wireless Telegraph and Signal Company, Ltd.—soon renamed Marconi Wireless Telegraph Company, to take advantage of his spreading celebrity—was chartered in 1897. That was the year, too, when the electron was identified, though its discoverer, J. J. Thomson, called it a "corpuscle." Before the turn of the century the Marconi Wireless Telegraph Company of America, a subsidiary of the British corporation, was chartered.

On New Year's Day of 1898 the indefatigable inventor succeeded in sending and receiving electromagnetic signals over a distance of eighteen miles. Eleven months later, in tests on the American side of the Atlantic with the cooperation of the U.S. Navy, he expanded the distance to a thrilling thirty-six miles.

Off the coast of England, near Dover, in 1899, a ship in distress was able to summon aid because it happened to have an experimental Marconi installation. The episode was widely reported, and it dramatized the first and what was to remain for a long time the primary use of wireless: for ship-to-shore and ship-to-ship communication.

The clinching demonstration of the new force came when Marconi was able to pluck a signal—the three dots of the letter "S" in Morse Code—from the air across two thousand miles of ocean. The test was prepared and conducted in great secrecy, for fear of initial failure. But on a December day in 1901, only a year after the boy Sarnoff had been brought to the United States, Marconi scored his greatest triumph. Standing on a hill in St. John's, Newfoundland, using a balloon to hold his aerial aloft, he picked up the agreed-upon letter. The signal had been sent from Poldhu, on the coast of Cornwall. The achievement was revealed to the press, then duly repeated with witnesses to convince doubters, and established Marconi's fame for all time.

Though the young Marconi was the first in the field, many other scientists were making vital discoveries, some of them not too unlike his own. Inevitably there were those who challenged his primacy. But Marconi's leadership, patents and legalities aside, was quickly confirmed by more and more evidences of his genius.

There were in that early company of pioneers, to name just a few, a Professor Alexander Popoff in Kronstadt, Russia—whose work provided the excuse for Soviet claims half a century later that radio was a Russian invention; Professor Ferdinand Braun in Germany; the youthful Reginald A. Fessenden and the even younger Dr. Lee De Forest in the United States. This aside from the legion of enthralled amateurs fumbling with the elements of the newborn science on homemade apparatus in every civilized land.

All these men and boys were tapping out destiny for the boy born in the second month of that decade so decisive for wireless. In the perspective of time we know today that his advent was among the most important events in the history of electronic communications.

2

Considering what life had in store for him, the place of Sarnoff's birth could scarcely have been less logical, less auspicious, and therefore more humanly dramatic. For it was a hamlet so backward and stagnant, so remote from the burgeoning modern world of science, invention, and industry, that it might have been on the dark side of the moon.

Uzlian, inhabited by several hundred Jewish families, lay deep in the Russian province of Minsk. It was the kind of forsaken corner described by the great Yiddish storyteller Sholem Alcichem: a ragged remnant of the Middle Ages steeped in poverty and piety. Recently audiences in New York have had a romanticized glimpse of such a *shtetl* (small town) in the hit musical *Fiddler on the Roof,* based on Sholem Aleichem characters. Uzlian was, if anything, a few shades more primitive.

It amounted to little more than a jumble of wooden houses, weary and discolored by great age, deployed unevenly along a few straggling and rutted streets and paths. Many of these houses had earthen floors; a wood floor, in fact, was a sign of comparative affluence. The streets were ankle-deep in mud part of the year, barriers of ice and snow in the long, harsh Russian winters.

The life of the hamlet was backward and ingrown, with the world beyond a blur of fantastic and incredible rumors. Like all such settlements in the Pale—the area delimited by the Czar's government for millions of its second-class Jewish citizens—it eked out a bitter and juiceless living by home crafts and petty trade with the surrounding peasant villages. Few of its inhabitants had ever seen a train or a ship, an electric light or a telephone; the few crude phonographs in better-to-do homes were treated as miracles.

But Uzlianers, for all the bleakness and isolation, had pride of place, tradition, deep roots. Most families had lived there for centuries, as attested by inscriptions in the jungle of tumbled headstones of the ancient cemetery. Above all, they were the Chosen People, custodians of God's Law, merely waiting patiently for the Messiah, never doubting that the more humble their station on earth—provided that they lived as "good Jews"—the more exalted the place in heaven that awaited them.

The center of Uzlian's life, of course, was the house of worship. In temporal no less than in religious affairs the highest authority was the rabbi; and his wife, the *rebetsin,* outranked all others among the women. Except in taxes, military service, and a few other matters, the *shtetl* was self-governing. But it neither had nor needed policemen—public opinion, a strong sense of community, took the place of coercion in enforcing the law as laid down by the rabbi and the most respected citizens.

Uzlian had a long-abandoned "old" synagogue, possibly dating back to the time of the Crusades, and little boys like David explored it in shivery but fascinated awe. A dank and dusty place it was, filled with darkness even in the daytime. Great canopies of cobwebs hung from vaulted ceilings and bats like flying rats sent chills down their backs. Boys also explored the old cemetery, trying to make out names and Hebraic dates on moss-grown, eroded tombstones. The more venturesome splashed, a few even swam, in a muddy pond far outside the hamlet.

But mostly life was too earnest for such indulgences. A boy went to the *kheder,* the Hebrew school, at the age of four or even younger. His day began early and lasted into the late evening, so that a lantern, usually homemade, with oiled paper for windows, was part of the *kheder*-boy's winter equipment.

Because they lived by the Book, many of Uzlian's people knew the prophecy in Job: "Canst thou send forth lightnings, that they may go and say unto thee: 'Here we are'?" But had anyone suggested that man-made sounds might actually be carried by lightning waves, he would have been adjudged insane and, what was far worse in that place, blasphemous. Tampering with God's Nature was not for mortal man.

In reminiscing about his earliest childhood, David Sarnoff would often use the word "Uzlian" as shorthand for his humble beginnings, for the morass of ignorance and wretchedness and isolation from which he had emerged. But there would be on his tongue no trace of condescension or contempt. He knew that whatever else his birthplace may have been, it was not contemptible.

Its people were hard-working, abstemious, innocent of evil, and dedicated to the accumulation of *mitzvahs*—good deeds inscribed in God's books. Among the 613 *mitzvahs* listed by ancient rabbis in the holy books, learning led all the rest—meaning, of course, sacred learning. Illiteracy, the inability to read the Bible and the prayer book, was accounted not just a shame but a sin. Secular education, if not exactly taboo, was suspect as worldly. The occasional "enlightened" teacher who instructed his boys to read and write Russian as well as Hebrew and Yiddish was looked at askance.

Ranking only below learning was charity. To turn away a hungry man or woman when you had bread to share was considered so sinful that few would do it. In times of sickness and trouble, neighbors would as a matter of course rally to help a stricken family. Life might be hard and its pleasures meager, but it was attuned to righteousness, the rewards of which, to be garnered in the shining Hereafter, surely were not to be despised.

Within the narrow limits of their centuries-old isolation these people were wise too, with the primordial wisdom of the weak and the persecuted. Their talents for survival were of necessity highly developed. An ability to take hardships in stride, to accept obstacles as in the nature of man's portion on earth, was part of little David's heritage.

Above all, in places like Uzlian, social status was based on neither money nor physical prowess but on education and goodness. Should a penniless Talmudic student marry the richest girl in town, it would be obvious to the community that the wealthy family was getting the better of the bargain. What people coveted most was *koved,* honor. And this did not come to a rich man unless he was also pious and charitable, especially in supporting the synagogue and needy students.

Thus the Privins, though they possessed only a big dilapidated house and had known the taste of destitution for generations, rated among the best families. Their line boasted rabbis and *shokhtim* (ritual slaughterers) and preachers, impoverished all but rich in piety and holy knowledge.

Indeed, Shmuel (Samuel) Privin, David's maternal grandfather, practiced learning for learning's sake, since his erudition rarely netted him a kopeck. From time to time, under the lash of his wife's tongue, he did set up a *kheder* for young boys, but the ventures never lasted long. He simply had little of the patience and none of the skills for teaching except those that resided in a stout leather strap.

Shmuel was content to leave the grubby business of earning a living for their constantly growing family to Rivke (Rebecca), his resourceful wife, while he devoted himself to prayer and the study of sacred texts, combed his handsome beard, and built up credits in heaven with a miser's zeal. No one, least of all Grandma Rivke herself, thought the arrangement unfair or unseemly.

Rivke toiled and scrimped and haggled with the local peasants to feed her husband and their nine children, eight of them—an eightfold calamity— daughters. She trudged the rough roads, muddy in summer and frozen in winter, from village to village with a peddler's pack over her shoulder. She prepared meat patties and syrup-waters for sale on market days, when Uzlian was noisy and loud with peasants who reeked of vodka. Yet she found time to cook and wash and sew for the ever-expanding brood.

But her good-looking, self-centered husband was rich in *koved.* He occupied a seat of prestige in the synagogue, along the eastern wall, engaged in disputations on points of ritual with the most scholarly Jews in the region, and sometimes delivered elegant Sabbath sermons, well studded with God's own words. So Grandma Rivke considered herself, on balance, a fortunate woman.

This doughty lady, as all her numerous progeny in due time acknowledged, was a remarkable character. David and other grandchildren, in assessing their inherited equipment for life, readily credited their good minds to Shmuel the erudite, master of pilpulistic logic. Even in his old age, in America, his razor-keen intelligence could make mincemeat of the infidel arguments of his college-trained offspring. But all other worthwhile qualities, especially the practical ones, they traced to Grandma Rivke.

She had immense courage and will power, backed up by shrewdness and ingenuity in dealing with the problems, privations, and misfortunes which were her lot. Her natural gifts for imperious management of those around her would under other circumstances have made her an organizer and a leader. Though she shunned pride as a sin, she was incapable of real humility and comported herself always as a queen in Israel. Had the need or occasion for it arisen, she would have confronted the local feudal landlord or the governor of Minsk himself as an equal, prudently concealing her inner certainty that she was really his superior.

Rivke's ministering love was a mantle wide enough to shelter not only her own family, which she ruled with an iron hand and a fiery tongue, but neighbors in need. In the course of time she followed her children to America and settled in Brownsville, then a ghetto section of Brooklyn. There she dominated her immediate neighborhood even as she had done in Uzlian.

Anyone who has read the great novel by G. B. Stern, *Matriarch,* will remember how its magnificent heroine, Madame Rakonitz, watched over and manipulated her wealthy family (modeled perhaps on the Rothschilds), scattered over five continents. Grandma Rivke in her American years would be another such matriarch, though the family she ruled and protected, sternly or subtly as required, was scattered only over the five boroughs of New York City. She shouldered its problems, chastised the erring, and exploited the successful. As a matter of right she exacted tribute in cash or in kind from those who had it—which came to mean in the first place her prospering grandson David—to take care of less fortunate relations. Grandma Rivke, in short, was an authentic ancestor.

Radio seemed to her, in the American portion of her life, some kind of trickery, but she held her tongue on the subject so as not to hurt her eldest grandson. Nor did she believe in medical science, relying on herbs and other therapies learned from her forebears. One morning in the ripeness of years, however, she astonished everyone by sending for a doctor. He examined her and pronounced that it was no more than a mild cold. "Young man," she said sternly, "I know more about life and death than you ever learned in your books. Before this day is over I will be dead."

The relatives within reach whom she summoned to her bedside that day asked why, for once, she had called a doctor. Grandma Rivke explained that "it wouldn't look nice for the neighbors" if she passed away without a doctor.

That night she died. Her will, distributing her few ancestral jewels and a few dollars, bequeathed her debts to David.

Grandma Rivke's funeral was one that clings to memory. For the mourners presented a tableau of two worlds. Along with the bearded Jews, Old World figures stooped from long study of Holy Writ, there were Americanized second- and third-generation members of the vast Privin progeny, and a flower-filled limousine sent by officials of the Radio Corporation.

This, however, is running far ahead of our story. Since 1914 the kind of all-Jewish hamlet known to young David has all but disappeared in Russia and Eastern Europe, wiped out by wars and revolutions. It lives on only in the memories of those who knew it and in literature. Its imprint remained deep on Sarnoff's mind and heart. In a hundred subtle ways it would affect his character, his values, his adjustment to a new land.

3

In Uzlian, a matriarch burdened with a houseful of daughters who had no dowries except the good name of Privin could not be too proud in the selection of husbands. One after another the girls were married off below their social station to simple, honest artisans, a saddler, a potter, a butcher.

The eldest of the girls, Leah, married a house painter, Abraham Sarnoff. He was a handsome young man with delicate features, unlettered but pious and not too robust in health. Soon enough the Sarnoffs were blessed with a son whom they named David. Two others, Lew and Morris, followed in due course. Their great-grandmother, Raisele, who acted as midwife, lived long enough so that David remembered her distinctly.

The sluggish waters of life in the Czarist Pale were then being agitated by a new impulse: the magnetic pull of far-off America. Close to two million Russian Jews would emigrate to the United States in about thirty-five years.

From a thousand bleak villages, Uzlian among them, the bolder young men made the journey. Mostly they went legally. For those determined to avoid the hated four-year military service for the Czar there were illicit roads of escape, greased with bribes. Soon their letters, recounting incredible but blood-stirring marvels, were being passed from hand to hand. All such letters from across the sea were addressed, in effect, to the whole community. They said that in America work and food were plentiful, buildings scraped the skies, there were no czars or Cossacks, and most thrilling of all, all men were considered equal—Jews had the same rights as Gentiles.

Now and then, it is true, an emigrant returned after a year or two with a minority report. America, he might insist, was a heartless land of slums, sweatshops and, worst of all, godlessness; it was a place where Jews began by cutting off their ritual earlocks and ended by shaving off their beards and working on the Sabbath; a place where children were rebellious and money counted for more than learning. One of these disillusioned returnees was David's maternal uncle, Schlomme Elkind, a baker by trade.

Disturbing as such strictures might be, they could not crush the hope of deliverance from the Pale and pogroms. The dream of America flourished. Before long Uzlian, too, had its contingent of "American widows"—women, that is, whose husbands had gone ahead to the United States to earn passage money for the rest of the family.

Abraham Sarnoff was the first of the Privin sons-in-law to undertake the fearsome journey. Perhaps there was more desperation than valor in the move. Because of his poor health, he was unable to earn a living for his little family in any case and might as well try his luck among those skyscrapers.

So in 1896 he bade a tearful farewell to his loved ones and set out for the Land of Promise, the Golden Land. These partings were always heartbreaking, a painful tearing up of deep roots, shadowed by the knowledge that a reunion would at best be years in the future. Leah moved back into the crowded maternal household with her three sons. There was little of enthusiasm in the letters that soon began to arrive from New York, and the dollars transmitted were pitifully few. Clearly Abraham was having a hard time in America, where so many others prospered.

Existence in Uzlian was much too austere to leave a margin for the pampering of children. Yet David, as the first-born of Grandma Rivke's first-born, held a favored place. He was handsome and bright. At an age when other boys were only beginning to learn their Aleph-Beth, he could already read and even recite by heart passages from the Old Testament. To his doting mother and grandmother and aunts—male opinion counted for nothing in that matriarchy—it was clear that the Lord in His infinite wisdom was adding another *lamdun*—a man of learning—to the family line.

Grandma Rivke therefore wrote to her brother, a rabbi in Korme, in the region of Borisov, suggesting that he assume the holy obligation of boarding and teaching the promising boy. The plan had the incidental virtue of reducing by one healthy mouth the number to be fed in her own household. Since a suggestion by Rivke had the force of a command for all her kin, the matter was quickly settled.

Thus David at the age of five, so soon after parting from his father, was torn away also from his mother, his two brothers, his bevy of adoring aunts, the youngest of them no older than himself, and his one uncle, Alter. Four cheerless years would pass before he would see any of them again. Although Korme was only a few hundred miles away, the cost of the journey as measured by the Privin resources was such that it might as well have been sundered from Uzlian by an ocean.

The granduncle under whose roof and discipline the boy now came was kind but too weighed down by duty and worry to show the affection he felt. He ministered to only a score or so of Jewish families in the Korme area, so that his earnings were minuscule. How he made both ends meet is a mystery Sarnoff cannot explain to this day, but he recalls that too often they didn't quite meet.

David found himself the lone child in a household of grownups, with few other youngsters in the immediate neighborhood. In time he forgot the very meaning of play or toys, forgot that childhood could contain anything more than the backbreaking, head-splitting drudgery of everlasting study in large, musty books with peeling covers, sustained by a meager diet in an atmosphere of clammy poverty.

From sunup to sundown, sometimes for twelve or fourteen hours a day broken only for a thin and hasty meal, he pored over the Prophets in Hebrew and before long the Talmud in Aramaic. The system of learning was as simple as it was archaic. You intoned a page in the ancient texts over and over again until you could repeat it by heart, not only letter-perfect but with precisely the singsong chanting prescribed by centuries of tradition. The tedium of it was like damp walls closing in, six days running, between Sabbath and Sabbath.

The subject matter of this eternal study ranged from exegesis on the Bible to profound and subtle laws of conduct, property, or adultery. Whether much of it made sense to a boy of seven or eight is open to doubt. But there is no doubt that it inculcated patience, built up powers of concentration and memory, and honed a naturally keen mind to a fine edge of sharpness. After all, as anyone who has tried both can testify, Blackstone is child's play compared to the Talmud.

On the other side of the ocean, meanwhile, David's father was still finding the going hard. America might be a land of opportunity for the strong and ambitious, but the elder Sarnoff was neither. Though he worked at his trade, painting and paperhanging, as often as failing health permitted, and denied himself even food, it took him more than four years to save enough money to buy steerage tickets for Leah and their three boys.

But finally the journey was arranged. In the early summer of 1900 David was brought back from Korme to Uzlian to rejoin his family and they became part of the great tide that was washing up millions of East Europeans on the shores of the United States.

Leah packed a big straw hamper with dried breads, smoked fish, and cooked meats for the long journey. These, she explained to her sons, must feed them until they reached the new country; obviously they could not risk their souls by eating anything prepared by any but orthodox Hebraic hands.

In the city of Minsk, while waiting for the train that would take them to the port of Libau, they witnessed a scene that David would never forget. Some kind of political demonstration was under way. "As we watched the surging people," Sarnoff would recall in his mature years, "a company of mounted Cossacks came charging down. They called on the crowd to disperse. No one moved. The Cossack leader barked a word of command, and the whole company rode into the wailing mob, lashing out with their long whips and trampling women and children under the hooves of their horses. The sight sickened me and I clung to my mother's skirts."

Though Minsk was a shabby provincial town, it was the largest David had ever seen. The tall buildings—some of them three and four stories!—the manikins in dusty shop windows, everything was new, exciting. In Libau, on the Baltic Sea, he saw ships for the first time and waters stretching to the horizon. How big and complex was the world beyond Uzlian and Korme! With mind and senses alert, he drank in all sensations like one long famished.

Then came Liverpool and transfer to another ship. He was on its deck when a sudden vision of calamity cut across his musings. For he caught sight of the life-sustaining straw hamper being lowered into the ship's hold, and was filled with panic. He knew he must act quickly and resolutely to retrieve his mother's food—already, at nine, he had taken on responsibility for the survival of his family. So he plunged into the hold after the hamper, a sheer drop of fifty feet. Luckily he landed soft on some bundles. One of the astounded sailors who extricated the dazed, skinny child exclaimed, "Boy, you'll do all right in America!" Rarely has an offhand prophecy hit the nail so squarely on the head. David, clinging to the hamper, was hauled back on deck by a rope, none the worse for the plunge.

From Liverpool, in the squalid bowels of a small and a slow ship, they sailed to Montreal, Canada. The memory of that sordid crossing would remain with them always—the human freight packed in like animals, the stench of unwashed bodies and vomit, the endless retchings and groaning. No immigrant by steerage could ever quite erase the horror from his mind, no matter how well he did in the adopted land.

But through the portholes David caught glimpses of the heaving seas which stirred his imagination. Looking up from the pit of the filthy steerage deck he sometimes saw first-class passengers, well-dressed men and women, lovely children as playful as puppies. These creatures from a distant world of comfort and beauty and happiness seemed a preview of the wonderland at journey's end, confirmation of a vague dream. Like many of his fellow passengers in the steerage misery, he was consoled and warmed by thinking of the spacious ease and abundance that awaited him.

From Montreal the Sarnoffs, laden with the awkward bundles of bedding and linen which were their share of the Privin poverty, traveled by train to Albany and then, on a Hudson River steamboat, to lower Manhattan. On July 2, 1900, still dressed in their warm Russian clothes, they stepped into one of those infamous sweltering summer days in New York.

The Montreal travel agent had wired the necessary information to the husband and father. But the message had been garbled in transmission, or perhaps badly translated. Abraham had made only slow progress in English during his American years. In any case, there was no one on the dock to meet the bewildered newcomers. The only address Leah had was that of an Uzlianer with whom her husband had recently boarded. It took hours of blundering on foot and by horsecar, staggering under their bundles, to find the place. But finally they did, and there that night the distraught elder Sarnoff, who had waited on the wrong dock, finally caught up with them.

It was a tearful reunion, and they were not all tears of joy. The years had not been kind to Abraham. He was haggard and melancholy. Already his neatly trimmed beard showed streaks of gray. Even David, the eldest of the brothers, barely remembered his father; to the younger boys this man who hugged and kissed them seemed at first a stranger. He had, of course, prepared a home for them—a narrow, three-room railroad flat on the fourth floor of a decrepit tenement on Monroe Street, in the squalid heart of New York's East Side.

Abraham could not conceal the low state of his health or his dread of the responsibility of supporting his family. Alone, one could skip a meal, while sharing a room with three or four other boarders. With a wife and three children, the prospects were terrifying.

3

Boyhood in the Promised Land

   David looked around him, in those first American weeks, with a sinking heart. So this was the fabled Golden Land! This fetid human anthill, this steaming Gehenna of a Manhattan slum in July.

The vision of beauty that had consoled him through the miserable ocean journey was shattered on the garbage heaps, the dirty cobblestoned streets, the dark slimy stairways, the one foul toilet in the hallway serving all the tenants on their floor. Jostling, unfriendly crowds, children in noisy swarms like the flies on the dirt piles, blotted out the dream of spaciousness.

To add to David's dismay, the boys and girls who were his new neighbors spoke an outlandish tongue, they mocked his foreign clothes and called him "greenhorn." Their manners and horseplay would have rated a birching by his granduncle's standards, and by his own as well. It was a brutish, sticky, dog-eat-dog world he was thrown into.

According to the American myth, all immigrants on arriving in the United States were filled with joy and gratitude, thrilled by the vistas of freedom and opportunity. The truth is that more often they were disappointed, dismayed, and above all, scared. They knew utter loneliness and a sense of loss. Having come in most cases from the countryside or small towns, they were ill prepared for the crush and clamor and pressures of industrial communities, especially in the tenement jungles of our big cities. In their native places, somehow, the problem of making a living had been less frightening, the compulsion to "succeed" had been less oppressive.

Leah wept for her exiled children and her sick husband and the hopelessness of their situation. In Uzlian poverty had a more familiar face and was easier to bear. There had been sympathy and a sharing of troubles. Besides, there they had been somebodies, people with names and histories. They had identity and belonged to a cohesive community. Suddenly in America they became nobodies, ciphers, lonely among throngs of anonymous strangers.

But her eldest son had never learned to weep. Evidently the Promised Land was not a free gift but something that had to be fought for and won. It was another, tougher page of Talmud to be learned and absorbed. Amazingly, for a boy of nine and a half, he told himself: "If I don't help my family, who will?" Within weeks after his disillusioning arrival, David was handing over to his mother little fistfuls of pennies each night, gathered by hawking Yiddish newspapers on those hostile ghetto streets against the competition of older and more experienced boys.

At the age of ten and eleven, his small earnings would frequently make the difference between eating and not eating, between gaslight and candlelight. Before he was thirteen, two more children were added to the brood, his brother Irving and his sister, Ede, while their father's earning power was swiftly dwindling toward zero. David faced up to the cruel fact that he was the main breadwinner, at that tender age, for a family of seven.

Another American legend, enshrined in endless books and movies, is the one that glamorizes a hard, poverty-ridden childhood as the indispensable prelude to the standard success story. Owen D. Young would say one day that Sarnoff had lived "the most amazing romance of its kind on record." But the rags-to-riches romance takes little account of the wounds inflicted by an unequal early struggle. It was only later, viewed in the perspective of time from the summit of his career, that David could discern—or pretend to discern—a nimbus of romance around the cheerless reality. The actual living of it was always somber, sometimes pathetic and soul-searing.

The boy Sarnoff was never to know, except at second hand, that childhood could be bright and joyful. He had put away childish things when he was barely five and had plunged into the worries of maturity—the eternal problems of rent and grocery bills—when he was barely ten.

The boys diving off the docks on the nearby East River, stealing rides on horsecars, or teasing girls on street corners seemed to him strangers, almost another generation. He never had the leisure to learn to play, to swim, to join friends in outings or exuberant mischief. He did not complain. He accepted his lot, he would later insist, without bitterness. But men have only one childhood. Its loss would leave deeper scars on his personality than he could possibly realize at the time or liked to admit later.

Poverty was only half the ordeal of immigrant children. The other half was the feeling of being aliens and intruders. It embraced a certain envy of "real Americans," an irrational kind of guilt about having been born abroad. In common with most other immigrant boys and girls David suffered the strange and disturbing dichotomy, only vaguely apprehended, of living as a matter of course in two contrasting cultures, two worlds that rarely touched.

There was the imported world of his Jewish home and its religious rituals—and the bigger outside world of school, streets, gang fights, American newspapers, movies, American customs. They had not only different languages but different modes of thought, values, standards of judgment. When you returned home you removed your new American self like an outer garment, to be put on again when you went outside. The very idea of parents and children sharing the same ideas and interests, the same games and enthusiasms, seemed incredible and rather bizarre.

This dualism, this living on two almost unconnected levels, confused and sometimes distressed even a youngster as perceptive and psychologically sturdy as young David. Few Americans with deep roots in their soil can quite understand the homelessness of immigrant children, the pathos of little aliens, the desperation of their yearning to become and to be accepted as Americans.

Land where my fathers died, Land of the pilgrims' pride—sung in the assembly hall by hundreds of Jewish, Italian, Slav, other foreign-born boys and girls whose fathers had never heard of the Pilgrims and spoke, at best, a broken English. In the pressure-cooker efforts to "Americanize" them quickly, the more sensitive among them felt an implicit disrespect for the ways of their homes and families. Often they came unconsciously to resent the imported traditions, good and bad alike, which seemed barriers to the new civilization.

The year 1900, when David was brought to the United States, was the threshold of a fabulous new century. The coming fifty years would see more material progress, more scientific wonders, than the preceding five centuries. But even dynamic America felt itself smugly on a pinnacle of history, rather than in the foothills of great beginnings. Why should it not feel smug? The Spanish-American War had left the savor of empire on the nation's palate. Not yet in a class with Great Britain or Germany, the country nevertheless was beginning to think of itself as a Great Power. The flamboyant Rough Rider, Teddy Roosevelt, was the Vice President. Industrial and financial titans (soon to be denounced as "robber barons") still bestrode the wide land.

And science was triumphant; nothing was impossible. Some uptown streets in New York were illumined by electricity. Electric trolleys were slowly pushing out the horse-drawn streetcars. The automobile was ceasing to be a curiosity.

But it was still the gaslight era. In the crowded Sarnoff flat candles were always on hand for the times—too frequent—when there was no quarter for the gas meter. There were those who actually believed that the automobile would soon make horses obsolete, but meanwhile cobbled streets echoed to horses' hooves.

The new century and the boy from Uzlian were destined to mature rapidly together.

2

In September, two months after he landed in America, David was enrolled in a public school. He was placed in one of the special classes then set aside for the latest immigrant children, regardless of age or previous education, before being assigned to proper grades. With the mental discipline acquired in his earliest years, the American lessons were scarcely a challenge. He was reading English and beginning to speak it with some fluency even before the year was out.

During his first February in school the teacher told a story that cut deep into his mind and left him with a feeling of excitement. She told it in its most elementary terms, in words that could be understood by the assorted little foreigners—the story of a boy born in a log cabin, poor and self-educated, who by dint of hard work and self-discipline grew up to be a great man and a great President.

David had a peculiar sense of personal involvement in the Lincoln legend. A sensitive historian who would himself become President, Woodrow Wilson, wrote in 1894: "Lincoln owed nothing to his birth, everything to his growth; had no training save what he gave himself; no nurture, but only a wild and native strength. His life was his schooling and every day it gave his character a new touch of development." In a later essay Wilson wrote of Lincoln: "He has felt that his life contained nothing for him but effort, effort from the rising of the sun to the going down of it."

These are the elements in the Railsplitter's story, of course, which have made it a source of courage for numberless young Americans. The immigrant boy absorbing and being absorbed by America felt its impact at once and responded to it increasingly as he learned the details of the Lincoln saga. In years to come, in times of doubt and difficulty, he would draw strength from it. When he had advanced far enough to rate an office of his own, two pictures always went up on its walls—an autographed portrait of Marconi and an old-fashioned steel engraving of Lincoln. Whatever the changes in decor as his office grew more impressive, those pictures remained on its wall where he could see them from his desk.

How quickly Uzlian and Korme receded! Soon they seemed as far removed in time as they were in space. David was much too busy to brood, always on the alert for the chance of earning a few extra quarters. Besides peddling papers, he was soon running errands for a butchershop, selling candy and soda pop in Second Avenue theatres, and picking up other chores.

The stigma of "greenhorn" faded out, he was more and more at home in the ghetto slums, and he learned to hold his own—sometimes with his fists—against other youngsters no less avid for those extra quarters. The jungle lost its terrors and became his natural habitat. He made a few close friends: the serious-minded boys tended to draw together against the loafers and toughs whom they both envied and despised. Now and then he ventured into the "uptown" world of comfort, cleanliness, and affluence, and he knew as a certainty that one day he would be part of it. The knowledge made present hardships more endurable.

In justice to the East Side it should be remembered that it decidedly was not all grime and crime. It was humanly and intellectually exciting, and produced not only gangsters but geniuses. Most of its inhabitants were honest and idealistic to a fault. The love of learning they had brought over from the old country found sustenance in the crowded libraries and social settlements, in public and private night schools. The Yiddish theatres were more than a match, in content and acting, for those on Broadway; in time they contributed outstanding artists to the English-speaking stage and to Hollywood. Idealistic urges found expression in a strong socialist movement, in trade-union activities, in musical and literary circles.

For an intelligent boy eager to learn and to improve his mind, there was no lack of opportunities. David remained undefiled by the meanness of his surroundings. Despite a killing schedule before and after school hours, he found time to soak up knowledge of the new land. He read everything that came to hand and was never without a book from the nearest library. Also, he began to attend a few evening classes at the Educational Alliance, a fine settlement house for old and young on East Broadway. For one thing, he joined a debating group that called itself the Paul Revere Club. In his first public appearance as a debater, he would always remember, he defended the affirmative on "Resolved: the United States should grant independence to the Philippines." His team won.

In the Educational Alliance today, a "hall of fame" proudly displays portraits of its most celebrated alumni. David Sarnoff is among them, along with Governor Alfred E. Smith, journalist George Sokolsky, actor Eddie Cantor, Judge Jonah Goldstein, and others raised on the East Side. The settlement was important in the boy's life. It was there, rather than on the streets, that he found his few congenial friends.

But a childish tragedy is connected with the institution. Some thirty-five years later, at fiftieth anniversary ceremonies of the Alliance, Governor Smith and others who had used its facilities in their boyhood made speeches. Sarnoff, by then a trustee of the settlement, was among them. As he recounted the episode from the rostrum, everyone in the large auditorium sensed that the old wound had never quite healed.

David, struggling to improve his English, was given a role in a pageant. Not a big role, to be sure, but to him invested with world-shaking importance. He was to walk on the stage on cue and declaim the single sentence, just five words, assigned to him. For weeks he rehearsed those words and the accompanying gestures, until not only he but his family and neighbors could recite them in their sleep.

Came the big night. Relatives and friends and neighbors were in the audience. He could see them while he waited with beating heart in the wings. At the proper moment he was pushed into the spotlight, took the rehearsed stance, raised his right arm aloft—only to discover that the sentence had vanished from his mind, utterly and irretrievably. He opened his mouth in panic but nothing came forth. The shame of it was overwhelming and would rankle for years.

"So tonight," he said thirty-five years later on the selfsame stage, "is my blessed chance to wipe out that humiliation. I shall now speak the words that then remained unspoken: *Cleanliness is next to godliness.*" He then proceeded to make the adage his text for an address about what the Educational Alliance had meant to denizens of the Lower East Side, in both cleanliness and godliness.

Peddling papers was a competitive enterprise, in which victory went to the fleetest and the strongest. From school you rushed to East Broadway, which was Yiddish newspaper row, to grab a bundle, then ran through the streets crying "Extra!" It was always Extra. The sooner you got your papers the more easily you sold them. There were no "returns" and an unsold surplus could spell a wasted day. Fifty papers meant a profit of twenty-five cents and if you were quick and lucky you might dispose of a hundred in an afternoon.

After a time David also worked up a "route," delivering papers to homes. That meant running up and down many stairs six days a week, and again on the seventh to collect. A good many people still owe him six cents.

Several of the newsboys were the envy of the rest. Because they had relatives in the press rooms, they obtained their bundles at once. Because the evening *Tageblatt* carried want ads, the jobless gathered around its doors or waited on the benches in nearby Seward Park. The boys who had their supply first therefore could dispose of it almost on the spot.

In David's second or third year in the trade, the newsboys faced a new species of competition. Four young men had invested in a horse and wagon and set up shop under the grand title of Metropolitan News Company. They delivered papers to newsstands and candy stores at the regular price—two for a penny—but charged twenty-five cents a week for their service. Naturally, as the biggest customer, they got their stocks at once, even before favored relatives.

David thought a great deal about this piece of private enterprise. He would do the same, on a modest scale! He built himself a small wooden wagon from packing cases and discarded bicycle wheels. Then he offered deliveries to the smaller stands and stores at only fifteen cents a week. In time he built up a nice business, improvised a larger wagon and was handling three hundred *Tageblatts* a day.

The activities of the twelve-year-old evidently annoyed the Metropolitan News. One day he was invited to visit its cellar office for a conference. The partners told him bluntly to quit—or he would be sorry. David didn't quit. Again they called him and this time there were no threats. This time they offered him $10 for his delivery business, and he could go on selling retail as in the past. That was a lot of money. It was not easy to reject, but he felt that he held the advantage. When he turned down the proposal, the purchase price was raised by stages to the dizzy sum of $25.

This was more money than he had ever possessed, and the temptation was strong. But David swallowed hard and made a counteroffer. They could have his delivery route free and for keeps. All he wanted in return was the privilege of buying the first three hundred *Tageblatts* that Metropolitan received from the press, at the regular half-cent price. The deal was closed and Metropolitan kept the agreement—every afternoon the first three hundred papers were David's.

That, however, was the beginning, not the end, of the little entrepreneur's ingenuity. He went to one newsboy and offered him fifty copies, at cost plus ten cents for the early delivery. Before long he had six boys participating in the arrangement—a clear profit of sixty cents for David and the whole afternoon free for other things!

In the time of his rising celebrity, in September, 1943, David Sarnoff was interviewed by the *Jewish Daily Forward*. Reminiscing about his East Side years he recalled, among other things, this boyish triumph. In the intervening decades the Metropolitan News Company had prospered hugely. Its owners, reading the interview, thus realized that the spirited little negotiator in their first cellar office had prospered too. Sarnoff received a letter from one of the partners, Louis Weinstock, inviting him to join them for dinner at a Second Avenue restaurant. He did and ever after counted these men among his friends.

3

By the time he was thirteen and celebrated his *bar mitzvah* or confirmation a more ambitious hope possessed David's mind. If only he could buy a newsstand the rent-and-bread problem would be solved. His brothers Lew and Morris were old enough now to take turns tending it and their mother could hold the fort while they were in school. Even the ailing father could lend a hand. Week after week David studied the ads of stands for sale and visited a few to assess their possibilities.

Finally he found one that seemed suitable but the price, unhappily, was forbidding. Two hundred dollars! It might as well have been two thousand, the sum was so far beyond his reach. Yet he talked about it to neighbors and friends, hoping for a miracle—and the miracle transpired. In most of the biographical articles and one book about Sarnoff, it has been said that little David managed to "borrow" the money. But the truth is different and a lot more dramatic.

One evening, on arriving home, he found a stranger waiting for him, a pleasant, soft-spoken, middle-aged woman. She introduced herself, a bit vaguely, and engaged him in conversation about his schooling, his work, his plans in life. Then she remarked that she had heard about how he was supporting his family and that he wanted to acquire a newsstand. She had come, she said, to make this possible. And she handed him two hundred dollars! She was ambiguous about whether she was making a gift or a loan. In his daze of excitement, David failed to write down her name and address, but he would remember her face for the rest of his life.

The newsstand, which included a "paper route" or delivery service, was on the corner of 46th Street and Tenth Avenue, and the Sarnoffs moved to a slightly larger flat near their business. They learned the hard way that they were in the heart of a section of Manhattan known as Hell's Kitchen—and that it amply merited the sobriquet. It was a district where Jewish boys with a trace of foreign accent were not exactly popular. The tough Irish kids helped temper the steel in David's makeup.

In all weathers he would rise at four in the morning to pick up his bundles of papers and complete deliveries before schooltime. From school he would rush home to cover the afternoon route, up and down literally hundreds of floors of stairway every week, with a repeat performance for collecting payment.

The $200 miracle had a sequel. About twenty years later Sarnoff was at a conference in the home of the philanthropist Adolph Lewisohn, called to plan a money-raising drive for ORT, a Jewish organization providing vocational training in European areas. Throughout the discussion he found himself staring at a sweet-faced, gray-haired woman, evidently a social worker—and remembering.

Sarnoff was pressed into heading up the organization of the campaign. In pursuance of that task, he asked to confer separately with each of the men and women present. He maneuvered the proceedings so that the gray-haired woman was the last. When they were alone, he looked at her with a flickering smile.

"How good is your memory?" he asked.

"Not too bad, I guess," she replied.

"Well, think back about twenty years. A shabby railroad flat on the fourth floor of a Monroe Street tenement. You have come to give two hundred dollars to a thirteen-year-old boy. . . ."

The woman thought for a long moment, her brows furrowed; suddenly she looked startled and burst into tears. Sarnoff thought she would faint, but she quickly regained control over her emotions. Then she proceeded to solve the old mystery, except for one element: she withheld the name of the real donor behind the gift.

She had been secretary at that time, she explained, to a wealthy, big-hearted man who wanted to help people anonymously. One of her duties was to seek out deserving objects for his solicitude. On her visits to the East Side she had picked up stories about a remarkable little boy and his dream of owning a newsstand for his family. Having taken the precaution of checking the facts, she went to his home and turned over the money.

Now the discovery that she had played a role in this man's successful career stirred her profoundly. It proved, she said, that her modest life of service had not been wasted. As long as she lived they remained friends and the boy grown to manhood repaid her old employer's gift manifold by helping her to help yet others.

For several years the young David added $1.50 a week to the family exchequer by singing in a synagogue choir, though it meant many hours of rehearsal on top of his other chores. He had a dulcet soprano voice and a natural musical sense. Now and then the choir was hired to sing at a wedding or banquet. That meant an extra quarter or fifty cents and, more important, a big free dinner. It was Cantor Kaminsky who awakened the boy's love of good music. As often as he could make the time for it, between the paper route, school homework, and choir rehearsals, David splurged the fifty cents for a seat in the uppermost gallery of the Metropolitan to hear an opera.

Kaminsky remained a lifelong friend, whom the former choirboy helped over rough economic stretches in the cantor's old age. One day in that future, when David Sarnoff was presiding over a board of directors meeting of the Radio Corporation, there was an urgent telephone call for him. He listened gravely. "Of course, I'll come immediately," the directors heard him say. Their president excused himself and hurried out.

The call was from Kaminsky's son, informing him that the old man was dead and the funeral services about to begin. At the funeral parlor, as soon as Sarnoff arrived, the officiating rabbi called upon him to "say a few words." He did, from the heart. The humble cantor, he said in substance, had affected American life and taste more than he had ever dreamed. The love of good music he implanted in a boy's heart had been responsible, decades later, for Dr. Walter Damrosch's "Music Appreciation Hour" on radio, for the first live broadcasts of Metropolitan Opera performances, for the Toscanini concerts on the air, and other Sarnoff innovations.

By the time David was in his last term of the elementary school, his father was totally invalided, cooped up in the narrow Hell's Kitchen flat. The marginal hope of going to high school had to be abandoned. Immediately upon graduating, the boy realized, he must look for a man's job in a man's world.

One unpleasant incident in his final school year is worth recounting. The subject of the lesson on that memorable day was *The Merchant of Venice*. The teacher, a Mr. M., was holding forth amiably on the characters in the play and in due course came to Shylock. Here was a typical Jew, he pronounced. Shakespeare knew the race, as proved by the fact that it still produced Shylocks, right here in our city. He then told about a bearded pushcart peddler who, when annoyed by Gentile youngsters playing on the street, called the cop—demanding his "pound of flesh," as it were.

At this point David rose impulsively to his feet and interrupted the learned discourse. "You're teaching anti-Semitism!" he shouted, tears of anger in his eyes and voice. Teacher and class were stunned. Mr. M. ordered him to sit down—or leave the class and never return. All right, the boy said in substance, he would leave and ask the principal if a pupil could be expelled for protesting an injustice.

The principal listened to the story and tried to make light of it. He summoned the teacher and attempted to effect a reconciliation. But Mr. M., still furious, insisted that he would not have this impudent pupil in his class again. At this juncture David interjected, with equal heat, that he thought the Jewish newspapers should know about anti-Semitism being taught in this school. Magically, that changed the complexion of the affair for the principal.

"David goes back to class," he told Mr. M.

"I'd rather resign!" the teacher exclaimed.

"Your resignation is accepted!" the principal decided.

David, badly shaken by the turn of things, did return to his class and Mr. M. didn't.

This, too, had a sequel, more amusing than dramatic. A great many years later Sarnoff went to a bank on some minor errand. He was directed to an elderly gentleman at a desk behind a marker identifying him as a vice-president. Even before he read the name, David recognized the long-ago expert on Shylocks. After their business had been transacted, Sarnoff said: "Mr. M., you owe me a debt of gratitude. Here you are, a successful banker, and you owe it all to me."

"What do you mean?"

"If it hadn't been for me, Mr. M., you would still be teaching school somewhere." He identified himself as the eighth-grader who had occasioned Mr. M.'s resignation from the school system. The two men met again often on business matters in the succeeding years and—such is the illogic of human nature—grew rather fond of each other. They had had an emotional experience in common, even if on different sides.

4

The one thing clear in David's mind was that the end of schooling would not mean the end of learning. If he had one fixed idea, it was that he would never allow himself to be lost in the common herd of the uneducated. It was an idea rooted in his earliest conditioning.

In the Privin ménage and with his granduncle the rabbi, the *ahmorets,* the ignorant man, had been regarded with a kind of pity, a pity edged with contempt. Poverty was merely a misfortune, but ignorance was close to a disgrace. David did not have to decide to become one of the elite of enlightened men—the determination had sprouted in the depths of his soul long before. And its motivations were not primarily economic; escape from the swamps of poverty would be a by-product but it was not the shining goal.

Like many another newsboy, young David wanted to be a newspaperman. The very word "reporter" was pulse-lifting. In general he loved words, collected new and strange ones the way other youngsters collected marbles or stamps or baseball cards. Having come to it only a few years ago, he could not take the English language for granted but treated it as a thing of endless beauty and endless challenge, something to be explored and digested. If only he could find a place in a newspaper office, no matter how lowly!

"When I was selling papers in Hell's Kitchen," he was to recall half a century later, "the dread of remaining an *ahmorets* was always under the surface of my consciousness. Often it came to the surface. It jelled in a determination to rise above my surroundings. Instead of selling newspapers, I thought, I shall one day write for them. I'll be a reporter, and then an editor, maybe a publisher."

This was the impulse that took him one Saturday morning early in the year 1906 to Herald Square, on 35th Street and Broadway, where James Gordon Bennett's *Herald* was located. He was wearing his one good suit, his mop of brownish hair was slicked down, and he looked rather less than his years.

In the lobby he approached a man behind a window and announced that he wanted a job on the paper, any job. He heard the clicking of telegraph keys in the cluttered room behind the window.

"I don't know about the *Herald*," the man said, "but we can use another messenger boy in our shop. . . . Five dollars a week and all the overtime you want, at ten cents an hour."

In his excitement, it appeared, he had blundered into the outer office of the Commercial Cable Company. Those ticking keys somehow intrigued him. If not on a newspaper, he would at least be in a newspaper building. Besides, he needed the regular income.

"All right," David said, "I'll take it."

By Monday morning he was in his messenger-boy uniform—and in the communications industry, delivering messages by bicycle. One of the most spectacular careers of our time thus began by sheer accident. Ever since, Sarnoff has remained a firm believer in luck, in "the breaks," leaving it to others to point out that he had the will, the intelligence, and the energy to make the most of every break. He still likes to quote his mother, who had a sharp wit with inflections of irony. Appraising her four sons, Leah would explain that this one was the handsomest, that one the smartest, the third, the kindest, and—pausing for effect—"and David has all the luck!"

While holding down his first job and piling up additional dimes in overtime, David continued to rise long before dawn to make newspaper deliveries. He also held on to his place in the synagogue choir. More than ever the family was now his personal responsibility.

From the first day he was utterly fascinated by telegraphy, by the feeling of the vast, mysterious world at an operator's fingertips. London and Paris, Tokyo and Johannesburg, Rio de Janeiro and Moscow—the very names on outgoing and incoming cables fired his imagination. The dream of newspaper work subsided faster than he would have thought possible.

Actually his messenger work did give him a close-up view of a metropolitan newspaper operation. Most of the cable and telegraph traffic handled by the office where he worked consisted of news dispatches for the *Herald*. One of his chores, when there were no messages to be delivered, was to make up the "flimsies"—fourteen thin pages with carbon paper between—on which incoming dispatches for the paper were typed. He became familiar with the hustle and bustle, the noises and camaraderie of a metropolitan city room.

He had no intention, of course, of remaining a messenger boy for long. His first tiny savings he invested in a dummy telegraph key and a Morse Code book and began to put in long night hours practicing. Often awe-struck neighbors looked in to "watch Dave telegraph," though more complained about the click-clicking that threaded their sleep.

Many years later, when he had already made a name for himself and the Sarnoffs were living in the Bronx, the two-dollar instrument was still on proud display on the family mantelpiece. Even today the manual telegraph key is preserved in his luxurious RCA office.

David denied himself pocket money to buy books on electricity and telegraphy. When things were quiet in the Herald Square office, friendly operators let him practice sending and receiving on its pony line. At the other end, in the company's central office at 20 Broad Street, a tolerant telegrapher, Jack Irwin, seemed willing to chat with the ambitious youngster and to answer his technical questions. They became Morse Code friends before they had met in person, knew each other's touch on the instrument before they had heard each other's voice.

The job as messenger came to an abrupt and ignominious end. The High

Holidays—Rosh Hashana and Yom Kippur—were about to start. For the cantor and his little choir it was the climactic season of their year. They had rehearsed intensively, they loved the day-long rituals, and there was the extra pay. David approached the office manager, a Mr. Shea, and explained that he would need three days of leave without pay because he had to sing in a synagogue. Mr. Shea responded with a brusque refusal.

"We have to deliver messages, holidays or no holidays!" he said.

"But I *must* sing," the boy said. "Without its solo soprano the choir would be crippled."

"All right," Shea agreed, "you can take the days off—but don't come back. In fact, turn in your bicycle—you're fired."

David had lost his first full-time job. He took it hard. There was the humiliation of it and, more important, the sudden loss of the family's largest item of income. Ironically, the singing which cost him his messenger's uniform came to an end that Yom Kippur day, for he could no longer conceal the fact that his soprano tones were cracking under the advent of manhood. Some weeks earlier the choir manager had docked him a nickel, after a wedding performance, for having failed to hit the high C.

In addition to studying the want-ad columns, David decided to consult his new friend at the other end of the pony circuit. They met in person for the first time. Jack Irwin was sympathetic. He thought he had heard that there might be an opening for a junior operator at the Marconi office—anyhow, why not find out? Neither of them doubted that the youngster was by now proficient enough to fill such a post.

David had heard about wireless, in a vague fashion. He betook himself at once to the Marconi Company at 27 William Street, the first and as yet only wireless office in Manhattan. There he approached a dignified-looking gentle-man at a cluttered desk. George De Sousa, then traffic manager of the small company, remembered the scene well and talked of it with relish all his life. He had good reason to remember, since he would in time become one of Sarnoff's subordinates and one of his most loyal admirers.

The future "generalissimo of the radio industry," a short, skinny, bright-eyed and snub-nosed boy, had a grown-up and confident manner, though he looked considerably less than his fifteen and a half years.

"He asked if I could use a man as junior operator," De Sousa told the story. "I looked him over in surprise and amusement and tried not to smile. No, I told him, Jack Irwin's tip was wrong. I didn't need a man, but we could use a boy—an office boy."

As they talked another man approached: W. W. Bradfield, chief engineer.

Yes, he confirmed, they certainly could use a smart office boy who wasn't afraid of hard work.

David grabbed the job. The starting pay was $5.50 a week. The date—September 30—would ultimately be celebrated by the Radio Corporation of America and its affiliated organizations (none of them yet born) as significant in the annals of the company and the industry. For it marked David Sarnoff's entry into the electronics world.

"It is not usual to make mention in any serious work of history the mere hiring of an office boy," Dr. Gleason L. Archer would write in his *History of Radio to 1926*. But, he went on, the acquisition of a new office boy by the Marconi Wireless Telegraph Company of America in September, 1906, is a momentous event "in any volume dealing with broadcasting," because the job went to David Sarnoff.

The boy born in a forlorn village in the Russian Pale had made contact with his "twin," the electron.

"I have never underrated the element of luck on what passes for worldly success," he would say in that future upon which he was now embarked. "I know it takes more than luck alone but I don't hesitate to acknowledge that I have been lucky beyond my deserts. It was luck that my parents had the pioneering instinct to bring me to this land of freedom and the opportunity that goes with freedom. It was luck for me that this opportunity materialized in an art and an industry even younger than myself. It was a lucky coincidence that I was born about the same time the electron was discovered."

There is a humanly interesting footnote to David's loss of his first job. Around 1919, when he was commercial manager of the just-formed RCA, needing an additional canvasser to call on potential customers, he placed an advertisement in a New York newspaper. It called for a man with experience in the field of communications. The traffic manager, Mr. Winterbottom, read the replies and handed the most promising to Sarnoff.

One of these gave him a shock of recognition, and he asked that the writer be brought to his office when he came for an interview. A few days later the applicant sat on the other side of Sarnoff's desk, no doubt puzzled by the smile playing around the commercial manager's mouth.

"Mr. Shea," Sarnoff said, "I can personally testify to your long experience with the Commercial Cable Company. What's more, I am very much indebted to you. Back in 1906, on the eve of the Holy Days, you fired me as a messenger boy. This led to my entering the wireless field. To show you I'm really grateful—you're hired. You can start at once."

Shea worked with RCA, on increasingly important assignments, for about ten years. His devotion to his former messenger boy never faltered.

A formal portrait of David at the time he was office boy is still extant. He is in a dark suit, wearing an oversized gray bow tie, a big handkerchief protruding from his outside breast pocket. His arms are crossed in a pose of self-confidence. Big eyes set wide apart dominate a pinched, boyish face, and he looks two or three years younger than his sixteen years.

4

The Formative Years

ᔑ At the time the seven-year-old American Marconi Wireless Telegraph Company hired its new office boy, wireless was in its swaddling clothes. But it was a precocious infant, erupting with theories and inventions, and often ill-tempered, howling through the courts of law in squabbles over patent infringements.

In December, 1901, as we have noted, Guglielmo Marconi had finally conquered the Atlantic. At St. John's, Newfoundland, he picked up three faint dots—the letter S—which had been sparked on the coast of Cornwall, England, 1,800 miles away. In the following months entire words were sent and received. The U.S. Navy was so impressed that it took under advisement the replacement of carrier pigeons by wireless.

That same year, too, Dr. Reginald Fessenden finally succeeded in transmitting and receiving the human voice without wires, in a Pittsburgh laboratory. The sounds were indistinct and snarled in static but the dream of wireless telephony was taking on the flesh of reality. Fessenden, and he was not the only one, was working on a detector that would pick up not only dots and dashes but continuous sounds.

American inventive genius had been deeply stimulated. Dr. Lee De Forest, Harry Shoemaker, and a dozen others were refining existing apparatus and developing new ones, each adding to the patent chaos but pushing the new science forward. By 1903 Marconi was able to transmit across the ocean an exchange of amiable telegraphic messages between President Roosevelt and King Edward VII. In an attempt to lay sound ground rules (or should we say air rules?) for the expanding enterprise, the First International Wireless

Conference was held in Berlin. It failed to agree on anything vital, thus presaging years of conflict and confusion on the airwaves.

By the end of 1904 wireless telegraph stations were blossoming on coastlines all over the world, twenty of them in the United States, and the challenge of transoceanic wireless in competition with the cables was exciting pioneers in several countries. In the Russo-Japanese War, 1904–1905, press correspondents and naval vessels were using seven different systems of wireless—a commentary on the vitality of the burgeoning science.

On Christmas Eve of 1906 wireless operators far at sea, listening through their earphones for dots and dashes, were startled to hear human voices—a woman singing, a man reciting poetry. It meant that Dr. Fessenden had made significant progress in continuous-wave radio. As requested, many of those who heard the program notified him at his Brant Rock, Massachusetts, station. A month later Lee De Forest applied for a patent on his Audion tube, which would bring the inventor a lot of grief but would ultimately prove itself a great boon to broadcasting.

With every year rivalry between and within countries in the wireless race grew more feverish. The American De Forest Company, organized in 1902, had equipped some two hundred ships with its system before it went into bankruptcy five years later. The International Telegraph Construction Company, also born in 1902, had sold its wireless products to the Navy, to United Fruit, and to others before succumbing in its turn to bankruptcy. Indeed, though wireless activities were booming, the profits (except to a few stock promoters) were nil. One after another companies foundered on the rocks of patent litigation and reckless financing.

The American branch of Marconi was the most prestigious in the field—Marconi was a name to conjure with, the company had been the first launched, and most important, it controlled indispensable basic patents. But it was neither the largest nor the most successful and many years would pass before its efforts netted any profit.

"The wireless business was not making money in those days," David Sarnoff would write twenty years later in the *Saturday Evening Post*. "Sometimes, indeed, when Saturday pay day came around, I would be sent out to friends of John Bottomley, our general manager, to borrow funds to pay off. Bottomley, poor fellow, did the best he could; but it was hard going; for there were only four ships—the *New York,* the *St. Louis,* the *Philadelphia* and the *St. Paul*—equipped with Marconi wireless, and only four land stations—Sea Gate at Coney Island; Sagaponack, Long Island; Siasconset, at Nantucket, Mass., and South Wellfleet on Cape Cod, Mass."

The Marconi organization was small, impecunious, handicapped by foreign control and a management that was often baffled by American competitive zeal. Bottomley and his British bosses were inclined to look upon energetic challengers in the business as poachers on their preserves.

Borrowing payroll money was only one of David's manifold duties as office factotum. He was starting, almost literally, from the ground up, since sweeping the floors was among his occasional chores, along with dusting desks, emptying wastebaskets and cleaning typewriters. He duplicated and filed letters, ran errands, announced callers. Yet he found interstices of time to practice on the telegraph key connecting the office by wire with the four coastal stations and with Western Union. Before long the operator, Mr. Gocking, was trusting the boy to send and receive dispatches.

Always David was prompt, hard-working, dependable. For fear that his employers might think him too tired for the job, he concealed the fact that by the time he reached the office, cheerful and alert, he had already put in four hours delivering papers. There were times when he had barely slept at all: the girls he sometimes dated never seemed to have the kindness to live in midtown, and so had to be escorted home to the far Bronx or Brooklyn.

But such is the abundant vitality of youth that his secret was never discovered. His associates were aware only of his unique enthusiasm, his boyish appreciation of their various talents, and his penchant for asking questions. Everything on the premises and in the wireless world beyond seemed food for his voracious curiosity; and in addition, he was rarely without a book or pamphlet on electricity or telegraphy in his coat pocket, for vacant minutes or travel time on the trolleys.

It was to curiosity that his betters charged David's habit of reading the correspondence he filed. But it went deeper, being part of a conscious design for self-improvement—one more device for studying English as well as exploring the mysteries of business affairs.

The youngster from Hell's Kitchen felt himself in a new and exciting world. He was in a business that embraced the whole globe, a science that stirred the imagination, among types of people whom he had not met before. The company then counted about a dozen men in the office, several officials outside, the wireless telegraph men at the stations and on the ships, and a technician in the small workshop on Front Street that served as an experimental laboratory.

In each of these people David discovered qualities of character or manners, knowledge or skills, which he admired and meant to make his own. There were the cultivated accents of Bottomley, the business acumen of De Sousa, the speed and clarity of Gocking's telegraphy. He was especially impressed by the fine sonorous writing style of the president of the American Marconi Company: John W. Griggs, former governor of New Jersey and a former Attorney General in President McKinley's Cabinet. To this day a little of the Griggs rhetoric, such as a weakness for polysyllabic words of Latin origin, adheres to Sarnoff's own style in writing and speaking.

But his interest was focused less on the important executives than on the men in the technical jobs. First of all, he had decided, he must acquire mastery of the craft and its instruments. The fact that few of the executives had a thorough grasp of the technical side of their business seemed to him their serious limitation. Of course, the technicians knew even less of the business side. There appeared to be a chasm between the two groups.

The man who made himself equally at home in both areas, the youthful Sarnoff thought, would have the widest and clearest view of the industry and the largest opportunities to affect its course. Thus half consciously, half instinctively—while still sweeping floors and running errands—he was preparing himself for leadership in the new art and science.

About once a month each of the four ocean going 'Coni men, when his ship was in New York harbor, came to the office to turn over his report and his cash. They were in uniform and brought with them the smell of the sea, the aura of far places. They were flattered by David's unabashed hero worship. He went with them aboard their ships. That meant a good free meal at the officers' mess and, more important, a chance to tinker with their wireless gear. They proved willing enough to let him clean the generators, make small repairs, or check the electric dynamo or transformer.

The laboratory technician, Jimmy Round, ranked high in the boy's private pantheon of heroes. Many an evening or weekend found David, self-invited, in the narrow cluttered lab in a loft on Front Street. Jimmy Round let him coil wire and do other jobs. "Since there was a good deal of dirty work a boy could do," Sarnoff recalled in later years, "he let me mess to my heart's content. I blew out dozens of fuses and have calluses on my fingers to this day where I burned them." Within a few months the technician was talking to the boy as to an equal about problems that needed solving and experiments in progress.

But the central niche in the pantheon, of course, was held by Marconi himself. The inventor first visited the United States in late 1899, only months before David Sarnoff reached the country. After that his sojourns in New York were frequent. David met him at the end of 1906 and could scarcely contain his excitement. The lines of destiny of a teen-age Italian testing electromagnetic phenomena in an Italian vegetable garden and a boy born in the Russian Pale had converged and thereafter would remain intertwined.

In September, 1936, there was a banquet to celebrate the thirtieth anniversary of Sarnoff's entry into radio. The Marchese Guglielmo Marconi, from Europe, sent a message of congratulation. He was especially proud, he said, that "Sarnoff's first connection with radio was in association with" himself, Marconi.

Those who heard the message read—officials and employees of the Radio Corporation of America gathered to honor its president—smiled knowingly. A few of the older men at the head table, like George De Sousa, chuckled. They were amused and touched, because they knew the lopsided nature of that distant "association." It had become a legend of the electronic age.

In late 1906 and early 1907 Marconi and Sarnoff—one already the world-famous wizard of wireless, the other an office boy. David tagged after the famous inventor, lugging his dispatch case and haunting the Front Street workshop where Marconi was making experiments. He delivered candy or flowers for the Italian genius and shared vicariously in the life of an elegant and lionized foreign celebrity.

It was in part from him that young David acquired a broad, almost poetic view of electronic progress and science generally. Almost from the first man and boy engaged in long, rambling philosophic discussions. Talk about a new tuner or the problems of static would somehow, again and again, carry them far afield to first principles of science and life, matter and spirit. One casual remark remained indelibly in David's memory, so that he quoted it again and again in his maturity. Marconi was patiently explaining to him the theory of the propagation of electromagnetic waves. "David," he said, "we know *how* things work. We don't know *why* they work." David Sarnoff sensed what he was as yet too inarticulate to express: the kinship between the creative impulses of the dreamer and the inventor and the mysteries beyond the grasp of science.

2

A life's pattern was already taking form in the boy's lively mind, a blueprint for personal growth. He was exceedingly conscious of his many handicaps—the lack of education and background, the poverty of his family, his status as an alien in the American land. There was no self-pity in this awareness—just inconvenient liabilities that he must turn into assets.

"I knew," he said once in a reminiscent mood, "that I would have to work twice as hard as most other boys, and that I would have to get my education, as it were, on the run. No, I didn't think it unfair and I wasn't bitter. I accepted the handicaps calmly, as facts of life, to be faced and overcome."

Those who counted most in the initial stage of his blueprint were the practical men, the doers, the craftsmen. For him they took precedence over the "paper" personnel, the pen-pushers. Far from coveting the executive positions, David saw them as potential traps. He made up his mind that, whatever the temptations of pride and pay, he would not allow himself to be tied to a swivel chair and a desk. After he had obtained the essential skills of the trade would be time enough to approach the organization and business aspects.

If David Sarnoff's new milieu was crowded with heroes, it was no less crowded with "firsts." Learning that a demonstration of Marconi equipment was scheduled at the Armory in Louisville, Kentucky, he talked Bottomley and De Sousa into assigning him to assist the technicians. The score was three unforgettable firsts in one: his first trip outside the New York area, his first ride in a Pullman sleeper, his first night in a hotel. These can be stirring experiences to a sixteen-year-old slum dweller.

Existence seemed to him full of exciting novelty. Sometimes he ran into former schoolmates, now in high school, with books under their arms. Or he glanced at the older boys playing ball on the streets near his newsstand. They seemed to him somehow juvenile; it took an effort of memory to recognize that they were more or less of his own age.

A few months after passing his sixteenth birthday, less than a year after joining the company, David was given the job for which he had originally applied. A new office boy came in—one who did *not* become president—and the old one succeeded Mr. Gocking as pony operator, at the heady salary of $7.50 per week.

That was when he finally relinquished the morning paper route to his younger brothers. Their father died soon thereafter. Before long the newsstand in Hell's Kitchen was sold, at a profit, and the family moved to the Brownsville section of Brooklyn. They lived in a $9-a-month walk-up flat in a five-story tenement on Thatford Avenue. The fact that the widowed Leah Sarnoff had to take on odd jobs to make both ends meet was an aching sorrow for her eldest son. The determination to extricate her from drudgery was never far from his thoughts.

One day there was an emergency. The 'Coni man on the S.S. *New York,* a Mr. Allen, had been taken ill just before sailing and a substitute had to be found at once. David eagerly stepped into the breach. Barely seven years after he had crossed the ocean in a foul steerage hole, he was back on the Atlantic, this time as a ship's officer in a glamorous uniform with a cabin to himself. The contrast was not lost on him.

The round trip came to three weeks of glory. He sent and received messages and chatted in Morse Code with operators on other ships. Some of these would boast in years to come that they had been among the first to hear the D.S. "fist" and to recognize its special qualities. His reputation as the fastest, clearest telegrapher in the business was to grow and grow, the marvel of generations of operators.

There was an evening, soon after leaving the harbor, when David was strolling on deck with a pretty girl passenger. He had not been told that junior officers were strictly forbidden to fraternize with the customers. Captain Roberts—Sarnoff still remembers the name and the scene—sent for him to administer the reproof. When the culprit stood before him, a skinny boy who didn't look his seventeen years, the captain did a double take.

"How in hell did *you* get here?" he thundered. "Is your company running a kindergarten? Well, go back to your cabin and stay there, and if I catch you mixing with passengers again I'll put you in the brig!"

"Aye, aye, sir," David said softly, and both of them smiled the smile of new friendship.

Back at William Street, David kept a weather eye out for the chance to work as a full-fledged wireless operator. By coincidence it was Jack Irwin, the same Jack Irwin whose tip-off nearly two years earlier had sent him to the Marconi office, who made this possible.

By 1908 Irwin was one of the four men who staffed the Marconi station at Siasconset, on Nantucket Island, Massachusetts. When he asked for a month's leave of absence, there was no rush of operators to pinch-hit for him. Siasconset was a notoriously dreary, lonely outpost, remote from civilized amenities. David was the sole applicant and he got the assignment. His friend was then, at his own request, assigned to ship duty and for David the one-month job stretched to eighteen months.

George De Sousa, having developed a fatherly concern for the boy whom he had hired, tried to dissuade him from going to Nantucket Island. Why, he argued, leave the headquarters of the company, with its larger associations and opportunities, for a forlorn outpost? But the youngster would not be swerved. It was not an easy decision. He was a city boy, had never been away from home for any extended period. Yet the shore post offered the kind of practical experience prescribed by his secret personal plan. Its isolation, moreover, had certain advantages. It would allow him to read and study to his heart's content, and he was eager to bridge the gaps in his education.

David's three associates at Siasconset, all seasoned telegraphers twice his age or more, met him with raised eyebrows. They had scarcely expected a seventeen-year-old. At first, he was to recall, they treated him with "exaggerated politeness," deferring to his opinions in open irony. One or another looked over his shoulder, pointedly, during his watch. But the irony and the doubts quickly gave way to cordial comradeship.

Starting as assistant operator at $60 a month, he was soon acknowledged a full operator at $70, of which $40 went to his mother in Brownsville. For Leah Sarnoff life was now a little easier. Her younger sons, too, were beginning to contribute their mite to the household.

At Siasconset, his appetite for work made David's youth an asset for the older men. The station equipment was crude. You generated your own electricity, made your own repairs. When the engine or batteries went wrong, it was the junior in the team who gladly did the fixing. He wanted to know every item of wireless gear inside out. His enthusiasm, as one of its beneficiaries wrote a good many years later, included a willingness to stand part of their watch when they wanted to play tennis or court a female vacation guest on the island.

The chief compensation for the bleakness of the outpost, for David, was its well-stocked technical library. He proceeded to devour it, volume by volume. Moreover, having acquired a secondhand bicycle, he often pedaled the seven miles to the Nantucket library for books of which he had vaguely heard and now at last could read. Books on the life of Lincoln topped the list; his psychological identification with the Railsplitter deepened with every extension of his knowledge of the man. In addition, he took correspondence courses in algebra and geometry. All in all, at the end of the eighteen months, he knew that the investment of time had paid off handsomely.

Next, in 1909, he was appointed manager at Sea Gate, Coney Island, the busiest of the company stations and nearest to New York City. He had asked for the post when it fell vacant. The fly in the ointment was that the change, despite its enhanced title and responsibilities, involved a $10 reduction in monthly salary, back to $60.

David worked up the nerve to ask Bottomley for the extra money. The sum, he explained frankly, made a real difference to the family budget. Moreover, wasn't it reasonable that as manager he be paid a bit more than the two operators under him? Bottomley seemed horrified by the young man's audacity. "I never heard such impudence in my life!" was his answer. Sarnoff could take the assignment or leave it—at the standard payment provided by the rules.

David took it, of course. But the incident rankled. Because of it he found himself listening with interest to a friend, a woman, who could get him work as a general factotum in a thriving clothing store in downtown New York. What future did he have as a telegraph operator anyhow? she argued. Now, the clothing business is something else—with his good sense and energy he was sure to get rich.

To test the project, he arranged to take the night shift at Sea Gate—midnight to 8 A.M.—and work at the clothing emporium daytimes. Two weeks of it convinced him that he could never be happy as a storekeeper, whatever the rewards. Unlike wireless, he tried to explain to the well-meaning woman, it had no "vistas." This was the first and the last time he would come even close to abandoning electronics.

To offset the cut in salary, there was support for his pride and self-confidence in the realization that, two years after the end of his office boy period, he was in command of a strategically located operation. He was continually making decisions which much older men carried out confidently. At the same time the fame of his "fist," his telegrapher's skill, was spreading among hundreds of wireless operators the world over.

David prided himself on punctuality. But once during this period he was late—under circumstances that helped embellish the legend of "Sarnoff luck."

A new dirigible, the *Vaniman,* was being flight-tested. It carried Marconi radio equipment. On its first trip the ship ran into trouble. Sarnoff, at his Siasconset key, was helpful in organizing a successful rescue of the crew, which included his friend Jack Irwin as operator. A new *Vaniman* was then built and another flight was scheduled to take off from Atlantic City, New Jersey. Sarnoff, by that time working at the Wanamaker station in New York, volunteered to serve as wireless operator. Because of some snag in transportation, however, he found it impossible to reach Atlantic City in time and, since it was to be only a short run, the dirigible took off without him. Disappointed and angry with himself, he returned to the station. By the time he got there the tragic news was already known: the *Vaniman* had exploded, killing all on board.

3

For all the weight of his job, there was enough of the boy in David Sarnoff to hanker for adventure. The lure of the sea was fed by his constant communication with widely dispersed ships and his friendships with ship's operators. In the first months of 1911 he reached out for an off-beat journey.

On the bulletin board in the home office one night he saw a call for volunteers to sail to the Arctic icefields. One of the sealing companies had been persuaded to try the experiment of equipping its vessels with Marconi wireless. The notice seemed to him a personal message. He applied at once, was signed up and thereupon resigned the Sea Gate post.

David reached St. John's, Newfoundland, a place already haloed in his mind as the site of Marconi's first transatlantic triumph. There the fleet was being made ready for its intensive hunting expedition, in the middle of February, 1911. He boarded the *Beothic*, the same ship on which Captain Cook claimed that he had reached the North Pole. Its sailors and sealers were a breed of rough-hewn, weather-tanned men quite unlike any he had met before. They looked on curiously, and sometimes gave a helping hand, as the slightly built young man from New York, so strangely polite and alarmingly grammatical, installed and tested the heavy wireless apparatus. They were a skeptical lot, for few of them had ever heard about telegrams without wires or cables, and not many of these believed the fable.

Under Newfoundland law the sealing season was restricted to a six-week period. Rivalry among the vessels was keen, bonuses being paid for the biggest catch. The traditional race from St. John's harbor, through its narrow mouth into the Atlantic, had attained a sporting quality. The entire popluation of the town lined the shores, bells were rung, and there was a great blowing of ships' whistles. The *Beothic* won that race and its 'Coni man, having entered into the spirit of the thing, was as thrilled as his shipmates.

The skepticism of the sealers turned into admiration a few days out at sea. It happened that the son of Captain Barbour, the skipper, was worried. He had left behind him a wife in the last weeks of her first pregnancy. A lot of crewmen and sealers were around when David plucked from the ether the glad tidings that a son had been born, mother and child doing fine. The news was spread and toasted throughout the *Beothic* and the 'Coni man was given credit, as if he had personally made the delivery. Now everyone solemnly agreed that the mysterious contraptions really worked.

David had promised a favorite girl friend in Brooklyn to keep a diary of the journey for her. It is still in existence: a stack of yellowed pages covered with his characteristic script, large, flowing, and cleanly legible. Mostly the writing is in pencil, since ink tended to freeze in the sealing zone.

In the perspective of more than half a century the diary makes interesting and often touching reading. There is curiously little romantic boy-to-girl persiflage; evidently his feelings were not deeply involved. Some of the entries are succinct, factual; others are quite technical accounts of the methods of killing the animals, then skinning and processing. He also records observations of the customs and characters of his shipmates. But the wide streak of philosophic speculation in Sarnoff's nature also comes through.

Ostensibly he was writing for the girl, but probably she never saw the manuscript. Actually it is a kind of soliloquy, under the spell of the sun-drenched icefields and star-filled night skies. Repeatedly he writes, with a catch at the throat, about the sad lives of his departed father and overworked mother. Hardly a day has passed since his father's death, he confides, without melancholy thoughts of him.

An entry on February 27 reads: "Good morning, Mr. Sarnoff, and many happy returns of the day to you." No one else was aware that he had just reached a momentous point in his life—his twentieth birthday. A snapshot of him on the sealer has survived and seems to belie that venerable age. It shows him lounging in a nest of crumpled tarpaulins, peering out from under the visor of an oversized cap, and looking more like a juvenile stowaway than a ship's officer.

Twice he came chillingly close to losing his life. When the expedition had been at sea some days, a sister ship signaled that its wireless had broken down, and Sarnoff's help was needed to repair it. David inspected the sheet of ice between the two vessels without enthusiasm but prepared to cross, after having talked the ship's doctor into keeping him company.

They were bundled up in heavy furs, wore sealskin boots with spikes on the soles to grip the ice and goggles against snow blindness, and they carried six-foot gaffs or poles for testing the ice. They made their way slowly, gingerly, reached the other ship in a few hours, and Sarnoff put its wireless in working order. But the return journey was another matter. Dusk had set in, an icy wind was blowing hard and, worst of all, the ice had broken into huge patches of slob or soft ice. Old-timers could have dealt with the problem easily enough, but for both the 'Coni man and the doctor it was a new experience.

"At every step of the way," Sarnoff would recount years later, in *Wireless Age,* "we fell in the water, grabbing the ice en route, which, after we had mounted it, promptly broke in half and gave us a thorough ducking. In a few minutes we were played out and lay gasping on an ice cake that held us for the time. The crew, which was watching our plight, yelled instructions and confused us more and more.

"Just at this crucial moment the captain of our boat set the bow of the vessel straight for us and ordered full speed ahead. I will never forget how I felt when I saw the big ship bearing down on us, smashing the very sheets of ice on which we lay. To be caught between two heavy sheets of ice and jammed into jelly wasn't exactly my idea of the proper ending for an ambitious young telegraph operator. The captain, however, immediately realized his blunder and sent out a dozen or more 'ice trotters,' as these expert sealers were called. The doctor and I were ignominiously handed from man to man and, as a crowning touch, the last man carried me aboard."

The second episode was even more frightening. On Sundays the killing of seals was rigidly forbidden and the *Beothic* rested. One Sunday afternoon the crew were on deck watching a seal family—father, mother, and baby—at play on the ice below and in a pool of water beyond. For David, eager to bring back snapshots, the scene was too tempting. He climbed over the side of ship. Camera in one hand and a gaff in the other, he approached stealthily within five feet of the baby, focused and clicked his camera. The father seal, in the water nearby, had seemed disinterested. But suddenly he pulled himself out on the ice and headed for the intruder, with amazing speed, considering his huge bulk.

"I took to my heels and ran," Sarnoff would write, "but I had sufficient presence of mind to follow a zigzag course. This gave me a slight advantage because it was difficult for my pursuer to twist his big body at every turn. We had progressed only a few feet and the seal, with murder in his eye, was gaining on me. But the strongest man could not hold out long on the jagged, slippery ice. I was near exhaustion. My breath came in gasps and my knees shook.

"Suddenly a shot rang clear in the still Arctic air. While the crew had watched my plight with awful fascination, one of the sailors had dared break the Sabbath law and shoot the seal. I think the captain believed privately that it would have been better if I had died a martyr to the law, but the man was never punished and all the men aboard heartily approved his action, none more heartily than I."

In the great hunt the first quarry were the young "white coats." Several times David joined the sealers on the ice, and, fighting the squeamishness that threatened to disgrace him, actually killed a few seals. Some of the men, he noted in his diary, cut out the heart of a seal, stuck it under their belt until it was frozen solid, then ate it raw. Others drank the warm blood of baby seals, ascribing to the libation all manner of health-giving virtues.

Weeks later, after butting through always heavier ice floes, came the turn of the hood seals. These were enormous creatures who fought for their lives. The pelt alone of the male hood—"the old gent," in the sealing jargon—weighed as much as 500 pounds.

Intership communication by wireless did all that had been promised for the innovation. It enabled the captains to keep each other informed where the pickings were fat and conversely where the going was tough and the crop thin. The *Beothic* visibly settled lower and lower in the water as the weight of its fresh-killed cargo grew. Its total haul at the end of the expedition set a record for the time—36,000 seals.

The wonder of wireless was once more demonstrated for the *Beothic* people when their 'Coni man picked up a message about a sailor on a ship a hundred miles away who had suffered serious internal injuries. There was no doctor on board. David therefore asked for precise details of the injury and the symptoms, submitted them to the *Beothic* doctor, then relayed instructions for treatment. The process was repeated several times in the next days and the patient was put on the road to recovery.

Other vessels possessing radio but no doctors, having followed the exchange, began to bombard the *Beothic* with medical inquiries and soon its lone physician was wirelessing advice and prescriptions, as Sarnoff subsequently put it, "for every complaint from bunions to bald spots."

It was on the return journey, however, that the improvised medical clinic reached its memorable peak. One day a message came to David from an operator named Jack Daw, at the wireless station on isolated, winter-bound Belle Isle. "I'm up against it," Daw said. "My assistant is terribly ill. His cheeks are swollen, his temperature soaring, and he is unable to eat. He has a toothache too and hasn't been able to sleep for a week." A Canadian government vessel would be coming with fuel and provisions, Daw explained —but not for another three months. Only a sealing icebreaker could cut through this time of the year.

The *Beothic* doctor, having asked for and obtained more information, diagnosed abscessed gums, evidently at an advanced stage of infection. He suggested therapy, but the medicine chest in the wireless station two hundred frigid miles away was depleted and now offered only calomel and liniment. The condition of the patient, a man named Barrett, was growing steadily worse.

"We were headed in the general direction of Belle Isle," Sarnoff would tell the tale some fifteen years later," but when the doctor and I begged the captain to turn the ship directly that way we got no encouragement. He was one of those silent, unemotional men of the north and the most expansive observation we drew out of him was usually a grunt or a snort.

"Meanwhile the news about Barrett was more alarming every day. Finally, in desperation, I advised Daw to address the captain directly. I worded the message myself: 'My assistant is dying. Unless you come at once with a doctor it will be too late.'

"I thought the captain showed a flash of feeling when I delivered this, but he said nothing. Several days dragged by. The doctor sent hourly advice to Belle Isle. Then came a report that made us wince in helplessness. Apparently blood poisoning was setting in. I carried this word to the captain myself and was starting on a last despairing appeal when the rocky-faced old fellow told me the vessel had been heading for Belle Isle all the time and should be there in six or seven hours."

The captain, it now appeared, had changed course for the sick man's sake when he first heard of the emergency. Something in his code kept him from confessing this touch of softness to the 'Coni man and the ship's doctor.

The *Beothic* was able to come within two miles of the island. Ten men, laden with blankets, pillows, medicines and other essentials, started across the steep and craggy ice. The station was some five hundred feet above sea level. Seven of the party turned back but three—the doctor, Captain Barbour's son, and Sarnoff—succeeded in climbing to the top.

They were greeted with shouts of joy by Daw and by the neighboring lighthouse keeper and his wife, the only woman on the island. On a rickety cot in a near-freezing room lay the wretched patient, convulsed with pain and almost a skeleton after twenty days without food. An operation, involving the drawing of three teeth, had to be performed immediately. Sarnoff acted as assistant to the doctor.

Before the *Beothic* resumed its course for St. John's everyone had the satisfaction of knowing that Barrett would recover. "It was tremendously exciting to me," Sarnoff later wrote, "that wireless had literally saved a man's life. Since then I have seen surgeons operate by wireless, dictating every move to some less skilled person. The time will never come when such a thing can seem commonplace to me."

At the journey's end David went in for a bit of impromptu salesmanship. He persuaded Job Brothers, owners of the fleet, to buy his entire wireless installation. This saved the Marconi Company the cost of shipping, and himself the job of dismantling the apparatus. His stock at the home office went up considerably when he delivered a handsome check instead of some secondhand gear. It was his first solo business transaction for the company.

A memento of the expedition—a mounted baby seal, pure white, removed from its mother's abdomen—long remained part of the decor in the Sarnoff parlor. A more important memento of his *Beothic* experience is the Marine Medico Service, which has saved hundreds of lives at sea in its decades of existence. The organization is generally regarded as a direct outgrowth of his pioneering, since it was on the *Beothic* that radio for the first time starred in the role of medical samaritan.

On his return from the North, Sarnoff did a tour of duty as operator on the

S.S. *Harvard,* and then applied for a post that was to have a great impact on the industry and on his own career. He became both operator and manager of a 5-KW station—then the most powerful in the commercial field—on top of the Wanamaker department store in New York.

A similar station had been erected also over Wanamaker's in Philadelphia. According to the announcements, these installations would speed up contacts between the two stores. Their unannounced function, of course, was to promote sales. The novelty of radio was expected to draw thousands to the stores, and that is precisely what happened. A good-looking youngster wearing earphones and tapping a telegraph key in the midst of mysterious equipment became one of the prime attractions of the New York department store.

For the young man himself the main attraction of the new assignment was its regular hours. At last he had his evenings free for some of the education he craved. Pratt Institute, in Brooklyn, was offering a special night course in electrical engineering, a course that telescoped three years of normal instruction into one. He was one of about fifty to enroll, but the course was so grueling that students fell by the wayside and at the finish line there were only Sarnoff and eleven others.

To the great public, wireless was still a thing of mystery. When Leah Sarnoff was asked what her eldest son was doing, she had a hard time of it making her answer credible. "Mother," David advised, "just tell them I'm a plumber." Evidently that is what she did, because for many years thereafter old Brownsville acquaintances, on meeting him, inquired how his plumbing job was going.

5

The *Titanic* and the Music Box

    David Sarnoff had reached man's estate, in the sense that he came of voting age, in 1912. Quite coincidentally, it was to prove a year of destiny for the radio industry, for the Marconi Wireless Telegraph Company, and for himself. Its high point, unfortunately, would be a cruel calamity at sea, the foundering of the British luxury liner *Titanic* on its maiden voyage.

The word "radio" derived from the fact that signals from the transmitters "radiated" in all directions. In 1912 it finally displaced "wireless" in popular American usage. The U.S. Navy had coined "radiotelegraphy" and "radio-telephony" to distinguish them from the wired types of communication; inevitably they were trimmed down to the prefix common to both.

From 1907 to 1912 the industry had continued to accelerate its pace of development. It was growing, if not yet prospering. The most important technical progress, in terms of future significance, was probably the work done over a number of years by the General Electric Company, in Schenectady, New York, first for Dr. Fessenden and then on its own. Its end product, announced in 1910 although it would not come to full fruition until the war years, was to be the vital Alexanderson alternator, a 20,000-cycle high-frequency alternator for radio transmission. It was to provide the necessary power, at last, for continuous-wave wireless communication over long distances.

Progress in the conquest of distance was being made through other means. British Marconi in 1907 undertook to provide commercial transoceanic service, by erecting 150-KW stations at Clifden, Ireland, and Glace Bay,

Nova Scotia, an interval of two thousand miles. The setup functioned erratically, depending on weather and atmospheric conditions; yet in time it was handling a sizable traffic.

At the same time radiotelephony was being brought closer, largely through the power of the De Forest Audion. When the American Navy made its historic round-the-world trip in the autumn of 1908 some twenty of its vessels were in telephonic contact with one another.

De Forest had a sharp eye for publicity values. In 1908 he broadcast music records from the Eiffel Tower. The program was heard in Paris in a radius of twenty-five miles. In January, 1910, he transmitted—"live," as we would say nowadays—the main arias of two operas directly for the Metropolitan stage, with Enrico Caruso in the stellar roles. His audience probably did not exceed fifty, wireless operators on nearby ships and a batch of reporters at the De Forest plant in Newark, and the reception was spotty and distorted.

Strange as it seems in retrospect, the public remained exceedingly cool to these wonders. Even exciting breakthroughs like the Caruso broadcast received little attention. Only those personally engaged in radio research and business caught glimpses of future greatness, and even among them only a handful, like the youthful manager of the Wanamaker station, had the instinct and imagination to see the vision whole.

An anecdote has come down which underscores the general failure to grasp the potentials of radio. A trial was under way in New York City, in 1910, in connection with allegedly fraudulent claims by officers of a wireless company. An eminent engineer, Max Lowenthal, was testifying as technical expert.

"Do you believe it feasible to telephone without wires from New York to Philadelphia, or say Chicago?" the judge asked him.

"It should be possible in a few years," the witness replied, "to telephone around the world without wires."

His Honor was distressed by such absurdity. He shook his judicial head sadly. "With all due respect to your intelligence and your record," he ruled, "I must ask you to step down, Mr. Lowenthal. Your statements are extravagant and you have disqualified yourself as an expert."

Unhappily it took an episode of horror and wholesale death to awaken the world to the importance of radio. On April 14, 1912, David Sarnoff was listening casually to the routine flood of dots and dashes. Suddenly he was stung to startled attention. The message was dim and faraway and choked by static, but he deciphered it notwithstanding. It was coming from the S.S. *Olympic,* 1,400 miles away:

"S.S. *Titanic* ran into iceberg. Sinking fast."

The *Titanic,* pride of the British shipbuilding world, had made headlines while it was under construction and when it was launched. It was the largest, fastest, most luxurious passenger ship of that time. Now it was on its well-publicized initial voyage to the United States, with a passenger list that included hundreds of prominent Americans and Europeans.

The operator at Wanamaker's signaled receipt of the message and asked the *Olympic* for details. He notified the press. Soon extras were being cried in the streets and the eyes of the whole world, it seemed, along with its fears and hopes, were fixed on young Sarnoff and his earphones. Reporters, then crowds of friends and relatives of those on board the liner, along with the curious, converged on the department store. Police had to be summoned to control them and give the operator the privacy and quiet that he needed.

Other coastal stations and vessels in the disaster area tried to help, which merely jammed the airwaves. This was to be a one-man job. President Taft ordered all other stations to close down so that the one at Wanamaker's might more easily maintain communications.

For three days and three nights, without sleep and virtually without food, Sarnoff remained glued to his earphones, while a horrified world hung on his every word. Only a few of the most prominent among the frantic relatives, such as Vincent Astor and the sons of Isidor Straus, were allowed to share the somber vigil at Sarnoff's elbow. Vincent's father, John Jacob Astor, and both of the elder Strauses were among the 1,517 who drowned.

The reports from the *Olympic* were primarily names, the names of survivors as they were hauled from the ocean by radio-equipped ships that had rushed to the scene. Not until he had given the press the names of the last survivors, seventy-two hours after he had picked up the first distress signal, did the exhausted operator relinquish his earphones.

"Much of the time," he was to write years after the event, "I sat there with nothing coming in. It seemed that the whole anxious world was attached by my earphones during the seventy-two hours I crouched tensely in the station.

"I felt my responsibility keenly, and weary though I was, could not have slept. At the end of this my tryst with the sea, I was whisked in a taxicab to the old Astor House on lower Broadway and given a Turkish rub. Then I was rushed in another taxicab to Sea Gate, where communication was being kept up with the *Carpathia,* the vessel which brought in the *Titanic* survivors.

"Here again I sat for hours—listening. Now we began to get the names of some of those who were known to have gone down. This was worse than the other list had been—heartbreaking in its finality, a death-knell to hope. I passed the information on to a sorrowing world, and when messages ceased to come in, fell down like a log at my place and slept the clock around."

The stark drama of the scene—a young man in Manhattan as the sole contact with a great catastrophe in mid-ocean—made a terrific impression on the public mind. What had been a scientific curiosity was raised in a few tragic days to the status of a necessity. Hundreds more could have been saved if ships in the area, several of them closer to the *Titanic* than those that did hurry to the rescue, had been equipped to hear the distress call. This sad fact was too obvious and too devastating not to register.

The *Titanic* disaster, Sarnoff once summed it up, "brought radio to the front," adding quietly, "and incidentally me." The limelight that played for three harrowing days on the twenty-one-year-old operator would rarely dim for him in the crowded decades that followed.

2

Life had been saved at sea by wireless in the past, without erasing public apathy on the subject. But the 1,500 who perished and the 750 rescued in the *Titanic* tragedy could not be ignored; the lesson was too clear. Congress quickly passed a Radio Act that made it mandatory for ships carrying more than fifty persons to install radio and to maintain a constant watch at sea. It also prescribed the licensing of operators and regular inspection of the equipment. Shipping firms until then stubbornly indifferent to the new instrumentality now ordered equipment and, for the first time, the investment capital the Marconi Company badly needed began to flow into its coffers.

The prestige of the organization zoomed. The managing director of the British parent corporation, Godfrey Isaacs (a brother of the more famous Lord Reading) came over to reorganize its American subsidiary. Luckily for him, the company which then led all the rest in aggregate business, United Wireless, had gone into receivership notwithstanding. Mr. Isaacs was able to scoop up all its assets, rights, and contracts, and with this handsome accretion Marconi—for the time being at least—assumed clear leadership in the field.

This was a circumstance, of course, for which Sarnoff deserved no credit, except to the extent that he had starred in the radio phase of the *Titanic* drama. But it provided him with an organization big enough to give his talents and energies larger scope. Beyond most others in the company, he was aware that its leadership was no more than provisional; that it would have to be defended against emerging challenges from many directions.

While in America Mr. Isaacs also launched the most ambitious project yet for overseas radiotelegraphy. Work was started on three powerful stations, two on the Atlantic and one on the Pacific coast, for communications with Europe and the Far East. This time the cable companies became really uneasy over eventual wireless competition.

The history-making year was notable, too, for another phenomenon. It was the year when the American boy, hundreds and then thousands of him, discovered the "crystal set." A plaything for some, a consuming passion for others, do-it-yourself radio became almost a national craze. Electrical manufacturers worked overtime to supply the rising demands for parts. Elementary handbooks for the radio tinkerers by Elmer E. Bucher (later sales manager and still later the historian of the Radio Corporation of America) became profitable bestsellers.

What made the craze possible was the crystal receiver. As first invented by General Henry H. C. Dunwoody of the U.S. Army, it was a carborundum detector; then others discovered that silicon and other crystals would serve the same function. Because the crystal was cheap compared to tube detectors, and far more durable, it stimulated and gave its name to the spreading amateur participation. Antennas blossomed on roofs all over the country. In cities and towns and on remote farms, teen-agers and many adults as well forgot that night was made for sleeping. The thrill of plucking dots, dashes, and sometimes even human voices from the ether was more than Morpheus could contend with.

David Sarnoff, after the *Titanic* events, remained with Wanamaker's only a few months. The Marconi Company recognized his value to larger enterprises and he rose steadily in its ranks. Toward the end of 1912 he became its radio inspector for ships in New York harbor and a few months later chief inspector for the whole country. Then the title of assistant traffic manager was added to the list.

At the same time he served as instructor at the Marconi Institute, a training school for radio operators, who were suddenly in urgent demand. In addition he organized a special course, with himself as teacher, for the company's business executives who might wish to know more about the apparatus they were selling and the science behind the apparatus. The result was that many of his superiors, including the man who had hired him as office boy and some for whom he had run errands, now became his pupils. Those endless hours of messing in the Front Street laboratory and doing dirty chores for ships' operators were paying off—to himself and to his associates.

Godfrey Isaacs had the good sense to acknowledge that the company needed some "Americanizing" and face-lifting if it was to take advantage of its new importance and opportunities. Reluctantly, he placed an administrator with deeper American roots and larger American experience over Bottomley. That man was a veteran in the communications field, Edward J. Nally, then vice-president and general manager of the Postal Telegraph Company. He was induced to move over to American Marconi, with the same titles.

The new general manager would play a large role in Sarnoff's career—and vice versa. Nally, too, had come up from abject poverty, starting out as a Western Union messenger and office boy. But there the parallel ended. Nally when he joined Marconi was fifty-four years old, Sarnoff was then twenty-two. And they were men of strikingly different mentalities and temperaments.

The older man was cautious, penny-wise, a conventional and settled personality. He had spent about thirty-five years in wired telegraphy, a business which had itself by that time become stable and muscle-bound by tradition, in contrast to the noisy, zestful, fast-growing wireless newcomer. Sarnoff was bursting with bold ideas for improving the company's services and boosting its business—ideas which usually called for risking money and risking major innovations.

Small wonder that Nally, appraising his new staff, was rather alarmed by the boyish dynamo injected into his life. Despite this, perhaps in the long run because of this, the two men eventually made a potent team. It was to be an association of nearly forty years—Nally, happily, would live into his nineties.

As is not unusual in expanding companies, there was some tension between the technical and the commercial personnel, which in this case meant primarily Frederick M. Sammis, the chief engineer, and George De Sousa, the traffic manager. As the one official equally familiar with both divisions, and blessed with a measure of instinctive diplomacy, Sarnoff became invaluable to them—and then to the new general manager—in easing frictions.

In the summer of 1914 Nally appointed the young man as his contract manager. It was a post, as Nally possibly realized and possibly did not, that Sarnoff had himself invented to match his needs. It had the advantage of straddling both divisions, since contracts involved the negotiation of new business as well as supervision of the equipment sold or leased. Every move upward was consistent with the plan he had blueprinted for himself when still in his teens.

An inventory of his titles, while impressive, does not begin to suggest the subtle but certain growth of his influence. Inevitably some of the older men, especially those his senior in the length of association with the company, took a wry view of this boy in seven-league boots. It is not always pleasant to be outstripped by a stripling. An element of plain jealousy probably entered into the human equation, now at Marconi and even more so in years to come in the huge Radio Corporation.

But try as some of them might to keep the quietly aggressive youngster in his place, the sheer force of his ideas and insights obliged them to turn to him increasingly for opinions and proposals on commercial and engineering problems alike. At the same time nearly everyone from the general manager down remained on guard against what sometimes looked like runaway youthful enthusiasm.

The fact is that, besides his prescribed duties, Sarnoff was making the whole of the unfolding radio world his personal province. Nothing affecting its present or its future seemed to him outside his sphere of concern. He was gripped by the feeling that he was witnessing the birth of something incalculably bigger, more meaningful for the future of humanity than others around him seemed to realize.

There is an indefinable sense of history that cannot be learned, though it is sterile without a foundation of hard knowledge, and David Sarnoff appeared to possess that sense in inordinate measure.

3

Sarnoff was watching with particular attention the advances in voice transmission—what was to become known as "broadcasting." A great idea was germinating in his mind.

The Wanamaker station was refurbished in early 1914 for experimental sending of phonograph music, and its former manager kept close to the tests. A good opportunity presented itself when he sailed on the S.S. *Antilles* for New Orleans, to attend a convention of Railway Telegraph Superintendents.

By advance arrangement with the ship's radio operator, the Wanamaker program was tuned in on the first evening at sea, when the *Antilles* was about sixty miles from New York. In the salon fellow delegates and other passengers watched as the young man donned a pair of earphones. The recorded music was being pulled in clearly, sweetly. Sarnoff then invited the onlookers to take turns listening. They were all impressed—Sarnoff himself most profoundly. His great idea was taking on the lineaments of reality, though he would allow it to mature for another year before putting it on paper.

In the meantime he was drawn into a telegraphic experiment which, deservedly, attracted wide interest in its day. It was an attempt to give moving railroad trains the kind of contact by wireless long available to moving ships.

The proposal was originated by Mr. Foley, the telegraph superintendent of the Lackawanna Railroad. Negotiation of the project and the conduct of the tests fell to Sarnoff. A number of fixed stations having been erected along the Lackawanna route, a crack passenger train was equipped with sending and receiving apparatus. On January 22, 1914, with Sarnoff at the key, and with some five hundred members of the Society of Civil Engineers on the train, the first radio messages were sent and received from a fast-moving train. The experiment was highly successful and, for once, amply reported in the press and the newsreels. In the publicity the center of the stage was held by "the wonder boy of radio," as he was beginning to be called.

Among radio inventors, at this time, a new giant was coming to precocious maturity: Edwin Howard Armstrong. He had been born into a comfortable Presbyterian home in New York City, about two months before Sarnoff was born into a poverty-ridden home in far-off Russia, and raised in a big Victorian house in Yonkers, New York. Sixty-five years after the birth of the two boys, in 1956, Carl Dreher was to write in *Harper's Magazine* that "as Armstrong was the technical genius of radio's second period, David Sarnoff was and remains its administrative genius."

One of the legion of American boys fascinated by wireless, Armstrong's inventive urge asserted itself when he was still in high school. By the time he entered Columbia College at eighteen he was already hot on the trail of new principles which would revolutionize radio. The boy from Yonkers was fortunate in finding at college the warm understanding and encouragement he had not always enjoyed at home. For he was taken under the wing of the world-famous and picturesque Professor Michael I. Pupin. Sensing the student's greatness, the scientist and teacher gave him the run of the Columbia laboratory and research facilities and, after graduation, obtained for him a largely honorific assistant instructorship at $50 a month that enabled him to continue his inquiries.

The first fruit of Howard Armstrong's genius was the "feedback" or "regenerative" circuit, also to be known as the oscillating audion and the ultra-audion. He had worked out a technique for feeding back a portion of the current from the plate of a vacuum tube to the grid, where it was amplified over and over again, to make existing tubes many thousands of times more sensitive. The new method yielded magnification that brought in signals across vastly greater distances.

There was to be no public announcement of the regenerative circuit until December, 1914. But rumors of its startling power had spread through the industry and inevitably reached Sarnoff, whose mind was always attuned to novel techniques. The result was that, accompanied by two Marconi engineers, he had been given a private demonstration of the Armstrong invention at Columbia College on January 6, 1914.

For a playwright minded to point up the extraordinary youthfulness of radio at this juncture it was a scene ready-made: a twenty-three-year-old scientist showing one of the epoch-making discoveries in the annals of radio technology to a twenty-three-year-old radio executive! Armstrong was tall, blond, slow-spoken, and reserved. Sarnoff was short by comparison, quick and emphatic in speech, already every inch the entrepreneur.

The demonstration was blind, in that the apparatus was carefully hidden in a black box, the visitors being allowed only to sample its effects. The young inventor was almost obsessively secretive, determined to protect his brain children against imitation. Ironically, he was to be involved for decades, to the hour of his tragic death, in heartbreaking patent litigation, as both plaintiff and defendant, that would sap his energies, dissipate much of the fortune earned by his discoveries, and turn him prematurely old.

Sarnoff donned the earphones and deciphered messages from points as far away as Ireland and Hawaii, normally inaudible in the New York area. His report to Chief Engineer Sammis the next day, still extant, rates as a historic document. Further testing for verification was essential, he said, but "the results obtained were, I thought, quite phenomenal." Several weeks later the two young men spent forty-eight hours at the Marconi receiving station at Belmar, New Jersey. The device was still discreetly concealed in its black box, but Sarnoff subjected it to every conceivable test.

This time his report to Mr. Sammis was frankly enthusiastic—"the most remarkable receiving system in existence," he called it. He recommended its acquisition without delay. When this advice reached the London home office, Sir Godfrey Isaacs lost his temper. The rash upstart, so ready to spend the company's money, ought to be fired, he declared. But the upstart's judgment would be amply justified. What could at this point have been acquired by Marconi for a song took a symphony in 1920, when Westinghouse bought the Armstrong patents for the feedback and related developments for about half a million dollars.

The careers of the two men were to be interlinked, stormy, and in later stages embittered. An ill-assorted pair in looks, temperament, and mentality, they nevertheless developed an intimate friendship. It endured for some thirty years—until changes in the radio art brought disagreements and misunderstandings. Their deep-down respect and admiration for each other, however, remained constant almost to the end. Although by 1935 their disputes had begun to make unpleasant industry headlines, the inventor rose gallantly to defend Sarnoff against criticism at the RCA stockholders' meeting that year.

"I didn't come here to make a speech," he declared. "I didn't come here to get into a row. I have been a stockholder since 1915, since the days of the old Marconi Company. I have seen the inside of radio from the beginning to the end. I want to say that the man who pulled this company through during the difficult times of the General Electric, Westinghouse, RCA mixup with the government was its president, Mr. David Sarnoff. I think you would have been wiped out if it hadn't been for him. . . . I don't agree with everything, for I have a row on with him now. I am going to fight it through to the last ditch. I just wanted to tell you what you owe to Mr. Sarnoff."

The president of RCA was touched. "Doubtless I have made many mistakes in my life," he wrote Armstrong after the meeting, "but I am glad to say they have not been in the quality of the friends I selected for reposing my faith."

But again I am running far ahead of our story.

Sarnoff's rapid rise in the world was, naturally, reflected in improved circumstances for his family. His brothers, too, had begun to earn a little and the pinch of the extreme poverty they had all known too intimately was ended. But partly through inertia they still lived together in the walk-up flat in Brownsville.

One day in early 1914 David called the family into conference. He tried to look solemn but a half-smile played around the corners of his mouth. He had an announcement to make, he informed them, and they must listen carefully. Well, in short, and anyhow—they were moving to a nice part of the Bronx! That was a big step upward from the Brownsville slum. Leah Sarnoff naturally wanted details: what about furnishing the new home, and packing, and getting a moving van?

"There will be no packing and mighty little to move," David replied mysteriously. "Just leave everything here—and I mean everything, the furniture, the oilcloth, the dishes, the linens. No, don't sell it, give it away."

A few days later, with the air of a necromancer, he unveiled the Bronx apartment to the wide-eyed, open-mouthed Sarnoffs. It had electric lights, a bath, hot water, steam heat, all of which then rated as luxuries. And every room was completely furnished, decorated and stocked! Despite the growing pressures of his multiple jobs, he had been working secretly for months on that jackpot surprise, which cost him every dollar of his savings.

The margins for a personal life, outside his business, were not too wide.

Yet he made the most of them. Now and then he managed to take in a show on Broadway, and more often an opera at the Metropolitan. And though the romance of radio held him more securely than the conventional variety, time could always be found for girls.

4

That sense of history to which I alluded earlier overflowed in numerous memoranda and letters by Sarnoff, addressed to his superiors. Reading them today, in the perspective of events, one marvels at the clarity of his vision, the accuracy of his analyses and forecasts—especially when it is recalled that they were written by a man in his early twenties who had been in the communications field only seven or eight years.

"Sarnoff was now convinced," Elmer E. Bucher would sum it up, "that the old Marconi Company traditions would no longer suffice, and that new equipment of higher technical efficiency, plus licenses under the patents of others, alone would keep the Marconi Company to the fore in the development of radio-marine services and international communication.

"He then plotted a course of action which was intended to awaken his superiors to the necessity of revising the company's technical programs and its commercial policies. Here he was already laying the basis for his future career, studying minutely the entire field of radio, seeing into the needs and requirements of the present and the future, projecting plans to meet these requirements, and then finding some way to convince his superiors of his convictions."

The opinions and suggestions he submitted, as Bucher indicates, were not random, impulsive affairs. Though the recipients could not know this, they were elements in a carefully thought-out plan—a plan that had in view nothing less than the rehabilitation of the company's equipment and attitudes. Without any official authority, working obliquely through those who did wield authority, David Sarnoff was attempting to steer the company—and through the company the entire evolving industry—in directions he considered wholesome.

In these missives to Sammis, De Sousa, Nally, and occasionally even Guglielmo Marconi, he was tactful and self-effacing. There was in them no hectoring or bravado; from their tone an outsider could never have guessed how young and inexperienced the author was. Sarnoff knew that by this pressure from below he risked offending higher-placed associates. When his advice and proposals were pigeonholed, he was not surprised; but neither was he surprised when eventually they were dusted off and acted upon. He counted on the cogency of his insights and foresights.

Thus by 1914—and increasingly in the following years—he became, *de facto* though not yet *de jure,* the company's most effective adviser on technological and commercial policies.

Where far more experienced men were inclined to rest on the Marconi laurels, Sarnoff lost no chance to emphasize the vitality of competitors. The American subsidiary of Germany's Telefunken (Atlantic Communication Company), the National Electric Signaling Company, the De Forest Radio and Telegraph Company, the Federal Telegraph Company of California—not one of them seemed a real immediate menace. But Sarnoff, observing their operations closely, kept his company apprised of their points of superiority.

True, the basic Marconi patents were thorns in the side of every competitor. Infringement, however, had become almost habitual in the radio world. Patent suits lingered in the courts for years, during which positions of advantage could be won or lost. Indeed, so many inventions and refinements overlapped that rigid observance of patent rights would have paralyzed all contenders, Marconi included.

More to the point, as Sarnoff patiently explained the matter, was that others possessed devices to which Marconi had no access, such as the Telefunken quenched spark transmitter, Fessenden's synchronous rotary transmitter, Armstrong's feedback technique, the Alexanderson alternator. Besides, General Electric, Western Electric, and other big corporations had research facilities and staffs beyond what Marconi could muster and, in the nature of things, were bound to attain technical ascendancy.

To meet this complex threat from many directions, Nally slowly recognized, required the kind of imagination and realism that his youthful contract manager seemed both able and eager to provide. Though congenitally a conservative, he repeatedly found himself siding with the younger man's radical therapy.

Sarnoff was not unmindful of the fact that his views, however diplomatically advanced, implied criticism of existing practices. He had to assume the almost automatic hostility of those responsible for current policies. Thus we find him writing to Nally, in March, 1914:

"Faith in certain production methods by the misinformed or the uninformed is often mistaken as a sign of 'loyalty.' To me, this does not seem to be the fundamental of loyalty. I think that whatever one might deem necessary and expedient to tell another, it should, nevertheless, be remembered that 'It is a great mistake to fool oneself.' No matter what we may determine amongst ourselves, the ultimate and most important decision is reached by the consumer and the people on the outside who are competent to judge."

On another occasion—and again with an awareness of the dangers inherent in criticism of seniors—he wrote:

"In conclusion I want to state that my views on the entire subject are given chiefly with the object of improving the present conditions. It is evident that while an apparatus may have been quite sufficient several years ago and probably sufficient at present to fulfill all requirements, it is nevertheless well to look forward to the future and this can be done by frankly discussing the viewpoints of all those who have suggestions to offer."

His strictures on the company's equipment finally led him to the logical but unpopular conclusion that it should be virtually scrapped in favor of competing devices, to be obtained by license or purchase. The daring proposal drew angry fire from heaven itself—from London headquarters, that is to say. For it meant discarding apparatus that had cost immense sums, and a loss of face to boot. But convinced that he was right and that the changes were inescapable, the young man stuck to his guns.

The letter containing the quotation about "loyalty" was by way of prelude to a memorandum in which Sarnoff asked fifteen "leading questions." A Technical Committee, comprising the company's top engineers, had been set up to appraise the state of Marconi apparatus and technology. Sarnoff asked that the committee be confronted with his probing queries—dealing with the design and efficiency of radio transmitters and receivers—but that his authorship should not be revealed. Though cast in the interrogative mood, the answers were implicit in each of the questions and hardly flattering to Marconi leadership.

The affronted engineers probably guessed the source of the queries. Who but that juvenile upstart would have had the gumption to impugn their collective wisdom? His views met with a barrage of opposition, some of it sharply worded. But, as Bucher later chronicled the facts: "The logic of the questions put the engineering forces on the defensive. The records of the succeeding two years show that the Sarnoff program had been adopted by the company."

More and more, also, Sarnoff was now beginning to act as spokesman for the industry as a whole. In a paper presented before the Institute of Radio Engineers in September, 1914, for example, the twenty-three-year-old Marconi man directed himself to an analysis of the rules and procedures, national and international, of routing messages between ships and shore stations. This involved intricate problems of the division of tolls collected, rates per word or per message, the importance or unimportance of speed in transmission, and other thorny problems.

All of his judgments, naturally, touched off heated controversy among the firms, the countries, the governments affected. The expansion of the wireless arts and business was so rapid that regulation of the traffic could not keep up with it. A study of decisions ultimately reached, according to historians of the industry, indicates that sooner or later Sarnoff's basic views came to prevail.

5

In the dossier of the Sarnoff memoranda of this period, one stands out above the rest. It has been acclaimed as one of the most remarkable documents in the annals of radio and certainly it has been the most publicized, quoted, and admired. Far from tarnishing its glory, the passing years have heightened its luster. Also, it mirrored those qualities of its author's mind and method that would in the future help shape the entire art, science, and industry of radio under his leadership.

The memorandum, composed in the late autumn of 1915 and addressed to Vice-President Nally, was decidedly not a flash of inspiration. It was, rather, the end product of years of watching, testing, discussing, and above all, thinking about radiotelephony.

Sarnoff was continuing to take part in the Wanamaker station broadcasts—those with which he had astounded passengers on the S.S. *Antilles*. Other such programs were being put on the air on an amateur basis by a brilliant young professor of electrical engineering, Alfred Goldsmith, at the College of the City of New York. Dr. Goldsmith (subsequently chief broadcasting engineer for RCA and still its engineering and research consultant) had built up an ardent audience of crystal-set enthusiasts within a radius of 750 miles. Meanwhile the giant electric corporations, such as GE and Western Electric, were making progress on the basic tools of radiotelephony.

The most impressive victory was scored by the American Telephone and Telegraph Company, through its laboratories. Having developed more powerful and more stable vacuum tubes, A.T.&T. combined a battery of them with the Armstrong feedback system for a giant transmitter installed at the U.S. Navy radio station at Arlington, Virginia. Some of the tests failed but those that succeeded were sensational. Voice programs from Arlington were heard in September and October, 1915, as far as Paris to the east, San Francisco and Honolulu to the west, distances from 3,000 to 5,000 miles. But while striking as an experimental demonstration, the effort opened no immediate practical possibilities; the process was exorbitant in cost and as yet too erratic in operation.

It was against this background that Sarnoff projected his historic plan for what he called a "Radio Music Box"—an extraordinarily accurate preview of the home radio receiver as it was to emerge in the early 1920's.

The very word "telephony" seemed to him to point to a failure of imagination. Experimenters were thinking almost wholly in terms of point-to-point communication: a wireless substitute, that is, for the existing wired telephones. The great commercial weakness of wireless in this connection, it was generally and sadly said, was its lack of privacy. The sound was sprayed indiscriminately in all directions, and anyone could eavesdrop on a conversation between Smith and Jones.

Sarnoff, of course, was not the first man to realize that this lack of secrecy, accounted an insuperable liability, could be turned into the greatest asset of radio by enabling one voice to reach thousands or millions simultaneously. As early as 1904 the great inventor Nikola Tesla had flirted with the idea, though vaguely and hesitantly. He wrote of a possible device which "will be very efficient in enlightening the masses . . . a cheap and simple device which might be carried in one's pocket" and set up to catch signals in the atmosphere. About a decade later Charles Steinmetz, the wizard of electricity, came much closer to the broadcasting concept in a magazine article.

But Sarnoff was the first to think this through to a concrete conclusion and to set it forth in the language of actuality. The memorandum is worth quoting *in extenso:*

I have in mind a plan of development which would make radio a "household utility" in the same sense as the piano or phonograph. The idea is to bring music into the home by wireless.

While this has been tried in the past by wires, it has been a failure because wires do not lend themselves to this scheme. With radio, however, it would be entirely feasible.

For example, a radio telephone transmitter having a range of say 25 to 50 miles can be installed at a fixed point where the instrumental or vocal music or both are produced. The problem of transmitting music has already been solved in principle and therefore all the receivers attuned to the transmitting wave length should be capable of receiving such music. The receiver can be designed in the form of a simple "Radio Music Box" and arranged for several different wave lengths, which should be changeable with the throwing of a single switch or pressing of a single button.

The "Radio Music Box" can be supplied with amplifying tubes and a loudspeaking telephone, all of which can be neatly mounted in one box. The box can be placed on a table in the parlor or living room, the switch set accordingly and the music received. There should be no difficulty in receiving music perfectly when transmitted within a radius of 25 to 50 miles.

Within such a radius there reside hundreds of thousands of families; and as all can simultaneously receive from a single transmitter, there should be no question of obtaining sufficiently loud signals to make the performance enjoyable. The power of the transmitter can be made 5 K.W., if necessary, to cover even a short radius of 25 to 50 miles; thereby giving extra loud signals in the home if desired. The use of head telephones would be obviated by this method. The development of a small loop antenna to go with each "Radio Music Box" would likewise solve the antennae problem.

The same principle can be extended to numerous other fields as, for example, receiving lectures at home which can be made perfectly audible; also, events of national importance can be simultaneously announced and received. Baseball scores can be transmitted in the air by the use of one set installed at the Polo Grounds. The same would be true of other cities. This proposition would be especially interesting to farmers and others in outlying districts removed from cities. By the purchase of a "Radio Music Box" they could enjoy concerts, lectures, music, recitals, etc. which may be going on in the nearest city within their radius.

While I have indicated a few of the most probable fields of usefulness for such a device, yet there are numerous other fields to which the principle can be extended.

The memorandum then went over to the technical and fiscal aspects of the idea:

The manufacture of the "Radio Music Box" including antenna, in large quantities, would make possible their sale at a moderate figure of perhaps $75 per outfit. The main revenue would be derived from the sale of "Radio Music Boxes" which if manufactured in quantities of 100,000 or so could yield a handsome profit when sold at the price mentioned above.

Secondary sources of revenue would be from the sale of transmitters and from increased advertising and circulation of the *Wireless Age*.

The company would have to undertake the arrangements, I am sure, for music recitals, lectures, etc. which arrangements can be satisfactorily worked out.

It is not possible to estimate the total amount of business obtainable with this plan until it has been developed and actually tried out; but there are about 15,000,000 families in the United States alone, and if only one million or seven percent of the total families thought well of the idea it would, at the figure mentioned, mean a gross business of about $75,000,000 which should yield considerable revenue.

Aside from the profit to be derived from this proposition the possibilities for advertising for the company are tremendous, for its name would ultimately receive national and universal attention.

To Nally and others who read it in wide-eyed amazement, the Music Box idea seemed more than a bit harebrained. Interesting but fantastic. So they shrugged it off, filed it away, and forgot it.

The industry was bogged down in a morass of patent conflicts and stock manipulations. There were exaggerated claims, heated counterclaims, and expensive legal wars. No less a pioneering inventor than Lee De Forest was brought to trial in 1912, accused of selling stock for his wireless system on fraudulent technical pretensions. Referring to an invention that would enshrine De Forest's name in electronic history, the prosecution called it "a strange device like an incandescent lamp, which he called an Audion, and which device was proved to be worthless." It is a measure of the confusion and public ignorance on the new industry that De Forest barely avoided going to prison. The court solicitously advised the young man to turn honest by "getting into a common garden variety job and sticking to it."

The valor of the Sarnoff proposal is underlined, therefore, by the background of patent chaos. In his memorandum he did not even bother to unscramble the manifold devices that would go into his theoretical "box" or to ascertain which of them the Marconi Company did or did not control. This, however, was no oversight. Now, as in the future, he proceeded on the common-sense assumption that the industry, being interdependent, would in due time have to enjoy full access to all devices. This was the prime and irreducible condition for its healthy growth.

Europe was already at war and before long the United States entered the struggle. No one could spare thought for music boxes. But in 1920 the memorandum would be drawn out of the file, and many would wonder that five years before the obvious had been obvious to only one man. In later years the press would get wind of the "prophecy" and it would become standard fare in historical articles and books about radio.

Because the actuality—with respect both to the "box" and to its uses—turned out to be so close to what he had sketched, the memorandum became the cornerstone of a remarkable edifice: David Sarnoff's reputation as a "prophet." The Music Box, the first and best known in a long array of predictions, was typical of that sense of the future which prompted Dr. Gleason Archer to call Sarnoff "the prophet in our midst." It was what Nally meant when he declared, many years later, that "wireless never caught up with him."

6

The Radio Corporation Is Born

❧ As of January 1, 1917, the Marconi organization brought large portions of its activities, until then dispersed in a number of departments, into a new, over-all Commercial Department. The move reflected the sudden growth of radio business as the government stepped up military preparations. Defense orders for millions of dollars in equipment, primarily from the Navy, were being placed with Marconi, as with other companies. Ground was broken in New Jersey for new Marconi plants tripling the manufacturing capacity.

David Sarnoff, not quite twenty-six, became head of the new department, with the title of commercial manager.

In the years since he left the Wanamaker post he had grown enormously. Within the industry he was widely recognized as a coming leader—his election as secretary of the Institute of Radio Engineers was one indication. In newspaper city rooms he was no less widely recognized as "good copy," so that his opinions were solicited and his public speeches increasingly reported.

During these few formative years he had tested and sharpened his inborn ability to sort out myriad conflicting ideas and data, discarding the dross and concentrating on the gold. He had learned the art of reducing complicated situations to a few basic and easily comprehended principles. He had engaged in negotiations of great importance, dealt intimately with the patent tangle, and helped formulate policies on rates, licensing standards, and other issues. Already he probably knew the technological intricacies of his trade as thoroughly as any other practitioner. Since he was not himself an inventor, his judgments on the unfolding science were not warped by the kind of ego drives and emotional reactions that unavoidably affected the views of men like De Forest or Fessenden or Armstrong.

As commercial manager he was now definitely in the upper echelon of the whole industry. His responsibilities were large and varied. Under him were 725 employees—the number was to grow rapidly—and the radio installations on 582 vessels. He negotiated all service contracts, supervised sales to the government and to private customers. His was the prime responsibility for providing operators, maintaining effective customer relations, regulating the movement of his company's radio and telegraph traffic. Under his direction, as Bucher would write one day, "the Commercial Department became the creative department, a new hub around which all the commercial activities of the Marconi Company revolved."

Once more, however, the title and its growing emoluments were no sufficient measure of his functions. In reality he was now second-in-command in the American organization, with Nally as his sole superior. The alliance between the two men was by this time firmly cemented. Older men, in tenure as well as age, whom he had passed on his way up were sometimes peeved; a few grumbled audibly, more tried to trip him up. In his mind Sarnoff filed such things under the head of Struggle, one of those facts of life.

In the closing months of 1916 Sarnoff had for the first time faced the lawmakers of the nation. His aim was to help head off the threat of government ownership of radio. He could not know that it was the beginning of a lifetime assignment—that ultimately he would be credited with doing more than any other one man to keep radio on a private-enterprise and incentive basis.

Washington, motivated largely by concern for military communications in a world at war, was reaching out for virtual government domination. In November, 1916, a plan worked out by an Inter-Department Committee on Radio Legislation was in the lap of Congress. Under its recommendations the Navy would be authorized to operate stations in competition with private firms even in peacetime; rates and regulations of traffic would be fixed by the Secretary of Commerce. In effect the plan would have made the industry an appendage of the government.

The very survival of private initiative in this sphere was at stake and industry leaders naturally rallied in opposition. Sarnoff, significantly, testified not for his own company but as spokesman for the industry, in his capacity as secretary of the Institute of Radio Engineers. Having presented the Institute's formal resolution indicting the proposed plan, as well as several statements by individual experts, he enlarged on the theme. He was cast in the role of a man concerned with the industry as a whole, seeking to solve its problems and guide its healthy growth.

Two months later there was a further Congressional hearing, this time on actual bills to implement the government plan. Again Sarnoff was in the fore among those who were warning that government ownership would stifle a great emerging service. The coming of war, however, soon made the issue academic. The armed forces took over on an emergency basis.

A personal anecdote of this period, just before the United States entered the war, seems worth telling, if only because Sarnoff himself liked to tell it in after years. A Russian commission came to New York to shop for radio equipment for its armed forces. It fell to Sarnoff to entertain the general heading the mission and they became quite friendly. When the deal was being wound up, the general proposed that his American host come with him to Russia to supervise the installations.

"Might be interesting." David Sarnoff smiled. "Have you forgotten that I was born in your country and emigrated as a child?"

The general instantly turned solemn. "In that case," he announced, "I would be obliged to place you under arrest just as soon as we crossed the three-mile line—for failure to do military service. Under Russian law you are technically a deserter."

In February, 1917, the United States broke off diplomatic relations with Germany. In the first days of April the country was at war. The government took control of all high-powered radiotelegraphy stations, including those of the Marconi Company. Said Sarnoff afterwards, "I was thrown in with the other liabilities and assets."

On the purely personal level, too, 1917 was an important date for him. On July Fourth he married a beautiful French-born girl, Lizette Hermant, blonde, vivacious, with a peaches-and-cream complexion. In the family circle the private little joke was that on Independence Day he surrendered his independence.

It was a Bronx romance made, if not in heaven, at any rate in its terrestrial environs—specifically, in a house of worship. There during the High Holidays two women met at prayers and, in the manner of their kind, proceeded to boast about their progeny. One of them, recently arrived from Paris, talked about her lovely daughter. The other, not to be outdone, sang the praises of the eldest of her four sons.

The matchmaking instinct was aroused on both sides. Two such prodigies, one of beauty and the other of success, they agreed, were made for one another. The mothers therefore in time contrived an "accidental" meeting to test their theory. It proved even more successful than either Leah Sarnoff or Lizette's mother had thought possible.

It was love at first sight on both sides, but the engagement was a long one. Lizette would recall, in the fullness of time, that David wooed her with "fairy tales about a little music box." Her cautious mother thought well of the prospective son-in-law but confessed that she was worried by his strange talk of "voices in the air," which seemed to throw some doubts on his fundamental sanity. Her daughter was no less apprehensive about his imaginative bent. But in the end love had its way and a modest wedding followed. "I could speak no French," David explained, "and Lizette could speak no English, so what else could we do?"

2

As soon as the United States plunged into the war David Sarnoff betook himself to the Brooklyn Navy Yard for enlistment, applying for a commission in the communications branch.

At first he could not understand the delay on his application. But after a while he became aware—and much disturbed—that his "case" had run into a roadblock of race prejudice in Washington. Meanwhile the machinery of the military draft was at work. Despite urging from Washington and from within his company, Sarnoff refused to ask his local draft board for exemption and he was duly certified for service in the Army. The local board, of course, at the outset knew nothing about the wartime implications of radio. It ignored a letter from Admiral R. S. Griffin, engineer in chief of the Navy, certifying to the young man's importance to the war effort. The Admiral then sent a second, more persuasive letter in which he told the draft officials:

"Exemption is considered absolutely necessary, in order that the Fleet will not suffer delays due to unsatisfactory deliveries in existing contracts."

The draft order was thereupon canceled. As for the commission, the application was turned down but the blow was cushioned by flattery. The Navy Department formally requested that he curb his patriotism and remain where he was; his services as commercial manager of Marconi Wireless were officially rated as indispensable to the war effort.

Great disasters have ever quickened the pace of invention and technology. The progress of wireless, as we have seen, had been repeatedly speeded up by catastrophes on the high seas. Now the all-encompassing catastrophe of a world war, even before America was in it, was giving powerful impetus to its growth and development. Under the spur of military necessity, historians of the industry would attest, many years of progress were compressed into every year of war.

The vulnerability of cables, and hence the value of the wireless alternative, was dramatized in the initial weeks of the conflict when the British severed all cables serving enemy nations. Then the Kaiser's U-boats, in their turn, succeeded in cutting British cables. Of necessity the warring countries fell back on radio, especially for contacts with their forces at sea. In radio-telegraphy, moreover, both sides found the most effective instrument for propaganda aimed at hostile and neutral public opinion.

During nearly three years of increasingly unneutral neutrality the moral of this story registered full force in Washington. The Navy, which had from the outset been keen on the new science, now gave it top priorities. Its chain of stations—in the Philippines, Hawaii, Panama, and on the mainland—was enlarged and its power boosted. All major electric companies had to work overtime and erect new plants to supply pressing government demand. A good many radio patents were bought by the Navy outright.

With the declaration of war in April, 1917, President Woodrow Wilson placed all radio facilities in the United States and its possessions, both commercial and amateur, under government control, which in practice meant overwhelmingly under the aegis of the Navy. Only the manufacturing end of the business and a dwindling portion of installations on merchant vessels remained in private hands. Almost overnight the U.S. government was thus operating a radio setup more formidable than that of the rest of the world combined.

The Navy, besides, commandeered all existing devices to make—for the first time—complete patterns of effective equipment. Personal preferences, considerations of commercial prestige, fears of patent infringement—all were swept aside. In the process it was demonstrated how seriously radio tech-nology had been hampered and hobbled by patent rivalries. At last apparatus could be used without reference to who owned what. The results were astonishing and the lesson would greatly influence the future of the industry.

The Marconi Company had been building its largest station for overseas service at New Brunswick, New Jersey. The government now completed the undertaking, with a 50-KW Alexanderson alternator in place; subsequently an alternator of 200 KW, the largest yet produced, was installed. The station became the most powerful then in existence and its call number, NNF, became familiar on all battlefields and behind their lines.

Through the new magic of radio, President Wilson's historic address to Congress on January 8, 1918, embodying his Fourteen Points for a just peace, was disseminated throughout the world in a few hours. The New Brunswick station and radio in general played a major role in the Wilsonian appeals over the heads of enemy governments which doubtless hastened the Armistice.

In the course of the hostilities, radio was America's main medium of communication with its expeditionary forces. Even in the forward trenches troops were provided with regular news bulletins. To meet the mounting need for radio operators, special schools had to be set up; those at Harvard and at Mare Island, California, gave training to an aggregate of over 5,000 students.

Through his personal dependence on the new force, both in war and during the Peace Conference in Paris, President Wilson was profoundly impressed with its destined role in human affairs. So was a dapper Assistant Secretary of the Navy named Franklin Delano Roosevelt. They realized, as did most other officials, that the United States, where the most significant strides had been made in wireless, must never permit foreign domination in this area. It was a realization which would help direct Sarnoff's career.

Of some twenty suppliers of radio equipment to the government, the largest was Marconi. Its sales for 1917 exceeded $5,000,000, an unprecedented total for the company. Chief responsibility for the efficient flow of this vital material rested with Sarnoff. In effect he became the coordinator and expediter between his firm and the armed forces, dividing his time between the Marconi plants and the national capital.

He was constantly called in by the Navy and the Army for consultation on problems of military communications. In addition, his was the guiding hand in engineering and research projects of tremendous pertinence to the conduct of war. Among the major Marconi accomplishments during the war period were radios on airplanes and devices for reducing static. Usually it was young Sarnoff who supervised official tests and always it was he who negotiated the government contracts for the new apparatus. The vast contacts and experience in government that he gathered at this time would prove extremely useful to him in the crowded years ahead.

At the war's end he received generous commendations from military leaders for his work. Typical was a letter from the head of the Radio Bureau of the Navy at the time, Commander Sanford C. Hooper.

"At the beginning of hostilities," it said, "this Bureau deemed it of importance to the nation's interest to request that you be denied the privilege of active duty with the troops, as your services were urgently required in connection with the supply of radio equipment to the Fleet. . . . Our constant association throughout this trying time led me to admire your work and your organization tremendously and I came to realize that I could depend upon you above all others."

Despite his numberless business duties, which allowed barely any margin for a personal life, Sarnoff throughout the war had kept a vigilant eye on the legislative chambers in Washington. The industry was almost unanimous in dreading the extension of military controls, inescapable in the great emergency, into peacetime. Simple self-interest was involved, obviously, and Sarnoff, concerned for the fate of his company, shared this motivation.

But his zeal went far beyond this. He was convinced in principle of the long-run superiority of private enterprise. More than any other representative of the industry, he had assumed the task of shielding it against government encroachments—precisely because, more than any of them, he sensed the limitless horizons of radio and therefore reacted against anything which might obstruct or slow down its advance. Nearly everyone, especially on official levels, still thought of radio simply as a medium of communication parallel with the telegraph and the telephone. Sarnoff, as his prewar vision of the Radio Music Box attests, thought of it in terms of unique services and influences far beyond the compass of older media.

The people pressing for government ownership had a plausible case in the fact that under government operation radio was making the most of all available inventions and technical improvements. Its relinquishment to private capital, they argued, would renew the prewar patent wrangle and would, besides, leave radio wide open to domination by foreign interests. But Sarnoff and others retorted that this was a passing phase, a species of growing pains, and that in any case the price was worth paying. In the end, they promised, the industry would evolve its own solutions for its problems.

Leading the campaign for government controls was no less a political personage than Josephus Daniels, Secretary of the Navy. His influence was usually behind the spate of bills in every session of Congress looking to regulation of radio so stringent that it came close to government hegemony. The young spokesman for the Marconi Company and for the professional organizations in which he was increasingly active became an expected witness at committee hearings, speaking calmly, always in command of the concrete facts, consistently defending the thesis that the private initiative which had produced radio must not be hampered in developing its full potentials.

For Sarnoff it was the prelude to a lifelong fight to hold radio—and therefore in due time television and electronics generally—within the free-economy pattern. Much of his labor in this context is on record, in Congressional testimony, speeches, and articles. Much more—his running debate through the decades with legislators, military men, and socialist-oriented theorists—is unrecorded.

3

Secretary Daniels was not a man to give up easily. Eight months after the Armistice he was still writing to Congressional committees in support of legislation which, however disguised, would have made radio the creature of officialdom. Again and again David Sarnoff appeared before those committees to plead the case for private initiative.

Yet the threat of government ownership was steadily receding. Americans had tasted a lot of official regimentation in the war and apparently they didn't like the flavor. Secretary Daniels himself tacitly acknowledged that the country was not ready for a fundamental break with its economic tradition, since he was permitting his subordinates to make dramatic plans for the future of radio on the premise of private control.

The immediate danger in the domain of radiotelegraphy and -telephony was that of foreign dominance. The victorious war had quickened national pride and sensitivity to security factors, and these sustained the rising sentiment for American autonomy. So did the unholy spectacle of the Paris Peace Conference, with its orgy of greed and grab, its cynical scramble for national advantage. The determination grew apace that foreign influence must be stripped away and that the United States must seek a position of leadership in international communications.

"Foreign" meant British and that in turn meant primarily the British Marconi Company. The restoration of world commerce was putting heavy strains on both cables and wireless channels. A boom in communication was clearly building up. Great Britain, with a virtual monopoly of world cable systems in its hands, was reaching out frankly and boldly for an equivalent position in the new medium.

This put the operating executives of American Marconi, Americans all, in something of a psychological dilemma. Basically they shared Washington's apprehensions over British ambitions. Some of them, indeed, saw even more sharply than did military men that Americans were about to be squeezed out of the world's major radio channels. Yet they were dependent, in the final analysis, upon majority stockholders in England. Theirs was an uncomfortable position and they were gratified when forces outside their company moved to extricate them.

The outlines of a rational answer to the British challenge were taking shape among those in the Navy closest to the picture. The first to articulate it was probably Commander Hooper and he at once won the support of the director of naval communications, Admiral W. H. G. Bullard, of Franklin D. Roosevelt, and of others in places of authority or influence.

Their plan envisioned the creation of a powerful private corporation, with the tacit backing of the government, to take over as much as possible of the radio patents and facilities soon to be released to their original owners. Licenses in inventions owned by the Navy could be added to the pool in the hope of providing a spectrum of equipment adequate both for domestic services and for energetic competition with other countries.

The issue was brought to a head early in 1919 when British Marconi acted to acquire at least unrestricted access to, and if possible exclusive control of, the Alexanderson high-frequency alternator, developed and owned by General Electric.

Back in March, 1916, David Sarnoff having concluded a study of the main existing methods of sending electromagnetic signals, reported that the one based on the Alexanderson device was "most likely to survive." The war experience bore out his judgment. Whoever controlled this alternator, it now seemed apparent, would have an almost insuperable advantage in the race for global leadership.

Actually the British bid for exclusive rights dated back to the spring of 1915. Guglielmo Marconi, in America on other business, spent a day in Schenectady inspecting General Electric manufacture of wireless apparatus and the Alexanderson alternator especially. He then wrote to the head of the GE legal department, Owen D. Young, suggesting that they meet in his New York hotel to discuss possible British purchase of the alternator patents.

For Mr. Young, destined to be neck-deep in radio, this was his initial contact with the business. In later years he would say whimsically that the first "wireless message" he ever received came to him from Marconi—by mail. His meeting with the inventor led to protracted negotiations, marked by long delays on both sides, until America's entry into the war canceled out the whole enterprise.

Now, three months after the Armistice, representatives of Marconi's company in England came over to renew the undertaking. Tentative terms were sketched, involving millions of dollars in alternator orders and an outright bonus of a million dollars for various exclusive rights.

Young, for GE, considered it his patriotic duty to apprise the Navy of the impending contract. The news touched off acute alarm in Washington, accelerating action on plans already formulated. Admiral Bullard, it appeared, had been alerted by President Wilson himself to the need to forestall foreign control of the high-frequency transmitter. So Hooper and others quickly intervened. In a letter signed by Assistant Secretary Roosevelt they asked GE to postpone action until the situation could be examined in an early conference. The conference took place in New York on April 8.

As a matter of highest national policy, Admiral Bullard urged that the electric company break off negotiations with the British, to which Young, for his corporation, agreed forthwith. He indicated the magnitude of the financial sacrifice being made by his company. The naval men thereupon brought out their design for an all-American organization, one that would be financially and technically robust enough to bid for both domestic and world primacy in radio communications. They proposed, moreover, that GE take the initiative in assembling the elements for such an organization.

Another company, too, had been considered for the task of forming the radio colossus: The American Telephone & Telegraph Company. It, too, held vital patents and disposed of the necessary financial resources. But the GE control of the critical Alexanderson device tipped the scales in its favor. Soon Young and naval officers were drawing up specifications for the new corporation.

The big electric companies—GE, Westinghouse, and others—were at this stage serenely disinterested in communications, except as a profitable market for the equipment they produced. A.T.&T. was concerned only with the use of various radio patents in its keeping for more effective transmission of voice by wire; wireless still seemed competitive and outside its realm.

Before long all these groups and dozens of others would come to covet a place in radio, particularly in its exciting new dimension of broadcasting for home audiences. Their struggles for supremacy in this realm would create protracted dramas of industrial competition and legal duels. But as of 1919 the only real radio organization extant, interested in all aspects of the enterprise and having the most experienced personnel, was American Marconi.

From the first, therefore, this company was acknowledged to be indispensable, the keystone of the new structure. Before it could be set in place, however, the parent company across the ocean had to be induced to sell its stockholdings to Americans. Edward Nally for the U.S. subsidiary and Albert G. Davis for GE sailed to England for this purpose. After nearly three months of strenuous argument and bargaining, they were finally able to apprise their home offices that they had succeeded.

Now the Radio Corporation of America, as it was already being referred to, was ready for launching. In effect it would be the old American Marconi Company in a revised corporate form, with major ownership and dominant control vested in General Electric. All that remained to be done was to spell out the details of the relations between RCA and GE. This entailed a vast amount of intricate negotiation in which Sarnoff, as the most knowledgeable official in the partnership, of necessity carried the main burden.

Finally, on December 1, 1919, the Radio Corporation became a reality, with Nally as president, George De Sousa as treasurer, E. F. W. Alexanderson, the scientist who gave his name to the alternator, as chief engineer. A few months later Owen D. Young was named chairman of the board of directors. Admiral Bullard was on the board, without vote, as liaison for the Navy. Sarnoff retained his old post as commercial manager but was not named to the board.

Under the terms of the advance agreement, not more than 20 percent of RCA stock could be owned by foreigners. All manufacturing was to be done by GE, all marketing and communications services rested with RCA. By means of a cross-licensing arrangement, each organization had full access to wireless patents held by the other. Not a word was said, forthrightly, about broadcasting; even at the end of 1919 its business potential was underrated or ignored—except by the commercial manager.

4

As chairman of the board of the Radio Corporation, Owen D. Young found himself in the top spot in American radio. The complexities of the industry were quite new to him. Fortunately for all concerned, what the lawyer lacked in technical and scientific training for his new responsibilities was soon being supplied, willingly and copiously, by that remarkable young man from the Marconi office who had suddenly come into his business life.

In the months of negotiations preceding the birth of the corporation and even more so in the critical postnatal months, Young discovered that he could confidently turn to David Sarnoff for elucidation and guidance. Even when he was dealing with President Nally or other of Sarnoff's superiors, he soon realized, the imprint of the younger man's mind was usually on their plans, documents, and arguments.

Sarnoff seemed to have a clear-eyed view of the total picture, along with an instinct for the vital points, as against the incidental and temporary. Some men excel in the grasp of detail, the facts and figures, the minutiae of contracts, patents, laws. There are others whose main gift is that of extended vision, men who not only see the landscape whole but apprehend its contours beyond the horizons of visibility. Sarnoff was the rarer individual who combined both capacities.

Young and Sarnoff, who were to become the heads of their respective companies, made a unique team. In the hectic beginning years of RCA each was to find the other a source of strength against detractors and intriguers. In background and temperament they presented a contrast no less unique.

Young was born on a farm in Van Hornesville, New York, and received an ordered, conventional education. From the time he won his law degree in 1896 through 1912 he practiced law in Boston, mostly in the fields of public utilities. Gradually he emerged as a respected specialist in the mysteries of high finance. When General Electric lost its chief counsel and cast around for a successor, it turned to Young, who took the post and in January, 1913, and moved to Schenectady.

When he first ran into the Marconi commercial manager Young was forty-five, a tall, spare, austere-looking man, deliberate in speech and rather reserved in manner, the very prototype of the solid corporation counsel. The slightly built Sarnoff then looked more boyish than his twenty-eight years. Always articulate, often exuberant, a dynamo of energy, he seemed to know everything and everyone in radio. He was prone to flights of commercial and technological fantasy, sometimes in the midst of scanning a column of figures or an organizational chart. For all his grasp of immediacy, he was a man obsessed by the future.

Between the two men there were thus few natural points of contact. To the seasoned, typically American lawyer Sarnoff must have seemed a new and slightly disturbing specimen. Mutual appreciation was almost instantaneous: each at once discerned the special competence of the other; but the friendship that in time grew between them would necessarily be of slow maturing. David was impressed and a bit overawed by the great reputation of the older man, his air of authority, of "belonging." As for Young, what could such a man understand of the alien world in which Sarnoff had his roots?

Then and throughout his career, in truth, the younger man was to find more admirers—sometimes grudging admirers—than intimate friends in the purlieus of business. He felt more at ease in a literary-theatrical haunt like the old Café Royal on Second Avenue than in the opulent clubs for exalted executives. His hunger for intellectual stimulus, for the education he had missed, drew him to men and women with unusual minds, catholic tastes, creative impulses; and apparently he met more of these outside the orbit of finance and industry where he spent the larger part of his active life. The few big businessmen who did become part of his social milieu would be those who shared his own serious interests in affairs outside business, in the arts, in the poetry of scientific exploration, and increasingly as he grew older in national and international politics.

The trait most often alluded to by those who worked with Sarnoff or in his shadow, in trying to assess his personality, was already sharply in evidence. It was what some of them called his "aloofness." One early associate, whom I interviewed, thought it was a deliberate "tactic," a desire to surround himself with an aura of mystery. But all other testimony refutes this judgment. The aloofness was not a pose but an expression of the man's character. He was making a virtue of his predominantly introvert character, his inability to play hail-fellow-well-met.

It has been said, in print, that Sarnoff is "too subtle to be a gladhander and too intelligent to be a back-slapper." But this misses the target. His restraint was a matter neither of subtlety nor of intelligent policy but inherent in his makeup. There simply seemed little room in his life for levity and persiflage. He had small gift for small talk. Even if he tried, he never could have passed himself off as "one of the boys." Baseball, golf, bowling, poker—he could not even pretend an interest in such diversions. For him a concert always took precedence over a prizefight, a classic over the popular best sellers, and earnest political discussion over a gossip session.

In any event, the result of what they called his aloofness was that he rarely won friendship by turning on charm, never won allegiance by flattery. These rewards came to him, and they did in abundance, as an appreciation of his qualities.

In his long tenure as head of a great corporation and the key figure in a great industry, only a handful of his subordinates—and these only after long collaboration—ventured to call him by his first name. They knew that he was intolerant of fumbling and fuzziness, impatient with sloppy thinking. They knew that his logic was inexorable, that he would listen intently and then would cut quickly through rhetoric and surfaces to the core of the situation. But once a rapport of mutual appreciation was established, associates found him warm, generous, and patient. Sentimental under a reserved exterior, he prized friendship too much to dispense it offhandedly to all comers.

And his superiors, too, in the relatively short period when he still had superiors, learned not to expect apple-polishing from Sarnoff, or poses of false humility. He would be correct, respectful, true to the amenities of the relationship, but never obsequious. Owen D. Young learned this in due time, found it refreshing, and came to like it well.

At one point in the initial period of negotiations between American

Marconi and GE, Sarnoff produced a full accounting of his company's fiscal position, then proceeded to analyze some of the items.

"Mr. Sarnoff," the older man said, "you don't have to explain the black figures. It's the red ones I'm concerned with."

"Well, Mr. Young," Sarnoff replied, "there are liabilities as well as assets in every honest accounting, but it is not always the figures that tell the story. In this case, I believe, the greatest of our assets doesn't even show up."

"What is it?"

This was the touch that tipped the sluices of Sarnoff's eloquence. "Our great asset," he said, "is the vast ignorance about electronics."

Young lifted an eyebrow that asked for an explanation.

"I mean it literally, Mr. Young. The ignorance is what remains to be explored and conquered—because that's where we have unlimited potentials for an industry, in fact for many industries, that are still in their infancy or as yet unborn."

He then went on to sketch the electronic future as he sensed it, a projection of things to come which held the lawyer spellbound. Sarnoff talked calmly, as if he were dealing with the obvious, of his Music Box, of information and entertainment flowing into millions of homes. He talked of the coming use of wavelengths as yet inaccessible, of worldwide wireless telephony, and other miracles. What were mere figures, black or red, against the vision of daily life transformed and enriched by the limitless magic of the electron?

Another time, toward the end of the first year of RCA operations, the two men were discussing the prospects of the company. The gross income of the new corporation for the year was expected to exceed $1 million. Inevitably comparisons were made with General Electric, whose income that year was more than $270 million.

"Do you realize," Young asked, "that GE does business at the rate of one million dollars for every working day?"

"I do. Now tell me, how old is your company?"

Young told him. "Well," Sarnoff said quite soberly, "long before RCA is that old it will match or surpass your present rate."

His tone conveyed that it was not a boast, not a hope, but a simple statement of reality, as plain to the speaker as any current fact of life. Young smiled. He was impressed by the young man's bold imagination but hardly by his prophecy.

But in August, 1947, Sarnoff sent the seventy-three-year-old retired chairman of GE a statement showing that RCA had reached an annual income rate of $300 million. In the covering letter he recalled the forecast he had made more than a quarter of a century earlier and added: "I congratulate you on being here to see this happen, and I am glad to be here too."

Young had not forgotten the prophecy and in a gracious reply insisted that it was Sarnoff's enthusiasm and ability which had made it come true.

Such was the stuff of which the fruitful collaboration of the two ill-matched men was gradually molded. There was more than a little truth in the wide assumption, during the difficult formative years of the Radio Corporation, that Sarnoff was Young's "protégé." The older man's faith in him weighed heavily in the scales in times of crisis, when Sarnoff was under fire, when he needed support for policies or enterprises that seemed to some board members—sometimes including Young himself—too risky.

This is the more significant because the interests of GE and RCA were not always identical and in time even came into conflict. Sarnoff would make no secret of his ambition to free his company from GE and other external corporate dominion. Early in the game he had decided to win for RCA complete financial and commercial independence.

7

"Sarnoff's Folly"

ᕱ "Within thirty days after it was launched," a company official of that period told me, "David was running the Radio Corporation." This is a palpable overstatement. Sarnoff was then junior in rank to several of his colleagues. For all his sizzling energy, he had a healthy sense of discipline. And all of them in the final analysis took their marching orders from Schenectady.

Yet the statement sheds light on the atmosphere in which David Sarnoff had to work. It indicates an impression from the start that the youthful commercial manager was "running the show." And it was an impression that did him considerable harm, for it kindled envies, resentments, ancient prejudices. Among the business conservatives around him it raised honest misgivings about his daring policies and goals. One day, they feared and said, his imagination would overreach itself and get them all into trouble.

Already he was freely charged with being "too ambitious." It was a charge he never bothered to refute. He was ambitious for the new corporation, for the art he was determined to guide, for the future of electronics—and for himself.

It is a difficult and a futile exercise to draw the lines between the personal and social drives in any story of achievement. Personal rewards, whether in power or glory or cash, are part of the psychological equation even in the most public-spirited careers. Overweening ambition can be imputed—was in fact vociferously imputed in its time—to an unschooled railsplitter who became President of the United States. The accusation never seriously troubled Sarnoff. He took it for granted that his own success and the success of RCA were indivisible, that his private destiny would be a function of the progress of the new industry.

President Nally, Treasurer De Sousa, and other old-timers by now relied on him ungrudgingly; they had long ago accommodated themselves to his youth and exotic background. Among those who remembered him as a snip of a boy sweeping the Marconi offices there were a few, like De Sousa, who even took a sort of paternal pride in the miracle of his rapid maturing. But they were not typical.

Everything affecting the company was now pertinent to Sarnoff's responsibilities as commercial manager and therefore a logical object of his concern and spirited intervention. Besides, his present post seemed to him merely a way station on the road to the top. His quotient of self-confidence was high. His role, he felt, was to foresee the future of the corporation and through it the future of the industry, and to formulate policies accordingly.

Though never articulated, this presumption of leadership was implicit in his ardor, his ubiquity, his wide-focused appraisals of events. It was implied, too, in the speeches he was now making more often before radio and engineering societies, at hearings in Washington, and to the public. For he addressed himself, in an accent of authority, not merely to matters in his own bailiwick but to the crowding problems and challenges in the entire field.

All of which aroused the admiration of some colleagues but affronted or worried others. In preparing the second volume on the history of the industry (*Big Business and Radio, 1939*), Dr. Archer talked to dozens of radio veterans and plowed through great piles of documents and correspondence. He found a lot of evidence, he wrote, that Sarnoff had been "the target for sharpshooters" within and outside the organization.

As the growth potentials of RCA became more impressive, after the boom in broadcasting got rolling, a number of Navy men who had helped form the company and particularly some officials in the older electrical corporations began to covet the opportunities it might offer. For the most part they had looked upon the young man as a holdover from the dissolved Marconi Company who would in due time yield to older and "more deserving" people. Instead they saw him gathering the reins in his own hands.

Dr. Archer wrote at one point:

"A former official of the RCA, closely associated with the young man at the time, has stated to the author that, in the early years of Mr. Sarnoff's services at RCA, if there were any particularly disagreeable job to be done by or for the management it was almost invariably turned over to David Sarnoff. Tasks regarded as impossible were likewise shouldered upon him."

Now and then these harassments took stupid forms. For instance, bores were steered to his office. Salesmen of lumber and other products for which RCA had no possible need, since it was not in manufacturing, were sent to Sarnoff. The intended victim was much too shrewd to miss the point of the malice, but chose to ignore it.

"Unfortunately for those who sought to discredit Mr. Sarnoff in the early days, but fortunately for the radio industry," to quote the historian again, "the young man not only kept his head but actually made good on the difficult or impossible assignments. He won the approval of the directors of the RCA. More than that, he made friends with those who were sent on wild-goose errands to his office."

Even what he learned about lumber and other raw materials, filed away in his retentive memory, was not without value when the company eventually did undertake manufacture. In short, as Dr. Archer summed it up, "the very efforts to unseat him enabled him to demonstrate how necessary he was to the organization and left him more firmly seated in the saddle."

In mid-January, 1920, when the corporation was only six weeks old, Sarnoff received a curious letter from Young's office. It asked him for a "prospectus" on RCA, its present and future needs, the likely dimensions of its business. These were the very things he had already and repeatedly discussed with Young. Why, then, the formal request? Was it fair and reasonable to ask for a long-range blueprint of an enterprise that had barely begun to operate? In any case, should it not have been addressed to the company president?

The letter had been inspired, Sarnoff surmised at once and later confirmed, by lower-echelon GE officials in the hope of embarrassing him. No doubt some of them were sincerely worried by his presumptive "immaturity"; the spectacle of a twenty-nine-year-old making decisions involving tens of millions of dollars—GE dollars mostly—made them jittery. Others were simply covetous or alarmed by indications of Young's high opinion of the interloper. It is a safe guess that the tactful Young wrote the letter with tongue in cheek—let none of the carpers suppose that he was shielding the young man. Perhaps, too, he foresaw that Sarnoff would treat the "impossible assignment" as another opportunity. This, in all events, is what happened.

Within two weeks the commercial manager delivered a 28-page report which, in the perspective of time, would be recognized as a tour de force of comprehensive planning and forecasting under the most difficult conditions.

It dealt with virtually every phase of the radio world of that day: its apparatus and patents, production problems, and prospective markets. And as usual in Sarnoff documents, it embodied elements that were to enhance his flourishing reputation as a "prophet." He made clear that even the combined rights of GE and RCA were not sufficient to provide products of a quality demanded by domestic and international markets; that access to patents held by others was indispensable. The next few years would, in fact, be devoted to breaking down the patent barriers.

In addition, Sarnoff exploited the maneuver to discredit him as an occasion to revive his Radio Music Box idea. Broadcasting as we know it today, which he had visualized and described five years earlier, was by then around the corner. It would be initiated—and to Sarnoff's chagrin, by someone else— before 1920 had run its course. But imminent as it was, few could discern it in the first months of the year. None could see it as concretely and on the breath-taking scale outlined in the Sarnoff "prospectus" in 1915.

2

The radiotelegraph stations and patents commandeered by the government for war uses were restored to their prewar owners in February, 1920. RCA inherited the far-flung facilities of American Marconi, along with its extensive ship-to-shore business and its many affiliates, such as Wireless Press, Marconi Cable, a minority interest in Pan-American Wireless and Telephone.

And David Sarnoff inherited a multitude of commercial problems, technical puzzles, renovation and construction jobs. If there was anywhere in America a busier young executive, there is no record of him. He found himself ringmaster in a ten-ring circus, working sixteen and eighteen hours a day.

Virtually all the facilities had been outmoded by engineering progress and new inventions. Millions had to be spent to modernize old stations and build new ones. The transition, all along the line, from government to private management posed personnel problems. There were traffic agreements to be negotiated with communications companies and governments in foreign countries; by the end of 1920 RCA was handling a million words a month in overseas messages. Wireless equipment had to be marketed abroad in competition with foreign and other American manufacturers.

General Electric had to re-gear for production of all sorts of apparatus until then turned out in Marconi plants or by outsiders. The job of guiding these preparations—almost as much diplomatic as technical—fell to Sarnoff. The interdependence of his new-born organization and the mature giant of electricity created problems of design and research and day-to-day adjustment of interests and viewpoints. When a spirited young corporation finds itself in double harness with a staid, tradition-crusted corporation frictions are to be expected.

But the prime headache, as always, was the patent stalemate. No one group controlled enough inventions to make a complete ensemble for superlative service; and every group controlled enough to make life onerous for the others. American Telephone and its subsidiary Western Electric Company— comprising the Bell Group—had been accumulating patents for some ten years. So had Westinghouse Electric and Manufacturing Company, the International Radio Telegraph Company, the United Fruit Company, and many other organizations.

A backlog of patent litigation over some of the most critical ingredients of the radio services had accumulated through the years. Patent piracy was practiced on an almost unmanageable scale. Much of this, too, spilled over into Sarnoff's lap, since it affected sales, marketing, competition, advertising.

Moreover, the entire technology was in a state of flux. Equipment was constantly being obsoleted even while in the process of construction, at a cost shocking to men raised in relatively stable industries. "Obsolescence is our business," Sarnoff has been obliged to explain to boards of directors throughout his business life. Also, because of inadequate or outmoded regulations, there was a traffic jam on the air highways. Both domestic and worldwide allocations of wavelengths had to be hammered into shape to head off chaos.

In the patent area the most pressing immediate need was for cross-licensing with the Bell Group. In theory the dividing lines between wired and wireless communications should be simple enough. In practice the overlapping areas were broad, the conflicting claims acute.

Who, for example, would have paramount rights to make and sell vacuum tubes and other apparatus equally important in both fields? What about the use of wires for transmission to link wireless stations, or between the points of origin of a message and the station? Telephony, whatever the medium employed, seemed to the Bell Group legitimately within its own sphere of business.

Yet a cross-licensing agreement was worked out. It was an achievement that added luster to Owen D. Young's reputation as a negotiator. Wire telegraphy and telephony, even when used in conjunction with wireless services, were reserved to the telephone group, space communications remained the dominion of RCA and its partners. There were loose ends, although Sarnoff was one of the few who realized it while negotiations were under way. They would show up soon enough in connection with the coming boom in broadcasting—an event that only few as yet visualized even as a theoretical possibility.

Sarnoff's carping concern with contract clauses pertinent to broadcasting in the modern sense deserves mention because it again underlined his awareness of things unborn. To many of his colleagues and competitors alike, his emphasis on the matter may have seemed captious if not eccentric—"Sarnoff's Folly," some called it. Although broadcasting was about to emerge from the radio cocoon, he was almost alone in RCA in taking its potential seriously. Had his foresight in this respect been given the attention it deserved in the negotiations, the Bell and Radio Groups might have been spared years of recrimination and litigation that drained off money and energy in a futile conflict.

Sarnoff's insistence did win for the Radio Group exclusive rights to produce and sell devices for the reception of "news, music and entertainment" by radio. But the other end of the process—rights in devices and stations for transmitting such programs—was left in an ambiguous contractual state despite him. It was destined to provoke one of the great industrial conflicts of that generation: a years-long contest between the telephone and electric interests for primacy in the broadcasting field. Ultimately it would end, as we shall see—and that primarily through the leadership of Sarnoff—by radio casting off corporate fetters and becoming an autonomous entity, independent of both those older interests.

As the principal competitor, Westinghouse naturally was not content to remain a passive onlooker as General Electric assumed a position of leadership in the radio field. Before long it concluded a deal with the International Radio Telegraph Company, whose patents and facilities added to its own made a potent combination. Westinghouse also had acquired rights and licenses from Armstrong in inventions sorely needed by RCA.

While it thus made itself a strong factor in the picture, Westinghouse still lacked too many pieces—the Alexanderson high-frequency alternator, for instance—to fill out its own radio jigsaw puzzle. Its attempts to round up some foreign communications business quickly revealed that the head start and superior equipment of RCA were insuperable obstacles.

In the end Young's business acumen solved the problem by drawing Westinghouse into the GE-RCA pool. Through an agreement that became effective in mid-1921, the Westinghouse storehouse of radio patents and licenses became accessible to GE and RCA. In return, Westinghouse won a 40 percent share in all manufacturing for RCA, with GE retaining 60 percent for itself.

For Sarnoff and his associates this added another dimension of trouble. Where they had been obliged to harmonize RCA needs and commercial preferences with only GE, they must now harmonize them with two colossal electric companies which, moreover, were too habituated to competition between them to lend themselves easily to the demands of teamwork.

Though it is running ahead of the story, it is pertinent at this point to quote from a lecture at Harvard some years later by Harry P. Davis, vice-president of Westinghouse. Davis had been close to the radio phase of his corporation business for a long time and consequently in continuous relations with RCA. Those relations, in the nature of things, were not always honey-sweet and on occasion were bitter as gall. Yet he told his audience, in tracing the development of radio:

"No history of broadcasting can be complete without reference to Mr. David Sarnoff . . . an early pioneer whose fine judgment, clear vision and high executive ability made him the guiding genius of the entire radio industry."

Illogical as it may sound, the United Fruit Company also was an important factor in the industry in the initial RCA years. Because swift and reliable communications between the banana plantations in the Caribbean, the warehouses, the transport fleet, and the company offices on the mainland were all-important to the fruit company, it had been among the first to latch on to wireless. Through a subsidiary it possessed stations of its own and controlled an array of patents. In March, 1921, by a series of mutual licensing contracts, United Fruit also became part of what was coming to be known as the Radio Group.

Thus, in less than eighteen months after the retirement of Uncle Sam from the field, private enterprise had put together a radio patent consortium comprehensive enough to support RCA operations as efficient as the state of the radio art then permitted. The chief credit for this success belonged to Owen D. Young. Behind him, playing a larger part than was apparent at the time, stood his young protégé.

The government, which had taken the initiative that brought RCA into being, was kept apprised of the contractual structure from the beginning and, indeed, brought its influence to bear to speed up the process. It had an observer on RCA's board. If officials suspected any infringement of antitrust doctrines, they certainly said nothing. The national interest at stake was so large that it ruled out a too rigidly legalistic approach. There seemed, in truth, no other way to cut through the paralyzing patent tangles. This, however, would not save RCA and those aligned with it, in the future, from expensive and time-consuming antitrust suits.

The heart of RCA business in the first period was international communications. To meet the needs of its fast-growing network of global radiotelegraph services, the corporation began construction of what it called a Radio Central, a forest of installations eventually covering ten acres at Rocky Point, Long Island.

The official opening of the first segment of the Radio Central—just one spoke of the projected giant antenna and two pairs of 200-KW Alexanderson alternators—was hailed as a milestone in wireless progress. The day was November 5, 1921. In the absence of president Nally, then en route from London to New York, Sarnoff supervised the formal ceremonies and Young made the principal address to the notables gathered at the site.

President Harding, in the White House, threw the switch that put the Central into operation. Stations clear around the globe had been alerted to tune in for a congratulatory statement by the President. "To be able to transmit a message by radio in expectation that it may reach every nation in the world," Harding said in part, "is so marvelous a scientific and technical achievement as to justify special recognition."

The expectation came close to literal fulfillment. The President's words were picked up in the principal European countries, in Hawaii, Japan, Australia, and New Zealand and in many Latin-American countries. Among the messages of felicitation that Sarnoff read to the assemblage at Rocky Point was one from the hero of his own teen-age enthusiasms and by now his good friend, Guglielmo Marconi.

Incidentally, as an indication of the rapidity of the evolution in radio techniques: by the time the Radio Central was completed, two years later, the massive Alexanderson alternators could be replaced by powerful new vacuum tubes, also developed by General Electric. The apparatus which, in a sense, precipitated the formation of RCA, was obsoleted only four years later!

Even while the patent reservoir was being filled and the world's largest radiotelegraph central was being built, something new was emerging that would quickly overshadow international communications: modern broadcasting was being born.

3

"I feel," David Sarnoff wrote to Young in the first month of 1920, "that the time is now ripe for serious consideration of the project." He was referring, of course, to the proposal in his old memorandum on the Radio Music Box, a copy of which went with the letter.

Soon thereafter he ventured to spell out the commercial possibilities of his dream. Writing to the president of General Electric, E. W. Rice, Jr., he forecast the sale of a million of these household radio receivers in the first three years of distribution:

Roughly estimating the selling price at $75 per set, $75,000,000 can be expected. This may be divided as follows:

First year—100,000 Radio Music Boxes . . . . $ 7,500,000
Second year—300,000 Radio Music Boxes 22,500,000
Third year—600,000 Radio Music Boxes 45,000,000
                                              _____
                                              $75,000,000

Not a single marketable Music Box, it should be remembered, was then in existence. Many technical problems remained to be solved before an authentic radio set could be presented to the public. Nevertheless, the Sarnoff figures proved to be remarkably close to the coming reality; his margins of error were on the side of excessive caution. RCA's actual sales of sets in the first three years were to be: 1922—$11,000,000; 1923—$22,500,000; 1924—$50,000,000, for a total of $83,500,000.

The Music Box that netted these results would be marketed under the name of Radiola, a word coined by Dr. Alfred Goldsmith. Though so sharply visualized in advance and so persistently advocated by Sarnoff, the Radiola would be a relatively late starter in the race. Had Sarnoff's Folly not been so long ignored, the Marconi Company and then RCA would have had a head start in the home radio market, instead of struggling to catch up with competitors.

At the time RCA was born, research engineers in Schenectady were concentrating on a transmitter for radiotelephony. Point-to-point communication still seemed the essence of the challenge. Almost at once Sarnoff began to press them to switch priorities, to concentrate their energies on apparatus for household reception and transmission geared to the same purpose. Those affected barely concealed their annoyance with his monomaniacal interference.

He instructed RCA's technical staff—now headed by the same Dr. Goldsmith who had pioneered in broadcasting experiments while still a member of the engineering faculty of the College of the City of New York—to prepare designs and specifications for a complete broadcasting station.

An experimental model of a Radio Music Box, he was apprised by Goldsmith and others, would cost between ten and twenty thousand dollars. Sarnoff asked the Technical Committee of the RCA board for money and was granted, reluctantly, $2,000 to squander on his obsession. This was only four or five months before modern broadcasting, in precisely the form the obsessed young man had sketched it years in advance, became a functioning fact. By 1929, let it be noted, this reluctant investment grossed $176,500,000 and netted RCA a profit of $15,800,000.

Dr. Frank Conrad of Westinghouse had long been an ardent radio "ham," one of the brotherhood of amateurs on the airwaves. During the war years he began to amuse himself at his Pittsburgh home with broadcasts of recorded music. The "station" was in his garage. Later he rigged up a similar station on the roof of the Westinghouse plant in East Pittsburgh. Amateurs in the area came to know and appreciate his licensed signal, 8-XK. Entire families, using homemade receivers and earphones, got the habit of listening. Requests for favorite records began to come in and Pittsburgh stores reported increased demand for records of the music he presented.

Though his audience kept growing, Conrad himself could not guess how soon and on what a sensational scale his labors—as yet more hobby than business—would bear fruit. The initial impetus, in fact, came from outside his own shop. On September 29, 1920, an enterprising Pittsburgh department store advertised a new service: a complete line of parts and gadgets for customers wishing to assemble receivers in order to enjoy the Conrad programs. The rush of business brought in by the advertisement impressed Westinghouse. Maybe Conrad's hobby could be exploited after all!

For the first time top executives in the company gave serious consideration, and then their consent, to the engineer's plan for a stronger station. Vice-President Davis would attest years after the fact that it was then he first began to wonder—as Sarnoff had wondered back in 1915—whether the apparent liability of radiotelephony, its lack of secrecy, could become its greatest asset. He backed Conrad's vision of a station which would send out not only music but news, lectures, sermons, and other program materials at regular times to be announced in advance.

Providentially, a presidential election campaign was then under way. It was decided to push work on the station so that it would be ready to broadcast the returns on November 4. When these plans were made public, the entire city, it seemed, was caught up in a radio fever. The shops were denuded of their stocks of electrical accessories for do-it-yourself receivers. People traveled to other towns to search for parts sold out in Pittsburgh.

That was how the world's first true broadcasting station, licensed before Election Day as Station KDKA, was born. It was in large measure an improvised affair, far from complete when the great night arrived. Housed in a crude clapboard "penthouse" on the roof of one of the plants, it was wide open to all the noises of the surrounding area. Its acoustics were atrocious.

But thousands of people, in their homes and on the premises of enterprising electrical dealers who had set up receivers for the occasion, tuned in hopefully. With the cooperation of local newspapers, the station collected returns from all parts of the country by telephone and telegraph and put them at once on the air. Pittsburgh radio fans were the first to know that Warren G. Harding would succeed the ailing Woodrow Wilson. The real thrill of their experience, however, was not in the speed but in the medium—the novelty of receiving the news over the air.

The press of the country told the Westinghouse story. The great boom was not to come for another eighteen months but a substantial boomlet was generated immediately. Licenses for thirty-two stations were issued by the Department of Commerce in 1921, for 254 in 1922. Hundreds of radio shops mushroomed around the country, selling the components for homemade receivers. Here and there electrical shops assembled sets for their customers, at prices that would soon seem exorbitant when mass production of the magic box got going.

Encouraged by its success, Westinghouse put more money and men into KDKA. The programs were put on a scheduled-time basis, so that listeners at last knew when to tune in for what. The first steps were taken in covering news events and in bringing national personalities to the microphone. The first celebrity to speak over the Pittsburgh station—in February, 1921—was Herbert Hoover, then at the crest of his worldwide fame as a humanitarian. Among those who followed him was William Jennings Bryan.

The prestige accruing to the corporation for the pioneering effort, Westinghouse executives decided, was well worth the costs of operating the station. Besides, they foresaw a stepped-up demand for the "makings" of radio receivers which they fabricated. Their engineers were rushing work on a factory-made radio set, ready to be attached to a battery, for those without the mechanical skills or patience to assemble their own receivers. The economics of broadcasting would not be solved for several years—not until a New York station stumbled, almost accidentally, on the fact that radio, like the press, could be supported by advertising.

Sarnoff was at once pleased by the Westinghouse triumph and disappointed that another company had stolen a march on RCA. It would be cited against him, in future accountings of his business record, that he was neither the first to broadcast nor the first to market radio sets. The evidence, however, is that he would have done both if he had been in full command of the company.

Searching for a way to retrieve some of the lost ground, he came up with an idea that was to make broadcasting history. The story was told in *Reader's Digest,* thirty-four years after the event, by J. Andrew White, at that time editor of the RCA-owned *Wireless Age* and subsequently one of the founders and the first president of the Columbia Broadcasting System.

White, about eighteen months Sarnoff's junior, had long been among the few who took seriously his vision of the Radio Music Box. When Sarnoff came to him with the current idea, which some of their superiors again thought harebrained, White reacted with unbounded enthusiasm. On Saturday, July 2, 1921, the heavyweight champion of the world, Jack Dempsey, was to meet a foreign challenger, Georges Carpentier, the "orchid man of France," at "Boyle's Thirty Acres" in Jersey City, New Jersey.

The fight was arousing more popular excitement than the Harding-Cox campaign had done the preceding autumn. Sarnoff proposed to broadcast the championship battle on the air, blow by blow. The chief trouble was that RCA had no station. Somehow a powerful transmitter had to be found and installed within convenient distance of the fight arena. There were only a few weeks for preparation. Sarnoff and White, feeling around for a transmitter they could purloin or borrow, discovered that GE had just completed the world's largest commercial radiophone transmitter—but it belonged to the Navy.

"We asked to borrow it," White would recall in his *Digest* article, "but found the Navy rather stiff-necked about lending it to some crazy amateurs."

Fortunately a man who had been Assistant Secretary of the Navy under Wilson agreed to use his influence with the department. Franklin D. Roosevelt, two months before he was stricken with polio, helped obtain the necessary permission and the apparatus was shipped to the Lackawanna Railroad terminal at Hoboken, two and a half miles from the fight ring. The telephone company reluctantly agreed to string a direct line between the two points.

Years before, the reader will recall, the railroad—with Sarnoff in charge of the enterprise—had experimented with wireless from moving trains. As a memento of that period there was still a radio tower at its Hoboken depot. It now proved a lifesaver. The transmitter was installed in a shack where Pullman porters changed uniforms. The swiftly improvised station was ready.

But plenty of problems remained to be solved before a championship prizefight could be put on the air for the first time. One of them was to mobilize an audience large enough to justify the $2,500 Sarnoff was splurging on the broadcast. Soon he was able to announce that the American Committee for Devastated France, headed by Anne Morgan, a daughter of J. P. Morgan, and the Navy Club, headed by Roosevelt, were sponsoring the broadcast and would get a share of the admission fees charged at movie houses equipped to receive the program. This gave the undertaking a strong public-interest façade. With the help of Marcus Loew, movie theatres in the metropolitan area contributed their premises.

A second problem was to provide amplifiers capable of filling a theatre with sound. The solution was found in the purchase of 300 outmoded "tulip" phonograph horns at 30 cents apiece. These were attached to hearing aids and, after days and nights of experimentation, induced to work. Several hundred radio amateurs had volunteered to man these devices and to install aerials at the gathering places.

Andrew White was at ringside, the first man to venture a blow-by-blow report of a championship fight for an unseen audience. By his side sat Sarnoff. They could only hope that the words being poured out in colorful description were reaching the target. And they could only wonder whether "listening" to a fast-swinging sports event, a brand-new experience, would make sense.

It did. Some 200,000 people in clubs, halls, and theatres as well as in their homes heard the fight and appeared content. Reports of adequate reception came from points 500 miles away. The news of what a Reuter's official present called "the world's first real broadcast" was reported throughout Europe. Shortly after the Frenchman had been knocked out in the fourth round, Sarnoff received a succinct radiogram from president Nally, who happened to be in London: "You have made history."

In America, only one newspaper, the *New York Times,* had considered the unique radio experiment worth a brief story in advance. Now that it was successful, the entire press reported the achievement. Sarnoff was asked no questions by the board of directors about the $2,500 he had borrowed from funds allocated to other purposes. Broadcasting—and RCA—had received another powerful impetus.

4

Time was confirming the wisdom of Sarnoff's Folly, his Radio Music Box, and what had been a term of derision became a term of praise. But not too strangely, human nature being what it is, his very vindication stirred vindictiveness in the hearts of those who for their various reasons continued to resent or fear his success.

Certain people in General Electric, abetted by others in Westinghouse, connived to bring about a study of broadcasting potentials by a supposedly qualified outside business specialist, drawn from the academic world. It seemed an innocent enough precaution against runaway optimism and even Owen Young approved. Possibly he did not grasp what was at once apparent to David Sarnoff.

The move, the commercial manager of RCA guessed, was inspired not by skepticism about broadcasting but, to the contrary, a belated sense of its gigantic promise. Why should RCA reap the rich harvests, as the "ambitious upstart" running the corporation would have it, rather than the electric companies themselves? Why should the promotions and fresh opportunities for individuals inherent in a booming new business accrue to RCA and not to the personnel of GE and Westinghouse?

In a few months the study was completed. The findings of the high-priced expert seem bizarre in the light of history, but they had at least the virtue of clarity. The expectations aroused by broadcasting, he concluded, were madly exaggerated; the new plaything was crawling with economic bugs and would never pay off. The official mainly responsible for the exaggeration and the profligate spending it entailed, he went on dead-pan, was one David Sarnoff. He was squandering his own and other people's energies and his company's limited resources on fantasy. Therefore he recommended that Sarnoff be fired forthwith!

Looking back on the shabby episode, Sarnoff has called it "one of the darkest moments" in his life. It was not, of course, a matter of holding on to a job. Several of the newly launched companies were pressing upon him offers of larger incomes, sweetened with stock inducements, to lure Sarnoff into their service. He was dismayed, rather, by the menace to his dream of the electronic future. As he saw it, RCA was the right and maybe the only vehicle for the fulfillment of that dream.

Sarnoff's reaction was direct and quick. He chose to stake his case upon the integrity of Owen D. Young. He therefore telephoned Schenectady and induced the older man to come to New York immediately for dinner. A private room at Delmonico's was at this stage scarcely Sarnoff's regular habitat, but that is what he reserved that night.

There were no polite amenities. Sarnoff began to talk at eight, before the hors d'oeuvres were served, and the conference did not wind up until midnight.

"Mr. Young," he said, "this report threatens my life's work, so I want to begin by telling you about that life. It starts in a drab Russian village called Uzlian."

The lawyer-industrialist, of course, was aware of Sarnoff's background in a general way. But this night at Delmonico's he heard the full story in all its pathetic, heart-warming, and exotic dimensions. He was given an insight, perhaps for the first time, into what it means to be an immigrant child, penniless, in a dog-eat-dog world. He began to perceive, again perhaps for the first time, the deeper springs of conscious or unconscious bias under an array of office intrigues dressed up as practical business.

Against this personal background, Sarnoff then came to the report directed against himself but calculated also to cut RCA down to size.

He did not attack the author, who was clearly beyond his technological depth and had taken guidance from insiders. He had brought to the assignment the conventional yardsticks used to measure conventional businesses and these had proved incapable of assessing a new enterprise in which imagination outweighed statistics. Neither did Sarnoff deny that, by eliminating RCA from broadcasting, the electric companies might make more money in the short run. But in the long run, he showed, they would pay heavy penalties because the whole radio industry would be hurt.

That evening of crisis marked the true beginning of friendship between the two men. When Young got back to Schenectady he filed the expert's findings in the wastebasket. In the nature of a complex business, the two men did not always see eye to eye in the years that followed. There were even intervals of strain. But those who sought to undermine Sarnoff thereafter came to know that usually they would have to take on Young as well.

Sarnoff's victory had an epilogue that, at least in retrospect, seems amusing. He was apprised by a Westinghouse official that they had a truckload of letters from the public—unanswered while awaiting the decision on the personal fate of Sarnoff. "You wanted to keep the business in RCA," his informant said in substance, without concealing his spite. "All right, it's your baby!"

True to the threat, a truck pulled up before the RCA offices in the Woolworth Building a few days later and some 40,000 letters were dumped, as it were, into Sarnoff's lap. He sampled them; nearly all were inquiries about or orders for radio sets, parts, equipment. Then he called in one of his brightest subordinates. "You answer these," he said with a smile.

And that was how Elmer E. Bucher, a writer with a technical background who had never sold anything in his life except his own articles and textbooks, became sales manager of the Radio Corporation. In the years of his incumbency he planned and supervised sales that ran into many millions of dollars.

8

The Self-Appointed Leader

   ᥦ   In May, 1921, shortly after his thirtieth birthday, David Sarnoff was named general manager of the Radio Corporation. His annual salary, until then $11,000, was raised to $15,000. It was a post especially created and tailored to his personal measure, to compass the diversity of his activities. About sixteen months later, in September, 1922, the board voted an honorific addition: he became vice-president and general manager.

He now wore titles more appropriate to his functions. They had little if any effect on his authority or orbit of operation, since in truth he was already the chief executive of the zooming business, its main planner, policy maker, and trouble shooter—and there never was any lack of trouble to shoot at. President Nally, reared in an older type of communication, gave most of his time to international wireless telegraphy, in itself an immense domain. Virtually everything else was under Sarnoff's direct supervision.

Late in 1922 Nally decided to retire from active duty, though staying on as a consultant. He was succeeded by General James J. Harbord, a military man of national stature selected from among many aspirants by the shrewd Owen D. Young.

The general took his office and responsibilities most earnestly. Understandably, however, the industry was at first a deep mystery to him and the conduct of RCA affairs of necessity remained in the hands of the general manager. Harbord's great personal prestige was an asset to the corporation in dealing with the government. But his role was essentially of a public relations and administrative character. From the outset he and Sarnoff worked harmoniously.

These were the years of the tumultuous growth of broadcasting and of the manufacturing and sales services associated with it. What had been a plaything for amateurs now became a household necessity—the "home utility" which had seemed so farfetched a fantasy in 1915. More than five hundred stations mushroomed across the land. Steel and wooden radio towers became a feature of urban skylines. In most newspapers the radio page became standard fare. A spate of technical and fan radio magazines came into being.

How can those born into the epoch of radio imagine the excitement caused by its arrival? For millions of families everyday existence seemed suddenly transformed, broadened, deepened. With a trivial one-time investment in a set, they bought access to whole worlds of amusement, discussion, events, and personalities until then beyond their reach. "With a twist of the dial," to quote John Tebbel, in his short biography of Sarnoff for young people, "they were transported to Carnegie Hall, to distant football fields, to night-clubs and ballrooms where new dance music was being played." For the first time they could hear the actual voices of national leaders and celebrities in every department of life. It seemed the greatest bargain in history.

Electric lights and telephones, even automobiles, had come slowly. There was time for psychological adjustment to their novelty. But home radio burst upon the country, or so it seemed, overnight.

In the absence of Congressional legislation, the Department of Commerce assumed the job of issuing licenses to broadcasters. Its authority was questioned and in many cases ignored. Eventually, in fact, the federal courts ruled that the department held no legal mandate to assign wavelengths. Meanwhile, however, it did so in far too casual and openhanded style, sometimes assigning the same channel to several applicants in the same community.

The result was that in many cities and towns stations shared time, one taking over when another signed off, with reverberating squabbles for bigger and better slices of the time pie. Wildcat stations, with small regard for patent rights and often on pirated wavelengths, added to the great and clangorous tangle.

Established electric firms and hundreds of new ones labored lustily to feed the growing hunger for receivers. Enterprising companies provided printed instructions for "rolling your own" radio receiver. Then complete sets—improved models appearing almost daily—began to pour into the market, to be hawked not only in electric and music shops but in drugstores, hardware and delicatessen stores, at prices ranging from $25 for primitive crystal sets to $400 for super-deluxe models.

The mechanics of marketing the magic box had still to be worked out. Meanwhile literally thousands pressed the manufacturers for local distributing rights. Hundreds of unauthorized shops sent their orders, running into large sums, to RCA. The whole thing had the feel of a gold rush. To understand its quality we must recall the background of runaway prosperity and the so-called Jazz Age. Radio was a turbulent phenomenon in a turbulent time, adding to and blending with its cacophony and explosive vitality, its feverish and fun-mad generation. Prohibition, speakeasies, F. Scott Fitzgerald, H. L. Mencken, blue-sky promotions, stock bonanzas, bucket shops—and radio.

The public and industrial demand for the vacuum tube, the heart of the radio set, overwhelmed the productive capacities of its manufacturers. At times the shortages were so acute that the big firms, and RCA especially, found themselves accused, for the most part unjustly, of deliberately restricting output to squeeze out smaller rivals in the set competition.

Responsible leaders of the industry realized that the boom would collapse in disillusionment unless reasonably attractive programs were provided. Initially the novelty of the thing, simple curiosity, was enough to support demand. But before long those who invested in a receiver would expect to be entertained, informed, and titillated. Indeed, two lean years followed the first two fat ones, and those who had plunged into the enterprise on the supposition that the boom would last forever were alarmed; dozens of them went out of business.

Only companies with large financial and technical resources, of course, could hope to meet the demands for effective programing. Westinghouse, while pushing its pilot station KDKA in Pittsburgh, built station WJZ in the New York metropolitan area. General Electric erected a station in Schenectady. RCA, which is to say Sarnoff in the first place, fought for and won the right to put up its own stations, and after Westinghouse joined the Radio Group, RCA also assumed management of WJZ. By 1924 the corporation had nine substantial stations under its direction.

Inevitably, the Telephone Group—comprising American Tel. & Tel. and affiliates like Western Electric and Electrical Research Products—had come wide awake to the possibilities of broadcasting. More than that, it suddenly discovered that one-way transmission of sound for a mass audience was really an extension of telephone service and should therefore be its exclusive preserve.

Broadcasting had been little more than a gleam in Sarnoff's eye when the agreements for patent exchanges and the allocation of areas of business activity had been worked out. Negotiators for the telephone interests were then concerned primarily with protecting exclusivity in devices directly pertinent to wired telephones. They had failed to understand Sarnoff's curious fixation on the problems of a wholly theoretical Music Box. Now that his foresight was vindicated, the provisions he had insisted upon putting into the agreements assumed prime importance.

It was Sarnoff, for instance, who had won a clause giving the Radio Group the right to build and operate broadcasting stations. But the formulation was ambiguous; the contracts appeared to confer upon the Telephone Group exclusive rights in telephony as a "public service," whether by wire or wireless. Was radio broadcasting a public service in the sense intended? High-priced lawyers came up with contradictory but equally plausible answers in line with the interests of their particular clients. Western Electric demanded a slice of the radio set market. The Telephone Group disposed of its stockholdings in RCA to free itself for a monumental war on these and related issues.

The A.T.&T. bid for dominion was symbolized by Station WEAF, in New York. Having been erected many months later than the RCA stations, it embodied technical improvements that provided a stronger and clearer signal. To make life more difficult for its competitors, the telephone colossus refused to lease its wires to RCA stations for pickup purposes, forcing them to rely on the technically less satisfactory telegraph wire systems of Western Union and Postal Telegraph.

In the epic contest for leadership between WEAF and WJZ that ensued, the listening public was the beneficiary. The struggle put a premium on initiative and ingenuity in providing programs and helped to shape the character of broadcasting. WJZ scored a "first" with the broadcast of a World Series in baseball and WEAF countered by broadcasting a major football game. WJZ, acting on Sarnoff's proposal, stole a march in another direction with the first broadcast of live grand opera. It was a direction in which Sarnoff was especially interested.

At both stations the employees, from office boys up, shared the spirit of battle. Indeed, they became emotionally involved, convinced of the wickedness of the competing staffs. Some of the personal feuds and passionate loyalties to individuals persisted years after the conditions that had engendered them ceased to exist.

Never before had a medium so quickly conferred fame—though not yet fortune; that was to come much later—upon those who appeared on it. Performers of established but limited reputations and new ones were turned overnight into radio celebrities. Many an accomplished actor or musician discovered that performing for an impersonal "mike" cramped his style, but others found that a small voice and a small talent could be made to go a long way when amplified by radio. The names of various announcers, news analysts, sportcasters became household words.

It was a new and incommensurable industry. It could not draw on conventional business wisdom but must find quick answers to unprecedented questions. For it was at once a manufacturing enterprise and a public utility, at once in communications and in entertainment, and before long in advertising as well. It could not draw on existing skills but had to develop them pragmatically under the pressures of time.

And Sarnoff stood at its stormy center. To add to his burdens, the RCA structure bristled with built-in handicaps, weaknesses, and booby traps, any one of which might have wrecked the fledgling corporation. For all its size and prominence, RCA was a fragile structure. Its destiny was subject to the interests—which became more and more competitive with RCA—of the nation's two largest electric corporations. Its natural fields of expansion were fenced off by barbed-wire entanglements of outside control and restrictions. Its very right to operate was disputed by the mammoth telephone monopoly.

That RCA survived at all, except as a relatively secondary wireless telegraphy business, is a true measure of David Sarnoff's resourcefulness. It was Sarnoff, long before he had the requisite authority, who cut through one entanglement after another and in the end won independence for RCA. This achievement required many years, immense labor and tenacity, and above all, business statesmanship.

As originally set up, RCA was in essence a sales agency in the radio fields for General Electric, and then for Westinghouse. It had no right to manufacture the products it merchandised. The arrangement was cumbersome and put the entire Radio Group at a serious disadvantage as against competitors. To cancel out the anomaly of divided functions, it would have been natural for the great electric companies to take over selling, and it was widely expected, in fact, that they would do so. Instead, the problem was ultimately resolved by RCA taking over manufacturing!

Sarnoff's business strategy, his logic and energy, prevailed against the fiscal controls and ambitions of the parent companies. And while building his own corporation he became the acknowledged pacesetter, philosopher, guardian, and prophet of the whole complex of businesses in which RCA increasingly exercised leadership.

What makes these accomplishments unique, moreover, is the fact that he did not then—and does not now—hold any leverage of financial influence, let alone control. Unlike the founders and leaders of most other great corporations, Sarnoff never had more than token stockholdings in RCA. He was always subject to the will of boards of directors, those of the electric organizations in the early years and of RCA throughout. He could have been dismissed without notice—and occasionally, indeed, he was menaced with removal by opponents. More often the process was in reverse, Sarnoff threatening to resign unless his view on some critical decision prevailed; invariably it did prevail.

His role was purely managerial. Long before the latter-day phenomenon was generally understood, the Sarnoff career exemplified what James Burnham many years later would describe as "the managerial revolution."

2

Because they tested the mettle of the man who, beyond all others, had to deal with them and overcome them, let us look a bit more closely at those built-in handicaps. Nearly all of them related to the fact that the Radio Corporation ran in tandem with two powerful but unwieldy electric corporations—this in a race for business against vigorous new contenders free from outside control, masters of their own maneuvers.

Both Westinghouse and GE, though they owned and dominated RCA, came to look upon it with some suspicion. They tended to develop, in the words of Sarnoff, "the apprehension that the recently born child might surpass in stature those who thought themselves its parents."

It was the advent of broadcasting, of course, that sparked the apprehensions. An unforeseen element had been added to the corporate equation. In the parental preconception RCA was to be a pliant adjunct of their business, a useful outlet for their manufactured products. But now they saw that, despite all restraints, by the nature of its operations, RCA was outgrowing the restricted original role. Second thoughts therefore sprouted in Schenectady and in Pittsburgh. As the immense potential of sales opened up by the radio boom became apparent, questions were raised: Did not all this business inherently belong to the electric industry? Why should not radio goods simply be integrated with other "lines"?

It had been assumed, for instance, that the existing distributors of electric products would merely add radio to their stock in trade. In the GE-Westinghouse view radio devices seemed in a class with refrigerators, washing machines, and other household appliances. But the merchandising functions were lodged in RCA, where a different estimate of the new "lines" was being promoted. Sarnoff was energetically exploring and explaining the need for specialized sales outlets. If treated like electric toasters or vacuum cleaners, he argued, RCA products would be surrendering the new and unique markets to those who concentrated their merchandising skills solely on radio.

When RCA eventually began to appoint its own distributors it marked the victorious end of a long and hard fight.

In theory RCA was the exclusive sales channel for radio products. This right was, indeed, the very foundation of its existence. But in practice it was not always easy to differentiate between items destined for radio use and those intended for other fields.

The electric companies, for instance, supplied the needs of the phonograph industry. But the vacuum tube and certain other elements of sound recording and reproduction apparatus were also ingredients in radio sets. GE and Westinghouse, even if they so desired, could not always control the uses to which these items were put. Tubes sold ostensibly for phonograph manufacture, for example, had a way of ending up in radio receivers and transmitters.

Millions of dollars' worth of products which, by the test of ultimate use, should have been sold through RCA were thus detoured in direct sales by the manufacturers. The electric corporations needed only to extend this practice far enough to eliminate RCA as a merchandising organization, leaving only its wireless telegraphy business intact. And that, of course, would have stunted the growth of the company and its prospects for the future.

Another factor operated to slow up and complicate life for RCA. The two electrical giants were traditional rivals. Their competitive instincts had been honed by decades of rivalry. Yet in one corner of the battleground, that of radio, they had a common sales agency and must cooperate as loyal partners. Try as they might to work together, they brought their ingrained hostilities to the common enterprise.

Upon Sarnoff therefore fell the difficult task of overcoming divisive tensions within the coalition, the clash of business egos, the honest differences of view on production and sales policies. The constant need to synchronize the views of GE and Westinghouse—and to do this without penalizing RCA in the process—siphoned off much of his time and energy. But it did give him, at the same time, enough bargaining power to win for RCA marginal rights beyond the strict wording of basic contracts.

The most distressing aspect of the awkward setup was that it gave serious advantages to newly hatched companies like Atwater Kent, Philco, Grigsby-Grunow, Zenith, a score of others. In meeting their competition, RCA was muscle-bound by dependence on the electric outfits. The separation of merchandising and manufacturing, which was in turn divided between two producers on a 60–40 basis, imposed on the company a straitjacket that gave the right of way to unencumbered rivals.

RCA was obliged to place firm orders for radio sets and other apparatus, totaling millions of dollars, six to eight months in advance of delivery, on a cost plus 20 percent basis. Once ordered, the goods had to be accepted, regardless of market changes in the interim. In a business in rapid flux, subject to overnight revolutions in style, price, and technical refinements, this freezing of production could have proved disastrous. As measured by its tempo of obsolescence, six months in broadcasting were the equivalent of that many years in older businesses.

Besides, the electric plants were geared to mass output of highly standard-ized goods. They pressed, as a matter of course, for standardization of radio sets and other radio products. "This effort to stabilize radio in a rapidly changing stream and to tie it to an immovable rock," Sarnoff would write years later, might have proved "a tombstone for RCA." The need to keep from being thus fatally tied down was also a constant in his load of self-assumed duties.

His competitors, by contrast, had the advantages of unlimited flexibility. With complete control of their own engineering, price structure, sales methods, manufacturing processes, they could absorb new inventions and experience at once; they could adjust themselves quickly to changing condi-tions and opportunities. It taxed all of Sarnoff's ingenuity, and his special sense for trends, to overcome this handicap even partially.

Matters were scarcely helped by the fact that products bearing the RCA label actually came from two autonomous manufacturing sources. Variations in their respective facilities and production techniques made it hazardous to guarantee that the goods under the labels would always be truly identical. At best the designs agreed upon had to be compromises.

Decisions were made by planning committees on which GE, Westinghouse, and RCA were represented, under a major committee of which Sarnoff was chairman. His job, year after year, was to reconcile the preferences of the two manufacturers without doing too much violence to his own convictions about what was best for RCA and the industry.

The arrangement was unrealistic and unwieldy and, more than anything else, it enabled the newly arisen radio firms to prosper as fabulously as they did. It enabled them to outmaneuver RCA even while using RCA parts to assemble competing apparatus. The Radio Group provided almost all the research, the inventions, the costly experiments. It dealt with Congress and the government in hammering out rules of operation to prevent chaos and to eliminate wildcat stations and unethical practices. But it was tied in an organizational knot that made the full use of the benefits of this effort all but impossible.

The new radio firms were constantly leveling charges of monopoly against the Radio Group and RCA in particular. The American public and press, habituated to supporting the "little man" against the big corporation, too often reviled RCA without understanding or caring about the facts. Repeatedly Harbord, Sarnoff, and other officials were hauled before federal agencies and committees of Congress. Threats of antitrust and fair-trade actions filled the very air they breathed.

The supposed monopoly in practice served the interests of the new companies all too well. RCA was forever plowing the fields, its rivals were busy gathering in the crops. Despite this Sarnoff emerged as the leading advocate of general access to patents. He counseled the electric companies against policies that would bar competitors from the fruits of techonological progress. He had faith in the long-term virtues of untrammeled competition, whatever its short-term penalties. Besides, he had a shrewd understanding that monopoly methods, however justified legally, could not in the long run be enforced in relation to a service of radio's universal appeal and influence in public affairs.

3

These views, of course, did not inhibit Sarnoff in exploiting to the full RCA patent advantages while they lasted. A case in point was the superheterodyne principle for radio reception, developed largely by Howard Armstrong.

The inventor's relations with Sarnoff had remained friendly through all the years since their historic first meeting at the Columbia University laboratory in 1914. After the war Armstrong so often dropped in at Sarnoff's home at breakfast time—"just for a cup of coffee"—that the Sarnoff children called him "the coffee man." He was frequently at his friend's RCA office, too, to discuss his work and plans.

Sarnoff's secretary was a tall, strikingly handsome girl, Esther Marion MacInnis. The inventor was smitten with her at once and laid a long siege for her affections. Though gangling and prematurely bald, Armstrong was a magnetic personality. But he had eccentricities that gave a sensible New England girl pause. One of them was compulsive speeding in the most high-powered cars he could find at home or import from Europe. Another, perhaps part of the same lure of danger, was climbing to high places.

RCA was erecting a new station on the roof of the Aeolian Building on

42nd Street, off Fifth Avenue. Two 100-foot antenna towers were set up, each with a crossarm at right angles on which a man could walk. Between them, attached to the crossarms but about fifteen feet higher, there was a large ball of scrap iron. Armstrong liked to come to the unfinished station, ostensibly to watch its progress, then climb up and balance himself precariously on the ball.

Sarnoff wrote him a sharp letter ordering him to desist. But at the formal opening of the station, while Sarnoff was speaking to distinguished guests down below, Armstrong climbed the tower, reached the iron ball and posed for a snapshot 350 feet above 42nd Street. (Some reports said he did a handstand.) A few days later both Sarnoff and Miss MacInnis received copies of the picture. Though it led to orders barring him from the station, the episode did not spoil the friendship between the two young men.

There was nothing eccentric, however, about Armstrong's genius. In 1922 he was ready with what he called a superregenerative circuit. The technical press greeted it, prematurely, as the answer to radio reception problems. Among the first to see a demonstration, Sarnoff was so impressed that he induced his board to buy exclusive rights, at what was then a sensational price—$200,000 in cash and 60,000 shares of RCA stock. With the company's equities booming, Armstrong was suddenly a multimillionaire.

Unfortunately, it soon appeared that the superregenerative system could not be easily adapted to mass production. For the moment it seemed that Sarnoff had compounded his first large-scale blunder. But the old "Sarnoff luck" came to his rescue. Armstrong was perfecting a related circuit, based on the superheterodyne principle, on which he had been at work since the war years. In 1923, at last, he judged it ripe for use. The system was so uncanny in its receptivity that the set based on it could bring in programs without an external antenna.

For an additional bundle of 20,000 shares—which made the inventor the largest single stockholder in RCA—the company nailed down exclusive rights to this as well. Accruing to Armstrong, though it was not included in the agreement, was Sarnoff's secretary; Marion MacInnis gave up her job to marry the inventor before the end of the year.

At the time the deal was made RCA was about to conclude its periodical negotiations with the two manufacturers for several million dollars' worth of an improved set designed by its own small technical staff. Having convinced his board that the "superhet" would revolutionize radio reception, Sarnoff canceled the negotiations, much to the disgust of the electric companies. He was willing to forego a season of sales for a new start in the set market later.

Chiefly because of the organizational impediments I have already touched on, RCA was limping behind the leading set makers in total sales. The new superheterodyne receiver, released to the public in early 1924, changed this almost overnight. The sensation of the season, it soon put RCA at the head of the frenetically competitive pack. The company dominated the market for three years, until a new patent era made the "superhet" available to everybody. Sarnoff's apparent blunder had thus been converted into a gold mine. The superheterodyne system is still embodied in nearly all radio receivers, though Armstrong's rights to it were later disputed by others and brought him a lot of grief.

In the sum-total of crises and conflicts confronting the corporation in the 1920's patent troubles were a constant. They soaked up countless man-hours of effort—especially Sarnoff's. The whole radio art, he later told an audience of Harvard students, was in danger of being removed "from the laboratory to the courts." The confusion was deepened by a Navy Department decision to issue licenses for a collection of German patents held by the Alien Property Custodian. There were endless RCA suits against infringers, interim agreements that fell apart, recriminations and threats keyed to the war cry of "monopoly."

In a memorandum in March, 1922, Sarnoff offered a blueprint for cutting through the ever more complex patent maze. In substance it embodied the plan finally adopted by the industry. But the process took five years of unceasing and frequently acrimonious negotiations.

The leading competitors joined in a united front against RCA through an Association of Independent Radio Manufacturers, with the president of Zenith, Commander Eugene McDonald, as its main spokesman. In this man Sarnoff found an opponent worthy of his mettle. But Zenith and other large firms, too, had a stake in bringing order into the picture, since there were scores of small producers, quite contemptuous of patent legalities, always nibbling into *their* business.

By 1927 a system of liberal licensing was established under which virtually all patents became accessible to nearly all comers. RCA under the agreements obtained modest royalties (which it shared with the electric companies) on total sales by licensees. Thenceforth all the fruits of RCA research and discovery, at costs ultimately running into hundreds of millions, would be accessible to its competitors. The royalty payments by licensees—a percentage on total sales which was constantly trimmed down—would help in part to cover research investments, of course. They remained too small, however, to give RCA any price advantage in the marketplace or to meet the handicap of a 20 percent profit to the electric companies before RCA could earn a penny for itself.

The patent pool so dexterously collected by Young and Sarnoff was thus opened up to their business rivals. Had there been no such central repository, every radio firm would have been forced to negotiate separate patent deals with each of the original holders and many of them, under such conditions, could not have remained in business at all.

The licensing policy evolved by RCA has been widely acknowledged as one of the most fertile developments in American economic growth, in that it made possible and stimulated free competition. Practically all who applied were granted a license and under it enjoyed the benefits of all existing discoveries not only by RCA research in the area covered but by the laboratories of other companies with which RCA has cross-licensing arrangements.

This method of encouraging—and in some degree even subsidizing—competition is no longer unique. It has been imitated and adapted by other strongly technological industries. But it was a bold pioneering venture when the leading electronics company first established it. And, in the words of Bucher, "the chief burden in formulating the initial RCA licensing plan fell to David Sarnoff." Through it Sarnoff to a notable extent molded the character of the entire electronics business.

His influence in the electronic world, however, went further and deeper. For increasingly in the mid-twenties he emerged as the interpreter of radio both to its practitioners and to the public. He became the tone-setter of broadcasting, its strongest voice vis-à-vis the government, the confident guide into the electronic future.

"David Sarnoff," Robert Norman wrote in an article about him in the *American Magazine* in 1923, "is conceded to have a greater all around knowledge of radio development and management than any other living man."

It was knowledge backed by the kind of insight that enabled him to pick out the significant lines in the maze of radio events and pursue them to their logical implications. He could see the inventions and services whole with his mind's eye years before they became actualities. Fortunately, too, he was highly articulate. The boy who learned his first words of English when he was barely ten years old now used the language with skill and eloquence. Few who did not know his personal history could have guessed that it was an acquired tongue. His natural talent for colorful expression and imagery enabled him to convey the drama of the adventure in which he was engaged so that others were infected by his faith and enthusiasms.

In the confusions inseparable from swift growth in many directions, the industry groped for advice and guidance. For these it began to turn, more and more, to Sarnoff. In examining the record of those critical years, one marvels that one man could have found the time, endurance, and mental resources to exercise leadership in the whole field while managing his own acreage—weed-infested and rock-strewn—in the Radio Corporation.

9

Prophet with Honor

In unguarded moments David Sarnoff has made remarks implying his leadership of the whole industry. There was his statement, for instance, already cited, that he was the fellow "on the bridge" steering the ship of radio through the shoals. It was the kind of assumption that infuriated some other leaders. But there is little doubt that he consciously took up the burdens of the industry, worrying about its troubles and glorying in its attainments.

Being no mystic but a hardheaded man of affairs, he had a simple rationale for this all-embracing sense of responsibility: the conviction that RCA would survive and flourish only if the whole convoluted electronics business achieved coherence and healthy development. Deliberately he adopted the stance of an interpreter of the new science, art, and business, clarifying its prospects and implications not alone to the American people but to specialists engaged in it. Eventually they would come to appreciate his role but at this stage, we may be sure, a lot of them resented it as upstage presumptuousness.

His public addresses of this period show him at once as the philosopher of radio and its prophet. Invariably, they trace lines of growth and are filled with predictions of things aborning. The wisest among the entrepreneurs flocking to these new fields of business, whatever their feelings about the self-important young man, learned to scan his every speech for hints and portents.

With growing frequency he was called upon to interpret the new art for the business community and for the consumer. The calls came not alone from within the radio and electric worlds but from other industries, chambers of commerce, clubs, universities, the press. Congressional panels tackling radio problems also provided him with useful forums.

Secretary of Commerce Herbert Hoover summoned three successive conferences on radio. By wide consensus the most significant of the contributions
came in the last of these sessions—from Sarnoff. The high esteem in which
Hoover always held Sarnoff dated from this time.

Addressing a convention of electrical supply jobbers at Hot Springs,
Virginia, in 1922, Sarnoff offered a comprehensive analysis of the new
broadcasting business, its opportunities, problems, pitfalls. To point up his
unlimited confidence in the potentials of radio, he revealed that, although its
gross was then only around four million dollars a year, RCA was embarked
on expenditures of twenty millions.

But the address, typically, went beyond commercial considerations. The
business opportunities, he emphasized, carried with them vital social responsibilities, because "in broadcasting we have a force, an instrumentality,
greater than any that has yet come to mankind." Only those who lifted their
minds above the current confusions, he warned, only those who made public
service their foundation concern, would survive among the hordes invading
the new field.

A Chamber of Commerce session in Atlantic City on January 26, 1923,
heard Sarnoff stress the need for government regulation of broadcast transmission to bring order into the airwaves. He proposed that the entire nation
be divided "into radio broadcasting zones having the necessary number of
stations required effectively to serve the territory and employing such bands of
wavelengths as will eliminate interference." Eventually, after five years of
temporizing and false starts, this is precisely what the government did.

On this occasion, also, he forecast the use of external microphone pickup
techniques which, in fact, soon came into universal use. "Your real artist,
orator or educator," he explained, "should not be obliged to go to the
broadcasting station. The broadcasting station should go to them."

The year 1923 had seen a decline in radio business. A pall of fear hung
over the industry. In an impromptu speech in Buffalo in November, again at a
convention of electrical jobbers, Sarnoff made light of the regression. The fact
that sales in 1922 had been at a level of only $75 million did not deter him
from a bold forecast of general and rapid growth.

"I believe," he said, "that this industry will go on for the next few years
virtually doubling in volume each year. Two years ago I made the prediction
that the radio industry would be equal in a few years to the phonograph
industry, which in normal times reached 400 million dollars a year. Today I
say that the radio industry will be worth within the next few years half a
billion dollars in consumers' prices."

His feeling for the industry's tempo of expansion was more than confirmed. The phonograph industry's figure was matched by radio in 1924 and exceeded, with a total of $430 million, the following year. It touched the billion mark by the end of the 1920's. In the slump year of 1923, Sarnoff's confidence helped dispel the prevailing gloom.

In the same Buffalo speech he sketched his vision, long cherished, of an all-national audience for one program. He was aware of the technological roadblocks but did not regard any of them as insuperable. Already, of course, it was possible to connect low-power stations by wires. The Telephone Group, with the Bell System network of wires at its disposal, was linking up many stations on special occasions. But the method was costly and uneconomic. Instead Sarnoff urged that the government authorize strategically located superpower stations of a capacity of 50 kilowatts or more, to be linked by wire or by short-wave radio relays for continuous nationwide service. He referred to it as "a chain of national broadcasting stations"—perhaps the first use of the term "chain" in this context.

He saw each of the connected stations "simultaneously radiating the same program, whatever it may be, to reach every city, every town, every village, every hamlet, every home in the United States; and with an organization capable of measuring up to the responsibilities of that character of a national service. All this, gentlemen, is in embryo today, but in my judgment, very certain to come about in time."

Various schemes for taxing the listener to help pay for broadcasting were then being discussed. Sarnoff attacked them all as a menace to the consumer and therefore to the industry dependent on an ever larger number of consumers.

Such taxes, he argued, would turn broadcasting into "narrowcasting," by denying its advantages to those who could not easily afford them. His own preference, he explained, was for constantly reducing costs to the listener: "a 15 or 25 dollar set in the homes of the slums, receiving the magnificent things in the air" without further expenses. Always he talked in the metaphors of carrying the great outside world—news, entertainment, culture—to the poor and the isolated, to families on farms and in far-off hamlets.

His favorite and oft-repeated mental image was of the walls of humble dwellings being thrown open to influences from without. At the University of Missouri, on January 7, 1924, for instance, Sarnoff declared: "Radio, which first came to dispel the mystery and isolation of the seas, and then link the earth by invisible chains of communication through the air, has now come to attune every home with the great world outside"; come to "relieve the farmer and his family from the sense of isolation which is perhaps the harshest handicap of the agricultural life."

Testifying in Washington two months later he explained that the indispensable official regulation required was technical; that nothing should be done by Congress to impair either freedom of speech over the airwaves or freedom of listening. "The air belongs to the people," he said. "Its main highways should be maintained for the main travel. To collect a tax from the radio audience would be a reversion to the days of toll roads and bridges; to the days when schools were not public or free and when public libraries were unknown."

In the course of this testimony, by the way, he startled the legislative committee by suggesting that vital Congressional debates be broadcast: a suggestion that was not to be heeded, and then only with respect to certain committee hearings, until two decades later.

Sarnoff's presentation before the third of Secretary Hoover's conferences, made to a subcommittee on October 9, 1924, was as nearly a complete survey of the radio world—as it existed and as it would develop—as could be produced at that crossroads of confusion. His description of coast-to-coast programing, backed by a bombshell offer to build a superpower station at his company's own risk, was what made news. But it was only part of his great design covering every phase of the industry.

"We can choose the broad road of further research and achievement that will carry the art to its highest destiny," he declared, "or we can take the primrose path of easy accomplishment and rest upon the facilities that already have been created. . . . The day is not far when technical developments in the art will enable our country, through superpower stations, to reflect its best thought to other nations of the world, and at that time the United States will take the same position of leadership in worldwide broadcasting that it occupies today in worldwide telegraphic communications."

At a time when many able performers were appearing on radio with little if any compensation, content to be paid off in publicity, Sarnoff demanded that they be adequately paid. And this, he went on to say, would become possible as soon as nationwide audiences were provided—hence the importance of forging "chains" of stations. "Far from sounding the death knell of the artist's opportunities," he said, "I believe that radio eventually will give the artist a higher compensation, a vastly greater audience and a wider appreciation than he has heretofore enjoyed."

These, of course, are random citations from public pronouncements that add up to many volumes of manuscript. Running through them all, giving them their authentic Sarnoff flavor, are the proofs of his gift for prognostication, to which—unavoidably—we return again and again. The instinct that led him to envision the Music Box (2,500,000 of which were already in use as early as the end of 1923, served by 523 stations) continued to spark with increasing force and in ever-new dimensions.

His enthusiasm for his special field of action seemed touched with awe. Whether in his own living room or on a public rostrum, Sarnoff appeared eager that others comprehend and share his enthusiasm. In a lecture at the Harvard Business School, in the 1927–28 semester, he promised the students their "greatest opportunities" in the purlieus of science.

"The protean part which a single art may play in modern industry has no better illustration," he told them, "than the position of the radio art and the radio industry, and its growth and development since 1920. For radio encompasses telegraphic communication as exemplified in our transoceanic wireless system; sound communication as accomplished in telephony; mass communication as inherent in broadcasting; sight communication as promised by television."

Although it was still almost a generation in the future, he included television in the inventory!

He went on to say that radio "is an art that embraces and goes beyond the arts of electrical engineering; that touches upon the photographic and dramatic arts and is infusing new ideas into both; an art that has definite relations to chemistry, to metallurgy, to physics, to astronomy, to meteorology, to acoustics and to dynamics." If others saw electronics in these sweeping dimensions, they were few, and not half as articulate.

He spoke of a "changing order of things in the world of business," and tried to convey it to that Harvard class: "Other motives than mere economic gain are beginning to influence industrial leadership. Men are contending not so directly for a share of the public dollar, as in an endeavor to develop and perfect those unlimited possibilities of achievement which science is breeding in the laboratory and executive genius is exploiting in the promotion offices of modern industrial organizations.

"The needs of the times will bring forth, perhaps, a new type of executive, trained in a manner not always associated with the requirements of business management. He will have to reckon with the constant changes in industry that scientific research is bringing. He will have to be able to approximate the value of technical development, to understand the significance of scientific research.

"He will be equipped with an even and exact knowledge of the relationship between his business and similar businesses in the same field; between his industry and other industries which it may affect or be affected by; between business and government; and even between business and politics, for no great industrial enterprise is safe from political attack. 'Mind your own business' is ceasing to be an all-embracing business axiom. It may be the other fellow's business that will determine the success or failure of your own."

Knowingly or not, Sarnoff was here describing himself, attributing to businessmen in general his own perceptions and attitudes. One notes, in perusing the massive record of his views and promises in the 1920's, this strain of idealism—of exorbitant expectations—which has not been as fully justified by time as his purely technical prognoses.

Continually he described the coming social impacts of mass communication in his own, rather than the average man's, appetites for knowledge, beauty, and uplift. His emphasis was on class rather than mass programs, on symphonic and operatic music, greater popular participation in the processes of government, more enlightened public opinion, and improved international understanding. Thus he wrote in 1922:

"As an internationalizing agency, radio broadcasting is an instrumentality which, if properly used, may well break down prejudices, help men to understand each other, sway and even govern national and international motives by bringing the personality and intelligence and the thought of the world's great men to millions of people everywhere."

In practice, unfortunately, the new instrumentality proved no less useful to the world's demagogues and dictators. The phrase "if properly used" suggests that his lofty expectations were not unmixed with doubts.

2

In reporting on his study of certain of Howard Armstrong's experiments with short waves, in January, 1920, David Sarnoff predicted their use in commercial services. A month later he followed up with a memorandum urging the company to undertake work at once on short-wave broadcasting.

This ran counter to prevailing engineering opinion, but neither then nor later would he allow the pessimism of technical specialists to brake his own expectations. In mid-1922, though the engineering fraternity was still cold or at best lukewarm on the subject, he was more than ever convinced of the coming importance of short and ultrashort waves. "Some day in the future," he wrote to president Nally, "we will signal and talk across the Atlantic and Pacific in short instead of long waves." The current dependence on "brute force" for long-distance transmission, he said in a radio talk later, would no longer be necessary when we learned to harness the short waves.

He was not speaking only on instinct or intuition, of course. Nearly always his previsions were related to solid scientific fact or indications provided by experiment. He knew that in December, 1921, a group of amateurs succeeded in flashing a brief message by short waves from Greenwich, Connecticut, to England. Then, in 1923, Dr. Frank Conrad at Westinghouse was able to report some progress with short-wave broadcasting. But the technique was still far from perfected and the industry, deeply engaged in profitable long-wave enterprises—themselves new and heady—was reluctant to sink capital into novelties.

Sarnoff's propaganda in this area was supported right along by Marconi, who was himself hot on the trail of short and ultrashort waves. The two men had become intimate friends and kept each other informed on inventive progress on both sides of the Atlantic. Now and then the Sarnoffs joined the Italian inventor and his wife on their celebrated floating laboratory, the yacht *Elletra*. What was ostensibly a Mediterranean holiday usually turned into nearly round-the-clock orgies of experimentation. For both men belonged to the fortunate species whose trade is also their hobby.

By 1927 their efforts, along with important contributions from other dedicated research groups, led to universal acceptance of short waves for long-range communications. The "brute force" required to project long waves across vast spaces was eliminated. If only because of his persistent emphasis on the inevitability of this development, Sarnoff was widely credited with a prediction that came true.

In August, 1922, in a letter to Dr. Alfred Goldsmith, Sarnoff sketched in words what he called a radiolette: a small, compact, easily portable receiving set for the individual in motion. Before long, of course, such a compact set was a working fact; then it was reduced to pocket size, though the complete fulfillment of Sarnoff's promise had to wait for the age of miniaturization made possible by the "printed" circuit and the transistor.

Would radio spell the doom of the phonograph? Majority opinion, especially within the alarmed phonograph industry itself, which was experiencing steep declines in sales and profits, was that it would. Sarnoff did not agree. He believed that whatever the immediate effects, the phonograph would in the long run benefit from the electronic powers of radio. He was the first to foretell the rejuvenation of that medium through cooperation, rather than competition, with radio. Specifically, he predicted the "marriage" of the old and the new musical devices, living in easy harmony in the same cabinet.

"A happy association of the two instruments, which should live under the same roof," is the way he put it in April, 1922. Radio, he said, "can be expected to produce inventions and improvements which may technically govern and control the future of the phonograph." This, of course, is precisely what came to pass.

As usual when he had the authority, Sarnoff proceeded to support his predictions with cash and research. He instructed RCA and its electric associates to design a combined radio-and-phonograph set, with a common speaker. Development of the magnetic pickup in 1924 made the "marriage" possible and ultimately highly lucrative. Any radio could—by the addition of a turntable, a driving motor, and the pickup device—add phonographic reproduction to its capacity for service. Despite premature funeral orations, the phonograph and record business was headed for unprecedented prosperity.

Sarnoff's optimism on the future of phonograph music set a pattern. He would consistently argue that the emergence of a new medium did not necessarily annul the old ones. After a period of readjustment an older form might even be revitalized by the techniques of its young competitor. Repeatedly he would reassure the leaders of the live theatre and motion pictures that radio, and then television, need not spell their doom. Similarly, when the broadcasting of serious music began to worry musicians, he explained that the appreciation of the art generated by radio would create demands for more live symphony orchestras and concerts.

Writing in the New York *Herald* of May 14, 1922, Sarnoff predicted something that then sounded farfetched—radio in motorcars. "It is reasonable," he declared, "to expect its eventual application to automobiles and in some cases to individuals." A year later he promised that "everything which moves or floats will be equipped with a radio instrument: the airplane, the railroad, steamship, motorboat, automobile and other vehicles." This prophecy took eight or nine years to mature. Radio in cars became a commercial fact in 1931 and a decade later some ten million cars were so equipped.

In the same *Herald* article he foresaw regular broadcasting between the American continent and Europe, which became a reality about six years later, chiefly through his own unflagging experiments in cooperation with the British Broadcasting Company and other European organizations. He also threw out hints of what would in due time come to be known as the walkie-talkie.

In May, 1924, Sarnoff told a National Electric Light Association meeting that before long radio receivers would draw their power directly from household electric outlets, thus dispensing with the dry or storage batteries then in use. This, of course, is what happened.

The dream of adding sight to sound in transmissions over the airwaves was engaging the interest of many scientists. Still or facsimile images had been sent, experimentally, for a number of years, but images in motion were another matter. Sarnoff, however, was among the first who dared talk of it not as a dream but as an inevitable reality. As early as 1922, we know, he was assembling in his mind the theoretical ingredients of television. By April, 1923, he was ready to put a forecast into documentary form. In a memorandum to RCA directors he wrote in part:

"I believe that television, which is the technical name for seeing instead of hearing by radio, will come to pass in due course.

"Already, [still] pictures have been sent across the Atlantic by radio. Experimental, of course, but it points the way to future possibilities. It is not too much to expect that in the near future when news is telegraphed by radio . . . a picture of the event will likewise be sent over by radio and both will arrive simultaneously, thus . . . we will be able to see as well as read in New York, within an hour or so, the event taking place in London, Buenos Aires or Tokyo.

"I also believe that transmission and reception of motion pictures by radio will be worked out within the next decade. . . . The problem is technically similar to that of radio telephony, though of more complicated nature; but within the range of technical achievement. Therefore, it may be that every broadcast receiver will also be equipped with a television adjunct by which the instrument will make it possible for those at home to see as well as hear what is going on at the broadcast station."

His conception of TV was steadily sharpened. Eventually, he said at the University of Missouri in January, 1924, every farm family would be able to "look in" as well as listen in on news events. And in an article in the *Saturday Evening Post* (August 14, 1926) he wrote: "The greatest day of all will be reached when not only the human voice but the image of the speaker will be flashed through space in every direction." It is not easy to realize, in the present television age, how unreal such forecasts sounded in the 1920's.

Two Sarnoff addresses to military men, in 1926 and 1927, make astonishing reading in the perspective of events. Nearly all of what he saw with his mind's eye of the application of radio, television, and other electronic forces in case of war came true in the Second World War and the Korean War. His own research laboratories, indeed, would take the lead in perfecting many important instrumentalities in this area.

The first of these addresses, on February 20, 1926, was delivered at the Army's Industrial College. Future wars, Sarnoff said, would be won "on the basis of brains and scientific devices rather than numerical preponderance." He added: "It is not inconceivable that a future war may last five minutes rather than five years, and yet be infinitely more destructive." Among other things he mentioned explosives placed at targets in advance and exploded by remote control; unmanned or "robot" airplanes, ships, submarines, and tanks; the massive use of radio for propaganda and counterpropaganda.

He went on to speak of destructive radiation that might defeat an enemy, alluding to the death-dealing potentials of X rays and heat rays. "An investigation of these and perhaps as yet unknown rays, as well as incendiary or disintegration agencies," he said, "may well lead to the development of powerful methods of warfare." Accordingly he urged that "now is the time to study intensively scientific agencies of destruction, and perhaps even more vigorously the countermeasures for combatting them on a wholesale defensive scale." He called for "coordination of the existing or the establishment of new optical, electrical, chemical, biological and research laboratories, and the placement of recognized experts in their respective fields on the staffs of such laboratories."

These concepts of war uses were further developed in his address at the Army War College on January 31, 1927.

"Far away as we may seem from the accomplished fact of television by radio," he told the assembled military specialists, "we have made sufficient progress to bring the goal within measurable distance. Practical difficulties, hitherto considered almost insurmountable, are responding to advanced technical solutions . . . [soon] we shall be able to transmit a picture by radio in the remarkable time of ten seconds. When that stage is reached, our consideration of the problems of television can well turn from fantasy to fact."

Given television, he then proceeded to visualize its potentials in warmaking. He foresaw, for example, scout planes soaring over enemy territory and transmitting instantly all that their television cameras saw below. "We may see the day when a fleet of aircraft, with no human occupants and loaded with bombs, may be sent against the enemy's lines, with all the controlling operations performed by radio. . . . As the principles of remote control by radio have already been determined, it is not impossible to conceive the radio-controlled tank of the future, without human pilotage, being driven toward the enemy lines. . . .

"Perhaps it would be too fantastic to consider the part that may be played by direct television in the war of the future, but it is not too early to consider the direction which laboratories should take in its application to military uses. It is conceivable that a radio-television transmitter installed in an aeroplane might be useful in transmitting a direct image of the enemy's terrain, thus enabling greater accuracy in gunfire."

With no less clarity he foresaw the struggle for the minds of men: "The next war will involve a great problem of mass education in which radio must play a dominant role. Through the institution of broadcasting, radio is the first universal system of one-way communication developed by man. No other agency can speak with a single voice at the same instant to millions of people. . . . The greatest problem of mass communication that is likely to face us in the next national emergency is the problem of counteracting the deluge of enemy propaganda that might pour in on us through the air."

He tempered his vision, again typically, with a conservative note: "While the radio art, in its present phases, has no more definite limits than the bounds of imagination, it is an admirable principle which commands men to keep their feet on the ground in discussing a subject of practical importance. Yet it is the anomaly of this age we live in that while men may desire to keep their feet firmly on Mother Earth, scientific progress may well whisk the very ground from under them."

3

It was thus that the label of "prophet" came to be permanently attached to Sarnoff. Decade after decade, the national magazines turned to him for those previews of life twenty-five or fifty years hence so dear to editorial hearts.

But the label can be utterly misleading. The word "prophet" carries overtones of the occult and esoteric, of some sort of sixth sense. In David Sarnoff's powers of divination there was nothing of the kind. He was not composing science fiction but dealing with hard scientific and technological fact. He was not peering into a crystal ball but projecting the known today into tomorrow.

We know that certain scientists, on the basis of a single bone, can reconstruct some long-extinct animal. Sarnoff had an equivalent but more rare ability—the same skill, as it were, in reverse. From a few bones of laboratory information, from a single attribute of the electron, he "reconstructed" technological developments into the future, clearly and concretely.

This enabled him throughout his life to speak of things still in the womb of time with the calm assurance of a meteorologist describing tomorrow's wind currents. A man who had ample opportunity to observe him at work from close range and through many years told me:

"General Sarnoff had a faculty of listening silently to the shop talk of engineers. He would pick up a hint, a half-thought, and would explore it, expand it, analyze its potentials for use. Frequently he pounced on an idea or a research indication which the engineers themselves thought of no importance.

"He would demand more information, suggest lines of investigation that sometimes seemed 'unrealistic' to the specialists. Again and again, I recall, these Sarnoff 'hunches' led to vital developments. He could visualize the finished product and the utility of such work, in practical detail, long before it was more than a vague notion to the very researchers working on it, and of course years before it reached the public.

"Along with this imaginative vision, he had patience. He was a radical in foreseeing things but a conservative in bringing them to the market. This balance of prophecy and caution seemed to me exceptional. He couldn't be pushed into premature announcements or marketing. 'When in doubt,' I heard him say again and again, 'say No.' "

Dr. Goldsmith, after a lifelong association with the man, once explained to me that Sarnoff has a highly analytical mind combined with a lively imagination—the amalgam typical of the great inventors and scientists. Having cross-examined those who held conflicting theories or worked on conflicting projects, he said, Sarnoff would unerringly choose the right alternative and then push its development.

A "practical visionary" sounds like a contradiction in terms. Yet it describes Sarnoff and helps explain his special contribution to electronics. Though he would accumulate a few patents to his personal credit, he did not regard himself as an inventor. His strength was in seeing the long-range implication of some line of research so acutely that he was able to guide the experimenters in his organization.

Uniquely among the tribe of seers, moreover, he did not leave the fulfillment of his predictions to chance. Having identified some coming wonder in the welter of technical laboratories, he liked to set a date for its perfection and unveiling. His forecasts thus have been in effect marching orders for his technical staff, specific goals to be reached at specific times. Unlike the run of prophets, also, he staked large amounts of capital on his personal vision— often to the discomfiture and against the opposition of more "practical" associates.

General Harbord once said: "An invention does not make its way alone. Its art must be guided in its development. It must be supported by an alliance to the world of business, and its application made to contribute to the welfare of mankind." That, he declared, has been Sarnoff's role in radio, electronics, and their related forces.

The Sarnoff imagination in effect paced the industry. His frequent speeches were at once reports to the American consumers on progress in this field and guides to the industry on directions for further progress. Thus he was not simply indulging in a propensity for prognostication. His purpose was plainly functional: to ignite others, especially in his own company, with the flame of his own vision, in order that they might make the inordinate efforts and investments he considered justified.

There is some danger, naturally, that any such conspicuous talent may be overstated and magnified beyond reality. His accurate forecasts have been hailed in print to the point of creating a myth. Because they embraced such epoch-making things as the Music Box and television, this has operated to obscure some Sarnoff predictions that have failed to materialize. What is more, his sure instinct in foreseeing tangible, technical developments did not as often hold true when he attempted to sketch the future on the trickier levels of political and social developments. An example, out of chronological order: In 1931 he said in a public address:

"When television has fulfilled its ultimate destiny, man's sense of physical boundaries will be swept away, and the boundaries of his sight and hearing will be the limits of the earth itself. With this may come a new horizon, a new philosophy, a new sense of freedom, and greatest of all, perhaps a finer and broader understanding between all peoples of the world."

Unfortunately this prognosis has not yet been justified. In fact the era of television has coincided with a steady and tragic shrinking of the areas of freedom on this earth, a rebirth of know-nothing nationalism, the triumphant advance of aggressive and obscurantist ideologies. He had the prudence to cast the prediction in the subjunctive mood. Still, his social optimism seems as uncertain as the next man's, in contrast with his technological visions.

As a footnote to this brief survey of his gifts of foresight, it is intriguing to recall Sarnoff's "debate" with another and more famous practitioner of these arts, H. G. Wells. The British novelist enjoyed a justified reputation for daring prophecy but it did not serve him too well when he plunged into the subject of broadcasting. In a widely quoted article in 1927 he dismissed radio broadcasting as an "inferior substitute" for older means of communication. He resented the innovation and regarded it as a passing fancy. With the authority of an established crystal-ball operator, he asserted that radio stations would soon be talking to a "phantom army of non-existing listeners."

This challenge to the new medium was quickly picked up by Sarnoff. In an address at Syracuse University on April 28, 1927, he directed himself to the meticulous demolition of the novelist's views. He found it "difficult to understand," said Sarnoff, "how a brilliant mind that could foresee so many modern inventions could have reached such extraordinary conclusions about radio." At the heart of the H. G. Wells forecast, as Sarnoff saw it, was the "intellectual snobbery" that disdained mass audiences.

"Broadcasting," he conceded, "cannot hope to thrill the intellectually overfed or the spiritually jaded, but it can and does fulfill a splendid destiny in the field of mass entertainment and education. . . . The critics who fix their thought upon the immediate limitations of the radio art are taking their places with those who guffawed at the possibility of the 'horseless carriage'; who considered the telephone a mere toy and the steam engine as merely a 'dangerous contraption.' "

He then sketched the extent to which radio had already brought millions of listeners into direct communion with great artists until then beyond their reach. In the preceding six months, he pointed out, vast audiences had tuned in on operatic stars like Maria Jeritza, Giovanni Martinelli, Rosa Ponselle, Beniamino Gigli, Titta Ruffo, Mary Garden; such concert artists as John MacCormack, Josef Hofmann, Mischa Elman, Frieda Hempel; master conductors like Arturo Toscanini, Willem Mengelberg, Walter Damrosch. "Through what other medium of communication could a musical, cultural and entertainment service have been rendered to many millions of homes throughout the world?"

History soon enough gave its decision on the Wells-Sarnoff "debate." The ever larger audiences of radio broadcasting were scarcely "phantom."

4

While charting a course for the radio industry as a whole, David Sarnoff was steadfastly shoring up the positions of his own corporation. Its problems grew in variety and magnitude but so, as he viewed the panorama, did the opportunities. The hallmark of his breed of business leadership, in fact, was that it so often detected opportunity in major problems, exploiting short-term troubles for long-term benefits. That he had that unique ability will become evident as we recount some of its concrete manifestations.

Faced with some immediate problem, Sarnoff's associates sought a solution as an end in itself. The general manager saw it as another chance to advance his larger plans. These envisioned: (1) unification—consolidation of all phases of the business, including manufacturing, research, engineering, chain broadcasting within RCA; and beyond that, (2) autonomy or separation— complete independence from the electric companies. He made no secret of his ultimate objectives, but what Dr. Archer called "the Napoleonic plan under his hat" seemed as yet too farfetched to alarm those who now exercised fiscal control.

Whatever the negotiations he conducted himself or masterminded through others, he was determined that they yield a bonus for RCA in the coin of enlarged scope of operation and ultimate sovereignty.

Thus the prolonged and often bitter contest with the Telephone complex ended in its voluntary retirement from the radio field—which in turn facilitated the birth of the National Broadcasting Company. The long impasse in relations with Victor Talking Machine led to its absorption by RCA. That consummation not only added gramophones and records to the corporation's business but, more important from Sarnoff's special vantage point, endowed it with manufacturing facilities and thereby helped RCA to win some rights to produce what it marketed. The endless harassments of fair-trade and antitrust investigations and suits led in the long run to the corporate independence of RCA. None of these gains was accidental. The general manager and vice-president was engaged in putting together a jigsaw puzzle, piece by piece, though not many around him recognized the whole picture before all the pieces were firmly in place.

His strategic and tactical skills were tested to the limit. At one and the same time he was integrating old and new entertainment media; pressing for superpower stations as building blocks for his radio networks of tomorrow; developing short-wave techniques for transoceanic telephony and relay stations on land; dealing with the Federal Trade Commission and the Department of Justice on legal problems; negotiating (in its climactic phases almost singlehandedly) with the Telephone Group; shaping up patent licensing agreements; building up distributor outlets; appraising the progress of radio in Europe in a number of time-consuming trips to that continent. Before long, moreover, as a direct extension of radio developments, sound was added to sight in motion pictures—a revolution in which Sarnoff of necessity became deeply involved.

And these, of course, were in addition to the normal responsibilities of directing a great domestic and foreign merchandising enterprise, a worldwide radiotelegraph network, enormous manufacturing and research programs; in addition to synchronizing the activities of the tension-filled Radio Group, while parrying threats to his personal position even inside RCA.

There were also the periodical testings and launchings of new services. One anecdote in this connection Sarnoff still tells with a lot of relish, although it was scarcely world-shaking:

He happened to be in London, in the mid-twenties, when the first transatlantic radiotelephone conversation was scheduled. He was apprised by New York that when everything was set he would be called at the Savoy Hotel, where he was stopping. On the crucial day he had been invited, through a Viscount Castleross whom he had met aboard ship during the crossing, to dine with Lord Beaverbrook.

He was told that the great press magnate expected guests to dress for his dinners—not simply black tie but in the full regalia of "tails." To an American this implied a gala gathering with many guests. Instead he found only his host and the viscount. They were deployed around a banquet table large enough to accommodate a score, and behind each of their chairs stood a butler in operatic uniform. Perhaps unfairly, it all seemed irritating pomposity to the overseas guest.

During the second course word was brought to Sarnoff that New York was calling him—on the telephone! But he was too annoyed by the pretentiousness of his host to give Beaverbrook the satisfaction of witnessing a significant technological "first" in his own home. With a *sang-froid* he decidedly did not feel, he therefore said that the call could wait, he would pick it up when he returned to the Savoy. Somehow he concealed his excitement and anxiety until the meal was ended, engaged in some more desultory conversation, then excused himself and dashed to the hotel to make history.

Sarnoff's workday often stretched deep into the night and he rarely knew a workless weekend or holiday. Luckily he was young, healthy, equipped with enormous physical stamina. Most important, he was fascinated by the unique business-art-and-science to which he was committed and actually relished the challenges and conflicts that he faced. Vitality and valor were his long suits. No soul-searching was involved in his rejection of the offers that came to him constantly, each baited with great immediate financial reward, to abandon RCA and join other flourishing radio firms. No matter how lush, they seemed to him irrelevant and therefore no real temptations.

10

Networks and Talkies

ᕇ His existence left Sarnoff small enough margins for a private life. Yet domestic and social demands could not be shirked. He managed to share with his lovely Lizette the burdens and decisions entailed by three lively sons—Robert who was born in 1918, Edward in 1921, and Thomas in 1927—and an expanding social life.

David's three brothers were by this time well established and his sister was married to a chemist, Herbert Baer. The two youngest brothers, Morris and the American-born Irving, early demonstrated a bent for business that eventually made them financially independent. Leah Sarnoff was at last enjoying surcease from economic pressure and with it the satisfaction of helping her sisters and other relatives.

The second-born, Lew, the maverick of her brood, had taken to the road and finally enlisted in the Army. He was with Pershing in the Mexican campaign against Villa as a cavalryman, then went through World War I in front-line combat in the Signal Corps. Eventually, when he chose to "settle down," he too lived up to the Sarnoff flair for affluence. In later years the four brothers would establish a joint fund, under Lew's bighearted management, upon which the neediest of their kin could draw for assistance.

To David's sons, growing up in a thoroughly American milieu, everything connoted by "Uzlian" was as strange and remote as tales out of the *Arabian Nights*. Always, along with their pride in their father's accomplishments and mounting renown, there would be an element of bewilderment. Their father as a boy had known the dichotomy between an immigrant home and the American environment. Robert and Edward and Thomas could neither know nor understand such problems. A very important part of their parents' world was inaccessible to them and almost incomprehensible—a fact that their parents acknowledged with a deep sigh.

But let us return to complex business under Sarnoff's guidance and manipulation.

2

For all the surge to new frontiers, the very first of the Radio Corporation's services, marine radio and radiotelegraphy, was not slighted. Though a steadily diminishing part of the aggregate business, it expanded year by year. The fulfillment of David Sarnoff's prophecies on short-wave communications brought more and more countries within the corporation's reach. He supervised and in many instances conducted personally negotiations with dozens of foreign firms and governments which produced for RCA a comprehensive global network of wireless telegraphy that was a match for the cable telegraph services.

At a meeting of the New York Electrical Society in November, 1922, Sarnoff dramatized the telegraphic aspect by exchanging messages directly from the auditorium with Paris, Berlin, London, and other European cities. The round-trip time was from one to two minutes. Within five or six years he was able to communicate not only with Europe but with the Far East and the Southern Hemisphere in a fraction of the time.

Broadcasting at this stage held first place in Sarnoff's thinking and planning. His concepts of this force, as in the case of the Music Box, ran considerably ahead of existing technology. Years before the techniques of coast-to-coast broadcasting had been perfected, he visualized nationwide networks in operation. "It seems to me," he wrote to President Rice of General Electric in June, 1922, "that in seeking a solution to the broadcasting problem we must recognize that the answer must be along national rather than local lines, for the problem is distinctly a national one." Therefore, he went on, "Let us organize a separate and distinct company, to be known as the Public Service Broadcasting Company, or American Broadcasting Company, or some similar name."

He did not expect, of course, that this idea, as yet so startling, would find early acceptance. It seemed too far beyond the technical and imaginative limitations of the time. In a public address in Chicago in 1924 he explained:

"It is useless to consider how broadcasting might be made to pay for the services of a premier artist before a method has been evolved of broadcasting the artist's program to the greatest economic advantage. From a technical standpoint, I believe the answer to the problem lies in superbroadcasting with a force that could be distinctly heard in every home in the United States."

Again and again he emphasized the fatuity of expecting five hundred small stations to generate five hundred good programs. The superior programs, he insisted, would follow, rather than precede, availability of vast regional and national audiences. This, of course, was a long-range motivation behind Sarnoff's pressure for official permission to erect a superpower station on an experimental basis.

The main opposition came from the small stations, fearful that the strong signals would drown them out and, worse, that public access to first-rate, high-priced chain programs might cancel out their own reason for existing. Sarnoff went out of his way to reassure them. "Such a system," he told the Hoover Conference, "would no more replace individual broadcasting stations than the national magazines of large circulation replace the local newspapers." On the contrary, local stations would be fortified by augmenting their own programs with network programs, just as the community newspaper offered dispatches and features of national press agencies.

At the aforementioned conference arranged by Secretary of Commerce Hoover, Sarnoff had pleaded for permission to build an experimental 50-KW station. To the consternation of more timid associates, he pledged to the government to dismantle the costly station if it proved to be a nuisance to existing stations or electrical services.

Hoover congratulated him on the speech and the pledge. In a few days, however, he informed Sarnoff that the industry itself appeared to be opposed to the idea. Hundreds of letters protesting the superpower proposal had reached him. "Looks like you stand alone against the industry and the public," said Hoover.

To offset this opposition Sarnoff decided on a direct approach to the public in a radio speech on several linked-up stations. Having painted his picture of nationwide broadcasting, he asked listeners to write in their opinions, addressed to Herbert Hoover in care of RCA. As a result Sarnoff was soon able to place before the Secretary not hundreds but thousands of letters in enthusiastic support of his project. Hoover was convinced and his department authorized the experiment.

Accordingly, in 1925, RCA began the construction of the country's first superpower station, at Bound Brook, New Jersey. When it began to function, all the fears voiced by opponents quickly faded out. Sarnoff had weathered his million-dollar gamble and was a long step closer to national broadcasting.

The thorny question as to who would pay for broadcasting was not yet answered. This despite the fact that Station WEAF, the Telephone Group's showpiece, had stumbled on the magic of advertising as early as August, 1922. That day it permitted a local real estate firm, the Queensborough Corporation, to talk about its housing project in a ten-minute program. The listener response was so impressive that department stores and others soon were asking for the privilege of sponsoring programs for a fee.

The innovation, however, met substantial and in some quarters passionate resistance. Among the first and most outspoken opponents of advertising on the airwaves—a notable instance of defeat in his long record of victories— was David Sarnoff. For a year or two he stuck to his preconception of broadcasting untainted by money-making. One of the tentative names he proposed for a network, as we have seen, was the Public Service Broadcasting Company. At various times he elaborated schemes for drawing support from philanthropic foundations plus prorated contributions by manufacturers of radio apparatus. None of them made much business sense.

At one point a committee was set up by General Harbord to study the economic phases of broadcasting. Among the questions it was instructed to answer was this: "Is there any way that the Radio Corporation can secure financial contributions and support for broadcasting without going into the advertising business?" The answer was unambiguous: "There is no way!" Sarnoff sadly capitulated. RCA stations, too, began to solicit sponsors and by 1927 the entire industry was suddenly in the advertising business.

The challenge of the American Telephone colossus was one of Sarnoff's main preoccupations in the earlier 1920's. It ranks among the great duels in modern business history. Sarnoff was perhaps the only one who sensed, even before he could see the relationship clearly, that its outcome was meaningful in connection with his dream of national "chain" broadcasting.

The protracted contest between the Radio Group and the Telephone Group was far too complex and tangled and technical for recital here. For long periods it simmered, then it would boil over in heated conflict. The ardor of the Telephone Group for a leading role in the new art mounted in proportion to the exciting growth of RCA sales of radio sets and apparatus—from $1,468,000 in 1921, to close to $50,000,000 in 1924 when the superhetero- dyne set was launched. Obviously the stakes were mouth-watering. While myriad other things were in dispute, the main prize, in dollars and cents, was the market for radio receiving and transmitting equipment.

Arbitration proceedings consumed several years. The decision was substan- tially favorable to the Radio Group. But its implementation was postponed on technical grounds to permit direct negotiations to be resumed. In April, 1925, the negotiators were reduced to two: Edgar Bloom, president of Western Electric Company, on one side, David Sarnoff on the other. To the astonishment of all concerned, they reached substantial agreement in a few sessions.

"During three years of intermittent effort," Dr. Archer would write, "the best brains of the radio industry had striven in vain for a common ground and now, in less than two weeks, two nimble-minded negotiators had completed the task—but one of them was the persuasive and dynamic David Sarnoff in the first of a series of similar triumphs."

Actually a lot of disputed ground still remained to be cleared. Not until July 7, 1926, could the critical treaty of peace between the telephone and radio giants be formalized. In the interim Sarnoff was successfully persuading the Telephone Group that it did not belong in the broadcasting field; that further expansion of what was already a near-monopoly could endanger its whole empire; that its own and the public interest would best be served if the Telephone Group stuck to its traditional orbit of business.

Throughout the years of negotiation and arbitration, he had exploited the very complications of the situation to project his idea of "unified broadcasting" from coast to coast. In the course of what he called a "Memorandum of Fundamental Considerations," for instance, dated February 5, 1925, he made the suggestion that the broadcasting facilities of both contending groups be vested in a single and separate company. It was a new, revolutionary idea and he had little hope of its acceptance. But he had no doubt that the seed would take root in many minds.

A telltale example of how Sarnoff converted trouble into advantage was provided by his ancillary negotiations with Edgar Bloom in the latter part of 1925 for RCA purchase of the Telephone Company station, WEAF. Only a handful of top officials on either side were cognizant of these secret discussions. The deal was made, the price: one million dollars. Though embodied in a separate contract, it was closely related to the final settlement of the larger conflict.

Relinquishment of the station marked, in principle, the retirement of the Telephone Group from broadcasting. And that, by no means incidentally, greatly facilitated Sarnoff's stubborn campaign for a great network.

The peace treaty with the telephone interests was momentous for RCA and for the whole industry. Either General Harbord as president or Young as chairman of the board could rightly have claimed the honor of signing the historic agreement. But both of them chose to stand aside and invited Sarnoff to be the signatory for the Radio Group. They knew, as did everyone connected with radio, that his had been the decisive role.

The hard-won settlement carried with it an agreement for the use of Bell System wires for linking RCA and affiliated stations. For this it guaranteed to the telephone company a minimum annual fee of one million dollars for ten years. It took exceptional confidence to assume this ten-million-dollar obligation and high salesmanship on Sarnoff's part to convince the corporation board to shoulder it, at a time when there was no regular network service to pay for it. But before the decade was over RCA had become the wire company's largest single customer; ultimately, in the 1960's, its "telephone bill" for broadcasting would exceed $15,000,000 a year.

With the Telephone Group eliminated and interconnections by wire assured, the ingredients of a national chain were at last available to RCA. The National Broadcasting Company was finally incorporated in September, 1926. It had required the pooling of GE and Westinghouse stations with those of RCA, and then the absorption of WEAF and its facilities. Fifty percent of the stock of NBC was held by RCA, 30 percent by General Electric, and 20 percent by Westinghouse. Merlin H. Aylesworth, long the managing director of the National Electric Light Association, was brought in as the first NBC president. WEAF was made the key station of what was called the Red Network; subsequently the Blue Network was developed around WJZ as its core.

The formal launching of the country's first and for some time only nationwide broadcasting organization took the form of a banquet in the ballroom of the Waldorf-Astoria in January, 1927. The one thousand guests included virtually all leaders of the industry, along with the most celebrated radio personalities.

The most impressive radio program ever attempted to that time was mounted in the ballroom and carried to twenty-five stations. Although it reached only as far as Kansas City, it was the biggest hookup yet assembled. The program included Mary Garden, Will Rogers, Titta Ruffo, Weber and Fields, the New York Symphony under the baton of Walter Damrosch, the Goldman Band, Vincent Lopez and his Orchestra. In reporting the celebration, the *New York Times* estimated its cost at $50,000.

Sarnoff was the hero of that climactic occasion. Everyone in the great hall, everyone in the radio field, knew that the National Broadcasting Company was largely the product of his foresight, his planning, his obstinate advocacy of the idea. He had done this, moreover, in the years when his authority within the company was still limited, even before he had a seat at the table of RCA's board of directors.

It would be said, after network programing had become commonplace, that its development was natural and inevitable and would have come in any case. This is true of most notable accomplishments. If Lindbergh had not flown across the Atlantic, assuredly someone else would have done so—but this did not detract from Lindbergh's achievement. The fact is that David Sarnoff recognized the inevitability years earlier than anyone else and years before it was technically possible. He had fought for it. He had staked his reputation and the capital of his corporation to make nationwide broadcasting a reality.

The network had more than its share of vicissitudes. The enterprise had no precedents to go by. Station relations, programs, advertising, the character of commercials—everything was a new problem to be solved by the heartbreaking processes of trial and error. As chairman of the board, Sarnoff in the initial years kept close to the operation. His time of fulfillment came in 1928 when the first coast-to-coast program could be broadcast—the dream he had nourished for so many years. For the first time the presidential candidates that year, Hoover and Al Smith, could talk to virtually the whole country.

A rival network had been organized soon after the launching of NBC. It was snarled in corporate tangles and did not seem to present any formidable competition—until a remarkably able and dynamic young Philadelphian, William S. Paley, took over toward the end of 1928.

Paley's father had come from Russia as a young man and made a fortune in the cigar business. His American-born son, after leaving college, joined the family firm. But at twenty-seven Bill Paley met radio and was "hooked." It was the demonstration that radio could sell cigars which first aroused the young man's interest, then his recognition of the financial, entertainment, and cultural potentials of the new service led him to concentrate on the new field. In the beginning there were few in the NBC offices who took his Columbia Broadcasting System seriously—proof that they had not yet taken the measure of the youthful millionaire's business talents.

At Sarnoff's suggestion, NBC set up an Advisory Council composed of prominent men and women whose credentials for public spirit and personal probity were of the highest order. Drawn from the fields of education, religion, social welfare, the arts, labor and industry, the Council provided advice and guidance on programs and commercials. What Sarnoff had in mind, of course, was to forestall hostile criticism and the always present danger of excessive government regulation. Years later he would take the lead in providing organization and a code of standards for the entire broadcasting industry.

An amusing sidelight: Once, during the pioneering period of NBC, a rumor spread that the network was anti-Semitic in its hiring policies. When this reached Sarnoff's ears, he instituted an investigation and got to the cause of the rumor. The personnel department, it appeared, had taken over bodily a job application form that had been used by the Telephone Company's station. It included a question on religion and church affiliations. Sarnoff at once called in George McClelland, then the executive vice-president at NBC. He pointed to the question.

"George," he said, "this certainly is not aimed at Catholics, since you're a Catholic. It can't possibly be aimed at Jews, since I'm a Jew. Why do we discriminate against the poor Protestants?"

The job form was revised at once.

3

It is not generally understood, even today, that sound motion pictures— "talkies"—are a by-product of the science of radio. Sound on film involves vacuum tubes, radio amplifiers, loudspeakers, photoelectric cells, and other elements perfected in radio laboratories. Talking movies were implicit in every refinement of sound recording and transmission yielded by electronic research. They had been foreshadowed by the invention, in 1917, of a device for "photographing" high-speed wireless signals on tape.

When David Sarnoff was alerting his superiors in 1922 that exploration of radio was certain to have a rejuvenating impact on the phonograph and record business, he added that the same was true of motion pictures. Along with his manifold other preoccupations, therefore, he had kept an eye on developments pertinent to this area.

Two systems for adding sound to images in motion were being researched in the mid-twenties. Western Electric Company, a subsidiary of the American Telephone Company, was concentrating on sound-on-discs, synchronized with the unrolling picture film. General Electric, on the other hand, was committed to all-electronic sound-on-film—in the early stages run separately and synchronized with the moving picture but eventually "photographed" on the picture tape itself. In 1922 and 1923 both systems were demonstrated to selected audiences, and in both cases it was evident that much remained to be done before moving pictures would begin to "talk."

The mechanical or disc process was the first in the field commercially. By 1926 Western Electric had formed an alliance with Warner Brothers, through a separate company called Vitaphone. After several experimental "shorts," they undertook the production of the first full-length talkie: a screen version of the successful Broadway play *The Jazz Singer*. Until then rather lackadaisical in its attention to this area, GE now sought to make up for lost time.

The new development was not contractually within RCA's domain, but Sarnoff looked upon it as a logical extension of his company's business. He believed and had long proclaimed that any by-product of radio research applicable to phonograph, cinema, and other established industries should be exploited commercially by RCA. This dogma, of course, did not sit too well with the electric companies; some of their officials saw in it another proof of Sarnoff's empire-building propensities. But in due time the new businesses branching from radio, talkies included, did accrue to the Radio Corporation.

Remarkable as the fact now seems, the motion-picture industry was apathetic, skeptical, and then increasingly hostile to the prospect of giving its pictures a voice. In those Roaring Twenties it was prospering too fabulously to welcome the change that unsettles. For Hollywood silence was golden, in the literal box-office sense. Industry spokesmen argued that silence was the chief virtue of movies, in that it engaged the imagination of the audience—the intrusion of sound, they actually believed, would wreck the illusion of real life on the screen. They feared, too, that the most idolized stars and top money-makers might not have voices or speaking skills equal to their reputations.

Hollywood was jolted out of its complacency when *The Jazz Singer,* starring Al Jolson, made its historic debut on a Broadway screen on August 6, 1926. It watched in alarmed distress as the talking picture, produced by Warner Brothers at a cost of only $100,000, piled up millions at the box office. Reluctantly it conceded that the era of silent films was coming to an abrupt end. In one respect Hollywood's fears proved justified: many of the most magnetic stars were demagnetized when they attempted to speak. Some screen actors, it was clear at once, should be seen, not heard.

RCA and its electric associates were no less jolted. The competition had beaten them to the punch in a new and lush field. Anxious not to be defeated by default, GE now accepted Sarnoff's view that RCA was better equipped than its own organization to make the race against Western Electric. In effect this piled responsibility for the new dimension of business on his shoulders. Dr. Archer, in telling the tale, would attest: "The driving energy of David Sarnoff was now an important factor in the contest."

In the very month when the Warner sound picture was released, RCA made a deal with Paramount to provide the sound equipment for the famous war picture *Wings*. The sound was still on a separate film, run simultaneously with the picture film in almost perfect synchronization. Released in 1927, *Wings* proved as satisfactory technically and as successful at the box office as *The Jazz Singer*.

Another new factor in the equation was the entry of Fox Films into the talkies sweepstakes. William Fox had acquired the rights to "phonofilm," a variant of sound-on-tape developed by one Theodore W. Case, a former associate of Dr. De Forest. By 1927 he was ready to launch Fox-Case Movietone. However, because it lacked many elements for a complete system, Fox was eager to combine forces with the RCA-GE system. An agreement was worked out in principle. But it happened that Sarnoff was in Europe in connection with further transatlantic radiotelephone tests, and Owen D. Young held the deal in abeyance for his return.

When he got back and read the agreements approved by his superiors, Sarnoff emphatically turned thumbs down. The Case devices, in his judgment, added little if anything to what they already possessed. At this point the distraught Fox invited him into his lair—for a private luncheon at the Fox Films offices on West 54th Street. He began by trying to convince his guest that together RCA and Fox-Case could compete with Vitaphone more successfully than either of them could alone. Sarnoff refused to withdraw his opposition. The movie magnate thereupon, as an inducement, offered to make him a very rich man if he would accept the agreement for collaboration. Sarnoff rejected the startling offer and terminated the negotiations.

David Sarnoff tackled sound movies (still called "squawkies" instead of "talkies" by many a doubting Thomas) with his by now celebrated energy. Under his prodding, research was expanded and speeded up. Upon his initiative, a separate corporation to deal with the new challenge was set up in March, 1928, under the name of RCA Photophone, with 60 percent of the ownership vested in RCA and Sarnoff as president. The manufacture of equipment, of course, was still in the hands of the electric companies on the old 60-40 ratio.

The sound in the RCA pioneering film *Wings*, it was widely conceded, was more authentic than Vitaphone's at that juncture. For the time being, however, the GE system was the Cinderella of the talkie-movies. Making the most of its wide headstart, the competition was cornering the market. Vitaphone licenses and apparatus were being marketed through a new company, Electrical Research Products, Inc.—ERPI for short. Under the direction of a hard-hitting executive, J. E. Otterson, it was reaching out for a virtual monopoly. Already it had signed up about 90 percent of the movie industry through long-term contracts with the Big Five of Hollywood, leaving only the small independents to others. In addition, ERPI had made an agreement with ASCAP, the association of composers, for the exclusive rights to its music for sound-film purposes.

The outlook for RCA Photophone thus seemed exceedingly bleak. The first imperative, as Sarnoff saw it, was to perfect the sound system. He diverted Dr. Goldsmith, now an RCA vice-president and chief broadcast engineer, to this task. At one point in the intensified experimentation, a sound film test was made with Gloria Swanson. To everyone's dismay the glamorous silent star sounded like a man! Within weeks, however, Dr. Goldsmith had revamped the electronic elements to the point where the actress, in a repeat performance, sounded like herself. The gallant lady went on to new triumphs on the talking screen.

The second imperative was somehow to get a foot into the door of the movie industry. Through a close friend in Boston, the department store mogul, Louis Kirstein, Sarnoff in late 1927 made the acquaintance of a forceful entrepreneur who had some interests in the motion-picture business, namely, Joseph P. Kennedy, the financier whose son would one day become President of the United States.

The meeting of the immigrant from Russia and the son of immigrants from Ireland led to a business association. Joe Kennedy had one supreme purpose to which his life was geared. It was to make money, fast and in great heaps, in any business that offered opportunity. He was the promoter par excellence, and with few equals in that calling. Sarnoff, dedicated to building a corporation and an industry, with little thought to personal enrichment, must have seemed to Kennedy a strange specimen of the business species.

Kennedy held substantial control in FBO (Film Booking Office), an independent producing agency. A pygmy among the Hollywood giants, FBO had the advantage of a close but informal relationship, through Kennedy holdings and manipulations, with the leading vaudeville chain, Keith-Albee-Orpheum, which owned several hundred strategically located theatres.

Sarnoff saw the opening in the door he was looking for. He had RCA invest $400,000 to purchase a stock interest in FBO. Vaudeville being then in steep decline, the bankers in charge appeared willing to merge the obsolescing theatre chain with FBO. Kennedy, who had a solid position also in Pathé Pictures, arranged to add this veteran organization to the amalgam.

In some quarters it had been assumed that the mastermind in assembling a new movie giant was Kennedy. The recent biography of him, *The Founding Father,* by Richard J. Whalen, refutes this. Whalen identifies the undertaking as "Sarnoff's grand design." Kennedy was in effect the fiscal technician carrying out the other man's design.

In any case, by October, 1929, the two men succeeded in combining the various elements to form a powerful company, well enough financed to challenge the Big Five. This was the origin of RKO (Radio-Keith-Orpheum), which, having lived through many troubles and a receivership, is still a major movie producer.

Kennedy, the first head of RKO, received $150,000 for managing the merger, along with various equities. He and a partner sold their remaining interest in FBO for $5 million. Having retained an option on 75,000 shares of the old Keith-Albee-Orpheum, he exchanged them for an equal quantity of RKO "A" stock, at $21 a share. That stock before long rose to $50. Kennedy sold at the top, clearing many millions for himself.

Sarnoff and RCA found themselves deeply involved in the motion-picture world. RKO not only provided a profitable outlet for sound equipment—both Pathé and FBO had signed contracts for the RCA Photophone system—but gave Photophone bargaining leverage in breaking down ERPI dominance. Among other things, Sarnoff instituted suits, on the grounds of monopoly, against the exclusive features of the ERPI agreements with the Big Five and ASCAP. In the end, Otterson yielded before the case came to trial. ERPI released its licensees from commitments to use only Vitaphone apparatus and canceled out the exclusive arrangements with ASCAP. In a remarkably short time, considering the handicaps at the start, RCA sound was thus able to compete on a free and open basis. ERPI's near-monopoly was steadily whittled down until, by 1935, Photophone came to occupy an equal and sometimes superior position.

In its first two years RKO made and distributed an impressive array of Hollywood's most profitable films and showed substantial profits. Then came the deluge, the market crash of October, 1929, and the cyclonic depression that followed.

Like other and more firmly rooted film companies, including Paramount Pictures, RKO was driven to the wall and finally into receivership. But that, chronologically, belongs in a later period in the Sarnoff story. He achieved his primary purpose, which was not the production of movies but a place in the sun of talkies for RCA Photophone.

11

A New President Is Born

In the "marriage" of phonograph and radio that Sarnoff had foreseen and proclaimed, the favored bride was the Victor Talking Machine Company which, however, fought desperately to remain in single blessedness. Early in 1921 Sarnoff wooed the firm with a model instrument embodying the latest improvements in both types of entertainment. He demonstrated it to Victor officials in his own home. They were impressed but not yet sold on matrimony.

RCA therefore entered into relations with the second largest phonograph concern, the Brunswick Company. The initial order for radio receivers to be housed in Brunswick instruments came to $1,500,000, and public acceptance matched the most optimistic prognoses. In 1925, after a long series of negotiations, Victor finally capitulated, contracting for a joint radio-phonograph under the famous listening-dog imprimatur, "His Master's Voice," and marketed through its own channels.

Although he was the prime negotiator, Sarnoff was far from content. He coveted not only the bride but the dowry: the Victor Company's production plants in Camden, New Jersey. The "Napoleonic plan under his hat" called for endowing RCA with manufacturing capacity, and the Victor plants, he realized, could be adapted to the making of receivers and other radio equipment. Outright purchase of the Victor organization was an element in his calculations but that had to wait several years for its consummation.

The radio industry was riding a boom. Technical advances in reception, improved programs, in a period of great and growing prosperity, made this inevitable. The more radio flourished the more persuasive were Sarnoff's

145

demands for consolidation. Now that the licensing structure gave all major manufacturers access to all Radio Group patents, competition in the field was being intensified. The handicaps under which RCA operated because of its dependence on an awkward, inflexible system of manufacture became more apparent.

Consequently many officials in the electric companies, among them Young himself, by 1927 were beginning to succumb to the cogency of Sarnoff's arguments. Partly to humor him, the board of directors of RCA designated a committee to examine the problem. In October, 1927, it recommended a separate manufacturing unit to which GE and Westinghouse would transfer elements of their radio facilities and staff. But the electric giants were still wary. A second committee was set up to study the matter further. Its report, in April, 1928, approved consolidation in principle but recommended that a ceiling of $25 million a year be put upon RCA production on this basis.

These were steps in the right direction—a welcome thawing of opposition —but a very long distance from the genuine unification sought by Sarnoff. At this juncture, providentially, the Victor Company appeared ready to consider the merger that the young executive had long coveted. The economics of the business, in the new radio age, called for closer integration in the radio-phonograph field. The company was by now under control of bankers, hardheaded men without sentimental ties to the listening dog. They realized that Victor must either invade the radio field on a full scale or arrange a merger with RCA.

The second of these alternatives was, of course, exactly to Sarnoff's taste and he encouraged the board to undertake exploratory discussions. The polite word "merger" in fact amounted to outright purchase of the great Victor organization. For RCA the deal would involve huge financial outlays, in cash (necessarily borrowed) and stocks that would be a lien on the future. But the prospects opened up to the younger corporation were dazzling: RCA would become at once the country's and one of the world's largest factors in phonographs, records, radio-phonographs, and related products. As a bonus of inestimable dimensions, RCA would acquire for its outsized subsidiary, NBC, and for its movie interests the world's most important "stable" of musical artists and orchestras, assembled through the years by the phonograph firm.

On January 1, 1929, David Sarnoff was named executive vice-president of RCA, a promotion that was extensively featured and applauded editorially in the nation's press. The deal for the absorption was set, though several months would still be required to draft the agreements. Sarnoff's principal concern was how the Victor potential would be applied.

Within the Radio Group it was generally taken for granted that the Victor plant in Camden, in addition to established lines of production, would become the nucleus for consolidated manufacture of radio sets and equipment under direct RCA management. Certainly Sarnoff had been explicit on this score from the beginning and had received at least tacit consent from the GE and Westinghouse men on the board. Only that, in his view, justified RCA in taking on the immense new fiscal obligations.

This was the situation in January when Owen D. Young, having been invited to serve as chairman of a momentous international conference on German reparations, drafted David Sarnoff to accompany him to Paris as assistant and consultant.

Young had developed an immense respect for the younger man's skill as a negotiator—his talent for cutting through tangential matters to the core of a dispute; his ability to generate mutual trust and confidence; his skill in reducing complex affairs and mountains of data to simple essences for easier handling. Now, faced with negotiations in which the stakes were (or so it seemed at the time) nothing less than the stability and even the peace of Europe, Young decided that Sarnoff's presence would be useful. It was surely one of the wisest decisions he ever made.

But the Paris proceedings, expected to last a few weeks, dragged on for more than four months. Sarnoff's protracted absence at this passage in the corporation's evolution led to mistakes and misunderstandings—his own words for them were much harsher—in the disposal of the facilities taken over from Victor. On his return he faced a full-blown crisis. The issue was unification and, since he would brook no compromises on the heart of that issue, his resignation became a serious possibility.

2

Because his first trip across the Atlantic was made in a vile, tight-packed immigrant ship, David Sarnoff, looking back on the panorama of his life, sometimes chose to measure his progress by subsequent crossings. In that inventory of significant ocean journeys the one on the S.S. *Aquitania,* in the first days of February, 1929, deservedly held an impressive place.

For one thing, he was in most distinguished company; his traveling companions included J. P. Morgan and Thomas Lamont, his famous friend and boss, Owen D. Young, the prominent Boston lawyer Thomas W. Perkins, and other conspicuous Americans. For another, they were bound for a conference of surpassing importance to their own country and to the world.

At Cherbourg the Americans were met by high French officials, escorted to shore on a government tender, conveyed to Paris in a private train made available by the authorities, and lodged in the Ritz Hotel. The press of the world would watch every move in the big international game, affecting the destinies of a dozen nations.

"This time," Sarnoff would recall, "no passport problems, no baggage problems, no customs problems. Our reception was conducted with the pomp and protocol that the French are so expert in providing. . . . I shall never forget the moment when I stood on the deck of that tender, reflecting upon this novel experience. The picture that flashed through my mind was my first crossing of the Atlantic in the steerage. I thought of the contrast between the two trips and the fact that this could happen only in America."

The United States, having at Versailles waived claims for German indemnities, was not one of the creditor nations. Technically, therefore, the American delegation was unofficial, although in continuous liaison with the State and Treasury Departments. Its mission was to bring Germany and the creditor countries to an agreement that would replace the temporary Dawes Plan and bring the whole matter to final definition.

But the American stakes were high, since the collection of huge war debts from the Allies was unavoidably related to German reparations: a relationship not formally acknowledged by Washington. If Germany defaulted, so would its creditors. Beyond that, of course, the United States was vitally concerned in heading off political-economic convulsions in Europe, with dangerous repercussions on the whole world.

In 1924 the American role had been paramount in working out the Dawes settlement on reparations. This would hold true no less, everyone was aware, in the formulation of what would be known as the Young Plan. The U.S. delegation to the multi-nation Committee of Experts, authorized to renegotiate the whole complex problem, consisted of Young and Morgan, with Perkins and Lamont as alternates. The others in the party, amoung them the executive vice-president of RCA, were aides and advisers.

The Allies had been warned repeatedly during 1928 by the Agent General for Reparations, S. Gilbert Parker, that the Weimar Republic was under dangerous and deepening pressures. Both the Communists and Hitler's National Socialists (Nazis) were making the most of the runaway inflation and unemployment, blaming all the woes of the country on the "vindictive greed" of the United States and the Allies. Unless the Dawes terms were radically revised to reduce the burdens on the economy, Parker feared, Germany was headed for catastrophe. It was to re-examine the whole economic and monetary picture that the Committee of Experts, with Owen Young as chairman, had been summoned.

On the *Aquitania* Sarnoff applied himself to digesting the large accumulation of data on the inflamed issue. It was understood that the Americans, on the day after they arrived in Paris, would submit a concrete plan as a basis for discussion. The celebrated financiers and business leaders, and Young in particular, had worked on this task. But the results were still fragmentary and had to be quickly pulled together. The job was far from completed when they reached Cherbourg.

On the train en route to Paris, Young said to his friend, "David, suppose you try your hand at collating the general plan." Sarnoff went to work. For hours he dictated an analysis and specific proposals, leaning heavily on the rough Young draft. This was the American Plan laid before the Allied plenipotentiaries the following day and, with many changes made by Young and Morgan, before the German delegates at the first plenary session on May 11.

The British contingent was headed by Sir Josiah Stamp of the Bank of England and Lord Revelstoke. Governor Moreau, head of the Bank of France, led the French delegation, and his opposite number in Belgium, Émile Franqui, spoke for that country's delegates. The German group was under the command of Dr. Hjalmar Schacht, whose astuteness was universally acknowledged.

A large room with four executive desks at the Hotel George V served as headquarters for the U.S. delegates and their alternates. The aides, including Ferdinand Eberstadt, Jeremiah Smith, Jr., Frederic Bate, David Sarnoff, were summoned to this *sanctum sanctorum* as they were needed. It was this pattern that led them to call themselves, good-humoredly, the Bellhops Club.

From the outset it was clear that the conference would be prolonged and stormy, its chances of success dubious. The gap between the demands of creditor nations and Dr. Schacht's estimates of German capacity to pay was even wider than had been foreseen. In addition, Germany advanced an array of conditions intended to reduce the load if that capacity were to decline. Probably the most important of these, from Berlin's vantage point, was what Dr. Schacht called a "safeguard clause," providing for almost automatic moratoria on payments if reduced German capability made it necessary. Moreover, perhaps inevitably, as the contest of wits, claims, and statistics continued week after futile week, the smoldering embers of wartime distrust and hatred were stirred into flame.

By late April the conference reached a dangerous impasse. The German delegation had in effect withdrawn. Insisting that the intransigence on the other side of the table made it useless, Dr. Schacht would make no counterproposals. Threats of "dictated" terms, to be enforced if necessary by military reoccupation of key points in Germany, were being openly discussed in Allied circles and echoed in the world press.

The mood of the American delegation, understandably, was black. Matters were made worse by the illness of the chairman, who was increasingly confined to bed. The delegation was thus deprived, in serious measure, of his oft-demonstrated brilliance as a negotiator. The low mark psychologically was reached when the delegates, emphasizing the stalemate, composed a message to Washington proposing that they acknowledge the brutal reality and return home. The text was turned over to Sarnoff for editing.

But Sarnoff pleaded that it should not be sent. He convinced the conferees that a "walkout" would put blame for the collapse of the enterprise squarely on the United States. The situation, he argued, was not as hopeless as it seemed. It was incumbent on the Americans, in his judgment, to act more firmly, curbing the exorbitant demands of the creditor nations, on the one hand, and recognizing the reasonable elements in the German position, on the other.

At one point in the days of discussion that ensued, Young said in substance, "David, since you think that an agreement is still possible, why don't you tackle Schacht yourself? You have not been involved in the heated discussions, so he can have no animus towards you." The others concurred and Sarnoff, convinced that "another try" was worth the effort, took on the assignment. Hopes were revived. Lamont, in a note dated May 12, said to Sarnoff: "The more I think of it, the more I am convinced that the way you propose handling the matter is the correct one. Good luck. If anyone can do this job, you can." J. P. Morgan, loudly impatient to go off to Scotland for grouse shooting—his yacht stood by in readiness—became more cheerful.

From then until its successful completion, the great international conference was transformed into a negotiation between just two men, Sarnoff and Schacht, with Young providing invaluable guidance from his sickbed. The two men met for the first time at the German's suite in the Hotel Royal Monceau, for dinner, on May 1. What was to have been a get-acquainted formality turned into a marathon negotiating session of nearly eighteen hours, until 2 P.M. the following day.

Sarnoff returned to the Ritz sleepy but exhilarated. He could report that he had found the German financier, in private, more amiable and accessible to reason than he appeared in the full-parade sessions. They had actually roughed out a possible settlement, though the figures still had to be agreed upon.

The next day a fifth executive desk was put into the *sanctum sanctorum*.

Sarnoff had been promoted out of the Bellhops Club. Quickly recognizing the altered pattern of negotiation, Allied statesmen and bankers now closed in on him with their pleas and arguments for a larger slice of the reparations pie being baked. One morning the head of the Bank of France arrived so early with his bill of demands that the American negotiator had to receive him sleepy-eyed and in pajamas. As a token of his rising esteem for the younger man, Morgan, having observed that Sarnoff liked the big French strawberries then in season, went shopping for them personally.

3

In the initial eighteen-hour session with Schacht, Sarnoff had begun by working out a "safeguard clause" which he knew would be acceptable to his colleagues but also met the major requirements of the German side. It provided for automatic postponement of payments if certain economic criteria should develop in Germany. One towering barrier to understanding was thus removed at once. He was able to slash through the entanglements of secondary matters, exaggerated in the plenary rhetoric, to identify the issues of genuine dispute, then demonstrated that the areas of common interest were larger than either side had cared to acknowledge.

More important for the enterprise than specific clauses, however, was the human element—the kindling of mutual respect, followed by mutual liking, between the young American and the outwardly forbidding, high-collared German. Protocol and formalities were out the window, leaving two friendly and intelligent men to deal with concrete problems on an uninhibited human level, in a spirit of practical give-and-take.

On many occasions Sarnoff and Dr. Schacht met for lunch or dinner at the German's favorite restaurant. Their long conversations, had they been recorded, would have made a fascinating document, for they ranged over everything from personal biography to world affairs. Some of these exchanges would have been especially interesting in retrospect, in the light of Dr. Schacht's collaboration with the Hitler regime and his appearance among the defendants at the Nuremberg war-guilt trials.

One evening, for instance, the German arrived at the private dining room that was their rendezvous so visibly flushed and angry that Sarnoff inquired, in some alarm, what was wrong. Dr. Schacht told him the story. He had been invited by a French lady and her husband to dine with them in Paris the coming weekend. He had accepted gladly, since they had been close friends before the war, when the Frenchman represented his country officially in Germany. It seemed to him a good omen of improved human relations.

"But this morning," the agitated Schacht recounted, "the lady called on me in great embarrassment. The Governor of the Bank of France somehow heard that I was to visit them. He phoned her husband to say that he objected strenuously to my being entertained in a French home and insisted that the invitation be withdrawn. She explained to me in great distress that they had no alternative but to comply.

"Mr. Sarnoff, how prejudiced can people be! Here I am, ten years after the war, representing the German government, which is expected to shoulder billions in reparations, to be paid by unborn generations of my people, and yet I am not permitted to dine privately with old friends in a French home!"

After his companion had calmed down with the first course and a glass of good wine, Sarnoff said:

"Dr. Schacht, don't take this exceptional incident so seriously. I can offer some comfort in this matter. After all, you're an amateur in the area of prejudice, but I have had two thousand years of experience with it. Besides, your people are not free from such feelings either."

When Schacht vehemently denied that there was any race prejudice in his country, Sarnoff laughed. "Germany is the cradle of anti-Semitism," he said, and went on to cite the rising Nazi movement and some recent instances of anti-Jewish discrimination. As the argument continued, Schacht suddenly interrupted with a question:

"Do you speak Hebrew?"

"No," Sarnoff replied, "but I understand it, because I studied the sacred books in my boyhood."

"Well, I'm not a Jew, but I do speak it!"

Whereupon he proceeded to recite the opening passages of Genesis in perfect Hebrew. Sarnoff expressed his amazement and learned that the "Doctor" before the financier's name had nothing to do with economics, as most people assumed. He had earned his Ph.D. in a German university with a thesis on the Hebrew language.

The friendship between the two men formed in these talks and in the reparations bargaining continued until the advent of Hitlerism altered so many human relationships. A footnote on that brief friendship can be told here, for the first time, out of chronological sequence:

After the conclusion of the Paris conference, the German delegate asked Sarnoff for his photograph. The younger man was flattered and provided one with a felicitous personal inscription. About sixteen years later, dining in Frankfurt with General Lucius Clay, then commander of the U.S. Army of Occupation in Germany, Sarnoff learned of the further fate of the photograph. When Clay and his deputy, General William Draper, came to Schacht's chalet near Berlin to arrest him under the Nuremberg indictment, the German declared that he was not anti-American. By way of proof he said at one point, "Look at the picture on the wall!"

It was the only picture on the wall. Clay looked and realized that it was his friend David Sarnoff, inscribed in Paris, 1929. He carried off the photograph along with the eminent prisoner. Whether it was returned to the German after his exoneration in the Nuremberg trial, Sarnoff does not know.

To return to the negotiations: The only other member of the American delegation who sat in on the Schacht-Sarnoff meetings on several occasions was Ferdinand Eberstadt, another of the "Bellhops" brought to Paris by Young. Eberstadt had known the German financier before the war, spoke German fluently, and was exceptionally well informed on German conditions. For Sarnoff and Eberstadt their common experience in the negotiations marked the beginning of a lifelong friendship.

The minimum reparations figures acceptable to the American group were known to Sarnoff. But up to this time Schacht had refused to suggest or accept any figure. Privately he told Sarnoff why. Once he indicated a figure acceptable to the Germans he was certain that the Allied negotiators would regard it only as a starting point. Sarnoff had the same fear from the other direction—the fear that any figure he might get Schacht to agree to would promptly be revised upward under pressure from one or another of the Allies.

To forestall being stranded on a limb, if and when he had persuaded the German plenipotentiary, Sarnoff therefore insisted upon a formal letter to himself signed by Young and Morgan pledging themselves to abide by the minimum figure the Allies had previously told the American chairman, privately, they would accept. He drafted the letter himself to make the commitment foolproof and it was duly signed. Armed with this assurance, he could meet the importunities of the creditor nations and knew the limits of compromise in dealing with the Germans.

Later in May a climactic session was scheduled between Sarnoff and Schacht in the Hotel Royal Monceau suite. The uneasy skepticism that still prevailed was reflected in a remark by J. P. Morgan, evidently far from casual, as the American was about to leave for the appointment.

"David," he said solemnly, "if you actually bring back a signed agreement, you can have anything you ask for that is within my gift."

Those who heard it, like Sarnoff himself, might have assumed that he was proposing to the young man a partnership in the House of Morgan—the most coveted place in the American world of finance, an open sesame to great wealth and great influence.

Sarnoff, of course, had kept to himself the knowledge of the minimal figures for which the Allied group was ready to settle. At this meeting he offered those figures to Schacht as a final concession and they were accepted. The settlement thus would be on previously approved terms, though it might leave the more demanding among the creditors grumbling. Among other things the draft agreement provided for a Bank of International Settlement, a mechanism devised during these negotiations which is still in operation.

When the draft was finished, Dr. Schacht dictated a letter of transmission confirming his acceptance of the terms. Whether to flatter his new friend or to needle the American delegation, he addressed it to Sarnoff and referred to the document as the "Sarnoff Plan." Sarnoff, of course, would have none of this. On his insistence the letter was readdressed to Chairman Young and the agreement properly designated as the "Young Plan."

It was far past midnight when Sarnoff returned to the Ritz. Early next morning the anxious top delegates were on hand at the George V to learn the result. "Well, here it is," Sarnoff said with a broad smile, nonchalantly tossing the envelope on a desk. While a lot of handshaking and congratulations was under way, J. P. Morgan slipped out and returned with a black Homburg on his head. Thus equipped, he approached the hero of the day.

"I doff my hat to you," he said, bowing low as he did so. "And I propose to stick to my promise. Ask for anything you want, and it will be yours."

"Yes, I know what I want," Sarnoff said at once. "Ever since we met on board ship I've admired your white meerschaum pipe. If possible, I'd like you to give me one like it."

This type of meerschaum, it developed, was fashioned only by an aging craftsman in London. He had made it for the first J. Pierpont Morgan and was now keeping the son supplied. That day Morgan sent a man in a chartered plane to London with instructions to the pipemaker. The man returned from London and the meerschaum—which is still in Sarnoff's possession—was delivered before the head of the House of Morgan departed to shoot grouse in Scotland.

On May 17, Lizette Sarnoff received a radiogram from Young which said in part: "David did the job of his life last night and if we succeed here it will be due to his persistence and skill intelligently applied. Mrs. Young and I send you our good wishes and appreciation of your generosity in leaving David with us."

The final plenary session, on June 4, officially confirmed the Sarnoff-Schacht agreement. The Young Plan entered history. Unhappily it was fated to be washed out by the rise of Hitler to power three years later. The

American delegates and others were aware of Sarnoff's decisive role and generous in recognizing it privately. But the American people and the world at large had no idea of the magnitude of his contribution.

On June 15, Young wrote a letter to Sarnoff, for the record, expressing appreciation for "the very great service which you have so generously rendered." Incidentally he noted that "Dr. Schacht has taken the occasion to tell me personally of his gratitude for the assistance which you have given to him and to the entire German Group."

And from the *Aquitania,* on the return journey, Lamont dispatched a radiogram to Mrs. Sarnoff: "I want to send to you direct my sincerest congratulations upon David's work. You must already know that for weeks past we relied upon him in extraordinary measure and his work was wonderfully effective and a great contribution to the final result."

A year later David Lawrence, in an article in the *Saturday Evening Post* (June 14, 1930), quoted Owen D. Young as saying:

"He was our principal point of contact with Dr. Schacht of the German delegation, and he did an extraordinary piece of work in negotiating for us with the Germans. Dr. Schacht had confidence in Sarnoff and believed in him. They worked well together.

"One could easily see that each man in the group of American delegates and experts was effective and at one time did a job that served the conference; each seemed to have a part in the crisis which prevented it from being wrecked, and that can be said of Sarnoff in particular. For there came a time when only one man could save the situation, and that arose toward the end with Sarnoff and the German delegation."

It should be noted that Young here gave Sarnoff the main credit for "negotiating for us with the Germans"—which, after all, was the real job of the conference.

4

Back home from his muffled Paris triumph, in late June, David Sarnoff tossed aside his laurels and plunged into battle. For he recognized, as most of his associates did not, a crisis in the Radio Corporation's and his own lives: the two had become indivisible.

Without a more rational manufacturing and sales structure, without true unification, he was convinced, RCA would be driven from its position by centralized, efficient competitors. It would then survive, if at all, only as a minor factor in an industry to which it could and should have provided inspired leadership. He had labored for the merger with Victor and consented to the assumption of the staggering monetary burdens this involved primarily because RCA needed a production base for unification.

This objective, he now charged, had been forgotten—worse, deliberately sabotaged—in the disposition of the Victor potentials while he was in Europe.

Terms for the purchase of the phonograph giant had been set in January, before his departure, and the transfer was completed on March 15, 1929. The "tab" picked up by RCA came to over $150 million. What his company received for its money, according to Sarnoff, was inadequate and in shocking contempt of prior understandings; in the division of the spoils, the two electric companies were taking all the cream and leaving the skim milk for RCA.

An agreement between the two companies and RCA had been signed. One of its chief architects was Paul Cravath, counsel for both RCA and Westinghouse and therefore, as Sarnoff viewed the matter, subject to a conflict of interest, no matter how honorable his intentions. The document required only ratification by RCA's board to take effect, and that was considered a mere formality—until Sarnoff appeared on the scene. Implementation of the agreement, in fact, had already begun, on the assumption that it was all settled.

Under the arrangement, which President Harbord—on the advice of counsel—signed for RCA, two new organizations were created:

1. The Radio-Victor Corporation, wholly owned by RCA. It was defined as the sole sales agency for all Victor products: phonographs, records, synchronized motion-picture records, combination radio-phonographs, as well as radio receivers of the Victor brand.

2. The Audio Vision Appliance Company (AVA). This manufacturing unit would be jointly operated by GE and Westinghouse in the Camden factory and additional plants as needed, on the established 60-40 ratio.

To Sarnoff this spelled perpetuation of the existing scheme of things. All equipment marketed by RCA, now including the newly acquired Victor lines, would continue to be fabricated by the electric companies as heretofore. True, RCA received a stock participation in AVA. But all the frustrating built-in handicaps of divided management, the old separation between production and engineering, on the one hand, and marketing, on the other, were merely extended to the enlarged business.

The executive vice-president was furious. General Harbord, realizing that he had gone along without quite grasping the implications of the arrangement, supported Sarnoff's announced purpose of thoroughly revising the agreement. Young, having had no direct part in formulating the final terms, also was inclined to side with Sarnoff. But Gerard Swope, president of GE, and Andrew W. Robertson, the chairman of Westinghouse, were outraged by the sudden opposition to what they regarded as a *fait accompli*.

Sarnoff was tough and blunt. He let both men know that he considered the signed agreement not only inequitable but iniquitous. No, he would not be content with doctoring the contract, as they suggested—it had to be scrapped. To prevent ratification by the board, of which he was now a member, he was prepared to vote and argue against ratification. If he lost the battle, he would resign—but not without a public airing of the issues, to be carried to the courts if necessary.

Robertson of Westinghouse was a dignified and haughty corporation head of the old school, long accustomed to giving orders and unused to contradiction. He came up from Pittsburgh to put the younger man in his place. He failed. Possibly he had never before been spoken to in such sulphurous language by a man who, technically at least, was his subordinate in the electric empire. Gerard Swope came down from Schenectady and fared no better.

Sarnoff pointed out that in 1927–1928 two successive committees, on which GE and Westinghouse were amply represented, had already agreed in principle that consolidation of functions was essential. He insisted that the Victor facilities had been treated, in the course of negotiations, as the instrument for reaching that objective. The Victor element aside, he argued, RCA would be edged out of the market—with consequent heavy losses to the electric companies themselves—unless the old relationships were revised.

As the battle proceeded, the sheer logic of Sarnoff's presentation convinced more and more of his opponents. His threat of resignation, too, helped to change the climate in his favor. The possiblity of Sarnoff's joining forces with one of the competitors in the lush electronics fields was one that could not be viewed without apprehension. His case was helped, moreover, by the fact that the Camden plant under its new AVA management was in an unholy mess. Three sets of officials and engineers (GE, Westinghouse, and RCA), each with its own ax to grind, each pursuing its own business concepts, amounted to a formula for failure.

In the end, Sarnoff had his way. The disputed contract was consigned to the wastebasket and his own proposals became the basis of new planning. On October 4, 1929, his blueprint for reorganization was adopted by the board of RCA, with the approval of the electric corporations. Two weeks later a new entity, the RCA Victor Company, was agreed upon and on December 26 it was incorporated. Fifty percent of its ownership was vested in RCA, 30 percent in GE, 20 percent in Westinghouse.

This consolidated company, substantially as Sarnoff had formulated it, was to take over all the manufacturing and engineering of the Radio Group, along with the sales operations of Radio-Victor and RCA Photophone. AVA was dissolved. Except for the fact that RCA had equal but not yet majority control of the new RCA Victor, unification was a fact.

Between the approval of the plan and its incorporation, however, disaster struck the country and the world. The collapse of the bull market signaled the start of depression. Though he could not guess, any more than others, how prolonged and catastrophic the bad times would be, Sarnoff did not ignore the signal. Competition, which had been so keen in a rising economy, was certain to grow fierce if the economy began to decline. To confront the coming storms, he was determined in his mind that loopholes must be closed and the unification made total.

At a special meeting on January 3, 1930, Owen D. Young proposed that he resign the post of chairman of the board to become chairman of a newly created executive committee. General Harbord resigned his presidency to become chairman of the board. Swope and Robertson, his recent adversaries in the bitter battle, then graciously moved that David Sarnoff be made president of the Radio Corporation of America. His election was unanimous.

The teen-ager who had made contact with the electron a little more than twenty-three years before thus became commander in chief of the world's largest electronics complex. He was five weeks short of thirty-nine years of age.

12

Double Trouble

ᕲ His elevation to the presidency of the Radio Corporation touched off editorial tributes to David Sarnoff. An industrial pioneer, so the verdict went, had received a fitting reward. His leadership had been long acknowledged, and now it was made official, as it were. He deserved—and as head of the world's outstanding radio communications and electronics complex now occupied—what was incontestably the number one spot in his field.

Once more the accent in national comment was on his youth. The "boy wonder" flavor lingered, this despite an encroaching portliness. Once more the tale of his rise from slum pauper to industrial prince was rehearsed in newspaper and magazine articles, with the inevitable salute to Horatio Alger. Through the years the Sarnoff saga was hardening as a legend to warm the cockles of the American heart.

Its main elements were familiar to nearly everyone: the foreign lad hawking newspapers, the office boy casing a new-born business, the young wireless telegraph operator reporting the *Titanic* catastrophe to a hushed world. And now there was the happy ending preordained for this genre of Americana—the presidency. It was all neat and satisfying, as all good fairy tales, even true ones, should be.

But the climax was marred by its timing. The parable of a private success ran headlong into national failure. The irony of it was particularly obvious to the hero and would have appalled a less ruggedly self-confident man. His enterprise, after all, had flourished in a time of unlimited optimism and easy money—but he was assuming formal command precisely when the country seemed headed for dismal depression. What should have been the completion

159

of his pioneering phase promised instead another and more desperate install-
ment of struggle.

In the most inclement economic weather America had ever faced, the top
of the ladder was hardly an enviable perch. There were those who thought
that the purported "Sarnoff luck" had run out. A few of them, the few not yet
reconciled to his rapid ascent, waited with secret glee for his impending
fall.

The Great Depression, of course, was not ended when Franklin D. Roosevelt succeeded Hoover. In truth the calamity continued, with brief and
illusory abatements, for nearly seven years more. It was not only the worst
but the longest depression in the nation's history. Strong signs of improvement
in mid-1932, the final Hoover year, raised hopes, but they petered out in new
and more tragic declines. The New Deal medicines helped deaden the pains
but they did not cure the disease. Its ravages persisted until the coming of war
in Europe, by turning the United States into the arsenal of democracy,
restored economic vitality.

This was the mean, bitter decade of the 1930's during which president
Sarnoff steered his company to safe harbor, not merely undamaged but
stronger than it had been when the storms first broke. It was a decade in
which he attained total independence for RCA; in which, despite the heavy
weather, he dared throw millions into the development of television and
fought, at times almost singlehandedly, for its release to the public. It was the
decade, too, when he came of age conspicuously as a public personality, over
and above his role in the electronics arts; when his participation in national
affairs and his impact on opinion outside his own economic-scientific domain
grew steadily.

We have seen that the unification of RCA—through assumption of functions until then shared with the electric giants—was the condition of Sarnoff's
acceptance of the presidency. His first concern, therefore, was to put that
condition into effect. Within two months, by February, 1930, he had worked
out the details in strenuous negotiations with the parent companies, and in
April it was all consummated in a three-way settlement.

General Electric and Westinghouse agreed to hand over to their precocious
offspring all their former exclusive manufacturing rights in radio equipment,
phonographs, talking pictures and the rest, along with their stockholdings in
NBC, Photophone, RCA Victor, Radiotrom, and General Motors Radio
Corporation. They gave up their 40 percent interest in royalties on RCA
licenses under which thirty-seven electronics manufacturers were using the

Radio Group patents. At the same time they renounced their claim to $32 million owed to the now-discontinued AVA in connection with the purchase of the Victor Talking Machine Company.

The surrendered stock and claim had a book value of $40 million. The physical assets turned over to RCA—plants, machinery, real estate—came to another $13 million. The worth of the manufacturing rights, of course, could not be calculated in dollars. For all of this the electric companies accepted 6,500,000 shares of newly issued RCA common stock. "Undoubtedly one of the greatest transfers of assets in industrial history," Dr. Gleason L. Archer called it, writing in the perspective of nine years; and the ever-ebullient Elmer Bucher, in telling the story, exclaimed: "David Sarnoff had wrought a miracle!"

Of course, in the context of a collapsing economy, the values turned over by the electric companies, already seriously depreciated, seemed sure to shrink further. Certain electric officials may even have believed that they were unloading upon RCA properties already eroded and possibly doomed.

But Sarnoff, taking the long view, was well pleased. He had attained what had long been his objective, for he was now on the road to a fully consolidated organization, master of its own household. True, he had reached his goal in a period of business crisis. But the crisis would have been far more hazardous, perhaps fatal, had the company been obliged to meet its challenge under the old conditions of splintered functions. Now, in Dr. Archer's words, he had "put the Radio Corporation of America in a position to battle for its industrial life in the midst of the growing chaos of a world depression."

When unification (as yet largely on paper) would be accomplished, General Electric and Westinghouse, until then its virtual bosses, would be reduced to partners in RCA, sharing its dividends. They would still enjoy potent representation on the board of directors of RCA and the leverage of immense stock ownership. But since they now had a high stake in the health and prosperity of the organization there should be no conflicts of interest.

President Sarnoff had not renounced his ultimate corporate purpose, which was complete divorce from the electric companies. That came in the next two and a half years through his strategy in what, in less dexterous hands, might have been a disaster: the intervention of the Department of Justice under its antitrust authority. The unification agreement, the cross-licensing patent edifice, the whole foundation of RCA's industrial-financial structure, were challenged by the government—and this in a time of unexampled recession. Sarnoff was facing the most dangerous business crises of his career.

2

The dinner party in the sumptuous apartment of his friend Frank Altschul, a prominent financier, was in honor of David Sarnoff, to celebrate his rise to the presidency and the successful attainment of unification. A number of top-echelon RCA officials were present, along with other business and banking leaders.

The after-dinner oratory, quite naturally, loaded laurels on the guest of honor for his well-publicized recent achievements. From now on, it was implied, he would have comparatively smooth sailing. But in that cheerful company only Sarnoff himself was aware of the irony of the proceedings. In his pocket was the cheerless news that the victories being eulogized had just been placed in serious jeopardy. A federal marshal had met him as he entered the lobby of the apartment house and served him with a copy of the Complaint which the Justice Department, just a few hours before, had filed in a federal court. He had had no previous information that the action was impending. He glanced at the document before entering the Altschul home and decided to keep the unpleasantness to himself so as not to dampen the festivities.

At the end of the party, however, he called a few of his colleagues into another room and showed them the papers. They all realized the gravity of the matter at once. The Department of Justice had filed an antitrust suit demanding changes that could amount to dismemberment of the corporation. The scope of the Complaint and its terms were more drastic than anyone could have anticipated.

The following morning, May 31, 1930, the suit was officially announced and made headlines all over the country. RCA stock nose-dived. Even in normal times it would have been a body blow. Coming in the midst of depression, then contested under the handicaps of worsening business conditions, it imperiled the very survival of the company. General Electric, Westinghouse, American Telephone, and various of their subsidiaries were named as codefendants.

Only a month after the signing of the unification agreement, when the transfer of assets had barely begun, the Justice Department in effect wanted the whole arrangement scrapped. It asked that the patent pool assembled with such immense effort in the preceding eleven years—with the government's knowledge and blessing—be unscrambled; that GE and Westinghouse not only divest themselves of all stock ownership in RCA but gear for all-out competition with RCA, and among themselves, in the production and sales of radio and other electronic equipment. It also demanded that all existing exclusive patent and traffic contracts with other organizations at home and abroad be made nonexclusive.

If Washington had its way, the radio organization would be stripped of most of the new advantages Sarnoff had won for it, along with older rights for which RCA had paid its parents and outside companies. Its industrial and fiscal vitality would be undermined. Nothing less than the demolition of the basic RCA setup was in prospect.

Within months after he took charge, the youthful president was thus engulfed in a legal battle of fantastic complexity. It was to absorb much of his time, thought, and energy for thirty months of slow-moving, tedious negotiation and maneuvering. Batteries of eminent and high-priced lawyers were kept busy, of course, but from first to last the guiding mind was Sarnoff's.

He directed negotiations on several levels simultaneously: between the Radio and Telephone Groups; between RCA and the electric companies; with the government in behalf of all the defendants. (Halfway in the proceedings American Telephone, whose stake was marginal, made a separate peace with the Justice Department.) At the same time he had to bolster the morale of his own organization in the face of legal uncertainties combined with deteriorating business.

Charges of monopoly were nothing new in Sarnoff's life. From the year of its birth the Radio Corporation and its associates had been subjected to attack as a "radio trust." Their conspicuous success made them a natural target for envies and political demagogy. A four-year investigation by the Federal Trade Commission ended in 1928 in complete vindication and dismissal of all complaints. The attacks continued notwithstanding.

For the most part they were instigated by competing radio manufacturers whose prosperity derived, in the final analysis, from the products of RCA engineering research and the very licensing system they were assailing. The Radio Group laboratories had scored a long array of "firsts" in ultrashort-wave communications, advanced methods of recording and reproducing sound, improved tubes and radio equipment. These and other advances were automatically available to competitors who had done little if any research themselves. The "restraint of trade" alleged seemed refuted by the fact that RCA was doing only 20 percent of the radio set business. In truth, the company had *advanced* trade by creating virtually a new industry in which others shared.

Whatever logic there might have been in the charge that RCA restrained competition in benign times, it had little now that there was a glut of

competition in a shrunken market. Washington's antitrust enthusiasm—other
industries were under fire too—seemed ill-timed, now that inventories were
piling up, factories idling, businesses going bankrupt. Whatever the government's motives, harassment of alleged monopolies operated to unsettle the
economy further. But in bad times scapegoats must be found and assaults on
Big Business were becoming conditioned reflexes.

From Sarnoff's vantage point there was a curious paradox in the suit. We
know that he had long dreamed of throwing off the corporate moorings to the
electric companies. Now the government not only proposed but was demanding that GE and Westinghouse remove themselves from RCA and its board—
substantially the separation that had been his ultimate goal. But at what
price? The loss of the very rights and facilities which he needed to make
independence meaningful!

The Justice Department petitioned the courts to order that RCA "divest
itself of any property, facilities and assets" acquired from the electric
companies "pursuant to the plan of consolidation" entered into in April. It
outlined far-reaching revisions of the patent establishment. On these terms,
separation obviously would be a calamity. RCA would remain too crippled
and debt-burdened to exploit, and possibly even to survive, the independence
it had long coveted.

Sarnoff tackled the problem with a show of self-confidence. As visible proof
of his essential optimism, he chose to proceed vigorously with the transfer of
assets, the centralization of engineering and manufacture, and other provisions of the unification scheme. This was not mere bravado. He was counting
on the realities of the equation to prevail in the long run over legalistic
technicalities.

After all, as he saw it, neither the electric giants, the industry, nor the
public would be benefited by wrecking the potential for world leadership in
electronics represented by RCA, and, at least in his view, only by RCA. Was
it not to make such leadership possible that the government itself had taken
the initiative in forming the corporation in the first place? These were the
factual considerations he must make clear to all parties in the suit, the
government and the public included.

His strategy was to accede to the order for separation—in itself desirable
and in any case unavoidable—but without abrogating the unification agreement or dismantling the patent structure. It was a job of squaring the circle.
What he undertook was in essence a task of education and persuasion,
directed even more to codefendants than to the government. It required over
two years of almost continuous conferences, correspondence, sometimes daily

redrafting of projected contracts to meet objections—in all of which Sarnoff was the main participant—before the logic of his position was made manifest and accepted.

Finally the electric companies and then the government were persuaded. Sarnoff convinced the electric companies that they had more to lose than to gain by setting RCA adrift to sink or swim in the angry economic seas of the time. Their own standing with the public, the new president of RCA argued, would be endangered if the electric companies ignored the interests of some 85,000 unaffiliated (as distinct from corporate) stockholders in RCA. Acquiescence on their part in the official accusations would unavoidably reflect on their own integrity. Moreover, the implied admission that their policies had been in any degree culpable would open them to triple-damage litigation by elements claiming to have sustained losses because of the "radio trust." Many such suits had already been brought in anticipation.

Once he had lined up all the remaining defendants in the case for a united front in resistance to the threat of dismemberment, Sarnoff had the larger half of the battle won. They agreed to a set of basic principles which he had formulated. One of these was that none of the parties should benefit at the expense of the private holders of RCA equities. Another was that "the Radio Corporation of America must remain an effective unit in the radio and associated fields." It also set forth that, in view of the depression, GE and Westinghouse, while agreeing in principle to compete in those fields, would refrain from actual manufacture long enough to enable an independent RCA to secure its commercial position.

The logic of this commitment to assure the viability of RCA, indeed, enabled Sarnoff to obtain concessions from the electric associates beyond those spelled out in the unification plan. For instance, they agreed to the liquidation of nearly $18 million owed to GE and Westinghouse—half of it by outright cancellation, about $5 million more through the transfer of the new RCA building on Lexington Avenue at 51st Street to General Electric, the rest by the issuance of debentures to the two companies.

Acting as a unit, the defendants could now demonstrate that it was possible to reorganize the patent picture to meet government strictures without paralyzing the radio company in the conduct of its legitimate business. They could now show that the retention by RCA of the fruits of unification would not hamper eventual entry of GE and Westinghouse into full competition. Step by step, the Department of Justice—represented by Judge Warren Olney, an Assistant Attorney General—retreated from its original intransigence. Finally it came to share Sarnoff's honest conviction that the enfeeblement or destruction of the Radio Corporation would be harmful to American communications and to the national economy.

Notwithstanding agreement on general principles, a lot of intensive bargaining was required to translate them into concrete contracts that would be acceptable to Washington. In the crucial final weeks in the autumn of 1932, with the case scheduled to go to trial on November 15, Sarnoff and officials of the electric companies were engaged in marathon conferences, on occasion deep into the night.

The business community was steeped in gloom just then, by reason of the presidential campaign and the election of the Democratic candidate. Although Governor Roosevelt and his party platform were pledged to moderate policies and sound money, the victor's entourage included a spate of peddlers of extreme panaceas and advocates of fiat money. Melancholy forebodings therefore shadowed the sessions of the Radio Group, as its spokesmen worked against the deadline of a court action that could no longer be postponed.

Two days before the trial, a Consent Decree was reached. The government could fairly claim a victory, since it obtained complete separation of the radio from the electric corporations. But none of the elements affected suffered a defeat.

RCA not only retained everything it had gained through unification but acquired various residual rights in fields where it had previously been limited or excluded, such as manufacture for foreign markets. It emerged, if anything, in a more rugged financial position. GE and Westinghouse agreed to a transition period of two and a half years before engaging in competition—after which they would operate under RCA licenses and pay royalties like other producers. They committed themselves also to distribute their RCA stock only to their own stockholders. The two companies, of course, were required to resign from RCA's board of directors.

The Consent Decree, overwhelmingly the product of his agile mind, was universally acclaimed as a personal triumph for Sarnoff. His company was sovereign at last in the formulation of policies, its board of directors no longer subject to dual interests. Having examined the mountain of documents in the case, Dr. Archer concluded: "It is not too much to say that, had it not been for the almost fanatical devotion to RCA of its president, David Sarnoff, the corporation might then have gone down in ruin—the common fate of many great corporations in those perilous days. David Sarnoff, by his skill as a negotiator, coupled with a bulldog determination, had achieved the salvation of the Radio Corporation."

Thurlow Gordon, a distinguished lawyer who had taken part in the defense, wrote to Sarnoff:

"May I say to you once more—as I have said to others—that the settlement would have been impossible but for your patience and your fairness under the most trying conditions, and your courage and inexhaustible resourcefulness when everything seemed again and again to have ended in impasse.

"The Attorney General had said that this was the most complex antitrust suit ever brought. More than that, it involved the most difficult legal and business problems I have ever seen. And while others played their parts (and some of them very important parts) the major credit for the successful outcome is yours and yours alone."

Captain S. C. Hooper of the U.S. Navy was one of the military men closest to the development of radio communications. He had played a considerable role in the government's behalf in the organization of RCA. Consequently he watched the monopoly action and its satisfactory resolution with a kind of paternal concern. In congratulating Sarnoff he declared: "I have a great feeling of contentment that our government with your cooperation and with many others involved could have worked out such a fine agreement. It places the RCA on its own feet and gives you your great opportunity."

The professional press was loud in its applause. One trade journal used the occasion to assert that "those familiar with radio history agree that David Sarnoff is one of the few who has earned the title of 'mastermind.' "

As for Sarnoff himself, his comment was succinct and from the heart: "The Department of Justice handed me a lemon and I made lemonade out of it." Excessive modesty was not among his cardinal vices. He did not, in point of fact, consider healthy self-esteem a fault in any man—provided it rested on accurate self-knowledge. The man of affairs who deprecates his own worth, he said, usually had good reason for it.

3

The Radio Corporation had its just share of the losses and frustrations of a sick economy. The depression, coinciding with the antitrust suit and the crowding tasks of full corporate autonomy, imposed seemingly intolerable burdens on David Sarnoff. But the company demonstrated great powers of recuperation—it was back on an even keel long before the country's economy as a whole recovered. And its president carried the multiple burdens without stumbling, even with an air of nonchalance. At the price of other things—such as some sacrifice of the family life he craved—he measured up to his reputation for all-absorbing labor.

RCA profits of nearly $16 million in 1929 were down by two thirds, to $5.5 million, in 1930. In 1931 they fell to $796,000, and the following two years, for the first and last time in the corporation's history, registered deficits: over a million dollars in 1931 and about half a million in 1932. Then the trend was reversed. Beginning with 1933 there was a sharp and unbroken accrual of gross business and gross profits. Technological breakthroughs improved quality while trimming the price of equipment. There was a boom in portable radio sets, phonograph records reached new sales highs. Income from royalties on licenses, too, was useful in the over-all financial picture.

The unexpected vitality of the broadcasting end of the business helped to limit losses in the bad stretches and expand the gains thereafter. Even in the darkest years there was no trace of red ink on the National Broadcasting Company books. The American people, worried and increasingly idle, evidently turned to their radios for free entertainment and some emotional relief.

New stars, new types of programs, the constant improvement of equipment at both sending and receiving ends, assured sponsor revenues notwithstanding the pervasive gloom. At peak moments the audience embraced virtually the whole population. The biggest star, unsponsored, was Mr. Roosevelt chatting at his radio fireplace. He decidedly helped build radio ratings to ever-new heights.

The movies were among the last to feel the full impact of the hard times. People craved—and had more time for—distractions. But by late 1930 the hurricane reached the cinema box offices too. Reduced admission prices, double and treble features, free dishes did not suffice. First the smaller producers and then the giants of Hollywood were driven to the wall. Bankers were reluctant to lend money. Paramount, the kingpin of the industry, went into receivership.

RKO, in which RCA had about 25 percent of outstanding stock, had been strikingly successful for a newcomer in the field. Founded in 1928, it piled up substantial profits in its initial two years. Then its fortunes declined. Unable to obtain banking support, it drew additional capital from the coffers of RCA. But the pressures were too great and RKO, in its turn, chose receivership.

Much of the blame for the temporary RKO collapse was loaded onto Sarnoff's shoulders. RCA contended with stockholders' suits based on the RKO failure; some of them dragged into the 1940's. The whole movie venture was cited by less friendly critics as the exception to the apparent rule of Sarnoff's financial ability.

But the magnitude of the debacle was exaggerated by those intent on reducing his stature. The aggregate RCA investment came to $16 million. Eventually about half of this interest in RKO was sold for more than $5 million. The rest was converted into new shares of a reorganized and revitalized RKO which, when finally sold, entirely recouped RCA's investment. More important, in the meantime sizable revenues were garnered—and continue to be garnered—from the sale of Photophone licenses and equipment. By 1935, as has already been noted, Photophone occupied a position equal and at times superior to that of ERPI.

Time thus washed out most of the myths clustered around the RKO episode. What had promised to grow into another important adjunct of the Radio Corporation, one not inconsistent with its massive role in the entertainment world, was withered by the economic drought. But it had won for RCA talking-picture equipment a commanding position, and that had been its original and primary purpose.

4

Sarnoff's personal fortunes in the initial depression years, aside from the effects on his business, deserve mention.

Like millions of other Americans, he had bought some stocks out of his savings in the fabulously bullish market, including a modest amount of RCA securities. By the time he went off to Europe with the Young reparations mission in February, 1929, he owned a portfolio of thriving equities that, for a salaried man, could be described as substantial. During his five months' absence he was too occupied with bigger affairs to give his private holdings a second thought.

When he returned in June he was in a deeply pessimistic mood. His recent experience, in continuous touch with key political and financial personalities, was far from reassuring. "I met all the great men of the period," he said in looking back, "and found that most of them weren't." And he had serious doubts whether the Young Plan could save chaotic Germany from its downhill course. Yet he found that in his absence his paper profits in Wall Street had multiplied. One banking stock, a new issue bought on margin just before his departure, had already more than doubled in value. America was still riding high on its prosperity tide.

The contradiction between his European impressions and the American optimism disturbed Sarnoff. His inquisitive mind groped for an answer to the riddle. Consultation with a number of the foremost investment bankers was no help—they shared and fed the rosy popular illusions and seemed impervious to arguments for caution.

Sarnoff decided that the runaway optimism made no sense. If he were making judgments affecting his corporation, in an equivalent situation, he would have been wary. Why not apply the same cool judgment to the stock market? In July, therefore, in the face of a booming market and in disregard of expert advice, he picked up the marbles and retired from the game: he sold every share of stock he owned.

In the following months, as he watched those equities climbing higher and higher, Sarnoff naturally had moments of doubt and aggravation. He wondered whether he had been foolish. It was a kind of test of his confidence in his own judgment and apparently it was going against him. But when the crash came he was one of the few who had salvaged his investments and pocketed large profits.

Then, in 1931–1932, the market apparently had reached rock bottom. He decided to risk another but more modest portfolio. His timing proved right—stocks did enjoy an interval of revival. By the fall of 1932, however, as the presidential campaign developed, skepticism again got the upper hand in his thinking. Once more he turned his securities into cash—just before the market slumped again. This was the last time in his entire career that he dabbled in the stock market. The gambling element in that enterprise was too strong for his essentially prudent instincts.

Sarnoff claimed no special credit for the two "killings" that left him with a comfortable nest egg in cash. He had merely applied to the market the same common sense that he would apply to a financial statement in his own business. But his acquaintances in the panicky financial world read into his conduct evidence of fiscal wizardry approaching genius. He was offered the directorship of a big New York bank and urged to accept a full partnership in one of the leading investment houses and, of course, refused both proposals.

In the years before his salary reached six-figure dimensions, there were people who thought he was living on a scale beyond his relatively limited income—and wondered how he managed it. The fact is that to a substantial degree he lived on the capital he had salvaged precisely in the years when others had been pauperized.

In June, 1933, the Radio Corporation moved from its former quarters on Lexington Avenue at 51st Street to the amplitude and shining elegance of the new RCA Building, the central structure in the complex of skyscrapers called Radio City. The names themselves amounted to an acknowledgment that, in a short quarter of a century, the radio industry and its leading commercial embodiment had won a central place in American life.

Radio City was an ambitious Rockefeller project. Undertaken in what seemed eternal prosperity, it was carried out and completed in a period of economic distress. Only capital on the grand Rockefeller scale saved the enterprise from the financial beatings suffered by the Empire State Building and other gigantic office buildings planted in balmy weather and harvested in the cyclone.

David Sarnoff had worked closely and continuously with the Rockefeller brothers on the Radio City venture. His friendship with the entire billionaire family, and especially Nelson Rockefeller, endured through all the years that followed. In predepression optimism Sarnoff had committed RCA to far more space than was now feasible, which required renegotiations and a payoff in stock for being let off the hook. Eventually, of course, RCA needed and took on even more floor space than it had originally contracted for.

Its new headquarters, where NBC and other ancillary organizations were housed for the first time under the same roof, represented the last word in resplendent, streamlined, assembly-line planning, and the decor was modern to match.

The president's office, modest in dimensions by his own choice, was paneled in limed oak, sparsely furnished and hushed. It somehow conveyed to callers a sense of aloof power under perfect control. The portraits of Marconi and Abraham Lincoln were on its walls; they had attained an almost ritual aura for Sarnoff. On a mantel, under a glass bell, stood the primitive telegraph key on which a twenty-one-year-old operator had kept his celebrated seventy-two-hour vigil during the *Titanic* disaster.

The young executive—only forty-two when he first took possession of the office he still occupies—sat behind the tooled-leather expanse of a clean desk. (Few who have written about him failed to refer to this uncluttered desk as a symbol of the man's love of order: the farthest remove from the Hollywood stereotype of the busy executive tangled in telephones in a wilderness of papers.) He puffed an outsize cigar. He seemed completely secure and at home. The convulsive splendor of Manhattan's man-made cliffs stretched for miles below his vantage point on the fifty-third floor. Beyond, westward, was the steel-blue ribbon of the Hudson and beyond that the flat landscape of New Jersey. It was a setting consistent with the saga of an industrialist peculiarly suited to the age of Marconi and Einstein and Norbert Wiener.

"Spectacular" is a word that was to become almost the special trade-mark of the radio industry. And spectacular, one may say at this juncture in his development, is the inescapable word for the career of David Sarnoff. Seemingly at its apex in the early 1930's, certainly without parallel in his own domain, it was to reach new heights and acquire new dimensions in the decades to come. He could not know himself, sitting in his bright new office, that though he had "arrived," it was also a commencement.

13

The Roosevelt Years

꿍 When the ship of industry is caught in a storm, the first ballast to be jettisoned is likely to be research. For research, whatever its long-range promise, is costly and a gamble by definition; at best it offers no prospects of early profit. Its postponement therefore seems to make good bookkeeping sense. Why invest in the pursuit of improved or new products when consumers are not buying?

David Sarnoff refused to be overawed by this bookkeeping. As the business crisis deepened, he imposed stringent economies down the line. In time, payrolls were pared by half, real estate commitments were reduced, inventories were stripped through drastic price inducements. He voluntarily cut his own salary from $80,000 to $51,000 a year—the same percentual reduction imposed on others. But his measures for economy ended precisely where they began with most other industrialists. RCA research was not only maintained but expanded. Grumbling within his own business family and stockholder protests failed to deter him.

A scene in his office, as he recalls it himself, suggests the quality of the muffled opposition inside the company. A newly hired executive called on president Sarnoff. He had surveyed the operations of RCA, he reported, and come to some conclusions.

"We can make money despite the depression," he said in substance, "provided we stop certain heavy drains on our resources. . . ."

Though he knew the answer—others had voiced the same complaint—Sarnoff put the question: "What are you referring to?"

"Well, let me be blunt, sir. The money we make at the sales end is being drained off by heavy outlays on television and other research. Plug that leakage, Mr. Sarnoff, and the whole company picture will change for the better."

Sarnoff looked at him a bit grimly. "That," he said, "is a matter of basic policy. If you feel that it's too much of a handicap, you're free to resign."

Then he proceeded to explain again, as he had done to others, that technological research was not a luxury for good times but a necessity for all times. If America renounced its traditional allegiance to the future, its free economy would be finished. Especially was this true of electronics, a new industry that, despite striking growth, was still in its infancy. RCA, he believed, must pace further development in order to maintain its leadership.

Such was the philosophy he was expounding during the bitter years to associates and also to the jittery business community at large. In speeches and articles he insisted that the depression called not only for brave men but "brave dollars." The phrase was applauded by some and derided by others, but it took hold.

There was no dearth of opportunities for exposition of the theme. Sarnoff was in ever-greater demand as the featured speaker at trade conventions, engineering conclaves, academic forums, commencements. From this time forward, in fact, the growing number of invitations—usually baited with awards and degrees—gave him problems both in the budgeting of time and in diplomacy. The speeches he did make were normally well reported in the press and on the air.

Addressing a forum conducted by New York University and the Investment Bankers Association, in January, 1933, he warned that it would be suicidal for America to throw away its compass of progress in the fogs of recession. The present troubles, he said, "should serve as a basis for still further progress along lines that will assure not only the maintenance but further improvement of the American standard of living."

On a subsequent occasion, in 1934, he declared that "Any attempt to freeze society and industry at a given point will be as ineffectual as undertaking to hold back the onward rush of time." He conceded that "progress, not retrogression, has created the problems with which we are now struggling." But surely we should not therefore impose a moratorium on science. Like it or not, American industry must learn to live with what he called "supplantive competition"—the competition, that is, generated by the creativity of the research laboratories.

More and more, David Sarnoff was talking to and for business. By now the press and radio turned to him habitually for opinions on economic issues. His by-line was becoming familiar to readers of magazines. And his opinions, moderate in that time of extreme counsel, were highly personalized.

Among other things he raised questions about the oversimplified concepts of competition. It was not, he said, "a graven image to be worshiped under any and all conditions." The kind of competition which makes a virtue of a hundred producers fighting fiercely to occupy the selfsame spot in the market could be socially wasteful and debilitating. "The principle of competition must be interpreted in the light of new methods of production, new forms of organization, modern methods of distribution, and new creative forces which have entered industry."

The creative element tended to become decisive in the new equation, as he saw it. New products were displacing old ones, wholly novel services were emerging without advance notice. "From the cauldrons of science new forces of supplantive competition are constantly arising. They stalk as pale ghosts of industrial obsolescence after every industry that has become so thoroughly 'stabilized' that it can only grow around the waist." In short, the true competition of the new age was "the competition between the old and the new." Consequently there could be no complacency on the basis of past performance, no renunciation of research even in foul economic weathers. No industry could be sure of its area of operation—radio in particular had broken the ancient maxim that commands the shoemaker to stick to his last: beginning as a telegraph communications service, it had reached out to compass manufacturing, broadcasting, movies, entertainment, education.

Once, under cross-examination at an FCC (Federal Communications Commission) hearing in 1938, Sarnoff described his corporation as a tree with three main branches: communications, manufacturing, and broadcasting. But more important than trunk or branches, he said, is "the part of the tree that is ordinarily unseen, the part that gives life and growth—the root, and the root of the tree is research."

Successful research brings obsolescence, but the "supplantive" processes in modern industry cannot and should not be stopped. By way of example he cited RCA experience with transoceanic radio. Marconi and others were experimenting with short-wave frequencies and Sarnoff himself was insisting that the "brute force" of long waves would eventually be supplanted by short-wave transmission. Meanwhile, however, RCA went ahead with employment of waves on the order of 12,000 and 20,000 meters, generated by alternators. Then these facilities, extremely expensive, were canceled out just about the time they were ready for use.

"In one case, at Port Jefferson, Long Island," he recounted, "we built a station with seventy-two 400-foot towers and ten square miles of land, with eighteen 200-kilowatt alternators, at a cost of about ten million dollars. And by the time the paint was on the buildings, it was obsolete because short waves came into existence."

2

His advocacy of constant search and growth, though unwittingly, ran counter to the profound pessimism of those years, expressed in a doctrine of the "mature society." The doctrine held that there were no more frontiers to be conquered; that the chief need now was more equitable division of what was already available, rather than the creation of new wealth. In the perspective of history, of course, the no-more-frontiers theory can be seen as a product of despair—in due time the country reached levels of productivity and living standards beyond the most optimistic forecasts. But in the 1930's the defeatist philosophy was fashionable.

Because of his own character and the nature of his involvement in science, David Sarnoff was unable to go along with the assumptions of the "mature society." Instead he talked consistently of new worlds of labor and leisure waiting to be opened by invention and courageous enterprise. Referring to space, for example, he said: "We have broken our earthly bounds and have started to hammer out a new frontier, vaster beyond all human imagination than any within human experience." Nor, to the distress of some colleagues, did he limit himself to rhetoric; he was actually putting millions of dollars into development of new products and services, from facsimile systems to television.

Thus he was basically out of step with many of the theorists of the New Deal. Nevertheless, he achieved a close personal association with President Roosevelt. He was frequently summoned to the White House and knew that the President expected him to announce himself when business took him to Washington.

Sometimes, after his talks with Roosevelt, Sarnoff dictated rough memoranda on what transpired and a number of these have survived in his files. They show that while radio and communications problems held first place on the agenda, their conversation took in a wide range of other subjects. They indicate, too, that Sarnoff neither concealed nor sugar-coated his disagreements with the New Deal party line. The press cliché that occasionally made him an "adviser" to the President was an overstatement. Yet those who considered him a moderating influence on both government and business could have found support in these private memoranda.

At a luncheon conference with Roosevelt in June, 1936, Sarnoff expressed his thoughts on the rising unemployment figures. The President suggested that he put his ideas on paper. Accordingly, the White House soon received a detailed analysis of the problem which the President, in turn, circulated to appropriate Cabinet officers.

The most striking of Sarnoff's proposals was that the government use its tax powers to "encourage capital to seek investment in new enterprises." This, he said, called for establishment of a "ratio of tax abatement to increased employment"—the more jobs an investment produces, that is, the lower the taxes. After a time he received a commentary from Frances Perkins, the Secretary of Labor. She enlarged on the difficulties of reaching such a formula but said that his plan "seemed worthy of consideration." If it ever was, in fact, considered, it did not lead to action. The idea, in any case, was typical of Sarnoff's penchant for specific proposals rather than generalizations.

Another presidential luncheon, on November 13, 1937, appears to have covered a lot of ground: everything from the prospects for television and the current economic picture to events in Europe and the Far East. Evidently Sarnoff argued that government spending could not arrest the renewed recession of that time. "Atmosphere," he told Roosevelt, was as important as "substance"—and the atmosphere was unhappily one of mutual distrust between government and business. Among other things he therefore urged systematic cooperation through the formation of a President's Businessmen's Council and, to make it effective, a moratorium on White House vilification of business.

Of particular interest in the Roosevelt-Sarnoff talks, because of its long-range consequences, was the radio executive's emphasis on the growing political importance of international broadcasting in the troubled world. "The struggle for the minds of men," as it would come to be called, was already well under way. Radio propaganda by the leading totalitarian states, Germany and Russia, was meeting only negligible counterpropaganda from the democracies. Since private American broadcasters neither could nor would do the job, he warned that unless the government took up the challenge on the airwaves, we would suffer defeat by default.

The President seemed "sympathetic with the problem and interested in its further development," Sarnoff declared many years later. In the fall of 1938, at Roosevelt's suggestion, he conferred on the subject with Sumner Welles, then Undersecretary of State, who referred it for study to experts in the department's Communications Division. In a covering memorandum left with Welles, the president of RCA stated the problem thus:

"The principal nations of the world are now busy strengthening and increasing their physical equipment for national defense, to meet changing world conditions. But it would seem that mental preparedness may prove as vital as physical preparedness. Radio, especially in the international field, is the instrumentality by which this can best be accomplished."

What he was saying, diplomatically, was that America must provide the means for political-psychological warfare along with the hardware of military defense. It took nearly a decade—and the dual stimulus of the World War and the cold war—for this idea to take hold. Sarnoff would return to the problem persistently during the war—in talks with the President, with Nelson Rockefeller, then Coordinator of Inter-American Affairs, with Secretary of State Hull—and after the conclusion of the war.

The documents show that he used the phrase "Voice of America" repeatedly, but they do not clearly confirm that Sarnoff coined the name. That he took the initiative in planting the seed that eventually sprouted as the Voice of America is quite clear.

It is significant, in view of his later emphasis on the Communist menace, that even in the 1930's Sarnoff as a matter of course bracketed Red Russia with Brown Germany in denouncing totalitarianism. That scarcely enhanced his popularity among those intellectuals who were then as ardently pro-Soviet as anti-Nazi.

In an era of crowding panaceas and isms, he was among those who pleaded for confidence in the larger American tradition. "The solution of our difficulties," he said, "can be sought with greater assurance within our present individual social and political systems, which may be modified and adjusted to meet new requirements, than through revolutionary methods which, if poorly conceived or executed, must sacrifice the progress already won and prove disastrous to our concepts of freedom." This kind of pronouncement, it is easy to surmise, did not sit too well with dyed-in-the-wool New Dealers.

Because the webs of radio communications covered the entire globe, Sarnoff was drawn into close contact with foreign government and industry leaders. His sensitivity to world affairs naturally was sharpened as the years passed. He was more and more intrigued by the tides of world developments and in time followed them with the relish of a chess amateur watching an international tournament.

It was, in a sense, an acquired taste. In earlier years he had been too steeped in immediate personal and company affairs. Now, upon returning from his frequent business trips abroad, his reports—to his own directors and in public addresses—dealt not only with radio but with the largest economic and political trends.

His mind was repeatedly engaged by problems far removed from direct RCA concerns. And he brought to them the same intense thought and time-consuming analysis that he did to business. An example of this sort of involvement is provided by a document, dated June 10, 1933, moldering in his files.

An economic conference, initiated by President Hoover and inherited by President Roosevelt, was due to open in London in July, 1933, with sixty nations taking part. Sarnoff had no role in it. No one had solicited his opinions. Moreover, as we know, he was then neck-deep in depression problems and costly research projects. Yet he found the time and the mental energy to think through and put on paper an elaborate plan for the economic rehabilitation of the world, no less! This he circulated among friends in government and in the financial community, with the apparent purpose of stimulating constructive thought on the eve of the conference.

He called the effort "a practical program" for dealing with the economic blights of the time, on a plane above purely national interests. Actually, he wrote, national interests could best be served through international action and thus there was no true contradiction. Justice Louis Brandeis once declared that "If we would guide by the light of reason, we must let our minds be bold." Sarnoff cited this advice in outlining action remarkably bold for its time. His proposals in many ways anticipated by more than a decade the foreign-aid philosophy and techniques in helping backward areas.

He recommended a series of fiscal and political innovations aiming to revive and then expand global purchasing power. Under his proposals the Bank of International Settlements—which he had himself helped devise under the Young Plan—would become a prime instrument in opening up new world markets by means of long-term credits. The "underdeveloped billion and a half people"—Sarnoff's phrasing—would be openhandedly financed not only in the purchase of consumers' goods but in starting local industry and thereby raising local purchasing power.

The London conference proved stillborn. This failure of what was the most ambitious attempt at international economic planning up to that time, very much as the Sarnoff document had warned, was the signal for a period of narrow economic nationalism, competing currencies, frozen credits, towering tariff walls, and know-nothing autarchy.

Sarnoff's cerebration was thus of no practical value. It would take another shooting war and the cold war that followed before statesmen caught up with his concepts of systematic aid to underdeveloped regions. They would then take courses not too far removed from those he had charted in 1933. But his plan, though sterile in its day, is meaningful for our story, since it points up a facet of the man's development.

What had prompted Sarnoff, unasked, to set forth his ideas on the economic rehabilitation of the world? The answer, I would guess, is that the strong sense of responsibility which led him to undertake the support of his family as a ten-year-old had been extended in some measure to the whole human family. We shall see this impulse moving him once more in the postwar years, in relation to the cold war.

This, however, should not encourage enhaloing illusions about the man. He was not what common parlance calls a "bleeding heart," grieving for the sorrows of mankind. He has not carried the weight of suffering humanity on his conscience. He was too much the realist, the technician of the possible, for that sort of thing. His plan for improving the economic health of the world was not, I think, sentimental in its inspiration. Having become aware of a challenging problem, whatever its scale, his instinct was to consider how it might be solved and to convey his conclusions to those whom they might concern.

3

In the fall of 1936 David Sarnoff returned from an extended sojourn in Europe. He sensed nothing unusual when his friend James R. Sheffield, a noted patent lawyer and long a member of the board of RCA, invited him and Lizette to dinner at the Astor on the evening of September 30. But instead of leading them to any of the hotel restaurants, their host steered them to the main ballroom.

Their entry touched off a huge standing ovation. The dazed president realized that he was the object, or victim, of an elaborate surprise party. Amidst the cheering and napkin waving, he was escorted to the seat of honor on the dais.

The inspiration for the testimonial had been Sheffield's and it was enthusiastically adopted by the board during their president's convenient absence. And the secret had been amazingly well kept, considering that it was known for weeks in advance to hundreds of people, including Sarnoff's office staff and members of his family. It had also been known to many of the nation's leaders, from the President of the United States down, since their assorted congratulatory messages were presented to the assemblage.

The first to be read, of course, was the President's, addressed to "Dear David." Having learned of the celebration, Mr. Roosevelt wrote, he wished to join in greetings and congratulations: "In an early day you visioned the possibilities of this new art both in the field of commerce and as a service to the general public. You have served with distinction in its progress not only in this country but throughout the world. The even greater developments in the years to come remain as a challenge to your energy and your intelligence."

This was the occasion on which Marconi sent the radiogram to which I alluded earlier: the one that attested his pride in the fact that Sarnoff's "first association with radio was in association with" himself. Those who remembered the character of that "first association" between the office boy and the famous inventor were touched and delighted.

The banquet, to quote the official program, was "tendered to David Sarnoff by employees of the RCA family in celebration of the thirtieth anniversary of his leadership in the art and industry." Which was a monumental exaggeration, since in the earliest of those years—as office factotum, telegraph operator, inspector of ship installations—he was hardly providing "leadership." In any case, the gala dinner commemorated his entry into the radio business, literally at the bottom.

One has to pause to savor to the full the implications of the scene. The observation of red-letter days in their history is customary in American business organizations. It may be the date of the founding of the company, the birthday of the founder, a variety of other anniversaries. But in this instance a great corporation, kingpin of a vital industry, was celebrating the day (many years before its own corporate birth) when a fifteen-year-old was hired to run errands and file letters! In the annals of solemn observances it was surely unique and in human terms uniquely dramatic.

In 1936 most of those who personally remembered the undersized, skinny boy of thirty years ago, with his untamed mop of hair and eager-beaver manner, were still alive and in attendance that night, men like De Sousa and Elmer Bucher, for instance. Some of them were by now of a venerable age. Two of the operators who served with the boy David at the remote Nantucket outpost, Charles Weaver and Jack Cowden, were present, along with other veterans of the old Marconi Company days. To all of them, looking down the long, long corridor of three decades, the metamorphosis of the boy they remembered into the mature and rather formidable president of the world's greatest radio complex must have been something to marvel at. They were inclined to take a possessive pride in having "known him when"—a senti-.nental bond which Sarnoff also cherished.

David Sarnoff

Abraham and Leah Sarnoff, David's parents

David Sarnoff,
age five,
with his mother,
in Uzlian, Russia

When he was delivering newspapers
and working as a messenger boy

Sarnoff in 1907, when he was
an office boy for the
Marconi Wireless Telegraph Company
of America

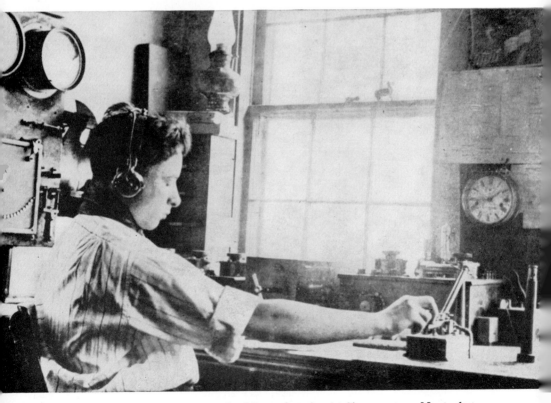

As wireless operator at the Marconi station at Siasconset on Nantucket

On the S.S. *Beothic,* in 1911,
Sarnoff was the wireless operator
on a sealing expedition
to the Arctic

On duty at the radio station
atop the Wanamaker store
in New York, 1912.
Sarnoff stayed at his post 72 hours
to report the *Titanic* disaster

In 1921, Sarnoff (front row, second from left) demonstrated RCA transoceanic station at New Brunswick, New Jersey, to distinguished scientists, including Einstein, Steinmetz and Langmuir.

Guglielmo Marconi and Sarnoff in 1933, at the RCA Communications transmitting center on Long Island

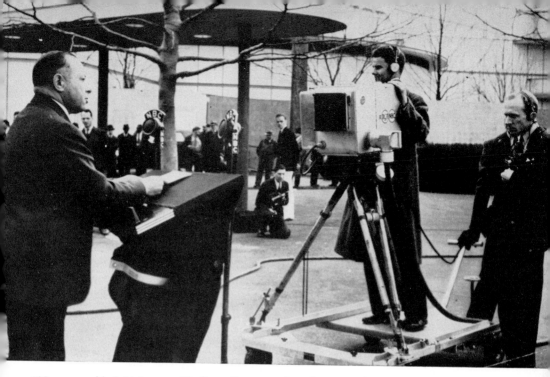

"Now we add sight to sound": Sarnoff announcing the start of television broadcasting, at the New York World's Fair, 1939

President Roosevelt with the original members of the Fair Employment Practices Committee in 1941; Sarnoff is second from the right.

David Sarnoff and Maestro Arturo Toscanini

A birthday greeting from Toscanini to his friend in 1944

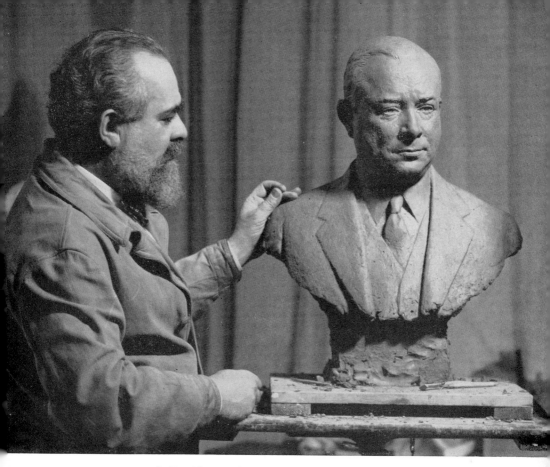

Jo Davidson and his bust of David Sarnoff

Vice-President Lyndon B. Johnson and Senator Jacob Javits with Sarnoff in Washington, 1961

Lizette Sarnoff and the three sons, Robert (upper right), Thomas (lower left) and Edward

Sarnoff, a Colonel in the Reserve, went into active service in World War II and was promoted to Brigadier General.

David Sarnoff in a rare casual moment

The David Sarnoff Research Center of RCA in Princeton, New Jersey

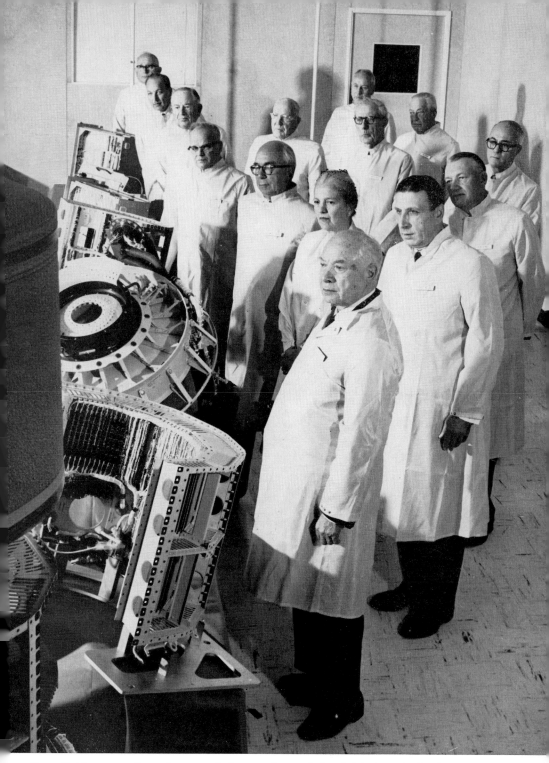

Sarnoff (foreground) and some of the members of the RCA Board of Directors at RCA's plant in Van Nuys, California, in 1964. (From upper left, front row) John T. Cahill, Robert W. Sarnoff, Frank M. Folsom, Elmer W. Engstrom, Lewis L. Strauss, Mrs. Everett N. Case, and Arthur L. Malcarney; (second row) Harry C. Ingles, Harry C. Hagerty, and W. Walter Watts; (rear row) Carroll V. Newsom, Paul M. Mazur, and Charles M. Odorizzi

The grandchildren: upper left, Rosita
and, above, Claudia and Serena,
daughters of Robert W. Sarnoff;
left, Danny and Timmy,
sons of Thomas W. Sarnoff;
below, Jimmy, Rusty and Johnny,
sons of Edward Sarnoff

Sarnoff, who went to work as a five-dollar-a-week messenger after finishing the eighth grade, proudly holds the high school diploma—honorary—bestowed on him in 1958 by Stuyvesant High School, New York.

Lizette and David Sarnoff in a family group

To Sarnoff, too, so unexpectedly reminded of how it all began, there were overtones of the miraculous in the celebration. Normally placid in ceremonial proceedings, he was visibly affected this night. There was a spate of oratorical encomiums—by General Harbord, then chairman of the board, by former president Nally, Sheffield, Winterbottom, Dr. Walter Damrosch. Sarnoff, the only man in the ballroom not in dinner clothes, responded with an impromptu speech suffused with nostalgia.

"Sometimes I feel that all of this simply cannot be true," he said. "I have never been much interested in yesterday, and seldom keen about today. My imagination is gripped by tomorrow." All the same, he talked of many yesterdays, from his bewildered arrival in New York as a boy of nine and his first assignments as wireless operator to more recent events, and saluted by name many of the men around him who had shared his odyssey. And he concluded with a tribute to another fellow passenger on that journey:

"May I also, before resuming my seat, ask you to indulge me in a very personal reference. There is present in this hall tonight a member of my family who has been impelled to the service of radio by what radio engineers would call 'induction.' The person has also served faithfully and loyally throughout the past nineteen years, and in one form or another has made many sacrifices in order that I might stay on the job. I should like, on this occasion, to express the deep feeling of personal gratitude I hold and the great debt I owe to the person who has made it possible for me, in more ways than one, to carry on. I refer, of course, to Mrs. Sarnoff, my wife, who is here."

One of the highlights of the dinner, again in the nostalgic mood, was an address by the president of the Veteran Wireless Operators Association, George H. Clark, come to present the guest of honor with a scroll. It happened that he had been on hand when the boy David first put on the "cans," professional slang for earphones, in the Marconi office.

"Thirty years ago," Clark said, "a young boy had just finished his supper, which he had brought with him, and was sitting down to 'listen in' for the first time to wireless signals. He knew the code at the time, but only a sounder, and now he was faced with the need of recognizing the dots and dashes in the form of twangs and shrieks.

"The lad worked until midnight at this new and delightful pastime, though the cans hurt his ears and the long drawn-out sending of the early wireless operators contrasted unfavorably with the snappy sending of the older cable boys. At the stroke of twelve he quit, not because he wished to but because he wanted to be in good shape for his second day of office-boying."

What Clark could not know was that between leaving at midnight and returning next morning, the boy would have to put in weary dawn hours climbing staircases in Hell's Kitchen to deliver newspapers.

As the speaker pointed out, Sarnoff was the first operator to be made a life member of the Veteran Wireless Association and his sending "fist" was still legendary in the profession. "He is an operator at heart," Clark guessed rightly, "and reverts to the good old days of code when he telegraphs back and forth on a buzzer line" instead of using the telephone. He also recalled the narrow margin by which the radio industry was saved from losing its fabulous leader at the time Sarnoff was tardy for the take-off of the doomed dirigible, the *Vaniman.*

The anniversary marked this night at the Astor was destined to become a sort of RCA institution, with a similar dinner in September ten years later and at five-year intervals thereafter. Thousands of employees, who had no idea when the corporation was formed, could tell you when a certain office boy was hired at $5.50 a week.

4

This is a convenient point at which to note again the extraordinary friendship that had flowered from that first lop-sided "association" between Marconi and David in 1906. The difference of seventeen years in their ages was soon forgotten. The boy-to-man relation turned rapidly into an equal man-to-man relation. The American's fascinated admiration of Marconi's inventive genius and philosophic bent was extended to the man himself and his family, and it was amply reciprocated.

Marconi was a shy, self-effacing person who shielded his private life from the public. He had few intimates and Sarnoff was one of them. As the years piled up, Sarnoff became the Italian's counselor and even his volunteer representative in negotiations on contracts and other financial matters, in which Marconi was an innocent. I have examined a file of the two men's correspondence through a quarter of a century. It is interesting to observe that the inventor's letters, at first rather formal and diffident, gradually grow warmer, more personal, in a sense ever more frankly dependent on the younger man's strength. In addition, of course, they managed to spend a week or two together when the Sarnoffs were in Europe or the Marconis in the United States.

Each of them kept the other informed on research and testing in progress, despite the fact that they now worked for competing companies. In one letter, as early as 1928, Marconi expressed his readiness to help the American engineers with any of the problems they were trying to solve. Interestingly, considering the date, he added: "I would particularly like to take part in the development or testing of television." Television was still treated by the press and the public, and in radio circles, as a dream with Sunday-supplement overtones. But two of the men closest to electronic magic, one an inventive genius and the other a great administrator, spoke of it as a reality.

Although he did most of his work in England, Italy was inordinately proud of its native son. He was awarded the title of senator and then was made a marchese. Repeatedly Marconi addressed the American people over NBC— for the last time on November 11, 1936, when he took part in ceremonies marking the tenth birthday of the network. The great innovator whose mark is deep on the modern world died on July 19, 1937, at the age of sixty-three.

All civilized nations mourned his passing and paid tribute to his accomplishments. In Washington, the House of Representatives adopted a Resolution of Sorrow. In the course of the special commemorative radio program, David Sarnoff said: "The world has lost a great man. Science has lost a great genius. I have lost a great friend." His friendship was manifested, for many years thereafter, to the Marchesa Marconi, their daughter Elletra and son Giulio, as well as to Marconi's two daughters from his first marriage, Degna and Gioia. They all turned to him, as one turns to a loving brother, for help and counsel, and the record shows that he never failed them.

The entire gross estate of Marconi, including his celebrated yacht, the *Elletra,* came to under $150,000. It was then that Sarnoff, shaking his head over the meagerness of the Marchesa's inheritance, coined his definition of an inventor, which he had occasion to repeat often in the future. "An inventor," he said, "is someone who makes other men rich." Many a radio and television entrepreneur spent more on himself and his family in a month than Marconi had accumulated in his lifetime.

While in Italy on business in 1959 Sarnoff made a special trip to Marconi's birthplace outside Bologna and placed a wreath on his grave. He was introduced to a gnarled and stooped peasant, ninety-five years of age, who remembered vividly helping young Guglielmo, nearly sixty years before, to plant poles in the Marconi vegetable garden and to string them with wire.

5

In chronicling the life of a man like Sarnoff, a biographer becomes immersed in the dramatic events and their impact on society. He tends to gloss over the prosaic everyday things which, after all, account for a large slice in any man's years. And in this he reflects a reality: the subordination, by the Sarnoffs of our age, of the private to the public man, the eclipse of home life by the life outside.

Yet the routines of existence must be mentioned at intervals if only to keep the portrait whole and human. Sarnoff had a home and a family and never knowingly shirked his obligations to either. He had his quota of domestic problems, squabbles, crises. He shared with his wife—though hers was incomparably the larger share—the care and education of three sons, each of whom early developed a will of his own and an ability, perhaps a compulsion, to stand up to a too famous father.

Fortunately the French-born Lizette Sarnoff proved herself a superb and devoted homemaker. In largely ignoring domestic affairs, her husband was acknowledging her superior competence in that sphere. On the whole he intervened only when she demanded his advice. Lizette, in later years, liked to illustrate his detachment from domestic detail with an anecdote.

"David almost never goes into the kitchen," she would recount, with a chuckle. "But one day he went there, looking for something or other. When he came out he asked me who was 'the strange woman' he'd found there. I told him—the strange woman had been our cook for many years!"

Sarnoff liked his comforts. The family lived well even before his income justified it. Perhaps unconsciously, moreover, he was impelled to provide his three sons with the things he had been denied in his own childhood. He gave them the best schools and homes he could afford, a superfluity of toys, even pets once he realized that they wanted and needed dogs, aquariums, and aviaries—things he had not learned to know or appreciate.

After the first two boys, Bobby and Eddie, were born, the Sarnoffs bought a small house in suburban Mt. Vernon in order to assure them the presumptive benefits of country life. The third son, Tommy, was born after the Mt. Vernon exile. For the sake of the children, David Sarnoff suffered the torments of commuting, which he hated, for six long years. Then the family moved to a large apartment on East 89th Street in Manhattan, and later to a spacious and expensive duplex apartment on East 68th Street. A separate small suite next door, for the exclusive accommodation of the boys and a nurse, was subsequently added to the ménage.

While their father gave the boys physical comforts and plenty of routine affection, he apparently did not really draw very close to them until they were old enough to be engaged in serious conversation. The truth is that during their earliest years Sarnoff lacked not only the time to cultivate a true intimacy but the talents for amusing children or entering wholeheartedly into their youthful enthusiasms. Having been deprived of a normal childhood himself, he quite literally did not know how to play with his own youngsters. He could not, except by an effort of the will, share their interests in baseball, football, bowling, swimming, Boy Scouting, since he had never come to know or feel those aspects of American folkways. In due time he came to recognize this with genuine contrition. He admitted sadly that he had in some measure failed his sons in their earliest years.

In the early 1950's he was interviewed by the late Dr. Bela Kornitzer, who was gathering data for a book, published in 1952 under the title of *American Fathers and Sons*. After talking to each of the three Sarnoff boys separately Dr. Kornitzer tackled their father, who readily admitted his shortcomings and mistakes as a parent.

"One of those mistakes," he said, "is that I did not find sufficient time to spend with my children when they were young. It is perhaps a common mistake with men in my position. Nevertheless, it should be corrected by those who still have the opportunity."

A second mistake, he said, was "to have expected maturity of thought from these, or any other boys, at too early an age." Not that he objected to their having fun, he explained, but he "expected definition and decision from them before their own processes of thought and decision had matured." This, too, he saw as a penalty for his own forced assumption of a man's estate when he was still a boy:

"I was required to think and decide at a much earlier age, in order to survive. Whether it was a mistake or not, it is a fact that I did not have the time to play when I was young. All my waking hours were occupied with working and trying to make a living. The result has negative as well as positive effects. For example, I could not meet my boys on their own level on the playground. While I went to baseball games with them, they knew so much more about what was going on that I am sure I made very little impression on their minds."

Then, characteristically, he drew a generalized moral from these personal experiences. He shook his head slowly, Dr. Kornitzer wrote, and the shadow of a sad smile played about his lips. "Another mistake parents make—and that includes me—" he said, "is the notion that the companionship you may lose with your children while they're young you can make up later when they are older and you have more time. A French philosopher, I think, has given the best answer to that and similar problems. He said, 'Happiness postponed is happiness lost.' "

As the boys grew older they began to observe the reflection of their father in the mirrors of the out-of-home world—in school, in the newspapers, in references to him on radio. Gradually it dawned on each of them in turn that Daddy was famous and special, somehow different from other daddies, and for youngsters this is not always a comfortable discovery. Their instinct is to conform, to avoid conspicuous difference. Apparently none of them was overawed by the mythological quality of his reputation but at the outset it hardly encouraged intimacy.

To this day the boys as grown men tell of times when their father unthinkingly turned off a program to which they were listening—a baseball game perhaps—in order to catch a news program. It never occurred to him that he was wounding their self-esteem. They tell of it affectionately, not in reproof.

Once, arriving home, Sarnoff found Tommy's shaggy Shetland dog sprawled on the couch in his workroom and shooed the animal out rather brusquely. His mind, no doubt, was on the thick file of work he had brought with him. "I suppose," Tommy said with some heat, "you wouldn't mind if you could talk television to the dog!" The fact that twenty or thirty years later neither father nor son had forgotten the trifling incident suggests that it was symptomatic of larger strains.

The one sin that Sarnoff apparently did not commit was to throw up his own hard childhood to his children. Yet it was at least implicit, sometimes, in things he said. Judge Jonah Goldstein, for instance, tells of a Sunday in the mid-thirties when he went along with Sarnoff and his sons on a drive through the Lower East Side, in one of the sentimental returns that David occasionally made to the scenes of his childhood. On Monroe Street their limousine stopped in front of the tenement which had been the Sarnoffs' first home in America. Time had not improved the face of the gaunt old building.

A batch of youngsters—shabby, not too clean, but high-spirited—were playing on the stoop and the sidewalk, some of them no older than David had been when he lived there. After watching them for a while he said to his sons, quietly: "Boys, you're not likely to have the economic problems I had at their age, or that these boys now have. But keep in mind that some of them may be smart enough to take advantage of the opportunities America offers. Your paths may well cross in the years ahead."

As in millions of homes, the subconscious resentments of the boys were expressed in a determination to steer clear of the radio business in which their father reigned all but supreme. They even showed small zest for the professions, outside radio, which he recommended—the law in Robert's case, engineering in Edward's—possibly because he did recommend them.

Robert was himself responsible, in some measure, for his father's stubborn hope that he would become a lawyer. In the summer of 1935 the family was living in an elegant home in Westchester, rented from Irvin S. Cobb. Robert, having been accepted by Harvard, was conducting a seemingly futile campaign to extract the "old man's" permission to buy an automobile. One day he cornered his father, prepared to argue his case.

"Dad," he said in effect, "I have analyzed your opposition to my getting a car. There are three main reasons, and none of them stands up."

Sarnoff was intrigued and willing to listen.

"The first reason," Bob said, "is that when you were seventeen you didn't have a car, so why should I? But please recall that you didn't have a lot of other things your sons have—a good home, spending money, this summer place, a chance to go to college, and so on. If your objection makes sense, why stop at the car? You might as well deny us all the other things you missed."

Conceding that this point was logical, the elder Sarnoff asked for the second. It turned out to be money. But he was not asking for any, Bob explained. He had $150 in his own savings account and had already found a good secondhand car he could buy for that sum. Then he tackled the third point:

"You're worried that if I have a car I may get into accidents. That's the most important objection, so let's look at it. You can't suppose that I'll be cooped up in the dormitory. If I don't have a car of my own, I'll be riding in the cars of my classmates. So the risk of accidents will not be any less. You know I don't drink and that I'm a sensible driver. So why do you have more confidence in boys you don't know than in me?"

His father was convinced. More than that, he was so impressed by the organized presentation that he decided, there and then, that his eldest son was cut out to be a lawyer. Incidentally, Edward and Thomas, when they entered college, did not have to plead for the right to acquire an automobile—their brother had established the precedent.

Eventually each of the boys in turn did find a place and fulfillment in electronics, Robert and Thomas permanently, Edward for a period of years. Increasingly, as they grew older and their father grew wiser, the vague strains to which Dr. Kornitzer alluded faded out and the Sarnoffs became what they are today: a close-knit, devoted family.

14

Quest for Quality

ə∫ Effective September 1, 1937, the board of directors of the Radio Corporation raised its president's annual pay to $100,000. The following November, on Thanksgiving Day, the Sarnoffs moved into the spacious house in the East Seventies they still occupy.

The two events were unrelated. The house had been purchased some six months before the six-figure salary was voted. But the coincidence was exceedingly useful. Sarnoff had bought the six-story, thirty-room structure at a bargain price; mortgage payments and taxes came to little more than the aggregate rental on the duplex and the boys' apartment. But he had to dig deep into capital to furnish and decorate the new home to his own and Lizette's taste. With the help of Mrs. Belle Lenert, a sensible and competent interior decorator, Mrs. Sarnoff achieved an elegance that was not overpowering or unpleasantly opulent.

The house had been built in the late twenties, when private city residences were still high-ceilinged and commodious, with carpeted spiral staircases and some facilities for outdoor living. Among those who specialize in such things, the Sarnoff home was rated as one of the showplaces among town houses. In fact Mrs. Sarnoff did "show" it on occasion to coveys of curious women in the interests of sweet charity. A number of magazines and Sunday rotogravure sections have photographed the interiors for their readers.

From the large paneled dining room French doors open into a landscaped patio. The living room, on the second floor, taking its cue from magnificent original Chinese murals, is Oriental in decor. On the same floor is a special projection room, where Sarnoff sometimes entertains guests with a documen-

188

tary or scientific film, and adjoining it is a compact "radio center," where he can tune in virtually any station in the world, as well as the rehearsal studios of NBC.

Each of the boys had his own room and bath, although at the time the house was occupied Robert was already at Harvard and Edward at Andover prep school. Only Thomas, then going on twelve, still lived at home. Like his brothers before him, he was attending the private Columbia Grammar School.

The fourth floor was Sarnoff's personal domain. That is where he still has his office-at-home, doubling as a trophy room. One wall is given over to shelves of gorgeously bound documents, records, speeches: a compendium of his life's work which one day, according to his will, will go to the Princeton, New Jersey, Research Center of RCA. The other walls are hung with plaques, diplomas, autographed photographs and scrolls. But the main display of his trophies is in the central hall of this floor. There are many scores of medals, cups, crystal beakers, bronzes—all the familiar and some unique exemplars of the many species of honors and awards, each inscribed to him in the high-flown style of formal eulogy.

On the fourth floor, also, is an emphatically masculine taproom, equipped with the regulation beerhall furniture, card tables, a well-stocked bar, mounted fish and wild game heads on the wall. This is a salute to the conventions of male entertaining, since Sarnoff himself, as we know by now, neither drinks nor plays cards and, despite his eventual title of brigadier general, has never fired a gun or snared a fish more dangerous than a flounder. Only the accouterments for smoking are in character; his consumption of oversized cigars is on the Churchillian scale.

Off the top floor there is an ample terrace, artfully furnished and decorated to give the feel of a cool, shaded garden. Nearby is proof of Sarnoff's one sybaritic touch—a fully equipped barbershop. He has one also in his office, concealed behind a secret door in the oak paneling. A psychologist, I suppose, might detect in this indulgence and his general emphasis on cleanliness and careful grooming a compensation for the grubby slums of his childhood.

From the outset, of course, the Sarnoff home contained an abundance of radio receivers and, long before they were available to the public, television sets in various stages of their evolution. Twenty is the usual estimate of the total collection, but the figure fluctuates as old models are removed and new or experimental successors are installed. Mrs. Sarnoff, who has acquired none of her husband's technological skills, likes to complain good-naturedly that no sooner has she learned to operate a new set than it is snatched away and replaced by another.

Her husband has radio and television apparatus in his bedroom. He can operate them by pushing buttons on a panel on the headboard of his bed— evidence of a distaste for unnecessary physical effort, he insists. He also has radio and television at his fingertips in the barbershop. Indeed there are few places on all the six floors, including the terrace, without instant access to sight and sound programs. Several of the television receivers are built into walls and concealed behind attractive paintings, landscapes and seascapes. He presses a button, the painting slowly rises into the wall and the face of the set is revealed.

And this inventory of the household leads us naturally to an intriguing question, considering his major life's work: what kind of programs does he enjoy?

2

The headman of the American radio-television world, when he turns on the instruments he pioneered and fought for, listens to news, political commentaries, good music, and serious theatre. Sometimes, in the early TV period, he watched a prizefight. But no one has as yet caught him in communion with one of the upper dozen or so top-rated programs, the big money-makers of broadcasting. He knows such popular confections, if at all, by general repute and their effects on the company balance sheet. The industrialist who organized the first national network has been concerned with plain business, not "show biz."

As a test of the country's listening and viewing preferences, the twenty-odd sets in the Sarnoff home would therefore be misleading to the gentry who sample and rate them. His tastes are high of brow and long of hair and, while he hasn't advertised this fact, he has not concealed it either. The popular programs, to put the matter plainly, have very little appeal for him.

There is nothing stuffy or patronizing in his preferences in air fare. His tastes simply don't run to comedians, quizzes, westerns, jazz bands, and electronic mayhem. But he has no objection to others indulging different tastes and, of course, has resolutely defended their right to choose shows which he personally dislikes. Sarnoff is no intellectual in the technical or egghead sense and certainly no intellectual snob. The true elite of the arts, the self-appointed Sanhedrin of culture, probably would condemn him without trial as a perpetrator of the "mass culture" they decry. Besides, he has stockholders, dividends, and competitors to think about.

"If we limited ourselves to programs that were entirely satisfactory to the professional newspaper and magazine critics," he told interviewers for *U.S. News & World Report*, "we'd be out of business. I myself dislike many things that are on radio and television. When I don't like them, I don't look or listen to them. . . . If more people prefer to listen to Bob Hope's jokes than to Toscanini's music, they should have the privilege, and they have it. It's nothing to cry about."

The public has the right and the freedom to be selective, he often emphasized, and should be encouraged to exercise these precious privileges more wisely. After all, he said once, "the world is not in need of more entertainment but of more enlightenment." "Given a chance," he explained in a public address, "the average man will move slowly, perhaps falteringly, toward a selection of the best." The duty of broadcasters, as he saw it, was therefore to make "the best" available.

And this is what he tried to do, especially when radio was the only broadcasting service—conscientiously, in some cases against opposition, and with a large measure of success. Others in his own and competing networks could claim personal credit for quantity and high ratings, David Sarnoff primarily for quality. The shows for which he was directly responsible, and they were many, are chiefly of the kind that pay off in prestige rather than immediate cash.

The paradox, since his commercial instincts are quite healthy, is that he has taken special satisfaction in his most unprofitable programs. This he rationalizes as expediency in reverse, so to speak; by adding respectability to the mix, he contends, the programs of superior quality have helped save broadcasting from government intervention and censorship. To have brought Dr. Damrosch, the Metropolitan Opera, and other such "class" productions to mass audiences—above all, to have made possible nearly seventeen years of Toscanini magic on the air—is balm for his spirit.

From the very beginning, Sarnoff's expectations for broadcasting were high-pitched and idealistic, perhaps romantic. His first sketch of the Music Box, years before its advent, listed sports and other popular titillations among the gifts it would bring into simple homes. But his emphasis was on education, good music, fine theatre, the improved functioning of democracy. In its formative stage, it should be recalled, he thought of radio as a "public service" financed by foundations, and resisted its dependence on advertising.

He was no less sanguine in his early forecasts for television. "There is little in the fields of cultural education that cannot be envisioned for the home through the new facilities of electrical communication," he wrote in the *New York Times* in 1930. "Assume sufficient progress in the television art, and every home equipped for radio reception may, at certain times, become an art gallery."

The great paintings and sculptures in the Louvre and other famous galleries channeled into humble city homes and farmhouses! "Television, advanced to the stage where color as well as shadow would be faithfully transmitted, could bring these treasures vividly to the American home. . . . Just as sound broadcasting has brought a new musical appreciation to millions of people, so could television open a new era of art appreciation."

A year later he said: "Television, when it arrives as a factor in the field of entertainment, will give new wings to the talents of creative and interpretive genius, and will furnish a new and greater outlet for artistic expression. . . . A new world of educational and cultural opportunities will be opened to the home. New forms of artistry will be encouraged and developed."

In the early thirties, when he was voicing these expectations, radio was just getting under way. Having made tall promises—not only to the public but, more important, to himself—Sarnoff set out to redeem them, as far as one man could, by stimulating programs closer to his original hopes. In the next two decades he was directly responsible for a large portion of the public-service offerings on NBC and indirectly, because they inspired others to follow suit, for many quality programs elsewhere. If those who credit radio with raising the country's musical literacy are correct, much of the credit belongs to Sarnoff. Much but decidedly not all—the long-term unsponsored presentation of the New York Philharmonic by Columbia Broadcasting merits particular notice.

In the course of testimony in Washington in 1938 Sarnoff listed what he considered examples of worthwhile programs. He could mention the Toscanini concerts, "America's Town Hall Meeting of the Air," the "National Farm and Home Hour," then in its ninth year, the Damrosch programs of musical education for the schools, among others. Speaking on the same subject to the Board of Regents of New York University a year later, he referred with satisfaction to the "University of Chicago Round Table," a spate of religious hours, programs fashioned to meet the special interests of women and children.

By the 1960's, to take a leap of twenty-odd years, American viewers were in fact seeing the treasures at the Louvre, in full color and with Charles Boyer as guide, just as Sarnoff had predicted they would.

3

In 1927 the famous conductor and composer, Dr. Walter Damrosch, who was then close to sixty-six, brought an idea to Sarnoff. He was startled by the alacrity with which the youthful executive embraced his proposal, refined it, made it his own.

Though it was addressed to young people in classrooms, millions of grownups eavesdropped. The broad, cultivated voice of the conductor saying, "Good morning, my dear young friends, and welcome to the Music Appreciation Hour," moved some uppity intellectuals to derision. But Sarnoff saw the program as a heart-warming venture in "universal education as well as entertainment," as an example of "the democracy of musical appreciation."

He could claim, and frequently did, that millions of Americans, young and old, were being initiated in the beauties and ecstasies of great music. At a gala celebration of Dr. Damrosch's seventy-fifth birthday, the president of RCA hailed him as "our outstanding ambassador of music." Five years later, at eighty, the great musician was still carrying on his embassy. His audience in schools was then estimated at six million, plus more millions of adults. Since the preceding year, in addition, the program had been regularly short-waved to Latin-American countries, the conductor's comments being translated into Spanish and Portuguese.

At his eightieth birthday party, in January, 1942, attended by the greats of the musical and electronics worlds, Dr. Damrosch told movingly how in 1927, "after forty-three years in public life," he "finally felt that he should retire." But, he said, "a remarkable pioneer, a genius, lured me back," so that for fifteen years he had been able "without any visible audience to play music from the great master composers over the air to millions who had never heard of Bach and Beethoven."

Turning to his host, the octogenarian exclaimed: "What a remarkable pioneer—and what a debt of gratitude we will all owe to David Sarnoff!" Several days later, in a private letter addressed to his "Dear Generous Boss," he wrote: "My talk expressed only very haltingly what I have so long felt about you—a man who is not only one of the greatest executives of all time, but who combines with it a passionate and understanding love for music—an all too rare combination." Dr. Damrosch continued to conduct his program until he reached eighty-four.

In Sarnoff's descriptions of the culture potential of radio, grand opera had always been in the forefront. It was, after all, the very symbol of culture for an elite, and he ached to bring it to the populace. A lot of technical problems had to be solved before grand opera could be picked up live and faithfully conveyed over the air. Also, the reluctance of the custodians of a tradition-bound art form had to be overcome.

When he first proposed to the Metropolitan Opera Company a weekly, unsponsored performance for a nationwide audience on a regular schedule, Sarnoff met with skepticism and soul-searching. Would the purity of operatic music be sullied? Might the general access to opera undermine its traditional appeal to the educated minority? In the end he convinced Giulio Gatti-Casazza, the celebrated general manager of the Metropolitan, that the certain benefits were vastly greater than the possible risks.

On Christmas Day of 1931 the first complete and live opera was broadcast by NBC directly from the Metropolitan stage, with a new luminary of radio, Milton Cross, explaining the music and the plot during the intermissions. It drew a reasonably large audience and spirited applause from the press. For the première, a light vehicle had been selected, *Hansel and Gretel,* but more formidable operas were staged as the season progressed and in the many seasons that followed. Eventually nothing on the Metropolitan repertoire was considered too heavy for the unseen Saturday afternoon audiences.

In 1934 Sarnoff became, and remained for about twenty years, a member of the board of directors of the Metropolitan Opera. Important financial support flowed to the organization, not only in payments by NBC but in contributions from newly minted music lovers. Despite this there were times of fiscal crisis.

A public appeal for a million dollars to subsidize the Metropolitan was decided upon in 1940. David Sarnoff served as chairman of the Radio Division, with Mrs. August Belmont and Lucrezia Bori as his vice-chairmen. On the air he challenged the new lovers of opera, won to the cause through nine consecutive seasons, to show their appreciation by sending in one dollar each. The response was overwhelming—the mails brought more than half a million dollars and the million-dollar goal was reached through contributions by private organizations and individuals.

Education, of course, ranked high in the quest for quality. In 1937 Sarnoff persuaded Dr. James Rowland Angell, former president of Yale, to emerge from retirement to serve as educational consultant for NBC. The experiments in education by radio that followed were vital pioneering efforts. Many of the techniques worked out by Dr. Angell and the network staff became standard pedagogical procedures on both radio and television.

These were a few of the highlights of Sarnoff's drive to raise the quality average. Other networks and individual stations, of course, were also providing notable public-service programs, but NBC under his prodding scored more impressive "firsts" in this department and he personally developed more of the conspicuous cultural shows cited when the subject was under discussion.

NBC officials knew that they could count on their chairman of the board when "class" projects were on the table. His influence was behind national hookups for concerts by leading orchestras like those of Boston, Chicago, Cleveland, Rochester, and by visiting European orchestras. The same influence was behind the formation of the NBC String Orchestra under direction of Dr. Frank Black, the NBC Quartettes, Music for Young Listeners, a string of such shows.

But the climax was yet to come. The last months of 1937 were notable, to David Sarnoff, less for the $100,000 salary or the acquisition of a luxurious town house than for the start of the Toscanini concerts on the air. Few events in his professional life have given him the same abiding glow of inner content. When he pauses to look back on a long life replete with excitement and achievement, it is still his main object of pride.

4

In *Toscanini, an Intimate Portrait,* a charming and colorful little book published in 1956, the late Samuel Chotzinoff told how it all started:

"In the fall of 1936, at a dinner party in New York, I met General David Sarnoff, then president of the Radio Corporation of America and chairman of the board of the National Broadcasting Company. We talked about music and discovered in each other an admiration for the great voices of the past, a brash addiction to melody, and a reverence for the art of Arturo Toscanini. 'What a pity,' I said, 'that America will never hear and see the Maestro again.' He agreed it was a pity and something should be done about it."

Chotzinoff ("Chotzie" to nearly everyone), then music critic on the New York *Post,* was not only sensitive and knowledgeable on music but a talented writer. He could not have guessed that the casual meeting with Sarnoff was about to divert the course of his professional life. They met, again accidentally, at a concert three weeks later and the RCA president gave Chotzie a lift home in his car. En route, without prelude or explanation, Sarnoff offered him a job at NBC.

The music critic protested that he knew nothing about radio but agreed to work on a part-time basis. Eventually he was to become the network's music director, but at first his duties were few and exceedingly vague. He wondered what Sarnoff had in mind. Several months later, early in 1937, he had the answer. Sarnoff called him in and announced that he had decided to induce Arturo Toscanini to come to the United States and perform exclusively for NBC.

"I could not help smiling in pity for his ignorance of Toscanini's character," Chotzie remembered. " 'He will never come back,' I said. 'He told me so himself.' I sketched for Mr. Sarnoff a verbal portrait of the Maestro, underscoring his absolute intransigence. I pointed out that once the Maestro made up his mind about something, he could not be budged."

And the Maestro had made up his mind, emphatically, not to take up the baton again in America. The peerless Toscanini had quit the Metropolitan Opera Company orchestra in 1915, after seven years of service. Otto Kahn, then the Maecenas of grand opera, begged him to come back on his own terms but could not even extract a reply. In 1925 Toscanini returned to direct the New York Philharmonic, which he conducted until early 1936. At that point some disagreement arose and he departed for Italy in high dudgeon, vowing that he was through with America. Now history was being repeated— he ignored all pleas to come back. And this time he had the legitimate excuse of advancing age, since he was on the threshold of seventy.

Sarnoff refused to be discouraged by this recital of history. He asked Chotzie, as an intimate and well-loved friend of Arturo and his wife, Carla Toscanini, to extend an invitation by cable. Chotzie shrugged and complied, and the prompt reply did not astonish him. It read: "Thank you dear friend no." Again Sarnoff was not deterred. He had been thinking about something spectacular enough to tempt the greatest living conductor. "Suppose," he said calmly, "we offered to *create* an orchestra for him—a *radio* orchestra. Would he go for that?"

An ingenious idea, but it would not work with the Maestro, Chotzie was sure. True, Toscanini's Sunday concerts with the Philharmonic had been broadcast, he explained, "but for him they were just concerts." He closed his mind to the invisible audience beyond the auditorium. Radio was mechanical, like recording. For many years he had refused all offers to record. He would surely refuse to be primarily a radio conductor.

"Very well," said Sarnoff. "I want you to go to Milan and get him. The American radio listener deserves the very best in music. All we can lose is a few weeks of your time and the expenses of the trip. No more cables. Get on a boat."

With his wife (the sister of Jascha Heifetz), Chotzinoff sailed on what he regarded as a futile assignment. The details as he recalled them in the memoir make amusing reading. The Chotzinoffs were warmly received in Milan and took almost all their meals with the Toscaninis. But two weeks went by and poor Chotzie had not yet dared broach the proposal. He had taken Carla, Mrs. Toscanini, into his confidence. While pessimistic of his chances under the best circumstances, she advised that he wait patiently for an opportune moment.

The moment came on the night of February 2. The Toscaninis entertained the Gatti-Casazzas. There were sad and hilarious reminiscences, amusing or sentimental memories of America, all copiously washed down with the local wines. When the Gattis left, the Americans remained for a nightcap of brandy. The Maestro was in a wonderfully mellow mood, and the American critic, though no drinker, had had enough to lift his courage. It was now or never.

Chotzie confessed that he was in Italy not as a tourist but on an all-important musical mission. America yearned for the Maestro's return. NBC would create a great orchestra especially for him, the best that money and devotion could produce. Instead of playing for a few thousand in a concert hall, he would play for millions on the air; and he would not have to compromise in the slightest in the choice of music.

Toscanini, almost sobered, stared at him incredulously, and Chotzie would not let him interrupt. Surely he, who revered the Master, would not risk his friendship by urging the proposal if he were not convinced that it would serve the cause of supreme symphonic music. By way of a clincher, he produced an old clipping: a magazine article according to which canaries in Cincinnati, under the spell of Toscanini's rendition of Beethoven on the radio, had sung the chorus of the *Ninth Symphony*.

The child in the great musician was excited by the miracle of the canaries. *"Incredible . . . meraviglia . . ."* he murmured. The American saw and pressed his advantage. If birds were touched, let the Maestro think of human beings, millions of them, who would be touched and comforted by his genius. Toscanini calmed down, pondered the problem, and made the historic decision. "Why not!" he exclaimed. "Canaries . . . the *Ninth Symphony* . . ."

At seventy, despite his vows and his known aversion to mechanical transmission of music, he would go to America once more. Not for long, of course—just ten concerts before retiring for good. After reassuring the alarmed Carla that the charges would be reversed, Chotzie there and then put in a call to his boss in New York. The president of RCA was so thrilled by the good news that he offered to come right over to Italy if necessary to conclude the deal.

It was not necessary. Toscanini made a perfectionist's conditions at the musical end: he must have a veto on orchestra personnel, absolute authority on programs, no sponsorship or other commercial nonsense. But his wife, the practical-minded half of the family, did not disdain commercialism at her end: she insisted that the $40,000 for the ten concerts would be the residue after taxes, to be paid by the network. Chotzie was able to bring home a signed and sealed contract.

Artur Rodzinski, of Cleveland Symphony fame, was engaged as assistant director of the projected NBC Symphony Orchestra. He and Chotzie began to put together the first orchestra ever assembled especially for radio. Toscanini, in a handwritten letter to Sarnoff, had listed precisely what instrumentalists he needed, and they added up to ninety-two. Price was no consideration in mobilizing these topflight artists. The result was close to a cross section of the best symphonic talent in the country.

Announcement of the prodigal conductor's impending return was the sensation of the musical world. David Sarnoff made this exorbitantly costly sustaining program his personal project. He was like a boy with a new toy, emotionally in high gear as the enterprise shaped up. The hallmark of his personal style was on the first press release: Toscanini's "incomparable genius," it said, "will further stimulate and enrich musical appreciation in our country."

Congratulations poured in from all over the country. Mayor Fiorello LaGuardia of New York told Sarnoff: "The city is grateful to you." Writers in music and editorial columns solemnly attested that radio was coming of age. But no congratulations came from top stockholders. They were too conscious of the price tag, and some of them murmured that, really, this time the man was overdoing it. About a quarter of a million dollars would be invested, with small prospect that any of it would come back. The board of directors gulped and swallowed the outsize financial pill but did not pretend that it was sweet.

5

Interest in the initial concert, finally set for Christmas Night, built up as the day approached. Tickets of admission to NBC concert hall, Studio 8-H, which seated only fourteen hundred, were in such desperate demand that they became almost a status symbol in the New York world of music, art, and social eminence.

Rodzinski was rehearsing the new orchestra and keeping the Maestro informed; short-wave apparatus had been set up to enable Toscanini to listen in on rehearsals at home in Milan. In early December, when Sarnoff and Chotzinoff walked up the gangplank to greet the gray-haired celebrity, his first words were: "NBC orchestra very good . . . first clarinetist not so good." Across three thousand miles his amazingly acute ear had caught a minute flaw in one of ninety-two players!

On taking over the rehearsals, he helped the first clarinetist to erase the fault. Now and then Sarnoff stole time from mere business and sneaked into Studio 8-H to watch Toscanini rehearsing: perhaps the greatest show in the world of music, as the compact little Italian pleaded, scolded, yelled, raged, then beamed and exulted. "With what a new fierce joy we played!" one of the violinists would write in an essay on Toscanini's genius.

It was one of the swankiest and most emotional musical premières in many years. Leonard Lieberling, writing in *Radio Guide* immediately after the event, suggested a little of its soaring mood: "Christmas Night, 9:58 P.M. No such significant minutes have been known in radio since Edward of England waited to begin his memorable abdication speech last year. Again a monarch arouses this magic interest, but a monarch of a more spiritual kingdom, whose people are the music lovers of the earth."

The audience that night, in the United States and Canada, was so vast that even Charlie McCarthy may have been worried for his supremacy. Never before in the annals of classic music had so many people listened to the best in symphonic music, as interpreted by the acknowledged master of the conductor's art. The aura of greatness and significance clung to the show after it lost the aura of novelty. The Toscanini concerts were, and in large measure remain, the peak against which quality productions on the airwaves are measured.

At the closing concert of the first season, in March, 1938, Sarnoff took the microphone during an intermission to announce that the Maestro would be returning at the end of the year on a three-year contract. "The National Broadcasting Company is an American business organization," he said at one point. "It has employees and stockholders. It serves their interests best when it serves the public best."

Editorial writers picked up this statement in their unrestrained praise of the enterprise. Here, they said, was American business at its best. The New York *Herald Tribune* made a point of the fact that there had been no interference with "the most fanatically uncompromising of musical idealists," and no trace of condescension toward the mass audience. This proved "that the vast increase in the popular appetite for the greatest things that music has to offer is neither a delusion nor a dream. It is an actuality." The *New York Times* editorially placed the laurels where they belonged. "David Sarnoff," it said, "who began life in America as a messenger boy, has again glorified his office."

Sarnoff was especially pleased to find, among the many congratulatory messages, a glowing letter from Dr. Lee De Forest, whom he regarded as only a notch or two below Marconi among the inventive geniuses of electronics. "I want to express to you once more," De Forest wrote, "my feeling of personal indebtedness to you for this last and greatest of all contributions to the radio broadcast art. Those Toscanini symphonies constitute the capstone to the structure of broadcasting, the realized perfection of my life's dream."

What started as a single-season ten-concert agreement stretched to nearly seventeen years. From 1948 forward Toscanini was also on television. The Maestro's prejudices against recording were gradually broken down, so that all his great music remains as an enduring legacy. Between seasons, except in the years of World War II, he usually went back to Italy and conducted some concerts in various European musical centers. Accumulating years seemed to have no effect on his physical and artistic vitality.

The ninety-two members of the orchestra and everyone responsible for putting the show on the air—especially Chotzie—adored the "old man," but their adoration was more than matched by dread of his unpredictable temper. He rehearsed his men to near-exhaustion. His sweet patience could suddenly collapse in a Homeric rage, when he stamped on his watch, broke the baton, shrieked in anguish that he was through—through!—with music. Chotzie and his staff, as rehearsals proceeded, got regular "weather reports" on his temper, like nurses watching a fever chart.

Toward the very end of one performance on the air there was some fumble in the playing, so trifling that apparently only the Maestro himself detected it. He rushed from the podium in tears, would not take the usual bows, and in his dressing room vented his feelings on everything breakable within reach. He refused to be consoled or placated.

Though he showed up at the party in his honor scheduled that night in the Chotzinoffs' home, his black despair turned the gathering into a wake. That was the awful night, as reported by Chotzie, when the great conductor was driven to drink—water! Through some impulse for self-punishment, he would not touch the champagne but demonstratively called for glass after glass of the liquid he had not been caught imbibing publicly for twenty years. But between storms the same man was gentle, charming, and endlessly considerate.

Toscanini's hatred of Mussolini and fascism was well known. Only his world fame saved him from arrest and worse. During the war his mood depended largely on the news from the fronts. Often the responsible staff connived to keep reports of Allied setbacks from him for fear he might be too dispirited to go through with a concert. Though he had rejected an offer of $250,000 for a single Hollywood film, the Maestro made one gratis—*Hymn of the Nations*—for the U.S. government as a contribution to the war effort.

A true and deep friendship sprang up from the first between Toscanini and Sarnoff, far beyond the call of business and duty. Their correspondence through the years, which has been carefully preserved, leaves no doubt on that score. The older man made his deep affection for Sarnoff evident with Latin and a musician's exuberance, and the normally rather reserved American responded in kind.

At the end of every season Toscanini would announce that he was too old to go on, that he must be forthwith released, but in the end agreed to just one more year. Indeed, he would have been mortally wounded if his resignation had been taken seriously. But in 1954 all concerned admitted that he was at the end of the line. At eighty-seven he could no longer be denied the leisure he professed to crave.

On March 5 that year he wrote to Sarnoff: "And now the time has come when I must reluctantly say good-bye to my orchestra, and in leaving I want you to know that I shall carry with me rich memories of these years of music making." His departure evoked ardent tributes to his genius by the press and prominent individuals, in which NBC and Sarnoff were commended for having brought Toscanini to a new worldwide audience. Three years later the Maestro died in New York and was buried in Milan.

His long years on the air were widely acclaimed as a high-water mark of musical history in the United States and perhaps in the world. But Sarnoff's enthusiasm was not shared by everyone in the industry. One episode, as recounted to me by Sarnoff himself, indicates the nature of the dissent he encountered:

The largest single client of NBC was George Washington Hill, president of the American Tobacco Company and reputed to be something of an eccentric genius in his own art, which was merchandising. The advertising mogul who handled this cigarette account, Albert Lasker, finally succeeded in bringing Hill together with Sarnoff for the first time. In making the introduction, the ebullient Lasker boastfully described his friend's achievement in luring the world's greatest orchestra conductor to the air.

George Washington Hill interrupted the panegyrics. "You know what I'd do if I were a stockholder of your company," he said, looking straight at Sarnoff, *"I'd fire you!* I'd fire you for wasting money on symphony music in a mass medium." As far as Hill was concerned, a program that couldn't sell cigarettes was by definition a waste of time, effort, and money.

Did the seventeen years of Toscanini magic "pay off" in the practical, business sense? The question, debated at the time in the trade press, left Sarnoff rather cold and considerably annoyed. Dutifully he worked up persuasive proofs of the enduring values of the venture to RCA and the broadcasting community at large.

A substantial part of the investment did come back in profits on the enormous sales of Toscanini recordings. Between seasons, the orchestra or parts of it were assigned to play on sponsored commercial programs. And the deficits that still remained, Sarnoff was convinced, were more than paid for in intangibles of prestige, image, respectability. More than any other single program, he argued, Toscanini became a symbol of quality and culture and provided an insuperable roadblock to those who would saddle broadcasting with more and more government controls. At times he grew eloquent in reproving certain competing broadcasting leaders for their failure to recognize and give due credit to NBC for having protected their medium by raising its reputation.

Doubtless his arguments have validity. But at bottom they were also rationalizations. His quest for quality was explained as a search for prestige, which is to say in terms of cold expediency, but in truth it derived from his natural preferences. No matter how logically he justified superior programs, he was in fact responding to his own hungers for beauty, music, culture, the education he had missed.

Very few of David Sarnoff's business associates, no matter how cordial the relations within the business pattern, became his friends in the intimate, out-of-office sense of the word. What some of them described as his "aloofness" barred the way to uninhibited familiarity. It is not without significance, therefore, that Chotzie, the rather unworldly lover of music and literature, became one of Sarnoff's most intimate friends. His death in 1963 left a great void in Sarnoff's life.

The quest for quality that Sarnoff brought to radio set a pattern that was carried over into the television era. His son Robert, nurtured in his father's tradition, exerted a similar influence on TV operations, even before he became the chief executive of NBC in late 1955.

As production manager he encouraged and guided the advent of television's first major documentary, "Victory at Sea," a series in twenty-six episodes for which the Navy Department awarded him its Distinguished Public Service Award. Other such special programs on a continuing basis have followed, the best known of these being "Project XX," documenting the key events of the present century. The precedents set by Toscanini and the Metropolitan Opera on radio have been followed on television by such musical firsts as the NBC-TV Operas in English and the original operas of Gian Carlo Menotti, commissioned by NBC, among them the timeless *Amahl and the Night Visitors*.

Before long, moreover, his son and NBC president Kintner were bringing into humble homes the world's great art treasures, precisely as predicted by

Sarnoff thirty and thirty-five years earlier. In May, 1965, when Bob Sarnoff—himself an ardent art collector—addressed his associates of the Friends of the Whitney Museum, he was able to illustrate his thesis through landmark NBC color programs such as "Vincent Van Gogh," "Greece—the Golden Age," "Michelangelo," "The Louvre," and the "Art of Collecting." The early experiments in radio education, too, came to fuller fruition in the television era with such major projects as NBC's "Continental Classroom," launched in 1958—the first nationally televised educational series for college credit.

Thus David Sarnoff's quest for quality, carried on by his son, has yielded a substantial measure of the "culture and enlightenment" which were his dominant concern in programing from the outset. He still has little interest in the routine entertainment that holds first place on the airwaves, but he refuses to join the fashionable attacks on the medium. He feels that first-rate shows are available on all the networks, and that more will be coming—for those who seek them.

15

Struggle for Television

ᴧ̃ Americans born since World War II can no more imagine life without television than their fathers could imagine life without radio or their grandfathers a society without motorcars and telephones. The petrified forest of TV antennae on the roofs of the nation is as familiar and ubiquitous as chimneys used to be. For good or ill—and probably both—television is symbol and substance of present-day existence.

It is easy to forget, therefore, how new and recent is this pervasive phenomenon. It takes an effort of memory to recall the general skepticism about television before it arrived and the thrill of its actual advent. Who any longer thinks of it as particularly remarkable? But initially it seemed a wonder of wonders.

And the human miracle within the scientific-engineering miracle is that one man above all others was responsible for the introduction of television. I do not mean that he was alone or that it would not ultimately have emerged without him. I mean only that David Sarnoff nurtured the development from unpromising beginnings to operational maturity, despite obstruction by segments of his own industry and small support from any source. This is what the press means when it refers to him, as a matter of course, as the "pioneer" of television or (in a *Fortune* phrase) its "prophet and principal backer." This is what inventor Dr. De Forest meant when in 1941 he wrote on the flyleaf of his own book, *Television—Today and Tomorrow:* "To my good friend David Sarnoff, without whose far-sighted vision, financial courage, faith, and persistence, television as it is today would still be a vague dream."

The brains and labors of hundreds of scientists, engineers, and business administrators went into shaping and refining the new dimension in communications. Although the preponderant inventive and development job was done by the Radio Corporation, elements perfected in other laboratories were built into the final apparatus. Yet more than anyone else it was Sarnoff who coordinated the effort, kept it going, then brought the end product to the public. The research he championed was of far larger magnitude than that of any other company. Most important, he put his terrific driving force behind the project, holding it tenaciously to a course that proved right and successful.

The television system as it exists today is substantially the one perfected by RCA under his direction. Pride and reputation meant a great deal to Sarnoff, and these he put on the line in the big gamble for television. A few of those who fought him bitterly came around to conceding his primacy. Others, having harvested huge fortunes in the new medium, conveniently forgot how violently they had resisted its cultivation.

Toward the end of 1944 the Television Broadcasters Association, comprising men who knew the story from the inside, would bestow upon Sarnoff the title of "Father of American Television." Not many at the time, and fewer as the years passed, seriously disputed that patent of paternity. Those who awarded it knew, of course, that others had made vital contributions; but they knew also that for some fifteen years Sarnoff had pitted his faith against the judgment of the majority in the radio community and even in his own company.

Year after year, in a time of economic troubles and pervasive defeatism, he had gone before the board of RCA to obtain the appropriations for a pale hope called television. Not until 1949 would TV begin to pay its way and return the investment. By then RCA, directly and through NBC, would have sunk close to $50 million into it. Rarely before, up to that time, had a single business organization put so much capital into a single project.

The search for television over wires had started long before the search for radio. As a concept it predated the idea of wireless, being related to telegraphy over wires. Attempts to send images through space were made in many countries in the second half of the nineteenth century. Imaginative men sought at first to transmit "still" pictures and documents—what would today be called facsimile—over wires. They used whirling discs or spinning drums of many types to scan the image, converting it into a flow of electrical impulses for reassembly at the receiving end.

The inventor of the telephone, Alexander Graham Bell, was one of several persons who in 1880 took out patents for television devices. In the following decade a German and a French inventor, independently, put together systems of mechanical scanning to send and receive pictures *in motion,* which is the essence of television. Neither of them was successful—the technical tools of their time were inadequate—but they defined the character of the problems for successors.

By 1911 a British scientist, A. Campbell Swinton, established in theory that the Braun cathode ray might be adapted for electronic scanning. The same idea was conceived at about the same time by a professor at the University of St. Petersburg, Boris Rosing. Historically the Russian's experiments were especially fruitful because they kindled the imagination of a gifted student in his classes, Vladimir K. Zworykin, who eventually brought his genius and dedication to the United States.

From the 1920's forward, crude but identifiable pictures—still scanned mechanically but now conveyed by radio waves—were actually sent and received in America and Europe. In 1927 both General Electric and the American Telephone Company succeeded in flashing images in motion across impressive distances. The illusion that television was "around the corner" spread in radio circles. In those years of frenzied prosperity, anything could be promoted. A few manufacturers put a small number of receivers on sale—they brought in vague images from experimental stations on a screen three or four inches square—which were bought for their novelty appeal.

Television was becoming an intriguing conversation piece. Now and then it was the subject of an article in magazines devoted to science fiction sensations. Only a few at this stage took its advent seriously and they timed it for a safely distant future. The most optimistic and voluble among them was David Sarnoff. For him the question was no longer *whether* sight would be added to sound but *when,* and he dared promise that it would not be long delayed.

He once heard a great scientist and teacher, Professor Michael Pupin of Columbia, say that the discovery of an important need was almost as great a contribution as the invention itself. Sarnoff often quoted that maxim in his own excursions into the future and it seemed to him especially pertinent to television. The need, he insisted, was beyond dispute. The disembodied voices and sounds on radio, he said, represented the lesser segment of a circle, which would not be closed until the speakers became visible as well as audible. Radio was still "blind," he said, and blindness is a more tragic disability than deafness. Human ingenuity and persistence were consequently certain to fill the need.

The first detailed description of radio broadcasting in the home, young Sarnoff's celebrated Music Box concept in 1915, was in the form of a memorandum addressed to his superiors. It was realized in full about seven years later. Another such memorandum, in 1923, may be fairly regarded as the counterpart of the Music Box for television. Its fulfillment would take more than twice as long.

Both documents had in common the fact that they presupposed the invention of indispensable pieces not yet in existence. To that extent they were acts of faith—faith in the limitless powers of science. I have already quoted the television memorandum in connection with Sarnoff's uncanny ability to visualize things unborn, but it bears repeating in the present context:

"I believe that television, which is the technical name for seeing instead of hearing by radio, will come to pass in due course.

"Already, [still] pictures have been sent across the Atlantic by radio. Experimental, of course, but it points the way to future possibilities. . . .

"I also believe that transmission and reception of motion pictures by radio will be worked out in the next decade. This would result in important events or interesting dramatic presentations being literally broadcast by radio and, thereafter, received in individual homes or auditoriums where the original scene will be re-enacted on a screen, with much the appearance of present day motion pictures. . . .

"The problem is technically similar to that of radio telephony though of more complicated nature—but within the range of technical achievement. Therefore it may be that every broadcast receiver for home use in the future will also be equipped with a television adjunct by which the instrument will make it possible to see as well as to hear what is going on in the broadcast station."

As a forecast, this lacked the clean-edged precision of the Music Box precedent, reflecting the incalculably greater problems posed by television. But the concept was clear enough and he held to it steadily thereafter. He "plugged" television at every opportunity, not as a possibility or a probability but as a certainty. He became, in the words of Elmer Bucher, "America's chief salesman of the potentials of a television service." Without conclusive scientific support, he treated television as the inevitable "next step" in the maturing of radio and the fulfillment of its destiny.

Talking to students and faculty at the University of Missouri as early as January, 1924, he could say:

"Let us think of every farmhouse equipped not only with a sound-receiving device but with a screen that would mirror the sights of life. Think of your family, sitting down of an evening in the comfort of your own home, not only listening to the dialogue but seeing the action of a play given on a stage hundreds of miles away; not only listening to a sermon but watching every play of emotion on the preacher's face as he exhorts the congregation to the path of religion."

In the August 14, 1926, issue of the *Saturday Evening Post,* Mary Margaret McBride quoted him as saying:

"The greatest day of all will be reached when not only the human voice but the image of the speaker will be flashed through space in every direction. On that day the whole country will join in every national procession. The backwoodsman will be able to follow the play of expression on the face of every leading artist. Mothers will attend child welfare clinics in their homes. Workers may go to night school in the same way. A scientist can demonstrate his latest discoveries to those of his profession even though they may be scattered all over the world."

In those years, too, he was outlining to audiences of military men the uses of the "television eye" in future war operations. Those who heard him at the Army War College in 1927, for example, could hardly be reproached if they discounted his forecasts as "Sunday supplement stuff." Ten years later, a few of these men were among the Army, Navy, and War Department officials who met with RCA engineers to plan actual design and construction of television adjuncts for aircraft and battleships.

But we are still in the twenties. "We have passed the point of conjecture as to its practicability," Sarnoff told the Chicago Association of Commerce in 1927. "It is an accomplished fact. Not only by wire but by radio the image can be instantly flashed from point to point, so that it appears as an animated or moving picture of the subject thus photographed."

It is noteworthy, again as an index to the boldness of the man's mind, that already he was frequently alluding to *color* television, although the simpler black-and-white variety was still only a phantom in the laboratory. "If we let our imagination plunge ahead," he declared in 1927, "we may also dream of television in faithful colors."

2

Nearly everyone concerned with the problem recognized that mechanical, whirling-disc scanning was inherently defective and waited for an electronic substitute. In this respect Sarnoff decidedly was not alone.

In the 1920's, of course, his authority in research was circumscribed. The main work was being done in the Bell Laboratories and those of GE and Westinghouse. Along electronic lines, the most hopeful probings were those of the man whom we mentioned as a student in St. Petersburg.

Dr. Vladimir K. Zworykin deserves to be better known in our Television

Age. His inventions are at the heart of the apparatus. In television he occupies a place roughly equivalent to that of Marconi in radio generally. He was already working in electronics and had made advances in the use of the cathode ray to transmit images when the First World War and then the Russian Revolution cut his experiments short.

At the end of 1918 he emigrated to the United States, arriving in New York on New Year's Day of 1919. He accepted a variety of small jobs to keep himself alive. For a year (1921-22) he worked as a research assistant in the Pittsburgh laboratories of Westinghouse. He left to join an electronics company in Kansas City, then returned to Westinghouse in 1923. By the end of that year he had brought his iconoscope—an "electric eye" for scanning pictures—to the point where he applied for a patent on it.

His further work, however, was gallingly slow and marginal. It called for a lot more resources and administrative backing, he felt, than he was receiving. In the Radio Group, one of the top executives did evince a keen interest in his labors. Sarnoff not only kept himself informed on Zworykin's progress but praised his work to the higher-ups in Pittsburgh.

Dr. Zworykin was excited, therefore, when rumors of an impending unification of RCA functions opened the possibility that some Westinghouse engineering and research elements might be taken over by RCA. He glimpsed a chance to work directly under the sympathetic Sarnoff. Early in 1929, accordingly, he sought a private conference with the RCA vice-president and a meeting in New York was arranged. It made history for both men and for electronics. The teaming up of these two Americans, by coincidence both born in Russia, in a true sense signalized the beginning of television as it came to be.

The inventor laid all his cards on the table. First he explained the principles on which his "electric eye" was based. Then he demonstrated that basically the instrument was already operative, but that it still required intensive—and expensive—development.

As both men subsequently recounted the interview—until it was woven into the tapestry of radio legends—Sarnoff was impressed but worried about the price tag. "It's too good to be true," he said. "What will it cost to develop the idea?" To which Dr. Zworykin replied: "Maybe $100,000." Sarnoff pondered the figure, then said: "All right, it's worth it."

In fact television before it was ready for commercial use would cost RCA $10 million; then it would absorb $40 million more before there was a dollar of profit on the investment. Sarnoff could point to these figures, in a jocular spirit, as evidence of the inventor's salesmanship and his own gullibility. On a public occasion when Dr. Zworykin referred to himself as the "dreamer" and to Sarnoff as the "sponsor" in the annals of television, the latter took good-natured exception. By accepting the $100,000 estimate, he argued, he proved that he was himself the dreamer.

Whoever the dreamer, a dream was launched. Dr. Zworykin had at last found a patron with fiscal valor equal to the challenge, and Sarnoff had evidence that an all-electronic answer was a realistic goal. Westinghouse apparently was not reluctant to release its obsessed, one-idea inventor and several of his associates to RCA. For the first time they were given adequate staff, facilities, and moral support.

Others in the industry were concentrating on mechanical techniques, variations of those used as far back as the 1880's. The temptation, if only for reasons of economy, was to follow suit. But Sarnoff had made one of the central decisions in the history of electronics: to cut loose from those whirling discs. He was thereby committed to a long and at times lonely struggle. The fact that Marconi, watching from afar, expressed confidence in the all-electronic approach and was eager to cooperate was a compensating source of strength.

Television needed, again quoting Bucher, "major sponsorship, interpretation, financial support, top-executive direction, and a long-range program of experimental research." These Sarnoff provided. He took full command, bringing together and synthesizing the many hopes, hunches, and crude devices. Undismayed by shoulder-shrugging among his own people and gibes from competitors, he proceeded to pour million after million into the project. It was not always easy to justify the dramatic expenditures, against a backdrop of gloomy economic news, without persuasive proofs that they would ever come back. But he stuck to his conviction that television, as he phrased it, is "the ultimate and greatest step in mass communications."

For anyone but specialists in the field who know the story anyhow, a full recital of the technical unfoldment of television in these pioneering years might prove tedious. A few highlights seem sufficient for the purposes of this narrative.

In November, 1929, Dr. Zworykin exhibited and explained his TV camera tube at a convention of the Institute of Radio Engineers at Rochester, New York—the first public demonstration of an iconoscope geared to a cathode ray tube. Because its limitations and the clutter of unsolved problems were all too obvious, industry leaders paid little attention. The general press did not consider it newsworthy.

High-quality pictures, through a larger number of scanning lines, called for channels that could be found only in the ultrahigh frequencies below ten meters. This complicated matters, since little was known in 1930 about the design of apparatus for ultrashort waves. RCA engineers, nevertheless, were able to produce a transmitter which operated at approximately five meters. It was installed on the roof of the RCA Victor plant at Camden, with a receiver to match located a few miles away. The results were considered encouraging.

The following year a 2.5-kilowatt television station was erected atop the Empire State Building. It began telecasting in 1932. A number of receiving sets, first ancestors of today's sets, were deployed within a fifty-mile range to observe and report reception. The face of the screen at that time was horizontal, the program being viewed in a mirror set vertically at an angle to reflect the flickering images.

Performance was constantly improved, the definition of pictures was steadily sharpened, the range of reception extended. Experiments confirmed that pictures could be relayed from one city to another with virtually no loss in clarity: a token that the medium, when perfected, could be put on a network basis. Because of the total interdependence of sending and receiving instruments, nearly every improvement necessitated redesigning of both stations and sets. When the number of scanning lines was raised to 240, for instance, the Empire State station had to be almost completely rebuilt.

Absolute synchronization of time elements in the television system, too, was indispensable. Even a variation of $1/10,000,000$ of a second could distort the received image. RCA engineers in the end perfected an electronic generator to meet this imperative. Each of the myriad problems similarly imposed months and years of labor by a small army of specialists.

The later implication that Sarnoff, in runaway zeal, was pushing for the introduction of television to the public "prematurely" is not sustained by the records. He had the ability to combine generalized enthusiasm with specific restraint. He rarely spoke or wrote on the subject without underlining that TV was not "around the corner." At the same time he argued against a defeatist attitude. "While the magnitude and nature of the problems call for prudence," he summed it up in a statement to his restive stockholders, "they also call for courage and initiative, without which a new art cannot be created or a new industry established."

By 1935 he judged that television was ready for more comprehensive testing. At the annual meeting in May he outlined a plan that included: (1) erection of "the first modern transmitting station, incorporating the highest standards of the art"; (2) production of a limited number of television sets, deployed at strategic points of observation; and (3) development of "an experimental program service."

The last point is revealing. Until then the interest was limited on the *how* of telecasting; now enough progress had been made to require attention to the *what* of telecasting. About a year later President Sarnoff could report that the plan had been implemented and that field tests were under way.

A number of the major radio companies meanwhile were stepping up experimentation of their own, for the most part using the iconoscope and other elements in the emerging art developed by RCA. Among them were the Farnsworth Company, Allen B. Dumont Laboratories, General Electric, Philco, and Zenith. But in the scope of research, aggregate investments, original inventions, and engineering refinements—in short, the elements that constitute pioneering—RCA was consistently in the lead.

3

Concentration on television provoked an incidental clash of interests that eventually affected Sarnoff acutely. For it would cost him the long-time friendship of Howard Armstrong.

At the end of the 1920's the inventor had suffered a devastating blow from which he never quite recovered psychologically. By refusing to review the scientific substance at issue, the U.S. Supreme Court in effect deprived him of the patent on his first and probably greatest achievement: the regenerative or feedback system for amplifying signals. The decision was a victory for Lee De Forest, after a dozen years of litigation. Leading electronic engineers deplored the outcome. Legalities aside, they had no doubt that the feedback, built into nearly all radio and television equipment to this day, was overwhelmingly an Armstrong development.

Deeply hurt, the inventor threw himself into a new area of exploration, working night and day. And he discovered what he was looking for: a system that came close to performing the long-sought radio miracle, the elimination of static. In 1933 he obtained a patent on Frequency Modulation, or FM. But where he had hoped to retrieve his prestige he found himself instead in new quagmires of frustration.

In patent suits, it is well to remember, all claimants may be equally honest. New inventions are linked to older ones in an endless chain, so that drawing a sharp line between contenders for prior rights is often impossible. Certainly Armstrong was a man of scrupulous probity. He did not himself insist that FM was wholly the product of his own mind. The underlying theory had been advanced by others and dismissed as unworkable. It was he who made it work. Dr. Gleason Archer, writing as a neutral historian in 1939—that is, before the FM facts had been smudged out of recognition by legal squabbling —said that "Major Armstrong did not invent Frequency Modulation." Archer did not, however, deny the inventor credit for its development as a functioning system.

In December, 1933, Armstrong invited Sarnoff to a demonstration of FM. The scene was almost a re-enactment of their first meeting as youngsters nearly twenty years before. Again the setting was the Columbia University laboratory, again the invention was concealed in a little box, and again Sarnoff was greatly impressed.

By this time RCA was thoroughly engaged in television, progress being tested in the station atop the Empire State Building tower. Sarnoff arranged for the inventor to share those premises for his further work on FM. But Armstrong was demanding that RCA commit itself to adopting FM—not as an auxiliary service but as a substitute for the existing AM (Amplitude Frequency) system. This Sarnoff would not and could not do.

According to Armstrong's subsequent testimony, Sarnoff had exclaimed, some time in 1934, "This is not an invention—it's a revolution!" Whether or not he spoke those words, they packed a critical truth. If adopted across the board, FM would have canceled out every existing radio receiving set and broadcasting station. True, Sarnoff had always defended obsolescence as the price of progress and would continue to do so. But obsolescence on such a gigantic scale—not for a new service but for an improvement in the existing service—was carrying a valid principle to an unprincipled extreme.

Perhaps fearing future complications, RCA in 1935 politely asked Armstrong to remove his FM gear from the Empire State station. Moreover, the company was still refusing to give him a clear-cut decision on his FM system. This was the dispute to which Armstrong referred when, notwithstanding, he made an eloquent defense of Sarnoff at the 1935 stockholders' meeting, as quoted in an earlier chapter.

The fracture deepened into a real break in the late spring of 1936. At issue was space in the ultrahigh segment of the frequency spectrum. At hearings called by the FCC to make allocations, Sarnoff and his technical man, Dr. Jolliffe, addressed themselves exclusively to television. They were, of course, under no obligation to support the FM case for a larger segment at the expense of television. Moreover, Sarnoff believed strongly that the establishment of a new service—the addition of sight to sound—gave television priority over a mere improvement for the existing service of sound.

Yet the inventor was disheartened and indignant. It seemed to him that somehow their friendship was being betrayed. Armstrong would charge, in season and out, with the vehemence of a man who felt himself unjustly treated, that a great corporation was trying to keep a major invention from the American people. He was too emotionally involved to recognize that the American people, like the industry, had no desire to scrap the whole existing radio structure.

The inventor went ahead to develop FM on his own, exploiting the thin slice of channels allocated to him. He built a powerful FM station at Alpine, on the Palisades, on the New Jersey side of the Hudson. Consumer demand for FM sets gradually increased. To meet it, some manufacturers obtained licenses from Armstrong. Others, including RCA, produced FM equipment on the basis of their own research in this field.

Though he denied any legal liability, Sarnoff in 1940 offered Armstrong a million dollars for fully paid-up licenses. This the inventor rejected in anger. His emotions had long ago outrun his judgment. What should have been a business dispute was transmuted, at Armstrong's end, into a deadly personal feud, fought in the courts to the end of his tragic life.

4

Around 1937 the accelerating rate of RCA progress in television touched off industry activities in preparation for its possible release commercially. Whatever the sentiments and policies of individual companies—and they ranged from conditional approval to unconditional opposition—they could not risk being caught short.

Under the licensing system by which it was bound, all RCA patents were available to competitors. Contractual obligations aside, Sarnoff was eager to draw others into the gigantic enterprise. Far from seeking exclusivity, he feared it. A healthy new industry, as he saw it, would be unthinkable without a proliferation of stations, receiver models, and telecast programs.

Actual and potential licensees were kept continually informed. They were not only invited but lured to see new television devices, and where necessary were given RCA help on their own design problems. The corporation stood ready to build experimental stations for anyone authorized to do so. As a matter of fact it constructed one, every bit as good as its own Empire State station, for the Columbia Broadcasting System.

At an annual meeting of the Radio Manufacturers Association, on October 20, 1938, Sarnoff declared that extensive field tests "have convinced us that television in the home is now technically feasible." It was his company's view "that the problems confronting this difficult and complicated art can be solved only from operating experience, actually serving the public in their homes." Accordingly, he announced, RCA and NBC would inaugurate a limited but true commercial telecasting service in the New York area, to coincide with the opening of the New York World's Fair in April, 1939.

The news was featured in both the general and the trade press. At last, it seemed, television was really "around the corner." The reference to unsolved problems meant little to the public, which assumed that the long promise was about to be kept. But the trade knew that president Sarnoff was alluding to a bitter war within the business itself that might—and in fact did—confine the new force to a no man's land of technical disputation.

The conflict revolved around honest and not-so-honest differences of opinion on the readiness of the medium. Ostensibly and publicly, the inflamed areas of disagreement were properly technological. They concerned "standards" or "specifications"—the density or number of scanning lines, the number of picture frames per second, the nature of synchronizing impulses, and other elements on which an industry-wide consensus was necessary for the orderly launching of television.

This had never been required for radio—why, then, was it indispensable for television? The answer lay in the fact that in TV, unlike radio, there is a lock-and-key relationship between transmitter and receiver. One is rigidly synchronized with the other. A set "locked into" one station would pick up telecasts only from other stations that conformed 100 percent to the same specifications. For the protection of the set buyer, therefore, standards had to be "frozen" for a reasonable period.

In 1936, in part on Sarnoff's initiative, the Radio Manufacturers Association (RMA) set up a committee to study available standards in an effort to reach a consensus. It represented the principal producers. In December, 1937, its findings were communicated to the FCC. The RMA attested that "the proposed television standards were submitted to and approved by the member companies of the Radio Manufacturers Association." No one was surprised that the standards accorded fully with the apparatus and recommendations of RCA, which had done the basic research and testing.

In making the announcement of a limited and tentative commercial service in one city, Sarnoff was thus proceeding on the basis of agreed-upon standards. In England television had already been made available on a restricted scale, using roughly the same RCA specifications. True, higher standards could be expected through the years, but already they seemed to Sarnoff and a few other industry leaders high enough to sustain a home service. If action were deferred to await near-perfection, they pointed out, the medium would be postponed almost indefinitely. At that stage the powers-that-be in Washington appeared to share this view. In any case, the widely publicized RCA plans drew no rebuffs from the FCC.

Sarnoff went ahead with his announced schedule. When the World's Fair opened in the spring of 1939, the RCA Exhibit Building, featuring television, whipped up enormous popular interest. In the following months hundreds of thousands of visitors to the Fair from all over the country were able to see TV in operation for the first time. The great number of inquiries about where and when sets could be purchased amounted to a vote of confidence—the public found the service acceptable. In this the press, by and large, concurred.

Standing before a television camera at the dedication of the building, on April 20, 1939, President Sarnoff declared:

"Today we are on the eve of launching a new industry, based on imagination, on scientific research and accomplishment. . . . *Now we add radio sight to sound*. It is with a feeling of humbleness that I come to the moment of announcing the birth in this country of a new art so important in its implications that it is bound to affect all society. It is an art which shines like a torch of hope in a troubled world. It is a creative force which we must learn to utilize for the benefit of all mankind."

Hundreds of people assembled at the World's Fair for the ceremonies not only saw but heard Sarnoff on TV receivers. So did about a hundred guests at the RCA Building in Manhattan, along with the handful who had experimental sets in their homes and watched the proceedings on nine-inch direct-view or twelve-inch reflection-type sets. The first regular telecasting programs were started in ten days, when a limited number of receivers—priced at $625—were placed on sale by retailers. A few hundred purchasers were given a limited program diet through 1939 and 1940.

Many years and many industry battles lay between the World's Fair inauguration and the full emergence of television in the middle 1940's. A World War would intervene, when large industrial innovations were of necessity deferred. Nevertheless, the record was established. April 20, 1939, was fixed as an epochal date in the history of the medium. Television for the home, though forced to linger in the laboratories some seven years more, was born that day and announced to the world by its proud and worried "father."

The attempt to initiate commercial television in general drew no hurrahs from manufacturers, other networks, and station owners. On the contrary, it touched off a chorus of catcalls. As long as TV was a distant chimera, the latest "Sarnoff's Folly" could be ignored, but the closer it edged to actuality the greater the alarm that gripped some of the men operating the radio gold mines. Just as Hollywood had been distressed by the sudden appearance of talkies, and the phonograph interests by sound broadcasting, so most of the radio industry was flustered and frightened by the intrusion of television. It seemed a menace to their established business; already there was some evidence that the talk of television was inhibiting the purchase of radio sets.

The Radio Corporation had as large a stake in existing radio manufacturing and broadcasting as its competitors, larger than most. It was not asking anyone to gamble more than it was itself gambling. In the short run the temptation for RCA, too, was to hide television in the closet. The difference was largely in the circumstance that its president thought in terms of the *long* run. Sarnoff faced up to what he had often called "supplantive" progress, and its logic turned him once more into a troublemaker, at least in the eyes of some powerful competitors. To the able and hardheaded men directing the destinies of CBS, Zenith, and an array of other fabulously prosperous radio businesses he seemed a willful fanatic.

An incidental semantic footnote for its sheer curiosity value: At an early stage there had been some loud dispute about a proper name for the new industry. Commander McDonald of Zenith liked "radionics," while Sarnoff stoutly held out for "electronics." Now "television" was challenged, McDonald having coined and defended the word "radiovision." Again the name favored by Sarnoff prevailed.

5

Notwithstanding former approval of the RMA standards, influential companies now professed to have undergone a change of heart. Sarnoff, they insisted, must be prevented from "jumping the gun." They badgered the FCC and Congress to crack down on him. RCA, supported by some newspapers and political leaders, charged that dissenters were engaged in a strategy of delay to safeguard their positions in radio. The truth of the charges and countercharges will long be debated by historians of the industry. The fact that the essential standards available in 1939–1941 were ultimately adopted and proved adequate tends to validate RCA's position.

The kind of personal vilification that is familiar in politics but exceptional in business was now directed against Sarnoff. Among those determined to block television there were certainly men of integrity, honestly convinced that they were protecting the public; others were rationalizing their business preferences in those same terms. With the rest, self-interest was hardly disguised. And all of them denounced Sarnoff as a selfish vandal, hell-bent on saddling radio with what, at best, must for a long time remain a deficit operation. This was the time when the president of RCA was cartooned in a competitor's advertising, under the caption of "Televisionary," as an ape smashing the radio industry.

Here is an episode which gives some measure of the bitterness under the technical debates. By sheer coincidence, at the peak of the controversy, Sarnoff found himself in Paris not only in the same hotel with another prominent radio entrepreneur—call him Mr. X—but in an adjoining room. He was drifting into sleep one night when he was startled into wakefulness by hearing his name on the other side of the thin wall. To his growing dismay, he could hear clearly the loud and angry voice of Mr. X venting his feelings to his wife.

"That arrogant son of a bitch," he was declaiming, in substance, "will ruin our business! Somehow he must be stopped!" And there followed colorful variations on this theme. Mrs. X, to her credit, tried to defend the victim against her husband's ire, though with scant success.

The following morning, when Sarnoff ran into the X's at breakfast, nothing in his voice or demeanor betrayed that he had heard the nocturnal diatribe.

Testimony before the FCC in January, 1940, showed that a majority of radio manufacturers still were willing to abide, with some refinements, by the standards approved by the RMA committee. But a strong dissenting minority was enough to arrest action. As against receivers for the 30-frame 441-line system developed by RCA and seconded by the RMA, Dumont now urged 15 frames and 625 lines; Philco held out for a 24-frame 605-line variant; Zenith declared that television was still so defective that its release would penalize the American people. A CBS executive spoke candidly about the heavy economic burdens TV would impose on sound broadcasters at this time. Despite their vehement strictures, these hearings disclosed that Zenith, Philco, and others had designed receivers to RCA specifications anyhow, as a hedge against all contingencies.

To deepen the imbroglio, Armstrong and his backers insisted that the right of way be given to FM rather than television. They demanded the use of channels already assigned to experimental TV. The FCC, in what outwardly looked like a stroke of spite, assigned to FM in New York the very frequency on which RCA-NBC had for years been conducting tests, compelling a vital TV station to rebuild its facilities.

But the Commission did propose limited and tentative commercial telecasting for September 1, 1940. RCA chose to utilize this partial authorization to mount a practical test of popular acceptance or rejection of television. It decided to produce only 25,000 sets in the area reached by its Empire State installation with regular programing to begin on September 1. A full-page advertisement announcing the plan was drawn up.

To avoid misunderstanding, Sarnoff took the precaution of showing it to the chairman of the FCC, James Lawrence Fly, in the course of a conference in New York. Mr. Fly read the text carefully and offered no objections. This Sarnoff took as consent, especially since the timing conformed with FCC rulings. And so the advertisement appeared in the principal New York papers on March 20, 1940.

To the utter bewilderment of the management, Chairman Fly at once unleashed a violent attack on Sarnoff, RCA, the whole plan. He branded the projected TV service as a bid for "monopoly" and a menace to the public. In a full hour of free time on the Mutual network, he represented himself as the champion of the "little fellows" being bullied by Big Business—though qualifying CBS, Zenith, and some of the others as midgets was a bit awkward. His FCC rescinded the authorization for September.

David Sarnoff was outraged and said so in sizzling language. He accused Fly of duplicity under pressure from vested interests seeking to deny the public even a test of the new art. The cry of monopoly, he said, was a mildewed red herring. If RCA had a marginal time lead, it was because others had chosen to hold back.

A memorable business battle, with strong political overtones, was thus started. The public was understandably confused and divided. New Yorkers who had put in their bids for sets felt that television had once again been snatched from their grasp. Senator Lundeen went on both NBC and Mutual networks to answer Fly. "A new industry," he said, "was being throttled by a Government Bureau exercising power never granted by Congress." Most of the press, in so far as it commented on the battle, was on Sarnoff's side of the barricades. The *New York Times* editorially called the FCC action "absurd and unsound." The Philadelphia *Enquirer* wrote indignantly of a "bureau-cratic blackout of television."

There were more FCC hearings. Then Senator Burton K. Wheeler initiated an investigation by the Senate Committee on Interstate Commerce, at which Fly and Sarnoff were the chief witnesses. Always the prognosticator, Sarnoff told the Committee that television, when finally unfettered, would be a billion-dollar industry, employing half a million people. When TV did hit its stride, a decade later, these figures proved realistic.

Mr. Fly stood his ground. Unwilling to abandon his "little fellows" to the horrors of premature television, he issued an FCC decision which, though its language was ambiguous, had the effect of cutting off commercial telecasting.

The United States was not yet in the war, but electronics manufacturers were gearing to meet its demands. President Roosevelt, concerned that the controversy might hamper this phase of stepped-up military preparedness, decided to take a hand in it. He summoned Sarnoff to the White House and, in his breezy fashion, urged some kind of compromise. "David," he said, "I'll pay for the meal if you and Fly take lunch together and settle the argument."

To Sarnoff it seemed that Roosevelt had not been adequately or accurately briefed. "Mr. President," he said, "this problem is not in the stomach but in the head. There's no room for compromise. The public either will or will not be allowed to have television. No useful purpose would be served by a good-will luncheon."

Meanwhile the embattled industry organized a new and broader committee, which once again made elaborate performance tests of the several systems available. Its report, forwarded to the FCC in January, 1941, recommended that scanning lines be raised from 441 to 525. Also, it ruled that for the sound portion of television FM was superior to AM. That the verdict was close enough to the RCA system to please Sarnoff may be gathered from his public statement that it marked "a day of scientific recognition and economic encouragement."

Presumably the marginal changes saved face for the FCC. In any event, Chairman Fly suddenly threw in the sponge. On April 30, 1941, the FCC authorized unrestricted commercial television, as of July 1, and assigned eighteen channels to that purpose.

The specifications now adjudged satisfactory were little different from those RCA had sought to operate since the opening of the World's Fair. Technically, therefore, nothing had been gained by the two years of delay. The whole dispute on standards began to look, in the perspective of time, remarkably like the stratagem for delay some critics had said it was.

Both for the public and for Sarnoff the belated authorization was an empty victory. For by that time the American economy was being mobilized for war production. The President declared a state of unlimited national emergency on May 27. Neither raw materials nor productive capacity could be diverted to a new industry. Doubts on that score were erased at Pearl Harbor on December 7.

The struggle around television was not settled. It was merely postponed. After the war it would break out again with renewed virulence.

16

At the Half-Century Mark

ᴧʃ During the Second World War, David Sarnoff gathered a spate of conventional military honors, including the star of a brigadier general. But his most important contributions to the victory were industrial and technological.

The Radio Corporation of America, when the conflict erupted in Europe, represented the foremost repository of applied electronic knowledge, research brains, and manufacturing skills in the world, whether measured in quantity or in quality. It operated the largest and most comprehensive system of global radio communications. Its laboratories had "in the oven," at various stages of cooking, literally scores of devices of known or possible importance in warmaking.

Just after the First World War, when the U.S. Navy and other government agencies reached out for an organization to guarantee American leadership in radio, this was the kind of company they had hoped for. Their hope would have been diluted and possibly wrecked had Sarnoff failed to win unification and then autonomy for RCA; had he failed to ward off the dismemberment threatened by the antitrust suit of 1930; had he abandoned vital research activity in the melancholy depression times.

In simple truth the reality far surpassed the hopes of the official sponsors and corporate founders. Referring to Sarnoff's report on his first ten years as president, Owen D. Young, the number one founder, wrote to him: "As I read it I could not help thinking how crazy everyone would have thought us had we in 1919 made even a 25 percent forecast of what has actually been done. I am very proud of you and what you have done for RCA and for the world through its development."

By late 1939 Sarnoff could place at the disposal of the American government a many-faceted organization superbly equipped to meet the inordinate demands posed by the new types of electronic warfare. His long fight to preserve and fortify the company, in short, was paying off in the coin of military vitality for the nation and its allies. By the war's end RCA would have doubled and tripled its production of military hardware and taken the lead in engineering an extraordinary variety of weapons. President Sarnoff would have ample right to speak, as he did, of the laboratories of RCA as "creative beehives of activity," of its manufacturing plants as "arsenals," of its communications facilities as "lifelines."

The platitudes of patriotism have it that an immigrant who makes good in America owes a staggering debt to the adopted land. If this be true, then the military assets represented by the company Sarnoff had built could be accounted as payment in full. This he knew and it was heart-warming knowledge.

Within hours after Nazi Germany invaded Poland on September 3, 1939, Sarnoff called the top executives of all production units into conference. There was no doubt, he told them, that the country's manufacturing and inventive potentials would be strained to the limit. American defense measures would surely be stepped up; Britain and France would turn to the United States for munitions, transport, and communications. Moreover, the likelihood of direct American involvement in the struggle should not be discounted.

The executives were therefore instructed to reappraise productive capacity, streamline operations, prepare at once for dramatic expansion, and proceed to convert from peace to war goods. Orders were immediately placed for additional machinery and equipment for the main RCA plants—at Camden and Harrison, New Jersey, and Indianapolis and Bloomington, Indiana. The engineering and research divisions were similarly alerted. A variety of products hitherto fabricated by hand must be placed on a mechanized mass production basis. Myriad electronic items with possible military implications still on drawing boards or in early prototypes must be brought to practical completion on a crash basis.

From that moment until the Japanese surrender six years later, the RCA empire remained on a war footing. In a sense David Sarnoff had been preparing for this emergency for many years. So, of course, had leaders in other industries related to military needs. But in his case the problem was substantially different, and perhaps a greater test of imaginative planning, because he was dealing with unprecedented products, some of them only sketchily realized and others little more than theories and hopes. "Our destiny as a company," he would say at the end of 1944, "was one of preparedness to win the Second World War."

He had been a lieutenant colonel in the Army Signal Corps Reserve since 1924, a full colonel since 1931, and in continuous touch with corresponding branches in the rest of the military establishment. As a matter of course he had been consulted on problems of communications, reconnaissance, and procurement impinging on his field. The military potentials of the tempestuous new world of electronics were thus never far from his mind and conscience.

He had been among the first (possibly *the* first) to alert military tacticians on the most important of these potentials. I have already quoted him on this but it needs reiteration here. Future wars, he told the Army's Industrial College in 1926, would depend in ever-larger degree on "brains and scientific devices rather than numerical preponderance." He therefore urged immediate and systematic research on such things as remote control of mechanisms by radio; direction finding on all wavelengths; destructive radiations—and protective measures against these new perils. Considering the date, this was an impressive intimation of things to come.

His recommendations to military planners became more explicit and more urgent with every year. Long before television was in shape as a mass medium, Sarnoff was apprising them of its possibilities for guided missiles, underwater detection, target finding. The electronic eye of the TV camera, he realized, could be adapted for reconnaissance, precision bombing, many other purposes.

In April, 1934, Dr. Zworykin had prepared a paper on what he called a "Flying Torpedo with an Electric Eye." It described a radio-guided missile equipped with a television camera and transmitter; released in the proximity of a target, a control crew on a ship or plane would "see" the path of the projectile and steer it to its mark. Sarnoff was so impressed that he immediately set up a meeting in Washington where the inventor explained his concept—revolutionary for that day—to skeptical members of the Armed Forces.

In 1937, two years before war came and four years before America was sucked into its vortex, RCA built the first television system specifically designed for use by aircraft. Soon thereafter television reconnaissance equipment for airplanes was reduced to suitcase dimensions. In November, 1940, the company blueprinted a proposed flying-bomb design. A month before Pearl Harbor the first three guided missiles built by RCA for the Armed Forces were tested at Muroc Lake.

Taking into account the lead-time between conception and production, it is obvious that the company had been at work on these and most of the other electronic weapons years before the advent of war. Even before the United States was officially a belligerent, RCA had licensed more than 140 manufacturers under its patents, thereby, in Sarnoff's words, "opening channels of supply for successful conduct of war." In addition to its own enlarged facilities, the company was feeding work to scores of subcontractors and suppliers.

As part of the process of streamlining for war production, RCA accelerated its timetable for centralizing all research enterprises, until then spread through half a dozen plants and laboratories. Princeton, New Jersey, was chosen as the site for a unified Research Center.

A company dinner at the Princeton Inn, on March 12, 1941, heard President Sarnoff explain the importance of the move, not alone for RCA but for the electronic arts generally. The world, he said, was on the threshold of its Electronic Age, as colossal in its consequences as the Electric Age and the Steam Age which preceded it. Just as industry and life generally had been "electrified" since the turn of the century, they would now be "electronized."

With the establishment of the new laboratories, he said, "radio quickens its pace along with the older industries—electrical, steel, automobile, wire communications, chemical, metallurgical. . . . No new industry in the history of this country has made greater strides in as short a time as radio, or contributed more extensive benefits to people in all walks of life."

Ground for the building was broken in August, 1941, and the cornerstone laid on November 15, three weeks before the skies fell in at Pearl Harbor. Construction and equipment were rushed, so that the official dedication took place only ten months later.

On the day the cornerstone was put in place, president Sarnoff was on the S.S. *Matsonia,* on his way from Honolulu to San Francisco. He not only listened to the speeches at the ceremony in New Jersey but addressed the assemblage by short-wave radio across five thousand miles. "We meet today with the solemn resolve," he said, "that the cornerstone we lay at Princeton shall help support that great cornerstone which went into the building of our nation: the freedom of the men and women of America."

By the time the Center was opened for operation in September, 1942, the United States was at war. The three-story structure in the modern style had long corridors leading to 150 separate laboratory bays, each fully equipped and manned for its special purpose. At the dedication ceremonies, in the assembly hall of the new building, Sarnoff spoke with more emotion than he normally allowed himself. "It is a great fortune that comes to very few in life," he said, "to see one's dreams of years actually in being. This is one of the dreams that has come to fruition."

"It is significant," he went on to say, "that the foundations of this building were laid in times of peace, and its superstructure has been raised in time of war. Similarly, the modern sciences of radio and electronics have their roots in peaceful soil—in the search by men of good will for ways and means to make the world a better place to live in. Yet these sciences, and all science, are now enlisted in a total war."

And that total war, he went on, has become "a contest between brains and imagination and teamwork of the scientists, engineers and production workers of one group of nations pitted against those of another group. While it is true that the decision ultimately will be made on the battlefield, the high seas, and in the air, the fighting men who have the greatest resources of science, engineering and production back of them will be the victors."

Research, as the seedbed of industrial progress, had always been Sarnoff's overriding concern. We have seen that he remained true to this faith through the gloomiest periods of economic recession, despite doubts and forthright hostility in his own ranks. Now, with the establishment of the Princeton Center, he presided over the greatest aggregation of research, inventive and engineering brains specialized in radio-electronics not only in the United States but in the world. This fact alone, whether in war or peace, made him one of the most influential industrialists in the country.

The creative complex in Princeton was destined to grow until by the 1960's it covered six acres of floor space and employed about thirteen hundred engineers, scientists, and service personnel.

2

The start of construction on the Research Center was one of many things that made the year 1941 memorable for Sarnoff. In May that year commercial television was finally authorized. In December came Pearl Harbor with its life-and-death tests for America and lesser but crucial tests for the electronics industry. But, aside from momentous public events, the year was important to him in irrevocable personal terms.

That year his mother died. Even while she was alive he was pierced with pain every time he thought of her, and now that she was gone the pain was more acute. Leah's harsh and joyless earlier life, when she carried the burdens of an invalid husband, five rambunctious children, and stark poverty, was indelible on David's memory.

Earlier in 1941, on February 27, he reached the age of fifty, which is a conspicuous and arresting milestone on any man's road. No outsider can ever guess its impact on a particular traveler. Sarnoff was too thoroughly engaged by his work to feel or voice the conventional laments on the passage of time. He had neither the inclination to brood nor the leisure to indulge it. But he did voice regrets that the margins of time for hobbies, for more diversity of human experience, and particularly for reading and study, had been so thin.

How often he had promised himself to browse in the treasure houses of literature, history, philosophy—to read, at the least, the best of the ancient and modern classics. A quick mind and a tenacious memory helped him to hold his own even in a group of the deeply read and erudite. He would say, at a later time, "The world is my *alma mater"*—it presented him with its special sheepskins and Phi Beta Kappa keys in abundance. But he was conscious that, outside his areas of specialization, there were large gaps in his education.

It is not likely, however, that he was disturbed by such regrets on his fiftieth birthday. Too many exciting challenges involving the interests of his company and the demands of his personal pride remained to be met and mastered. He was passionately absorbed in his extraordinary life's assignment. The panorama of electronics still seemed to him limitless in its possibilities, a maze of intricate branchings, with the promise of surprises around every bend. In addition, because it was so closely related to the most significant events and personalities of his time, Sarnoff had a strong sense of "making history," which for most businessmen was only a spectator sport.

Fortunately his physical constitution was a match for these large commitments. He had never had a serious illness. Though he continually put in exhausting hours, he was rarely exhausted. Except for the tendency to overweight—which he fought intermittently, under Lizette's affectionate policing—he was in first-rate condition. His mother, who masked her pride in her son with irony, was watching him at the dining table one night. "Ekh, David," she said, shaking her head sadly, "half your life you struggled to earn a piece of bread—the other half you struggle to avoid eating it."

Sarnoff was a thriving refutation of the article in the American credo which asserts that exercise is mandatory for good health. For he engaged in no sports and where possible bypassed physical exertion. "I am physically a very lazy man," he confessed to an interviewer. "I don't like to do things with my hands." The fact is that he was strictly the indoors, sedentary type endemic in New York's concrete-pavement civilization.

For a period in his thirties, all the same, he allowed himself to be persuaded by General Harbord—to whom daily exercise was a law of life—to join him in horseback riding mornings in Central Park. With the help of his cavalryman brother Lew, David acquired a horse, which he kept in a stable in the East Seventies, near his home. Conscientiously he met the general at seven every morning; but he persevered in it as a duty, not a pleasure. On rainy mornings, Lizette revealed in a magazine article, he would look out the window and announce cheerfully, "Thank goodness I don't have to ride today!"

The two men would meet at the 59th Street entrance to the park and the general was annoyed because Sarnoff was occasionally late. One morning, as they were riding side by side, Harbord had a suggestion. "David," he said, "why don't you join the riding academy to which I belong, and stable your horse there? Then we could mount together and it will not be necessary to wait for each other at the park entrance."

"General," Sarnoff replied, "my horse is eligible, but I am not."

Himself without a grain of race prejudice in his system, Harbord did not at first grasp his companion's meaning. He did not know that the riding academy to which he belonged was an "exclusive" club, and Sarnoff had to explain the facts of life to him. The general was so impressed with the poignancy of his reply that he repeated it to friends for years, and Sarnoff's offhand quip attained a certain fame.

At the half-century mark, Sarnoff was solidly built, square-shouldered, with an utterly masculine presence. Despite thinning hair and a thickening midriff, he was accounted a handsome man and women found him attractive. His light-blue eyes, set far apart, could be chill and piercing; but usually they seemed curiously boyish and mischievous, tempering the severity of his expression—and reputation. His mouth was firm, though it broke readily into an infectious smile. He had the hallmark of all Sarnoffs: a short, almost snub nose which set them aside in looks from the mostly long-nosed Privin tribe. It was a decidedly strong face.

That he had exceptional practical intelligence, boldness, and creative imagination has been made abundantly clear by the narrative this far. But beyond that there are the intangibles of character and personal relations not so easily identified. These are matters of nuance and of subjective reactions in the observer. A man may mellow as he grows older—Sarnoff was among those who did mellow—or he may become sour and crotchety. But in either case the main lines of his personality are sure to be set by the time he is fifty.

Essentially Sarnoff was a serious man, austere in his tastes and habits. Only rarely did he enjoy true, uninhibited holidays; normally he carried a large baggage of work, worries, and plans wherever he went. He could not easily, that is to say, throw off cares—his own and the world's—for any protracted period. He disliked night clubs and overly plush restaurants and avoided, when possible, miscellaneous social gatherings. While he did not object to the rumpled, bohemian looks of some of his musical and artistic friends, he was himself well groomed in conservative accents, favoring dark-blue or brown suits, white shirts, and sober ties. His wardrobe was large, the accessories ran to gold and ivory. He expected neatness and conventional attire from associates and employees.

But if this leaves the impression that he was stolid, stuffy, and unbending, the fault is with the telling. Actually, he was often in a lighthearted mood and when relaxed fun was on the agenda he readily fell into its spirit. He appreciated risqué anecdotes, if they were clever, and in the appropriate company could top the next man in an exchange of off-color stories. His youngest brother, Irving, who specialized in the commodity, sometimes telephoned him to share a "good one" he had just heard. Sarnoff's sense of humor was close to the surface and easily ignited, and in the private dissection of events and the men behind them he wielded a sharp scalpel of irony.

In the nature of things, the lighter side was not too evident in his everyday business environment, nor in his public "image." There, it was the serious Sarnoff who predominated.

The normal climate around him was one of preoccupied earnestness, a no-nonsense climate in which intimacies do not often bloom. But those in continuous touch with him, from personal secretaries to top-shelf officials, soon discovered that they were dealing with a friendly and understanding human being, far removed from "the remote and almost legendary figure" sometimes depicted by outsiders. With few exceptions, they developed a deep liking for the man, expressed in fierce loyalty to him.

Sarnoff, at his end, frequently demonstrated a personal interest in the private lives and problems of subordinates, extending quick help when specific cases of hardship came to his attention. It was no secret that he kept men and women on the payrolls, sometimes assigning them less demanding chores, when deteriorating health or other causes made them unequal to their jobs.

At the same time, he was a demanding taskmaster and drove others, if only by example, as vigorously as he drove himself. He was hardheaded, high-pressured, and efficient to an extent that disconcerted men and women with only moderate drives. The fact that he could not conceal an impatience with the slower-paced, less gifted breeds operated to upset them even more.

His passion for order, plan, relevance ("I don't make my mind a waste-basket") has been remarked by most of those who have tried to pin him down on paper. It was evident in his immaculate one-telephone desk, his succinct letters and memos, the subdued voices of secretaries. The insulation of calm around him, however, was not always reassuring to underlings; it seemed to them deceptive, like the eye of a hurricane.

Nevertheless, Sarnoff in general enjoyed the affection of his associates in the Radio Corporation to a degree rare in industrial life. In 1965 he would cite with pride that the forty principal executives of his organization averaged more than twenty years of service with the company. They joined the team as relatively young men and never left it, forging through the decades strong personal as well as professional bonds with the boss. This two-way tie of loyalty, as he frequently attested, was one of the most emotionally satisfying aspects of his career.

Within the larger electronics community, even among competitors, he had a great many admiring friends. At the same time, inevitably, he acquired some outspoken enemies. Sometimes the enmity was a kind of inverted admiration by people whom he had bested in one or another of the intense industrial contests.

"Competition brings out the best in products, and the worst in men," he once quipped—and he did not exempt himself from this dictum. Especially in an industry so young that it had few fixed rules and precedents, competition and disagreement on technical matters often bred rancor and feuds. The very vastness of the Radio Corporation, its ubiquity, its control of thousands of patents, tended to evoke hostility. Besides, the more spectacular a man's career the more envy it generates along with the acclaim.

But detractors and admirers alike would probably agree that Sarnoff was a man of enormous personal force, touched by a magnetizing quality. His good opinion of himself was implicit in the self-confidence he radiated. Whether at a small negotiating session or a large shareholders' meeting, he seemed to assume at once, by his mere presence, the dominating role. Invariably he had done his homework and knew the facts at issue as well or better than anyone else.

He was fluent, his diction near-perfect, and above all, his reasoning was clear, organized, and persuasive. "Like watching a precision instrument at work," one who had seen him often on such occasions told me. "These who had come to oppose him somehow found themselves subdued—if not won over, at least with a fading faith in their own views." A man with such a weapon at his command can disdain the little trickeries of blunter minds.

His assertive presence at meetings and conferences veiled the fact that he was essentially an introverted and reflective man. He sought and enjoyed solitude. The vocation of a college teacher, I heard him say more than once, would have suited him fine. Yet he was engrossed in communications, entertainment, advertising, surely the most extrovert of activities. This was a paradox of his character and career.

3

Sarnoff was elected president of the influential Economic Club of New York toward the end of 1940. The first discussion dinner under his gavel has a certain historical piquancy.

A letter from President Roosevelt was read that night in which there was, as those present in due time realized, a sort of preview of the celebrated Four Freedoms. The letter, dated December 2, 1940, had a lot of kind words for the private enterprise system, stressing that "it is only by keeping our economy socially conscious that we can keep it free." Then it declared:

"In our American way of life political and economic freedom go hand in hand. Our freedoms must include *freedom from want, freedom from insecurity, freedom from fear.*"

The italicized phrases, of course, are close to what the President, in his address to Congress on January 6, 1941, propounded as the Four Freedoms. Two of them—"freedom from want" and "freedom from fear"—are identical with the formulation in his Economic Club communication. What makes this circumstance relevant to the Sarnoff story is that the letter signed by Roosevelt had actually been composed by Sarnoff.

The subject scheduled for discussion at the dinner was "National Unity for Defense." In view of the persisting lack of unity between the business community and the Administration in Washington, the new club president thought it would be useful if Roosevelt sent a message to the gathering calculated to help ease those tensions. To this suggestion the President agreed at once—and asked Sarnoff to draft something he considered appropriate, the sort of thing Roosevelt was often doing. With only a few minor alterations that did not affect the substance, Sarnoff's draft was the letter read to the club.

When the President, only a month later, unveiled the Four Freedoms, Sarnoff naturally assumed that he had contributed to the felicitous formula. In time the Four Freedoms were woven into the Atlantic Charter. As they emerged as the principal war slogan in American and Allied propaganda, he took a pardonable pride in part-authorship. After the war, however, others claimed prior authorship. Since Sarnoff, in preparing his draft for Roosevelt, had drawn the idea and its wording from his own mind, it may have been a unique case of coincidence.

Another "Dear David" letter from the President, dated March 12, 1942, and addressed to the Economic Club of New York was read at a subsequent club dinner. This one, too, had been suggested and drafted by Sarnoff. The United States by then was in the war. Among those in attendance to participate in a discussion were representatives of the principal Allies, including Maxim Litvinov for the Soviet Union.

"We are united," Roosevelt said, "against those who willfully and deliberately and with every weapon of force, propaganda, and terror, are aiming to destroy man's right 'to think as he will and to say what he thinks.' We are united to maintain man's religious heritage against those who would destroy the great spiritual resources of resistance to injustice. We are united against those who would enslave humanity by substituting terror for law, treachery for statecraft, and force for justice. We are united against the tyranny that has created untold want, privation, and suffering in a large part of the world. These are the pledges inherent in the Four Freedoms which are the essence of the Atlantic Charter: freedom of speech, freedom of religion, freedom from fear, and freedom from want."

Litvinov would have been more than human if he had not squirmed inwardly as he listened to this presidential sermon. In drafting it, Sarnoff had been thoroughly aware that it was an indictment of the Soviet no less than of the Nazi dictatorship.

17

Another World War

On Sunday afternoon, December 7, 1941, which is to say before Congress had declared war, David Sarnoff sent off a terse message to President Roosevelt:

"All our facilities and personnel are ready and at your instant service. We await your commands."

Actually, the company's machinery, manpower, and research priorities had already been switched to military requirements for radio, radar, special tubes, acoustical devices, navigation systems, and an array of other electronic appurtenances. President Sarnoff was able to tell the first post-Pearl Harbor shareholders' meeting that "National defense was given the right-of-way in all RCA activities long before Pearl Harbor," and that "ordinary commercial production was voluntarily curtailed to make way for government requirements, far in advance of official restrictions." He emphasized the fact that RCA had not waited for orders from Washington to begin gearing for war:

"As far back as 1939, the company's management foresaw that RCA must be prepared to enlist for an important role in the national preparedness program, and in war production. Conversion of RCA plants, machinery, materials and manpower to meet the Government's requirements were planned far in advance of this country's entrance into the conflict."

He tried to make his audience, and the country, conscious of the tremendous role of radio in the struggle. "Radio is more than a strong arm of defense," he said. "It is a powerful weapon of offense. Wherever the Navy, the Army and Air Force go, there radio also goes. In fact, it not only goes but it guides as well. Radio watches over the convoy, it protects the fleet, and is

232

the ear and voice of the fighter plane and the tank. It helps to carry the war to the enemy's territory."

The hunger of the war machine for electronic goods was all but insatiable. Hundreds of other companies and institutions helped to satisfy that appetite, among them the Bell Laboratories, General Electric, Westinghouse, Sperry Gyroscope, the Massachusetts Institute of Technology, Stanford University. At the peak of the war effort 550 radio and electronics manufacturers produced equipment for the Armed Forces, and about a thousand more provided components of the equipment. Their output, measured in monetary values, came to more than $10 billion.

What follows, therefore, is not intended to give undue credit to the empire directed by Sarnoff. MIT, working with government agencies, was especially important in coordinating radar developments. It produced, among many other things, the centimeter wave radar equipment. Before the war ended, both the Bell Laboratories and GE were turning out electronic goods in greater quantity than RCA. But primary responsibility in vital military fields did fall to RCA. This was particularly true of innovations involving television devices and techniques.

Soon after Pearl Harbor the company scientists and engineers received a memorandum from Sarnoff. "The potentialities of television-directed weapons seem to be of the greatest importance," he told them, "and it is possible that demands may be made for delivery of units beyond our present capacity." In this area, he pointed out, all defense elements "consider RCA the only presently qualified supplier and the one able to solve remaining problems." Wartime advances in television weaponry were, in fact, spearheaded largely by RCA and its subsidiaries, in collaboration with the Office of Scientific Research and Development of the Armed Forces.

The heart of radio and electronic equipment, of course, is the endlessly versatile electron tube. RCA was not only the world's biggest producer of tubes but paramount in developing special types for scores of specialized uses. As many as 400,000 tubes a day were turned out by American industry, and RCA necessarily stimulated other qualified companies to help meet the demands. It manufactured and delivered to competing plants during the war tube-processing machinery worth some $18 million. A 99-acre manufacturing setup in Lancaster, Pennsylvania—financed for RCA by the Navy and subsequently purchased by the company—was devoted solely to tube production. RCA turned out two thousand types of tubes in the war years, including 20,000,000 miniature tubes.

Much of the electronic development, naturally, was wrapped in secrecy until after the war. Proximity fuses, for instance, were not used in combat action over hostile territory for fear that a dud might fall into enemy hands for study and imitation. Not until the war was over was it revealed that in 1943 the factory in Bloomington, Indiana, was reorganized for production of this one item, of which it assembled over five million units.

The contributions of the Radio Corporation and its subsidiaries to the war effort are of a magnitude that precludes any attempt to describe them here. They are so highly technical, so crowded with new scientific concepts and esoteric nomenclature that a layman is overwhelmed. Besides, they are more relevant to a history of RCA than to a biography of its president. In any event, what follows is little more than a random and incomplete listing— simply to suggest the gigantic scope of the work—always bearing in mind that Sarnoff stood at the center of authority, leadership, and crucial decision making.

Warfare was not yet at the "push-button" stage envisioned by science-fiction writers. But it was taking on some of its aspects. Radio and electronic robots were doing jobs previously performed by men. RCA developed and produced airborne and shipborne missiles guided by television; precision electronic bomb releases; many varieties of equipment embodying radar principles, including radar altimeters; electronic navigation systems such as shoran, loran, and radio homing beacons; electronic gunfire control devices; infrared telescope and signaling systems; sonar—underwater sound-detection and communications equipment; ultrafax or high-speed radio facsimile apparatus; electronic means for measuring projectile velocity, pulse radio systems, radio-controlled land mines, techniques for jamming or distorting enemy electronic devices; small-image orthicon camera tubes; magnetrons, which produced powerful bursts of high-frequency energy for radar mechanisms; thyratons and optical range finders.

RCA also took the lead in perfecting a variety of personal communications apparatus, such as the handie-talkie and the walkie-talkie. Instantaneous voice communication between units of an army or compartments of a battleship soon became commonplace. Familiar devices like the loudspeaker were toughened for the rugged needs of combat, and electronic means were found to send and receive messages clearly through the din of battle. For the Navy alone, RCA produced twenty-six different intercommunication systems.

The company developed radio-frequency heating equipment used by muni-tions plants, airplane factories, and shipyards for welding, annealing, bonding, and soldering. It contributed importantly to antenna experiments for micro-wave transmission. To compensate for manpower shortages, it automated machinery for making automated devices; and to meet deficits in conventional materials, it successfully developed a number of substitutes.

All the Armed Services drew on RCA staffs, when necessary, for communications and electronic specialists. An RCA expert was rushed to England to help the British develop jamming equipment to deflect German V-2 rockets from their course. Unique methods for pretesting new products and principles were pioneered in RCA plants, through laboratory duplication on a reduced scale of conditions encountered in practical operations.

The inventory is only partial. The Radio Corporation was engaged in wartime enterprises of incredible complexity and prodigious scope. Its communications and broadcasting branches were as fully dedicated to the drives for victory as the research and manufacturing facilities. The utility of every invention and development, moreover, was multiplied manifold by being made immediately available to other manufacturers and suppliers. RCA Institutes trained thousands of servicemen in radio and electronics techniques.

"Among the companies which gave our fleet the power to attack, yours has been pre-eminent," James M. Forrestal, as Secretary of the Navy, informed the president of RCA when the war was over. Equivalent commendation came to the corporation and to Sarnoff from spokesmen of all the other Services and from two Presidents of the United States. On March 18, 1946, in a White House ceremony, President Truman awarded Sarnoff—by then General Sarnoff—the highest government honor open to a civilian or member of the Reserve, the Medal of Merit; the Citation dealt exclusively with his services as head of the Radio Corporation. Aggregate RCA output for war usage came to hundreds of millions of dollars in monetary terms, but there is no arithmetic to measure its contributions in brainpower and patriotic devotion.

2

David Sarnoff, of course, was deeply dedicated to winning the war. His detestation of the Nazis knew no bounds. In public and in private he enlarged upon the importance of a clear-cut, unambiguous victory over totalitarian aggression, not only for his country but for all mankind. On a more mundane level, as a business executive, he summed up a self-evident truth when he declared:

"The safety of a company can never rise higher than its source, which is the safety of the nation. Therefore, until we win the war, no individual, no business, no investment is secure."

But single-minded concentration on war necessities, in his view, neither required nor justified neglect of postwar possibilities. On the contrary, he considered it the duty of economic leaders to plan and prepare to meet postwar problems and opportunities. His own pronouncements from 1939 to the war's end continually assessed wartime technological progress, especially in his own fields, in terms of their long-range promises, come victory and peace.

The projection of current fact into the near or remote future was an exercise congenial to the Sarnoff mind. It had become for him, with time and indulgence, almost second nature, a kind of intellectual game, over and above its practical values. Now that science and invention were boiling over in the pressure cookers of war, he had plenty of scope for its practice.

But it is evident from his addresses in that time of mass slaughter that Sarnoff was perturbed by the perversion of electronic and other scientific victories for malign and murderous purposes. Was he not one of those who had glorified the science and technology which were now spawning ever more deadly weapons and agonies? His frequent defense of science suggests an uneasy conscience—a mild case of the malady which later, after Hiroshima and Nagasaki, would bring anguish to some nuclear physicists.

In general he exonerated science, placing the blame on men and conditions. Speaking at the University of Virginia in June, 1940, he said "it is the abuse, and not the use, of the instrumentalities which science has created for civilized living" that has contributed to wars. After all, "civilization is made or broken not by machines but by men." He returned to this aching-tooth theme frequently. As if by way of consolation, he held out high, often quite exaggerated, hopes for constructive benefits tomorrow from today's technology of destruction. It was an optimism, one suspects, heightened if not consciously prompted by deep-down gnawings of guilt feelings.

A case in point is Sarnoff's reaction to the news of the splitting of the atom in 1940. In a speech in October, before the American Life Convention in Chicago, he said:

"History may record the most momentous happening in 1940 as having taken place in the laboratory rather than on the battlefield. I am thinking that the truly epoch-making event of the year may be man's first successful attempt to release atomic energy, through the isolation of Uranium 235."

He then described—rather extravagantly, as viewed a generation later—the wonderful gifts for all mankind likely to flow from the coming of atomic power. It would provide "energy on an unbelievable scale," so plentiful and so cheap that the biblical curse of labor laid upon Adam would be almost lifted: "A myriad of new products and services will become available to all. Many of the old hardships and deprivations, the sources of social and economic unrest, will disappear. A new society, dwelling in a new economy of abundance, will be born."

It seems curious, given his record for percipient technological foresight, that he failed to mention or even allude to the nightmares of annihilation inherent in the release of atomic force. Or was his rose-tinted vision of a "new society" based on atomic energy proof that he did grasp the horrors and was trying, in anticipation, to balance the score?

The Eden of Abundance which he foresaw is still, alas, very far from reality. His prophetic touch was more sure in dealing with the implications of wartime developments in more conventional dimensions, especially in his own electronics domain. About two months after Pearl Harbor he spoke to the Chicago Association of Commerce on "New Horizons in Industry." What he glimpsed beyond those horizons was in effect the displacement of men by machines which would in due course be hailed, or howled at, as "automation." He promised a far-reaching new industrial revolution through electronics: "Controlled by these new radio devices—as if they were the brains that operate the individual machines—mass production in the United States should find it possible to increase its output, with increased quality, accuracy, and safety."

The promise (or threat, as others would see it) was inherent and already visible in the extraordinary versatility of the electron tube. This device and its related mechanisms, he showed, were capable of starting and stopping, guiding and supervising, machinery. The electron now opened doors, brought elevators to level standing, operated timing devices, rang burglar alarms, counted and sorted merchandise, measured humidity and atmospheric pressures. It could be made to respond to light, to color, to a wisp of smoke, to the faintest sound or the feeblest touch, and could distinguish colors more accurately than the human eye. It could maintain calibration in machine tools more precisely than with mere human control, to tolerances hitherto considered impossible. It could measure speeds—of bullets, for instance—to 1/100,000 of a second.

And technical developments growing out of the tube-of-all-tasks, he made clear, promised far-ranging results. The electron microscope which RCA produced was opening new worlds of knowledge and progress in medicine, biology, physics, plastics, chemistry. At the same time radiothermic instruments, though still in their early embodiments, were already speeding up industrial processes in a large number of fields. In most of these areas of change, for defense now, for constructive abundance when the war was over, his own company, he claimed, was providing crucial leadership.

In 1943 the war in both Europe and the Pacific was at a dangerous stage, raging like a runaway forest fire. The facilities, energies, and brains of the Radio Corporation empire were committed to the limit and beyond. Twice in 1942, for a total of three months, Sarnoff had donned his colonel's uniform for emergency assignments in Washington, and he was constantly consulted on procurement and communications problems by all the Services, as well as by the Secretary of War and the President. In short, he was one of the busiest civilians in the country, concerned day after day with urgent immediate tasks and problems.

Yet he made the time for several ambitious efforts that year to examine the postwar era. In an address on February 4, 1943, before the Chamber of Commerce of the state of New York, he said:

"This war has demanded a total of human and material resources without precedent in history. Nothing ever happened before to compare with this titanic mobilization of manpower, of creative genius, of natural resources, of ability to create synthetic substitutes where natural resources are lacking, and the ability to manufacture and distribute this material wealth. The gigantic effort now is dedicated to the task of worldwide destruction. Yet after all of this treasure has been spilled across the globe, there will still remain enough natural resources to feed, clothe and house the world's population."

He professed to discern, beyond the holocaust, "bread in place of bullets, farm tractors in place of tanks, fertilizer in place of explosives." He believed that "the millions of tons of cargo ships, now built for the war, one day may carry the products of farm and factory needed by world peace."

The old world frontiers were those of geography; the new frontiers, he said, will be those of science. An economy of plenty was inherent in the wartime surge of industrial science. There would be more and better food, housing, and clothing; improved lighting, heating and refrigeration; better health, educational, and recreational service.

Production of aluminum and magnesium, he went on, would be enormously expanded. New steel alloys of unprecedented tensile strength, amazing plastic products, high-octane gasoline, synthetic rubber and artificial textiles, hundreds of other types of goods on a scale hitherto undreamed of could be expected. In addition there were the scientific revolutions represented by the production of clothing out of wood, dyes and chemicals and medicines out of coal, fertilizers out of thin air. And, of course, he rehearsed once more the all but miraculous role the electron tube was preparing to play in reshaping the industrial economy, and television in reshaping entertainment and culture, once the war was won and out of the way.

This conviction that vast improvements in living standards would follow the peace, not only for Americans but for humankind, colored nearly all of Sarnoff's public expressions at this time. In endless ways, he assured an audience in Lancaster, Pennsylvania, on November 11, 1943, wartime developments in electronics, chemistry, metallurgy, and physics would enable industry to enrich everyday life in America and provide surpluses for battered peoples elsewhere. Then he plunged with zest into the kind of specific predictions his audiences had come to expect when Sarnoff let out the reins of his imagination on technological matters, as he did on this occasion:

"The day may come when every person will have his own little radio station tucked away in his pocket, to hear and to communicate with his home or his office as he walks or rides along the street. We have much to learn about the microwaves, in which is wrapped up this new world of individualized radio. Tiny electron tubes may make it possible to design radio receivers and transmitters no larger than a fountain pen, a cigarette case, a billfold or a lady's powder-box. Someday people will carry television screens on their wrists, as they now carry watches. As the useful spectrum of radio approaches the frontiers of light, the apparatus will become simpler and more compact."

Radio, which has been blind, is acquiring sight, he went on: "By this I do not mean only that we shall look at pictures in motion that travel through the air. Television will have many uses. It will serve wherever sight is needed. For instance, it will be used to prevent collisions on highways and railroads, on sea lanes and on the airways of the world. Radio will be the new eye of transportation and commerce. . . . Radio, which made the world a whispering gallery, will turn it into a world of mirrors."

Nor did he limit his incandescent visions to electronics. He let himself go on the new amplitudes of living implicit in plastics, light metals, synthetic rubber and textiles, luminescent lighting, dehydration of foods, a dozen other scientific victories over matter. Pioneering and research create wealth and employment, he said—and not merely on the surface and beneath the ground. "We must lift our sights to the skies!" There he saw "new adventures and pioneering by a new generation" in the air space which he described as "a universal chemical and physical laboratory."

"We are challenged to look upward for our future. Horace Greeley, if here today, might say, 'Go up, young man, go up and grow up in space!' There lies the unfathomed West of this century, with no last frontier. There lies a vast wilderness rich in resources, opportunities, and adventures. The Forty-Niners of the present decade will be prospectors in research. They will travel through the air to stake their claims to fame, fortune, and freedom."

This was the Sarnoff style when the mood for peering into the future was upon him. Through the ages prophets of doom have tended to go to extremes —evidently prophets of glory are subject to the same tendency. Much of what he saw with his mind's eye has come to pass or may do so eventually; the rest can be checked up to the occupational hazard of excess enthusiasm. Sarnoff was and remains a romantic of science and technology, sensitive to the poetry of research and invention, fascinated and moved to a sort of science-fiction eloquence by their more remote and fabulous potentials.

He has been especially responsive to the drama of the "leap in the dark," the sudden intuitive recognition said to be common to art and invention. But even his less felicitous predictions, it must be conceded, have been consistent with the facts and portents of science; never, that is, spun out of thin air.

Sarnoff's ability to visualize tomorrow proved immensely rewarding in molding a new art and industry. It has been no less rewarding subjectively, adding to his life dimensions of excitement of a kind rarely open to other successful men of affairs. He watched the spectacle of society being transformed by science and got a thrill out of taking part in the process. The unfoldment had for him an aura of "adventure"—one of his favorite words— aside from economic values and business opportunities.

Thus in the midst of the bloodiest war in history, under the cumulative burdens of a key place in a key military industry, he could evoke compensating visions of peace and plenty to come. "Personally," he said during these years, "I have faith in the irresistible urge of the human spirit to survive and go forward." He would need that faith when peace came, and with it the rise of a new totalitarian challenge in place of the one just defeated.

3

To meet the acute shortage of nurses, the Red Cross mobilized and trained women volunteers. Mrs. Lizette Sarnoff had been on the Board of Trustees of the New York Infirmary for a dozen years. She now became chairman of the Red Cross Nurses Unit in this hospital on a full-time schedule and for the duration, with some 150 nurses under her charge. She looked exceedingly handsome in her officer's uniform, as proved by a photograph that still enjoys conspicuous display in her home. Her interest in hospital work was unabated after the war was over, when she continued to give two or three days a week as director of the women volunteers in the Infirmary.

The eldest Sarnoff son, Robert, graduated from Harvard in 1939. Largely because he knew that his father hoped one of his boys would become a lawyer, he enrolled in the Columbia Law School. Since he had no sense of vocation for the law—his thoughts were then veering to a career in advertising —he was not unhappy to leave the school to enter government service. Subsequently, he joined the Navy, serving first in Washington and then in the Pacific theatre as a communications officer. At the war's end, leaving the Navy with the rank of lieutenant, he did not return to the study of law.

Brother Edward had some military training, also in communications, at Brown University. Soon after Pearl Harbor he enlisted in the Army Signal Corps and saw nearly four years of intensive service in the Pacific, including a number of the key battles in that theatre. He was a captain on assignment on the battleship *Missouri* and an eyewitness to the climactic scene of the war, when General Douglas MacArthur accepted the unconditional Japanese surrender.

The youngest, Thomas, was ten weeks short of fifteen on Pearl Harbor Day. Like his brothers before him, he was then studying at Phillips Academy in Andover. Upon graduation, in 1942, he entered Princeton. In late 1944, before he was eighteen, he too joined the Army Signal Corps, being accorded the rank of sergeant on the basis of previous training in communications. Before the war's end, despite his extreme youth, he was assigned for a period as instructor in radio at West Point. When he was offered a commission he declined. "There's enough brass in the family already," he said. Proving that he had plenty of brass of another order.

Thus the whole Sarnoff family was enlisted in the war effort. Their home and their lives, like RCA, were on a full war footing.

18

In the European Theatre

ᴈ David Sarnoff, who was nearing his fifty-first birthday when the United States entered the war, at once offered to join up for active service wherever he might be needed.

Ever since the war broke out in 1939, apparently, he had talked about possibly switching to military or government service. He could hardly have been too serious, but at least one military man was concerned enough to implore him not to do so. Having been among the first, back in 1918, to advocate the formation of a great American radio organization, S. C. Hooper —by now a rear admiral—regarded himself as a kind of godfather to RCA.

In a personal letter to Sarnoff in September, 1940, he argued with some warmth that because of its importance to national defense the corporation was now "a ship-of-war," and exclaimed: "Should the skipper be changed during the storm?" As he saw it, "RCA is David Sarnoff," whose overriding patriotic duty was therefore to continue in command.

Others in the military establishment might not have been so emphatic or so flattering. But the prevalent view was that Sarnoff, like many other key figures in war industries, could best serve by staying put. He was officially advised, as he had been in the First World War, to remain at his post in industry.

Several times, however, he was mobilized for direct military tasks. In the aggregate these intervals in uniform came to almost a year, more than seven months of it overseas, the rest of the time in Washington. During his absences he was not only formally on leave from the Radio Corporation but, to obviate conflicts of interest, cut himself off completely from its affairs. Although he was under no legal obligation to do so, he refused to accept his RCA salary while on active military duty.

Never before had a war machine demanded so much precision equipment in so short a time. By the middle of 1942, Army Signal contracts with radio and electronic suppliers ran to billions of dollars. The problems of procurement were vast and fantastically complicated. Most of the products involved were of recent invention and evolving in new directions with disorienting rapidity. Orders for equipment were virtually all of emergency character and fulfillment was under frenzied time pressures.

The situation bred confusions, duplications, and assorted snafus. On the one hand, there were delays in delivery; on the other, bottlenecks in distribution that piled up many tons of essential apparatus at depots. Along with the problems of coordination, manpower, allocation of deficit materials common to all war industry, there were others unique to the fledgling electronics business.

Colonel Sarnoff was among the Reserve officers called in by the Signal Corps to help rationalize procedures and untie knots. He was summoned to active duty in the capital on June 25, 1942, for only a two-week stint and again on August 27 for a two-month period. In the first of these tours of duty he ran through two titles in the two weeks: as vice-chairman and then as chairman of the Army Signal Corps Advisory Council to the Chief Signal Officer. In the second and longer tour, similarly, he carried a variety of imposing titles, reflecting transfers from one area to another on troubleshooting assignments.

The most durable designation was that of executive assistant to the Director of the Signal Supply Service. To indicate the immensity of this Service we may note that funds appropriated for Signal Corps equipment in 1943 would come to $5 billion, and that by 1944 it would have jurisdiction over some 32,000 officers, enlisted men, and civilians. This division also supervised and coordinated Signal research in both Army and private laboratories.

In the last month of the second tour Sarnoff was transferred to new duties, as special executive director to the Chief Signal Officer—a spot in which he could help expedite some of the procedural reforms he had worked out while with Supply Service. Among other things, in the final weeks, he served as president of a Special Board of Officers selected "to investigate certain allegations of deficiencies within the Signal Corps." The report that he drafted cleared the Corps of most of the alleged sins but found others plausible and proposed measures for their correction.

Colonel Sarnoff performed no miracles. The Signal Corps, like most other branches of the military apparatus, would continue to suffer headaches to the very end. But he did achieve ameliorations that plucked praise from superiors.

His suggestions for simplifying procedures and standardizing some types of equipment were all adopted. A central statistical agency within the Corps to provide dependable data for the coordination of procurement was set up along the lines he proposed. He inspected and reported on radar and radio training schools.

One of the thorniest technical problems in 1942—the chronic gap between demand and supply for electron tubes—was dropped in his lap. The fact that RCA plants alone that year had on their books 25,000 orders for more than 150,000 different tube items is an index to the size of the problem. Sarnoff arranged conferences of key Signal Corps officers and representatives of related military agencies from all the Services. Under his guidance some twenty specific recommendations for speeding up production and expediting distribution were agreed upon. Technical surveys were initiated that led to considerable standardization of tubes and of machine tools for their manufacture. If the ailments were not cured—new varieties of the electron tube to match new uses continued to proliferate—they were decidedly less inflamed when RCA's chieftain wound up his missions.

In all this work he had the advantage of being a civilian temporarily in uniform, without inhibitions in defining errors that might reflect on the brass. While politely ruling out criticism of the past or of personalities, he spoke out sharply. "Requirements to date have not been met," he said in one report to the Director of Supply Service. "Unless practical solutions are found promptly to the many pressing problems of facilities, materials, components, balanced production and distribution which beset the program of the Signal Corps," there could be dire consequences for the whole war effort.

But his forthright warnings were always matched with concrete ideas for curative action. Nearly two years later, when he was operating in the European theatre of conflict, Sarnoff often had to deal with officers from whom he was now demanding immediate results. The fact that they had developed a healthy respect for his judgment and courage in 1942 would prove useful to him.

One incidental service that Sarnoff performed in the final month figures in the annals of espionage and counterespionage of the period. In the long formal citation of his contributions, supporting the recommendation that he be promoted to brigadier general, this incident is prominently listed.

Colonel Sarnoff, it attested, "initiated a report to the Chief Signal Officer under date of October 19, 1942, on the subject of 'Secrecy of Communications.' In that report attention was called to the possibility of enemies tapping undersea cables and dangers therefrom in our war effort. Recommended an experiment to prove this possibility. As a result of this recommendation, and at the direction of G-2, this experiment was carried out by the Navy Department, substantiating the conclusions in the above report."

The suspicion that underseas cables could be tapped by an enemy was not born in Sarnoff's mind. It had been raised by electronics experts as far back as 1920 but somehow had failed to register in the military establishment. Once aware of the possibility, however, Sarnoff never forgot it. Meanwhile the refinement of electronic powers tended to raise the suspicion to a near-certainty.

The Atlantic was swarming with German submarines. The geographical pattern of ship sinkings showed that the enemy hunted close to the transocean cables. Why, then, did he refrain from cutting the cables, as the Germans had done promptly in World War I and were expected by the Allies to do in the new war? Colonel Sarnoff's answer was simple and startling—President Roosevelt, who was briefed on the subject, was among those startled.

If Hitler's U-boats were siphoning off valuable information by tapping and decoding cabled messages, Sarnoff pointed out, they would scarcely wish to interrupt their flow. His merit was that he had focused attention on the danger so persuasively that it led to immediate experiments by the Navy. These confirmed the old suspicion and that in turn led to revised coding and other preventive measures.

At the end of October, Sarnoff returned to the piled-up tasks and the backlog of postponed decisions in his corporate office, practically all of them related to the war effort. While he was frequently consulted on confidential military matters, he did not again don his uniform until the home-stretch spring of 1944.

2

On March 10, 1944, Colonel Sarnoff reported, as ordered, to the Commanding Officer, Plant Engineering Agency, in Philadelphia. There he was instructed to touch base with Signal officers in Washington, then fly without delay for sixty days' service in the European theatre. He arrived in London on March 20, a chill, blustery day. Motoring from the airport to the city, he observed the bomb-torn body of London and sensed its mutilation of spirit in the fifth year of war.

Sarnoff, as mentioned before, sometimes gauged his progress in life by certain successive journeys across the Atlantic. It was a gauge of progress he used from time to time—more in wonder than in boastfulness—both in private conversation and in public speeches. Because it all began with his traumatic crossing in steerage as a child of nine, he was touched by the symbolism of the ascending series.

There was the Atlantic trip as 'Coni man on a passenger vessel, in slick uniform and with officer rating, only seven years after the bewildered ordeal by steerage. There was the trip in 1929 with the reparations mission, when he was so frankly impressed by the celebrity of his companions and the ceremonious official reception in France. There were others. But the journey in March, 1944, would cap and crown the list; all subsequent crossings would be anticlimax. The symmetry of the graph was spoiled a bit by the fact that this time he crossed by airplane, not by ship, but the principle of dramatic contrast was not impaired.

The war service he was called upon to render, as special assistant on communications to General Dwight D. Eisenhower, Supreme Commander of SHAEF, would give him deep and lasting satisfaction. He was to make a direct, personal contribution to American victory, over and above the contributions through his company. It would be recognized and rewarded with official honors.

Aside from the fact that it was related to communications, he was not told in advance of the nature or scope of his assignment. His initial guess was that it involved some urgent matters of procurement, as on the two previous occasions when he was drawn into active duty. From the inauspicious approach via Philadelphia he could not surmise that he had been tapped for a role, as difficult as it was important, in the grand denouement of the war with Germany; nor that the sixty days' duty would stretch to over nine months, the first seven of them overseas.

After a while he was able to piece together the circumstances that landed him in the very thick of that spring's war events.

With preparations for the invasion of Hitler-held Europe gathering impetus, General Eisenhower and his staff were increasingly concerned about the communications aspects of the plan. Besides the needs for military purposes, there were multiplying problems with respect to the press and radio reporting of D day and its aftermath to an anxious world. Full and fast coverage of the assault on Fortress Europe was rated by all Allies as second in importance only to military victories. But facilities were plainly inadequate. To make matters worse, radio and cable channels, mostly in the hands of competitive companies, were not coordinated for efficiency under emergency traffic loads. Also, there was within SHAEF some duplication of responsibilities on these problems.

Meanwhile the pressures of journalistic competition, between agencies and between nations, were on the rise. Organizations and hordes of individual correspondents and commentators were jockeying for inches of advantage, come the great day. In some cases private deals had been made at the American end and between news outfits and communications companies. The British were disinclined to combine their communications resources with the Americans', and the French under de Gaulle had their own ideas of control of communications inside their country once its liberation was under way.

General Eisenhower therefore requested Washington to send him the best communications expert in the country, someone competent and big enough to take the convoluted problems off his shoulders. To the Signal Corps and to others involved in the selection, this spelled David Sarnoff; there was no runner-up, no alternative choice. President Roosevelt independently suggested his name.

The man designated had to be a top-notch negotiator as well as a strategist of communications in the technical sense. Sarnoff fitted the specifications. Probably he knew more about the global webs of communication, wired and wireless, than any other man alive. Through the years he had dealt with all the radio and cable interests in the United Kingdom, France, and the rest of Europe. He knew from the inside the physical setups, the personalities, and the national quirks in every area of communication.

At the time Sarnoff reached London the city had suffered through long months of bombing and privation. It was a grim metropolis. But people drew consolation from the knowledge, no longer secret, that "the balloon was going up" soon—the popular euphemism for the coming invasion. The long-deferred "Second Front" was about to be opened.

Quartered at the Claridge and provided with offices at the MOI (Ministry of Information) Building, Colonel Sarnoff was at once put through the formality of a security check, emerging fully "bigoted," the curious code word for "cleared." Thereupon he was briefed by Major General Rumbough, Commander of ETOUSA (European Theatre of Operations) on his assignment. It embraced inspection, analysis, reorganization, and expansion where indicated, of every phase of communications preparedness, for combat and news coverage, related to the invasion and liberation of Europe.

The president of RCA, of course, was not starting from scratch. Hundreds of men had worked on the problems for months, some of them for years. But everything now needed testing and acceleration. The undertones of doubt, the feeling that the communications picture was still murky, were justified by the reality as Sarnoff appraised it. In a candid accounting to Washington superiors, soon after D day, he wrote that he had found "a picture of confusion":

"With no compass or chart to guide me and with no one in P & PW [Press and Press Wireless] or PRD [Public Relations Division] familiar with the technical and traffic problems of communications, I pitched in and tried to do the best I could, at a time when the clock hand was moving uncomfortably close to twelve. Some things had to be undone and changed, and others had to be created."

As a mere colonel he was outranked by droves of American and Allied officers in his arenas of activity. None of them, however, questioned his technological and administrative superiority. With the full weight of the Supreme Commander's support behind him—and, before long, that of Winston Churchill as well—Sarnoff came close to justifying the exaggerated reference to him in a press article as "communications czar."

Early on the morning of his second day in London he reported to General Eisenhower at SHAEF headquarters, being introduced by the Commander's Chief of Staff, General W. Bedell Smith. It was the first of several meetings in the ensuing months. Their acquaintance would ripen as an enduring friend-ship—in their frequent postwar correspondence it would be "Dear Dave" at one end "Dear Boss" at the other. Sarnoff was encouraged to learn that the Supreme Commander appreciated the critical importance of communications and appeared aware of existing deficiencies. He outlined to Sarnoff three pressing tasks:

First, he wanted the creation well before D day of an independent SHAEF broadcasting station for contact with his troops in all European and Mediter-ranean theatres. He considered it necessary to end dependence on the British Broadcasting Company for this purpose.

Second, Eisenhower wanted a comprehensive inspection of existing and planned military communications systems being readied for the great assault and the subsequent struggle on the Continent. It was recognized that early communications for the press, from the battle areas, would have to be provided by the military authorities. Hence a check of equipment, manpower, training, everything was indicated, as basis for corrective measures where necessary.

Third, and most important, Sarnoff was to appraise the facilities and capacity for every type of news coverage, including electronic transmission of still pictures, from the scenes of action. While there could be and should be no favored treatment for American reporters, General Eisenhower wished to guarantee that the American people got the news as soon and as amply as anyone else.

"That's the story, Colonel Sarnoff," the general said in substance. "Don't hesitate to use my full authority in dealing with our own or Allied officials. Requisition all the men, equipment, and transport you need." He grinned and added, "In case of roadblocks you can get to me at once through Bedell here."

"Yes, sir!" Sarnoff said. He rose, saluted, and left.

He had asked no questions. It was now *his* job, not Eisenhower's. He realized that the assignment, though neatly divided into three tasks, actually blanketed the whole field of communications, from mobile transmitters on beachheads and battlefields to worldwide radio networks. He took the measure of his responsibilities and found it exhilarating.

3

Before the end of the day of his first briefing by General Eisenhower, Sarnoff had selected a site for a powerful SHAEF broadcasting station and had seen the planning for its construction started. A separate organization and staff had to be set up while the building was under way. The station was in operation before D day.

The task forces being prepared for the invasion included communications units, for radiotelegraph contacts with London under combat conditions. Personnel for this function were being trained in special British and American schools. Since this was an all-important link in the communications chain, Sarnoff visited several of the schools, selected almost at random, without delay. The experience was discouraging. In theory the trainees should already have been able to send and receive at least twenty-five words a minute. Sarnoff began by testing one of the teachers—outside the classroom to avoid possible embarrassment—and discovered that the man could barely manage ten words a minute. The showing by students, understandably, was even worse.

Colonel Sarnoff summoned the responsible officers and read the riot act. Abler teachers were quickly assembled, inept trainees were eliminated, and the whole undertaking tightened. He kept an eye on it thereafter and could note gradual improvement. When the telegraph units on battlefields, in the time of test, performed adequately—as with some exceptions they did—he had special reason to be pleased.

With respect to facilities and procedures for press and radio reporters, the word spread quickly as to who was "the man to see." The heat was diverted from SHAEF headquarters to Sarnoff headquarters. The news media, the respective official agencies (MOI and OWI), broadcasting officials, everyone converged upon him with problems, complaints, proposals, occasionally with camouflaged schemes for outwitting competitors. Sarnoff's obligation was to cut through such maneuvers and assure for the fourth estate absolute equality of opportunity in covering the impending drama.

This, however, could be achieved only if transmission facilities were equal to the expected traffic. As of mid-April the American companies, Western Union and Commercial Cables, and the British monopoly, Cables & Wireless, Ltd., were sending a maximum of 130,000 words a day and were not equipped to handle much more. In conferences with Sir Edward Wilshaw, top executive of Cables & Wireless, Sarnoff was assured that two additional transmitters already under construction would be completed by June 1. This would provide a daily radiotelegraph capacity to the United States (beyond, that is, the company's own needs for the British Empire) of 200,000 words. The combined facilities of the cable companies could transmit another 200,000.

The best estimates Sarnoff's staff could obtain anticipated a news volume of at least 500,000 words on D day—a total unprecedented in the history of transoceanic journalism. (The actual count on invasion day proved to be 570,000 and it remained close to the 500,000 mark on the following days.) To take up the surplus traffic, Sarnoff proposed the use of U.S. Army Signal Corps channels. This required permissions from Washington, which came through quickly, and acceptance by commercial companies, which at first were apprehensive of the arrangement but grudgingly agreed.

More important, he insisted upon the pooling of all American and British facilities under centralized management for the period of emergency. His goal was total coordination. Also, because the capabilities for electronic transmission of pictures were still extremely limited, he encouraged the formation of a common Photo Pool. At two successive meetings of representatives of all the civilian and military groups concerned, Colonel Sarnoff outlined his plans for a single and unified Signal Center. Located in the MOI Building, it would centralize and thereby expedite all the filing of dispatches, censorship, and the allocation of transmission facilities to avoid overloading any one channel.

Despite some initial resistance, the plan was adopted and the necessary construction of special studios and traffic control systems was ordered on a crash basis. A Traffic Control Committee was set up to work out equitable and effective regulations, and Sarnoff, as a member and then as its chairman, provided the continuing leadership.

Facilities for direct broadcasting across the Atlantic, too, required expansion. There was only one short-wave circuit between London and New York, serving the four American broadcasting chains. By hard bargaining and some political pressure Sarnoff got the British Post Office to lease one of its circuits for American use. The Signal Corps, at his urging, erected a new transmitter. In the end at least three of the American networks could thus broadcast simultaneously from England, and from the Normandy battlefields by London relay.

One of the chronic bottlenecks, the records of the time indicate, was British reluctance or inability to go along with some of the SHAEF communications arrangements being pushed by the American colonel. In part this was due to pride of service and concern for British prestige. Possibly there was also some uneasiness that excessive credit and glory for the reconquest of the Continent might accrue to the Americans.

"The BBC people were suspicious," Colonel Edward M. Kirby, one of the officers engaged in the negotiations, declared after the war. "They feared an American effort to achieve a dominance on the air in ratio to the greater number of troops the United States would throw into the assault on Fortress Europe."

Whatever the reasons, the British were sticky about pooling BBC with American channels. When Sarnoff proposed that all the facilities of the American Forces Network be merged with other Allied facilities in a renamed Allied Forces Network, the Ministry of Information demurred. BBC even required a lot of persuasion before it would lease its transmitter at Start Point to the Allied Forces Network.

Since the difficulties were political and psychological, rather than technical, Sarnoff decided to go to the top of the British hierarchy. At his request, Eisenhower set up a conference for him with Winston Churchill. He had met the Prime Minister socially in the United States through their mutual friend Bernard Baruch. Churchill, despite his titanic responsibilities in that critical time, appeared well informed on the communications squabbles. He listened patiently to the American's presentation, declared himself sympathetic with at least some of the contentions of his own countrymen—then brushed everything aside in the interest of unity for the invasion.

Thenceforth Colonel Sarnoff could invoke the authority of the Prime Minister, along with that of the Supreme Commander, in sparking action or removing obstructions. He consulted with the seventy-year-old leader on a later occasion, at a private luncheon with Winston and Mrs. Churchill at 10 Downing Street. In fact, though he had scant enough margins of time for socializing, Sarnoff felt it expedient in the interests of his job to meet many British leaders, among them the Postmaster General, the First Lord of the Admiralty, and a number of prewar acquaintances like Ernest Bevin, then

Minister of Labour. He attended a luncheon in his own honor given by the Board of Directors of the London *Times,* and a meeting of the British Institute of Radio Engineers, presided over by Lord Mountbatten, at which he was elected an honorary member.

Well before "the balloon went up," British communications were substantially integrated with other Allied facilities, though BBC remained openly unhappy about the Allied Forces Network. Its spokesmen argued that broadcasts aimed at both the American and British troops would miss one audience or the other. The British Tommy, the Information Minister, Brendan Bracken, once explained, will no more understand jokes by Bob Hope than the American GI could understand the jokes in *Punch.* The primary purpose of the network, however, was not humor. On the whole the Sarnoff plans prevailed, with semantic and command-post concessions to assuage British doubts.

To avoid burdening this narrative with too many technical details, suffice it to say that Sarnoff, between his arrival in England and D day about ten weeks later, found himself ringmaster in a three-ring circus. He dealt with military, commercial, and political problems and performers.

He saw to the creation of a mobile Army Signal Headquarters equipped and staffed for advancing into Europe in pace with the hoped-for military advance. Private companies in the transatlantic cable and radio business had to be coordinated with their British counterparts. The Signal Corps facilities had to be fitted into the pattern without alarming commercial interests. Preparations had to be made for tying VHF wireless and cable links on the English side of the Channel with their terminals on the French side if they had not been wholly destroyed by the enemy. Above all, the highly complex Signal Center must be finely tuned for faultless action when the great torrents of news descended. On May 25 a "dress rehearsal" was staged and the results were judged to be satisfactory.

When everything appeared fixed and ready, the affable, redheaded Brendan Bracken invited Sarnoff to call upon him. To the American's perplexity, the Minister of Information chose to lecture him on the vastness of the British Empire, the special burdens of communications this imposed, and the wholehearted help BBC had extended to the U.S. Forces. Then he came to the point.

His country wanted and deserved, Bracken said, a minor concession of immense political value to the Empire—namely, just five minutes' head start for BBC in flashing the first news of the invasion! Sarnoff concealed his astonishment as best he could. His orders from the Supreme Commander himself, he said, were explicit: to guarantee absolute equality. A five-minute, or five-second, advantage to anyone was therefore out of the question.

"Well," the Information Minister laughed, "my job was to ask you—and I've asked."

Colonel Sarnoff was not among the few who shared the central secret—the date of the invasion. But when he was instructed to make a final inspection of installations along the coast of South England, beginning on May 29, he realized that the time was near. These installations were geared for contact with the invasion armada and the beaches, some for immediate service and the rest on a standby basis. The tour also included inspection of the U.S. battleship *Ancon,* equipped as a floating electronic system. Scheduled to be anchored at a mid-point in the English Channel, it would be capable of taking over if communications were bogged down on the beaches.

Colonel Sarnoff was accompanied on this assignment by the Chief Signal Officer of the British Army and his American opposite number, General F. N. Lanahan. Traveling by car, the three men examined equipment and checked on organizational readiness at Plymouth, Torquay, Taunton, Somerset, and a number of other places.

The high point of that expedition was the visit aboard the *Ancon.* Aside from the normal naval contingents, about a thousand trained men were deployed for electronic jobs. The ship's main studio was actually larger than the largest at BBC or back home at NBC. But amusing trifles sometimes cling to memory long after big and solemn affairs are forgotten:

The visiting brass was being conducted through the *Ancon* by a young Signal lieutenant. In the main studio there were long lines of radio receivers of a large variety of makes, among them a good many of RCA manufacture. "Which of these receivers do you consider best?" Sarnoff asked disingenuously.

"Not one of them is worth a damn, sir," the lieutenant replied, "except this one, that I built myself."

The generals, roaring with laughter, thereupon informed him that their companion was president of RCA. Though he blushed with embarrassment, the young man, to his credit, stuck bravely to his verdict. In telling the story Sarnoff points out that it is typical of radio amateurs to believe that only their own handicraft is ever good enough—and, he adds, "quite often they're right."

About twenty-four hours before the invasion, Colonel Sarnoff was ordered to man all equipment and "stand by" for the agreed-upon signal, due when the first human waves hit the beaches of Normandy. The tension in the MOI Building was almost unbearable. But he was confident that communications— which ten weeks earlier he had considered "a picture of confusion"—were now in good order.

19

D Day and After

◈ The Allied invasion of Hitler-held Europe, like all historic turning points, looked different from differing angles of vision. For the hordes of journalists and editors and photographers poised to report the invasion, it was "the greatest coverage of a single event in the history of the world"—the quotation is from a postwar speech by an American military man close to the operation at the London Signal Center. The "story" was told to a keyed-up humanity both swiftly and amply.

The first flash that the invasion had begun came at 7:32 A.M. Greenwich Mean Time. The news circled the world before 7:33 A.M.

In their natural jitters as the release of the "balloon" came closer and closer, correspondents and broadcasters had feared technical and administrative bogdowns, which were not exactly rare in military campaigns. The forebodings proved unfounded. From the invading vessels and the beaches, from command posts, from London editorial mills, hundreds of thousands of words flowed smoothly into the Signal Center and thence across oceans and continents.

Colonel Sarnoff and his associates could inform headquarters in Washington within twenty-four hours that everything had got off to an "exceptionally successful start"; that all facilities and personnel were functioning according to plan; and that the U.S. Army Signal Corps, by taking up surplus traffic, had prevented a logjam. It was an unprecedented performance in the gathering and transmission of news under unprecedented tensions.

Considering the size of the action and the confusions inherent in desperate battles on extended fronts, SHAEF communications seemed a triumph of intelligent planning. The general public accepted the scope, speed, and precision of the reporting and the eyewitness broadcasts as a matter of course. It was not aware that this represented a near-miracle of technological efficiency and, of course, could have no idea that one American specialist played a decisive part in making this possible. The professionals, however, knew the facts and were generous in acknowledging them.

Forty-eight hours after D day, for example, the manager of the London Bureau of the Associated Press, Robert Bunnelle, wrote to Colonel Sarnoff:

"We've had hundreds of messages from all over the United States applauding the invasion coverage. Since no story is any good until it gets to the newspapers and radio stations, hats are off again to Colonel David Sarnoff who not only knows how to deliver news and picture copy to the ultimate consumer but how to cut through red tape that might delay such delivery. All your friends in New York asked me to pass along to you 'our gratification and appreciation.' "

On June 16 the London offices of the four United States broadcasting networks dispatched a collective letter to the Chief of the Public Relations Section, SHAEF, conveying their thanks for its splendid cooperation during "the frenzy of the first few days of invasion coverage operations." It was signed by Edward R. Murrow for Columbia Broadcasting, Stanley T. Richardson for National Broadcasting, John S. Steele for Mutual Broadcasting, George Hicks for the Blue Network. A top executive official of Columbia Broadcasting in New York, Paul Kesten, addressed a message of thanks to Sarnoff. It referred to his "heroic work in providing additional facilities, which made it possible for all networks to do a job of invasion coverage which you can be properly proud of."

Approbation also came from SHAEF and from Washington. The Chief Signal Officer at the home base, General H. C. Ingles, wrote to Sarnoff after D day: "It was apparent to us here that the requirements for press and broadcast communications associated with the invasion were of such magnitude as to point directly to your selection for this assignment, and to require all the resourcefulness, experience and organizing talent which you possess. . . . It is apparent that your estimate of the situation and your performance of a difficult and exacting task has been outstanding." The gist of the matter, perhaps, was expressed by General Stoner in the course of a transatlantic telephone conversation on July 18, the text of which is on record. "Dave," he said, "you got us out of chaos there." This was the prevailing judgment at SHAEF.

A formal recommendation that Sarnoff be promoted to brigadier general was made, through channels, by General Lanahan, Deputy Chief of the Signal Division at Supreme Headquarters, on June 29. The timing, about three weeks after the invasion, indicates that it was in recognition of the services connected with that event. But the military mills grind slowly; a number of subsequent successful activities would be added to Sarnoff's dossier before the promotion came through.

His assignments, as outlined by General Eisenhower in their initial conference, were accomplished. He had never before been completely out of touch with Radio Corporation affairs for such a long period. But if he had illusions about an early return to civilian status, they were soon canceled out. A number of urgent matters in his area of competence, in France and in the Mediterranean theatre, needed his attention. Though they were quickly given the belittling nickname of "doodlebugs," the sudden downpour of Hitler's V-1 missiles, beginning on June 12, dampened the spirit of Londoners, and served as notice that the conflict was far from over.

For some weeks, as chairman of the Traffic Control Committee, Sarnoff remained responsible for the Signal Center. As the tensions of D day subsided, the competitive impulses in press and broadcasting sharpened, creating new complexities. Mobile transmitters of the American, British, and Canadian armies were sending some ten thousand words a day from the battlefields. Directly from beachheads, by means of VHF transmission, broadcasts were pouring into England for relay to other countries. News was being rushed from the Continent by nearly every conceivable means—teleprinters, telegraphy, a Dispatch Rider Service, an Air Dispatch Service. Even pigeons were used successfully in the first days of combat, especially by reporters with paratroopers dropped behind enemy lines.

Nearly all of this traffic was funneled into the London Signal Center for processing and release. And for Colonel Sarnoff there were incidental stints from time to time, such as his inspection of radio installations at Portsmouth.

Much of his time and energy, too, were devoted to negotiations with a French Mission in London on problems of communication in the rapidly expanding liberated areas. Regulations for the management of facilities—some destroyed by the Germans, others reported in good preservation—raised not only technical but political problems. French telegraph and radio services obviously had to be marshaled for the needs of the Expeditionary Forces, and at times this imperative collided with General de Gaulle's ideas on national prestige. At the same time civilian communications had to be opened up as soon as possible.

A formal agreement was finally reached with the French PTT (*Postes, Télé-*

graphes et Téléphones). Colonel Sarnoff left no loopholes on the basic principle that in the military zones any disputes on priorities and maintenance would be resolved by SHAEF. At this stage he did not know that some of the burden of activating French communications would soon devolve upon himself.

As early as July 15, moreover, Sarnoff began to concern himself with telecommunications in Germany, looking ahead to the time when Allied armies would advance beyond the French frontiers. The invasion of Germany was still very much in the future, but he believed that the special problems posed in the enemy homeland must be thought through well in advance. He therefore formulated for the Signal Corps a series of guidelines. These ultimately became the basis for a full plan of operation he himself would be called upon to develop.

Sarnoff had his baptism by fire, his first experience on the actual fighting fronts, during a two weeks' mission of inspection in France, beginning on July 18. Close as he had been to the military enterprise since he reached Europe, direct confrontation with the gory business of killing and dying affected him more profoundly than he had expected.

From France, at the end of the month, he was ordered to the Mediterranean theatre. He flew from England, on a freight plane, to North Africa. There he diagnosed and prescribed for the distempers of military communications in Algiers and Morocco, presumably in relation to the new Allied offensive against southern France. Then he made his way to Italy, catching up with General Mark Clark north of Rome and participating briefly in the American advance toward Florence.

That duty finished, he was recalled to SHAEF and attached to General Eisenhower's Headquarters in France, at Granville. These dizzying shifts of mission usually necessitated new titles. For a time he figured in the official orders as Special Assistant to the Deputy Signal Officer, SHAEF; and in the final period of overseas duty as Deputy Chief, Army Communications Service. He was scarcely aware himself, as he was rushed from one trouble spot to another, what his current official label might be.

2

Restoration of French radio and telegraph services at the earliest possible moment was vital for both military and psychological reasons. Particular significance was attached to the renewal of direct radiotelegraphy from Paris to London and to New York, suspended ever since the Germans had occupied the capital. Primary responsibility in this connection was assigned to Sarnoff. With his arrival in Granville, he was thus committed to a task that, among his assignments for SHAEF, was second in importance only to his D day job.

Allied divisions were approaching the Seine on August 24 and rioting against the Germans, led by the Resistance movement, erupted in Paris and its environs. The German occupying forces were hurriedly withdrawing. That evening the first French troops, an armored formation, rolled into the city. Throughout the capital radios blared out the good news and all church bells rang. The following day, August 25, the U.S. Fourth Division drove into Paris, to be greeted by wild, hysterical crowds.

When word had reached Granville headquarters that Paris was being liberated, Sarnoff set off at once by jeep for the capital, a distance of about two hundred miles. He was accompanied by Major Hays, a nephew of the Will Hays who was then "czar" of the American movie industry. They made what speed they could through a terrain recently under bombing and bombardment, still littered with corpses and wrecked vehicles, the air heavy with the odors of decay and charred houses.

They reached Paris on the night of August 25, a day before General de Gaulle made his triumphant entry. There were still rear-guard German snipers on rooftops and sounds of blasting in the distance as evidence of demolition activities by the retreating forces.

Early next morning, after a few hours' sleep, Sarnoff made a rapid survey of the local situation. He established contact with American military headquarters, surmising correctly that he might need its help before the day was over. Then he headed for the old offices on Boulevard Haussmann he had known so well before the war, those of the French Wireless Company (CTSF), of which Radio France was a subsidiary.

He was in field uniform and helmet, unshaved, with muddy boots, a pistol on his hip. He went straight to the director's sanctum, where he had so often in the past visited to discuss business, and unceremoniously threw its door open. He was most curious as to what he would find.

What he did find was utterly unexpected and astonishing. For the scene was unchanged, precisely as he remembered it from his last prewar visit, as if preserved in deep-freeze through all the years of carnage and chaos. There, behind the same desk, sat the same man: Émile Girardeau, a radio pioneer who had occupied a place in the French industry roughly equivalent to his own in American radio.

The Frenchman rose and stared in disbelief, then burst into tears. He embraced and kissed the American and, still weeping, tried to give an account of his ordeal. The foreign conquerors had ordered him to remain at his old post, but working under German surveillance and stripped of all real power. His joy at the reunion, the living proof of his liberation, was apparently diluted by fear—Sarnoff's first intimation of the panic that was already gripping those who had collaborated with the conquerors, even if under compulsion.

"I am here in the name of the United States Army," Sarnoff said. "You're a free man again, and all I want you to do now is to get your staff and operators together at once and restore short-wave contact with London and New York."

"But I have no authority over my men," Girardeau said. "Why should they obey me? Besides, I am informed that a demolition squad has destroyed our station at Ste.-Assise, and the Radio Central in the city has also been badly wrecked."

As Sarnoff knew, Ste.-Assise, a suburb of Paris, was where the main Radio France station was located. He would have to ascertain quickly the extent of the damage. But first he must stiffen the morale of Girardeau, whose help was of crucial importance.

"In the name of the Supreme Commander of the Allied Forces, General Eisenhower," he declared, "I hereby give you all the authority you may need to locate and direct the necessary men. Every hour is important. The American Army will provide you with the equipment and protection you need to reopen the Radio Central and the station at Ste.-Assise."

To get his program rolling, he instructed Girardeau to send messages immediately to all present employees as well as former officials and technicians of his company who might still be alive and within reach. He was to invoke the authority of General Eisenhower and threaten military arrest of those who failed to report for duty without delay. Sarnoff at once requisitioned from the U.S. Army supplies of food, cigarettes, and other necessities for the personnel of Radio France. He arranged for soldiers to guard these supplies when they arrived and had several U.S. officers stationed with Girardeau for his personal safety.

Then he set out to inspect the wreckage of Ste.-Assise. Nearly everything depended on whether and how soon the station could be salvaged. To his delight, he quickly established that the Germans had botched their job of demolition. Evidently without technical background, and working against time, they had smashed all the large and conspicuous equipment—the 200-kilowatt long-wave alternator, the 400-foot towers supporting its antenna systems. But they had not bothered with small stuff: a 15-kilowatt short-wave tube transmitter and the smaller towers and poles of its antenna, which were the heart of the station's long-range communications. It was a lucky break.

Back in Paris, current and former radio employees were beginning to show up and Girardeau, his self-confidence returning, was rounding up other essential manpower. The prospect of American food and supplies worked magic. Colonel Sarnoff ordered that the transmitter tube set be put into commission, and the circuits between Ste.-Assise and Paris Central be repaired immediately or sooner. Work, he said, must be carried on in shifts around the clock.

While the repairs on Radio France were under way, a report reached Colonel Sarnoff that a large electronics warehouse on the outskirts of the city was being looted. It was an incident typical of that time—mob action against goods produced and stored during the Nazi occupation. At Sarnoff's request, a detachment of American soldiers was rushed to the scene, luckily in time to save some equipment he and Girardeau were able to use in the restoration of Radio Central.

The requisitioned supplies arrived at Ste.-Assise in truckloads. Under Girardeau's command, salvaging moved forward so fast that, from the purely technical standpoint, short-wave service could have been resumed in two or three days. But there were entanglements of red tape to be cut: questions of licensed wavelengths, Inter-Allied regulations on frequencies and handling of traffic, reopening of terminals at the American end, to mention only a few. Every item called for decisions and permissions by government and military officials in London, Washington, at the Supreme Headquarters locally.

It also meant long and sometimes frustrating discussions with newly designated French officials. Sarnoff put hours and days into negotiations by telephone, by telegraph, and in personal conferences. Meanwhile he had placed a rugged WAC in charge of the Paris Central Operating Building, with plenty of cigarettes at her disposal to keep the wheels turning.

Despite the bureaucratic delays, Radio France opened its message service to London on September 8, barely two weeks after the American colonel reached Paris. The service to New York was initiated a week later, on September 15. This restoration of direct communications, after the long and tragic isolation of Paris, was greeted in the free world press as symbol and substance of the return of France to independent nationhood.

Colonel Sarnoff took a hand, though not the leadership, in the general revival of domestic communications in the reconquered parts of France. Also, at the request of the Allied Network in London, he obtained from newly installed French officials the use of a Paris station equipped to rebroadcast automatically the SHAEF programs, originating in England, to Allied Army units in France. But the accomplishment singled out for special commendation was the revival of the international short-wave service of Radio France. On October 12, in a ceremony at ETOUSA headquarters in London, he was awarded the U.S. Army's Legion of Merit decoration "for exceptionally meritorious conduct in the performance of outstanding service" from August 23 to September 16, 1944. It went on to say, in the stilted language of such citations:

"Colonel Sarnoff was largely responsible for reopening communications in Paris, thus enabling press communications to resume both to the United Kingdom and the United States. His ingenuity and resourcefulness made it possible to restore cables which had been severed by the enemy, and allowed French radio experts who had not worked for many years during the occupation to return to their former duties. Sarnoff's outstanding devotion to duty, courage, and great diplomacy in handling French citizens have aided materially in overcoming the great difficulties in attaining this objective."

After the war, when conditions in their country had been normalized, various official and private French groups found or made occasion to express their gratitude. Sarnoff had been an officer of the French Legion of Honor since 1937. In September, 1947, in recognition of his contributions to the liberation, he was given the Legion's Cross of Commander. At a dinner in his honor in Paris two months later, Émile Girardeau, who had weathered the political storms and resumed the leadership of his country's radio industry, was the main speaker. He recalled Sarnoff's and his own labors in the hectic time of the liberation. After telling how "high capacity communication with London and New York" was accomplished under the most difficult conditions, he said to the guest:

"Since those days, one of my strongest wishes, so far as you are concerned, was recently accomplished when the Government of the French Republic promoted you to Commander of the Legion of Honor—the thanks of France to the man who took such a part in re-establishing our transatlantic communications."

Several years later the leading French engineering society, *Association des Ingénieurs-Docteurs de France,* presented Sarnoff with a special diploma, its Grand Medal Award, for his wartime help to the country. In fact, as often happens in an age of mythmaking publicity, he feels that he was credited both in France and at home with considerably more than he had actually done. Sarnoff had merely carried out, with conspicuous speed and success, a number of specific and limited assignments in that area. He was the leader of an efficient French-American team that had taken the initiative in restoring certain crucial French communications facilities with remarkable dispatch.

3

Although by mid-September American forces penetrated Germany at two points, beyond Eupen and north of Trier, the defeat of Germany was still in the future. Hitler would mount his last-ditch counteroffensive in the Battle of the Bulge in December and the final Battle of Germany would be fought, mile by mile, in the first months of 1945.

But planning for the administration of a wrecked and sullen enemy homeland was underway on many levels, all of it geared to the great illusion that Stalin's Russia would be a cooperative partner in the occupation. Under the aegis of the U.S. Army, a Group-Control Council had been set up, charged with organizing the nonmilitary aspects of life in Germany—civil administration, the management of food and medical services, civilian transportation, and other essentials.

David Sarnoff was brought in by the Council as chief of its Communications Division. Two months earlier, on his own initiative, he had submitted some thoughts on likely occupation problems in his special field. Now he was asked to draw up a detailed program for all German facilities, from radio to postal services.

This was his last assignment before leaving Europe. He assembled a small staff, worked intensively, and on September 23 turned over to the Council a complete blueprint. In view of the many imponderables involved, it was a remarkably concrete formulation. His Table of Organization called for 94 Allied officers and 150 enlisted men and women to supervise the local civilian contingents. For the top posts he nominated an array of officers by name.

On October 9, he was advised in writing by General C. W. Wickersham for Group-Control that the plan had been reviewed by both the Council and the Signal Division of SHAEF. Their verdict: "a first-class piece of work which provides the correct start for the planning and control of civil communications in Germany." In the actual event, in 1945, the Sarnoff plan would be followed in substance, though adapted to meet the mounting Soviet strictures and harassments.

The warmth of personal comments by General W. Bedell Smith and other key officers raised the risk that Sarnoff might be commandeered to put his concepts into operation. This he was determined to prevent. Already by October his sixty days' mission had been protracted to seven months, and he was more and more concerned about the affairs of his company. In his absence command had been assumed by the former president, now chairman of the board, General Harbord; but during the past two months he had been seriously ill.

The war production of RCA was then at its crest, with a growing backlog of orders on the books unfilled and the Princeton laboratory working overtime on research and engineering projects considered critical by the Armed Forces. In addition, an assortment of corporate problems required the president's personal attention; problems of financing, expansion, manpower, raw materials. Sarnoff's superior officers on both sides of the Atlantic understood his anxiety to get back to his "home front."

When permission to return was obtained, General Eisenhower took note of his imminent departure. In a personal letter he said in part:

"Your contribution in anticipating and preparing proper communication facilities for the press prior to D day and immediately thereafter was notable, and your initiative in reopening Radio Paris deserves commendation. You have, as Acting Chief, Communications Section, with the United States Group-Control Council, placed the benefit of your years of experience in the field of world-wide communications at its service, and this guidance will undoubtedly contribute to the Council's future success."

Colonel Sarnoff sailed for home on October 21, arriving in New York on October 28. After a brief visit with his family and a hurried survey of company matters, he went on to Washington, where he put in nearly two additional months on time-consuming Signal Corps jobs chiefly related to his experience in the theatre of war. Among other things he was instructed to prepare a report on the work of the Corps in Europe, as he had observed it from within. Though commendatory as a whole, his analysis dealt mainly and frankly with a number of specific faults.

4

In this last period Colonel Sarnoff evidently was allowed leeway for a number of "personal appearances" not directly related to the war. He was able, for instance, to take part in the twenty-fifth birthday party of the Radio Corporation on December 1, 1944, at the Waldorf-Astoria. Brought into being in consequence of one World War, the company was winding up its first quarter of a century in the midst of another. The significance, or tragic irony, of this fact was not lost on the resplendent gathering of military brass and prominent civilians.

President Roosevelt, in a warm letter read by Dr. James Rowland Angell as toastmaster, recalled that the corporation was formed "while soldiers were returning from the First World War." He added: "During these twenty-five years your company has played an important part in achieving pre-eminence of the United States in radio. I congratulate you personally for splendid leadership." Spokesmen for the Army and Navy played variations on this obvious theme, with special martial flourishes for the RCA president. A few of them mentioned the fact that Roosevelt, in behalf of the Navy, had been active and influential in the organization of the company back in 1919.

In acknowledging the compliments, Sarnoff turned them into "a tribute to radio men and women in the Armed Services, in communications, and on the production line." He did not consider it a "celebration," he said, because "only by victory can we win the right to celebrate." The nostalgic notes pertinent to a birthday were struck by old-timers like the eighty-five-year-old Edward J. Nally, the first president of the company, and the seventy-year-old Owen D. Young.

But the thrill of the evening—for David and Lizette Sarnoff in particular—was a congratulatory talk by radiotelephone from an undisclosed location in the Pacific theatre of operations. The speaker was a young Navy lieutenant named Robert Sarnoff. His mother wept openly and his father, those with him on the dais observed, had trouble composing the muscles of his face.

Later that month, on December 12, the title of "fatherhood" in television was bestowed on the president of RCA. Some days earlier, however, he had received a more conventional and to its recipient more important title.

His military promotion, first proposed at the end of June, was still stuck in War Department pipelines when he got to Washington four months later. Naturally he was impatient for the completion of the action. The War Department's recommendation finally reached the White House in mid-November. President Roosevelt made the nomination and on December 7 the Senate confirmed his appointment as brigadier general, Army of the United States.

At the end of the month he was back on "inactive status" in the Army and exceedingly active status in civilian enterprise. The nimbus of war heroism around his head was of rather low voltage. After all, he had merely applied to military electronics the same talents and focused energies for which he had long been famous in private enterprise. But the general's star he brought back to the fifty-third floor of the RCA Building was another matter. It glowed with an inner light that would not dim or lose luster through familiarity.

The president of RCA became at once "the General" to everyone around him and then, in widening circles, to the rest of the world. He was addressed as "General Sarnoff" in personal conversation and correspondence, at board and shareholders meetings, through the length and breadth of the RCA empire, and beyond, in the press and on the air. Before long people forgot that he was ever without the title.

None of this was the result of a conscious decision on his or anyone else's part. Everyone simply sensed that he enjoyed the title. More important, it fitted so neatly into the pattern of his personality, his position of authority, and above all, the incandescent Sarnoff legend, that it was automatically accepted as right and even inevitable. He looked the part of a general and he wore the star in unabashed pride.

An incident in the final months of war again underscored Sarnoff's powers of imaginative projection from the known to the unknown in technology:

He accepted an invitation from the *New York Times* to write an article on what he saw ahead for science in war and peace. On July 2, 1945, as a matter of routine and without any misgivings, he submitted the completed manuscript to the War Department for clearance. To his astonishment and mystification, the reaction was swift and sharp. A colonel came up from Washington to deliver to Sarnoff by hand and for his eyes only a message from General George C. Marshall himself! He was instructed not only to withhold the article from publication but not to discuss its contents with anyone until further notice.

The notice came immediately after the atom bomb was exploded over Hiroshima on August 6. General Marshall personally telephoned to inform him that the article was now cleared. Clear now, too, was the cause of Washington's alarm.

Although Sarnoff had had no intimation of the Manhattan Project, he had come dangerously close to an accurate forecast of the atomic bomb. In England he had seen the German "doodlebugs" in action. He remembered the splitting of the atom in 1940. Putting these things together, he deduced the possibility of missiles delivering nuclear explosives of incalculable power and innocently set it all forth for newspaper readers.

Because of its heightened significance, the *Times* rushed the article into print. It appeared on August 10, under the title "Science, for Life or Death," with an editorial note indicating that it had been written prior to Hiroshima. The author, under what was probably his first by-line as a brigadier general, described as among the deadliest "secret weapons of the future" what was already a deadly present reality.

He foresaw "an explosive projectile like a giant meteor from the atmos-
phere," whereby "great cities may be destroyed before a nation knows it is being attacked." "To supply the terrific driving force required by such a

weapon," he wrote, "we find men struggling with Nature to learn the secret of atomic energy. . . . Scientists tell us that a few pounds of suitable metal, atomically detonated in a metropolis, would convert the city into a column of incandescent gas flaming high into the sky. This is not destruction—it is annihilation! . . . It is no more fantastic now to believe that science will release and control atomic energy than it was in 1900 to believe that the radio waves could be useful for world communications." The article went on to describe "a bomb of this sort landed in a city" and converting "a large region surrounding it into gas and debris."

Sarnoff had reached these conclusions independently and without the slightest knowledge of what was going on at the Manhattan Project. It was a lucky precautionary act on his part that he had submitted his article to Washington before releasing it to the press. His remorselessly logical mind, where technical facts were involved, had stumbled on the most closely guarded national secret. Small wonder that General Marshall had acted personally and with firm dispatch to shut him up.

20

Father of Television

ᴈ⫯ So recently a general—five days, to be exact—that he was still in his colonel's uniform, David Sarnoff came up from Washington to New York on December 12, 1944, to attend the first annual convention of the Television Broadcasters Association. He was the guest of honor, slated to receive an award and to pay for it with a speech.

This award, which has been mentioned in previous chapters, was, to say the least, unusual; not a plaque or a medal but a title. The new organization in a new field had decided to name him "Father of American Television." The formal citation affirmed "his initial vision of television as a force and the steadfastness of his leadership in the face of natural and human obstacles to its present state of perfection."

The perfection of its present state, however, was still being heatedly disputed, as Sarnoff himself pointed out in his impromptu response. In pleading that the going arguments about frequencies, lines, panels, dimensions, and other technical details be buried, he acknowledged that they were still lively corpses—that his "baby" was not yet, as the war was grinding to its end, out of the incubator.

For many years opponents of television had contended that it was not ripe for commercial exploitation. This was still the main forensic weapon of those committed to imprisoning it in the laboratories. "Surely," said Sarnoff, "we know that television is not a finished art. We hope that it will never be finished, for when an art is finished the industry is finished." There would be further advances, he conceded, "but we cannot wait for the unknown to reach a point of perfection before we make products availabe to the public."

His paramount task in the postwar period, Sarnoff knew, would be the

268

unfinished business of overcoming hostility to the introduction of full-scale telecasting. More than any other of his company's enterprises, television had become identified with his name and his personal responsibility. A *Fortune* summary several years later (September, 1948) put this fact tersely: "In a sense he bullwhipped his RCA organization into making good on it. So television is a personal (and cosmic) mission with this determined man."

How the mission was fulfilled will be recounted in some detail. But first we must touch on a few other biographical data, if only to avoid a bogdown of chronology.

The Radio Corporation and its chief executive came out of the war with immensely enhanced prestige and power. Military necessity had transformed electronic technology, making it more versatile and sophisticated. Refinements on prewar products and services to meet combat conditions could now be used for civilian purposes. Technology developed for the military during the war could now, in many instances, be adapted for commercial use. Projects sidetracked by the emergency could now be revived.

The company quickly plunged into an across-the-board conversion of its expanded plant, redeployment of machinery and men, revision of the corporate structure. For Sarnoff these early postwar years were therefore as crowded with work and conflict as any that had preceded them. The trajectory of his career showed no signs of leveling off, nor had its motorpower suffered any loss of thrust. Besides superintending the return to a peacetime economy, he faced mounting demands for services far beyond the frontiers of his professional and business provinces. The proportion of his energies diverted to civic and government chores and to inescapable speechmaking kept growing.

No other leader in electronics, and few in any industrial sphere, were as well known, as often heard, as persistently quoted in the press and on the air. The invitations that poured in on him were not always easy to evade. Requests for services from the White House multiplied in the years ahead and they had the force of command performances. Many from less lofty sources, too, were hard to turn down. Sometimes, moreover, opportunities to speak came, or had to be improvised, when a forum was needed to convey vital information or offset harmful attacks.

Radio in its manifold manifestations was dependent, in the last analysis, on government licenses; public sentiment was an important element in the fight for television, then for color TV. Practical considerations thus compelled the head of RCA to take on more time-consuming public assignments than he relished.

Called in to arbitrate a tugboat strike in New York harbor early in 1946, he managed to obtain a settlement. This success had the effect, a few weeks later, of throwing a threatened subway strike into his lap, after normal negotiations had ended in deadlock. The metropolitan press and millions of worried straphangers watched anxiously while General Sarnoff, for several days, held the opposing parties to nearly round-the-clock bargaining. Finally an agreement was signed at Sarnoff's home at five in the morning on February 26 by Mayor William O'Dwyer and Mike Quill, president of the Transport Workers Union.

Sarnoff was on the governing council of New York University, a trustee of Pratt Institute, a director of the Metropolitan Opera Association, past president and an active member of the Economic Club of New York; he was on the boards of the Educational Alliance, the Pan American Society, the Thomas A. Edison Foundation, the National Foundation for Infantile Paralysis, to mention a few on the list that would continue to lengthen. In 1946 the Armed Forces Communications and Electronics Association was formed to maintain the industry-military ties built up in the war effort; Sarnoff was its first president and, after two years' service, remained on its board of directors.

Of necessity he participated in nearly all the commercial, engineering, military and social organizations directly or indirectly relevant to his business. Some of these posts and memberships were largely honorific, but others did involve a share in decision making, along with public oratory on ceremonial occasions.

During the first postwar years Sarnoff came in for a few windfall dividends on his war services. In February, 1947, as already noted, President Truman in a White House ceremony presented him with the Medal of Merit. Then came the formal bestowal, in New York, of his Cross of Commander of the French Legion of Honor; the French consul general specified that it was "in token of our gratitude for your war services in the liberation of my country."

The actual, physical Cross had been brought over by Geneviève Tabouis, an outstanding French political journalist. She had run into some trouble with U.S. customs officials, Miss Tabouis reported at the ceremony. They wanted to classify the item as jewelry and hold it in custody until she left the country. "But when I explained that it was a decoration for General David Sarnoff," she said in substance, "the name worked like magic. The scowls changed to smiles and I was allowed to bring it in."

Ever since 1938, it will be recalled, Sarnoff had been urging the creation of an effective American riposte to totalitarian propaganda. At President Roosevelt's request, he had discussed the problem with Sumner Welles, then Undersecretary of State. Soon after the United States entered the war, he conferred

on the subject several times with Nelson Rockefeller, then Coordinator of Inter-American Affairs. When time passed and nothing happened, he once more
raised the issue at a meeting with the President, who referred it to Secretary of
State Hull.

International broadcasting from the United States at the time was under
control of the Office of War Information. But what of the postwar period? In
a long session with Secretary Hull, Sarnoff stressed his conviction that a potent
American "voice" would be no less important when the conflict was over.
When the Secretary suggested that he submit a detailed memorandum on the
subject, the president of RCA reached into his portfolio and handed it to
him—he had prepared an analysis, including organization and costs, in
advance.

"We shall be called upon, doubtless," it said in part, "to help feed, clothe
and shelter war-torn Europe and Asia. We shall be called upon to assist in re-
establishing law and order." We shall therefore need the means for explaining
our policies and actions quickly, in tones audible around the world.

He proposed the creation by government and private industry jointly of a
special organization to do this job. Congress, he wrote, "should not only
authorize the undertaking but define its scope and goals—representing, as it
would, to the rest of the world the 'Voice of America.' " Sarnoff had used the
phrase himself years before and this probably was the first appearance of the
name in a formal document. At any rate, he had not seen or heard it
elsewhere.

At the war's end the question was still unresolved. Unwilling to accept
defeat by default, Sarnoff used various forums to focus attention on the
problem. Speaking at Princeton University in October, 1946, he again
emphasized the need and estimated that meeting it effectively would cost, at
the outset, about $20 million a year. It proved to be a good guess, a close
approximation of the actual cost of the "Voice" phase of the larger information program adopted in late 1947.

Meanwhile he had extended his concern for international broadcasting to
the United Nations. In a memorandum to the UN he proposed that "Freedom
to Listen" be added to the other freedoms championed—in theory, at least—
by the international body. He recommended, at the same time, that the UN
"establish an independent international broadcasting system to be known as
'The Voice of UN.' " In later public statements, television having broken
through its chrysalis, he added the principle of "Freedom to Look" to
"Freedom to Listen."

This one-man campaign, conducted through nearly a decade and in the face of official disinterest and vacillation, is an apt example of the man's sheer tenacity. When satisfied that his ideas were right, neither temporary failure nor boredom could persuade him to let go.

At least part of the credit for the establishment of the Voice of America—how large a part seems open to dispute—accrues to Sarnoff. And during the observance of the first anniversary of its "Declaration of Human Rights," in New York's Carnegie Hall, the United Nations presented him with a "diploma" for his "contribution in the field of Human Rights through the advocacy of concepts of freedom to listen and freedom to look as fundamental expressions of the Freedom of Information." Unhappily the UN has been unable to enforce these concepts and the human rights of which they are a part, but that is another and sadder story.

2

In September, 1936, the board of directors had thrown a surprise party for Sarnoff, to greet the thirtieth anniversary of his association with radio. Ten years later, in September, 1946, another party, larger and more glittering, took place at the Waldorf-Astoria in observance of the fortieth anniversary.

This one was no surprise. General Sarnoff did not himself suggest the repeat performance but obviously it could not have been arranged without his consent and collaboration. By this time, of course, the Radio Corporation had a high-powered Information Department under its special vice-president, busy in molding and burnishing the public image of the company. All big corporations have similar departments, often supplemented by outside public relations counsel, and all take advantage of anniversary occasions for their purposes.

The difference in RCA was that, as in very few others, the company and its chief executive had become indivisible in the public mind. Publicity technicians went on the theory that what was good for Sarnoff was good for RCA, a rationale of which Sarnoff was the captive rather than the author. His prestige had in effect become a corporate asset, to be guarded, enriched, and exploited. What began, ten years earlier, as a surprise party evolved into a sort of corporate ritual, the practical effect of which would be to keep alive the *Wunderkind* aura around the man into his maturity.

David Sarnoff's wife and their three sons, all safely back from the wars, were present, along with his three brothers, his sister Ede and her husband, Herbert Baer. In the ballroom that evening they again heard the eldest and most famous of their family extolled in full measure. The NBC Orchestra and several Metropolitan Opera stars provided a musical setting.

Laudatory messages were read from the President of the United States, the governor of New York, the mayor of the city; from the Secretary of War, the Secretary of the Navy, and other highly placed officials. Mostly these adhered to the familiar formulas of official eulogy, but at least one had a more intimate touch. From Moscow the U.S. ambassador to Soviet Russia, General Bedell Smith, cabled "affectionate good wishes," then added: "I still regret that you were not able to take over the job of running communications in Germany but I will always be grateful for the magnificent work you did while a member of Supreme Headquarters Staff."

A number of statements destined to be quoted and overquoted in scores of articles about Sarnoff for years to come—some have already been used in these pages—were first heard at this gathering. General James G. Harbord said: "Surely no runner in life's handicap ever entered a race with more burdens and fewer advantages than this man." Dr. Karl T. Compton declared that "it was a happy coincidence that David Sarnoff and the electron grew up together, because much of their subsequent careers has been in very close association."

This was the night, too, when Owen D. Young said:

"It takes about three men with their feet on the ground to one man with his head in the clouds to go forward and save the company from bankruptcy on the one side and make progress on the other. David has that rare combination of permitting his head to be in the clouds and keeping his feet on the ground. In one single package you have those several men whom I have been describing."

Forty years after he blundered into the electronics world and proceeded to take it over, the Sarnoff legend—and I use the word in its most creditable connotations—was thus rounded out, reaffirmed, verbalized. His address of response, too, was in character, filled with inspiration and cautious optimism on a plane of "business statesmanship."

Sarnoff alluded to the fabled beginnings. The man who started the whole thing by hiring young David, George De Sousa, was present and the ex-office boy called on him to take a bow. But for the most part he used the anniversary not primarily to look *back* forty years but to look *ahead* that distance. His audiences had come to expect a brace of titillating predictions, and this one was not disappointed.

He lifted a corner of the curtain that usually covered his deeper feelings. "My friends," he said, "radio is a possessive mistress. And so during these forty years I haven't had as much time as I should have liked to give to my family, my friends, and my associates, who have made it possible for me to survive these years. Perhaps tonight you will permit me to say that I recognize that my attention has not been equal to the devotion which I feel for all of them."

At another point he said:

"Forty years ago radio was so young that even a boy of fifteen felt that he was a veteran. As one of the youngsters within whose heart and mind the spark of wireless kindled a great enthusiasm, I must confess that even now as I look ahead I feel very little older, for radio today appears no less filled with opportunity for growth than it was in the early days when dots and dashes were music to a young man's ears. Our descendants will look back upon the radio services of this era and compare them, as a candle to the electric light, the horse-and-buggy to the automobile, the ocean liner to the stratoliner."

It was a mixed bag of goodies he held out to those descendants, sensibly hedged with "ifs" and "maybes." They might expect, by 1986, "a radio-mail system"; deserts turned into "habitable and productive regions" with the help of atomic energy and possible manipulation of ocean currents; "rain or sunshine by pressing buttons." There was also the familiar pocket-set for instant communication "with anyone anywhere in the world." (This prediction would be periodically revised to embody newer techniques—instant sight as well as sound, for instance; one might as well furnish a dream with the latest improvements.) At this writing the assorted forecasts still have twenty years to prove themselves, and on the basis of his scorecard during the four decades being celebrated, their chances are better than even.

It was evident that night, and would become more so in years to come, that Sarnoff was tempering his visions of technical wonders with misgivings about the fate of man among his awesome new toys. He had seen enough of the horrors of war to be disturbed by the prospect of all God's children playing with electronic and atomic matches.

"Unfortunately new forces are being released by science," he said, "which threaten to bring an abrupt end to all progress unless they are properly controlled and usefully applied. . . . Only three weeks ago I returned from the grim and unhealed battlefields of Europe. There amid the misery and still-smoldering ruins, one feels acutely the dread with which mankind nervously contemplates the threat of biological warfare, atomic bombs, and guided missiles with warheads pointed toward death and devastation."

He cautioned against American complacency: "The Atlantic and the Pacific are no more protection to our country today than the English Channel to the British Isles. Pilotless planes and rockets flying six thousand miles an hour in the stratosphere can carry explosives, poisons, or germs half way around the globe to wipe out entire cities in a deluge of radioactivity, fire, mist, dust, debris and disease. . . . The most difficult problems facing mankind are social and political rather than technical. Unfortunately, in the social and political spheres our imaginations cover a rather limited radius."

Such was the fortieth observance of the time when a slum youngster had got a $5.50 job as office boy. There would be forty-fifth, a fiftieth, a fifty-fifth. The birthday being commemorated was not biological but functional, the beginning not of a life but of a career. One is tempted to read symbolism into this singular fact. Has not career, for millions in our time, tended to transcend life?

3

But to return to television: The wartime truce exploded in renewed hostilities, in some respects more violent than in the past. There had been lusty skirmishing in the war years despite the cease-fire. Now it was open and full-scale battle.

The forces were perhaps more evenly matched. RCA's drive for television before long had the support of GE, Philco, Dumont, some smaller companies. But the opposition was formidable too. What it lacked in numbers it made up in fervor and fine generalship. The assault was spearheaded by the Columbia Broadcasting System, with Zenith covering the flanks; which spelled command respectively by William S. Paley and Commander Eugene McDonald, two of the shrewdest and boldest strategists in the radio business. Sarnoff had a healthy respect for their abilities.

At the war's end nine part-time semicommercial telecasting stations were on the air. Put together they reached only about 7,500 set owners, 4,500 in metropolitan New York and 3,000 more in the Schenectady and Philadelphia areas. These transmitters and receivers were locked into the 525-line system authorized in 1941. Yet another industry committee to review the standards had been set up in late 1943. The changes it recommended were so minor that the FCC in May, 1944, confirmed its prewar authorization.

One of the wartime stations, built for them by RCA, was operated by CBS. Its every telecast was preceded with a cryptic announcement:

"Good evening. We hope you will enjoy our programs. The Columbia Broadcasting System, however, is not engaged in the manufacture of television receiving sets and does not want you to consider these broadcasts as inducements to purchase television sets at this time. Because of a number of conditions which are not within our control, we cannot foresee how long this television broadcasting schedule will continue."

CBS denied that its intention was to downgrade and sow doubts. But the message was not exactly calculated to whet popular appetite for the new medium, which is what RCA and NBC were trying to do. Sarnoff missed few opportunities to focus favorable public interest on the service aborning. Speaking before the New York Chamber of Commerce in February, 1943, for example, he declared:

"When the curtain of war is lifted, television will be ready scientifically to go forward as a new service of public information and entertainment. We can expect to have intercity networks of stations as we have them in sound broadcasting. Eventually they will be nationwide."

With the advent of peace the road to television seemed wide open. Official barriers had been removed. The capacity of the electronic plants, in part idled by the cessation of hostilities, was available for new uses. Most important, accelerated research and engineering in all major laboratories, with RCA indisputably in the lead, had brought striking technical strength to television. Important improvements in the brilliance and sharpness of the images, in the size of the delivered pictures, and in other essential quality elements could now be carried over to home television—within the existing standards.

Technically and legally, in short, there seemed to be no reason for withholding television from the public. But Sarnoff and others still hoped for a larger industry consensus, because that would give television greater chances of success. The potential business was far too big for one or just a few companies. In order to build audiences of a magnitude to tempt advertisers, the widest participation by manufacturers, sales organizations, and broadcasters was required.

The consensus was absent. On the contrary, the FCC and Congressional leaders were importuned to forbid or delay the "premature" coming of television. Local merchandisers were complaining that the noise about the new medium was undercutting sales of receivers for the existing medium. As a battle tactic, CBS was assiduously promoting a system of TV standards of its own—"wide-band and fine-screen"—and, since it was still wholly theoretical, demanding time to construct and demonstrate its system.

Under such pressures, the FCC in January, 1945, staged new hearings and demonstrations. The result was merely a reaffirmation of the prewar specifications. With respect to CBS's demand, the agency ruled that television could not "be held in abeyance until a wide-channel system in the ultrahigh frequencies can be developed and proved."

Of some of those who sought to postpone the new industry, it is fair to say that, having invested least in its development, they had the least interest in its early emergence. That CBS seemingly lacked faith in the prospects of television was evidenced when the network rejected four of the five licenses assigned to it by FCC. It was an expensive gesture of contempt—in due time CBS would buy these discarded licenses for telecasting stations for sums running into tens of millions. An insurance company similarly refused to take a proffered license in Hartford, Connecticut, and subsequently paid millions to buy the rejected station. The National Broadcasting Company, by contrast, promptly accepted the five licenses assigned to its Red Network and five more to its Blue Network.

Reluctance to assume the responsibilities that went with a license was widespread and understandable. Immediate large-scale investments in equipment, organization, and programs were the certainties, everything else was guesswork. As compared with radio, the operation was shockingly expensive. The cost of TV programs was so high, the medium's appetite for materials so voracious, that the financial barriers appeared insuperable. And what assurance was there that advertisers, conditioned to spending thousands on the airwaves, would be willing to pay hundreds of thousands and even millions when sight was added to sound? From the purely economic vantage point, enthusiasm could not easily be whipped up, and it was constantly dampened by opposition propaganda impugning the technical maturity of television.

CBS had made a comprehensive study of the TV potential. The unpleasant verdict was that, whatever its ultimate values, the medium faced "seven lean years"—a barren stretch of huge outlays and meager returns, while radio income dwindled. Why starve for seven years when you can continue to feast on radio profits? This was the underlying psychology in an important segment of the industry and explains the wrath focused on David Sarnoff.

The president of RCA did not deny the likelihood of lean years, though fewer than the biblical seven, and the risks of obsolescence. Yet he believed that the promise of the new industry—and the right of the American people to enjoy what it had to offer—justified the investments and the risks. In August, 1945, the *New York Times* quoted him to the effect that television would be a billion-dollar business by 1955; the figure was reached years earlier.

While local telecasting was still an object of doubt, General Sarnoff did not hesitate to speak confidently of coast-to-coast programing. "Networks," he said in December, 1945, "are in prospect as automatic stations are being built to relay television from city to city. At the same time the coaxial cable, another artery of television, is being extended—already New York is linked with Washington and it is moving into the South as far as Dallas, Texas."

His self-assumed task was to dispel doubts and generate faith. The records of the period show that, beginning with 1944, he continually pressed the American Telephone Company to prepare without delay for the colossal business of interconnecting TV stations from coast to coast—a function he regarded as rightfully devolving upon that company. Doubtless his insistence speeded up the laying of coaxial cables and the building of microwave relay points without which television on a national scale would have been delayed for a great many additional years.

A new and, in the light of what we now know, rather remarkable argument for deferring television was added to the old inventory. While continuing to insist that ordinary monochrome TV was not ready, CBS now contended that *color* television was around the corner. The public, it implied, should not be forced to buy the "intermediate" black-and-white stage, but asked to wait for the completed package.

The color system constituting that package was one that CBS itself had been perfecting for many years. It was the traditional mechanical process, based on motor-driven whirling discs adapted to color. GE and RCA engineers had also done a lot of work on such color devices through the years but put them aside in favor of all-electronic research. Zenith's McDonald was so impressed with the CBS color equipment and the cogency of its argument that he vowed publicly never to produce a single black-and-white set. The "never" proved of short duration; soon enough Zenith was not only making and selling millions of these sets but at times outselling RCA. Despite a brief and sterile triumph in the form of an FCC certification for its color machine, CBS in the end bowed out, accepting the all-electronic color system, as did the rest of the industry. The postponement it sought would therefore have deferred television until the 1950's.

Sarnoff was not disoriented by the attacks and counterproposals. With official barriers removed, RCA took up after the war where it had left off on Pearl Harbor Day. Its facilities were converted to the point where by late 1946 it could begin to produce both TV transmitters and receivers in limited quantities. Television, though deeply in the red, was an actuality by 1947, and more emphatically than ever Sarnoff remained its chief champion and salesman.

He did not have to sell the public. Popular acceptance was excited and overwhelming, limited only by the absence of stations in most cities and inadequate capacity for the production of sets. The target of his drive was the industry. He tried to convince radio people to get in on the ground floor of what, he assured them, would soon be a business incomparably larger and more profitable than radio at its peak. Those who heeded his advice had cause to be grateful. Channel allotments, still to be had almost for the asking, would soon be valued in millions.

Addressing a national meeting of radio manufacturers in Chicago in June, 1947, he urged them to build modest local stations in their areas, with minimum facilities, even before network services were available. At that point ten TV stations were in operation in eight cities, and an eleventh about to go on the air in Washington. Coaxial links between Atlantic and Pacific communities, he said, were just a matter of time: "The East will see the West and the West will see the East. Television will project pictures across the prairies, over the mountains and into the valleys." True, profits may be slower in coming than they were in broadcasting—but "suppose it does take a few years . . . is that a reason for pessimism?"

In that speech Sarnoff made a special appeal to leaders in the movie industry to board the TV gravy train. Too many of them, he complained, were "strangely indifferent to the new art—or perhaps they are waiting until television delivers itself on a silver platter to the motion-picture industry." Television, in his judgment, could be "as great a boom to the movie theatre as sound was to the silent picture."

Specifically, he described theatre chains regularly presenting TV programs on large screens. It was a Sarnoff prophecy that would fail to come to pass. Closed-circuit theatre presentations did develop for special events, such as a championship prizefight, but as one-shot operations rather than the continuing entertainment he had visualized.

In the fall of 1947, speaking at an NBC convention in Atlantic City, he asked his listeners to rule out the phrase "around the corner"—the corner had been turned. Though only 30 million Americans were as yet within viewing distance of transmitters, about 175,000 television sets would be in homes by the year's end. By the end of 1948 he foresaw 750,000 sets, with fifty stations on the air. The public in the first two full years, 1947–1948, he estimated, would spend $375 million for receivers, and equally large sums would go into stations, operating costs and programing—"and that will be only the beginning!"

In these respects his predictions were fulfilled with big margins to spare. Not 50 but 127 stations were on the air before 1948 was over.

It was popular acceptance that won the long television contest for RCA and Sarnoff. Demand for equipment and sets canceled out skepticism. Gradually industry opposition subsided and then faded out. That it lingered in some quarters as late as May, 1948, may be deduced from Sarnoff's report to stockholders that month. "Television is too powerful a force for the public good to be stopped by misleading propaganda," he stated. "No one can retard its advance any more than carriage makers could stop the automobile, the cable the wireless, or the silent pictures the talkies."

He was right, on a dramatic scale. By 1948 the new industry was booming—"the explosive arrival of television on the American scene," as one writer put it. The decisive breakthrough came in 1949—the year, in Sarnoff's words, "when television shook off its adolescence and came into man's estate."

Of the $50 million RCA staked on television, $20 million were for plant and machinery. This unmatched readiness to produce gave the company a highly profitable head start in sales in the initial years. Figures for the industry's aggregate output of sets tell the story of rapid growth. In 1946, only slightly over five thousand were produced: in 1947—160,000; in 1948—944,000; in 1949—nearly 3 million, and in 1950 a whopping 7 million.

Not all the manufacturers combined could keep up with the clamorous demand and in the first years RCA accounted for more than half the national sales. In 1949 television products represented the largest single category of RCA income. "It is difficult to dodge the profane thought," a *Fortune* article said in September, 1948, "that RCA stands to make a pile of money out of the television industry."

A mighty big pile, it turned out to be. The millions Sarnoff had been accused of "wasting" were flowing back faster than they had flowed out. At the telecasting end, the process of recouping was slower. NBC television was operating at a heavy loss before turning its special corner in 1950. By 1952 it had made up its losses and showed a profit on a cumulative basis, after which TV supplanted radio as the major source of NBC earnings.

The rest is fairly recent history. The U.S. Census of 1960 reported that of the country's 53 million dwellings, over 46 million had television sets and 5 million of these two or more sets. Since then something close to a saturation point has been reached. Never before in industrial history has a new service caught on so quickly and on such an impressive scale.

When reminded how desperately they had fought to head off the bonanza, some industry leaders winced. A number of those who had been most fanatic in trying to block television—men like the Mr. X who had berated Sarnoff in a Paris hotel—made the largest fortunes on the new medium. Not many of the financial beneficiaries, alas, acknowledged their debt to the man whose leadership had made it all possible—and who personally was deriving no monetary benefits from his own triumph. A few, however, did recognize his paramount role: Richard A. O'Connor, president of Magnavox Corporation, for instance. In a letter dated October 25, 1948, Mr. O'Connor told General Sarnoff that his "many years of pioneering" had made television possible. He went on to say:

"The foresight and courage which you, and you alone, manifested in the days of skepticism and doubt is directly responsible for the creation of the service to mankind, the horizon of which is truly unlimited. . . . It must gratify you to know that your course in the expenditure of millions of dollars is now bringing its just reward."

Sarnoff *was* gratified. His reward—and he had expected no more—was a sense of accomplishment. His policies, his patience, and his stubbornness had been fully vindicated. In his first forty years of struggle, the success of television was his most dramatic victory. His personal stature and authority were raised to new heights, at a time when he needed them for the bigger and more costly struggle ahead of him. Already the fight for color television was in the open and again the chief protagonists were RCA and CBS.

Inevitably, some RCA people resented the fact that companies which had shown neither courage nor wisdom with regard to television were now getting fabulously rich on it. They spoke in bitterness about individuals in the opposition ranks. And sometimes, when the mood was upon him, General Sarnoff himself could be caustic enough on the subject.

"The American credo," he said to me in substance one night, "glorifies the Rewards of Leadership, and that's all right with me. There *are* rewards, not only in money but in inner satisfaction and public credit. But someone should write an essay for the benefit of ambitious youth on *The Rewards of Followership*. I'm sorry to say that radio history will give him lots of good materials.

"Let's face it. Most of those who made the biggest 'killings' in radio know nothing and care less about the hardships and heartaches of pioneering. They haven't led radio progress but followed it. The wealthiest of them had no part in initiating radio or broadcasting or television and even blocked the birth of both black-and-white and color television. Like so many others, they have reaped the Rewards of Followership. But if there had been no pioneers, no leaders, they would have had no one to follow. Surely they are too intelligent not to know this, even if they won't say it openly."

As of January 1, 1949, the Radio Corporation of America had a new president, Frank M. Folsom, with Sarnoff assuming the title of chairman of the board. While the reshuffling meant an increase of authority for Folsom, it signified not the slightest decrease of power for Sarnoff. He remained the chief executive officer and indisputably "the boss."

Folsom had joined the company immediately after the war—when he had held important procurement posts in the Armed Services—as vice-president in charge of the Victor division. This made him the number one executive at the merchandising end. His whole business background had been in buying and selling in the mass market, as vice-president of Montgomery Ward until 1939 and then as the top merchandising official in Goldblatt Brothers.

Unlike Sarnoff, whose quintessential interests were in the creative dimensions of electronics, Frank Folsom thought and planned and lived by sales and profits. He was three years younger than Sarnoff. A tough-talking, golf-playing, gregarious extravert, Folsom was as close to the stereotype of a dynamic businessman as Sarnoff was far from it. Many years later a perceptive *Fortune* writer said that Folsom could swear and storm without seeming to be an autocrat—but "when Sarnoff swears knees tremble."

The two men complemented each other to a remarkable extent. Though too different in mentality and temperament to avoid spats, the friendship that grew up between them has never been seriously strained. The enlistment of Folsom and his growth within the organization took the edge off some of the widespread—and much exaggerated—impression among investors that "the General" had little talent for, and even less interest in, piling up profits. The naming of Folsom as president consequently met with favor in the financial community. It was taken as a portent that the emphasis in RCA would thereafter be on higher dividends, rather than expensive "pioneering." Those who thought so were reckoning without the demands of color television.

Folsom remained president for eight years, until 1957, then retired with the title and emoluments of chairman of the Executive Committee. Sarnoff then invited John L. Burns, a senior partner in Booz Allen & Hamilton, a well-known firm of management consultants, to assume the presidency. Having done considerable work for RCA in the past, Burns was thoroughly familiar with its structure and problems. Toward the end of 1961 he resigned "for personal reasons," according to his statement. It was no secret within the corporation and the industry, however, that deep-reaching conflicts of policy and personality had developed between himself and Sarnoff.

Burns was succeeded by Dr. Elmer Engstrom, long the head of all RCA research and generally regarded as among the most universally liked and esteemed men in the organization. *Fortune* has described him as "low-keyed, realistic, cautious and precise." As a young engineer he had transferred from

General Electric to RCA in 1930, at the time of unification. He was thus, aside from Sarnoff himself, the only RCA president to have come up from the ranks. His rise to the presidency has been cited by the business press as typical of a trend in American industry—the assumption of managerial leadership by technological experts.

21

Roster of Setbacks

⌘   The cover of *Newsweek* for December 5, 1949, featured a recent portrait of David Sarnoff, by Karsh, over the caption: "Besieged on Three Fronts." He didn't seem worried. Smiling broadly, bright-eyed, thumbs hooked nonchalantly into armholes, and youthful on the edge of fifty-nine, he seemed a very picture of confident power.

In the inside pages the report said: "After a quarter of a century of almost unquestioned dominance of his industry, Sarnoff . . . is now waging a bitter, stubborn war on three fronts. In recordings, radio broadcasting, and [color] television he is being challenged by organizations with spirit, flexibility, and dash."

The account was typical, in that for decades news about Sarnoff had been cast in the metaphor of military action: sieges, battles, fronts. In this, as in all metaphor, there was a lot of hyperbole. At bottom the "wars" referred to were merely the rivalries inherent in a competitive economy. Yet the imagery of war did suggest the exceptional tensions, the atmosphere of recurrent crises, in which Sarnoff had to operate most of his life. In part this was due to the nature of the new industry and the importance of the issues being decided. The major conflicts in electronics, after all, were not of the same order as those between competing motorcars or breakfast foods; they involved the birth pains of totally new services with incalculable effects on society.

Of the fronts listed, the third is the principal concern of this and the next chapter. Color television was shaping up, as *Newsweek* headlined it, as "The General's Biggest Battle." As of December, 1949, the contest was in an early stage but gathering momentum. It would balloon into the longest, costliest, most emotion-packed conflict in the history of electronics.

On the other two fronts, however, the fighting was really over, except for boastful publicity by the winner and face-saving fusillades by the loser. In both, RCA and its chief executive had suffered embarrassing setbacks. They were too limited to dim the glory of the recent triumph in television but conspicuous enough to point a moral of humility. RCA had fought spirited battles and lost—and to the same adversary whom it had just vanquished on the issue of monochrome TV.

Despite its initial dread of radio, the phonograph and record industry had expanded steadily and was still growing. Paradoxically, the strongest positions in records had been captured by the biggest radio-and-broadcasting companies, RCA and CBS. Along with others in this intensely competitive field, they were constantly improving sound reproduction and the physical disc itself.

In the winter of 1948–49 RCA Victor proudly announced that, after nearly ten years of work on a longer-playing record, it was about to present the fruit of its research to the music-loving public. For generations the standard disc had spun 78 times per minute. The new one was geared to 45 rpm (revolutions per minute), giving more than twice as much music per square inch of record surface. But before this prodigy reached the market, Columbia Records got there first with its LP (for Long Playing), a disc that revolved even more slowly—at 33⅓ rpm. Actually RCA had also developed a 33⅓-rpm record, as one of a number of variants, but had chosen to lodge its faith in the 45 rpm.

The war of recordings was under way. Tens of millions of dollars were at stake. Whichever the bewildered public went for, 33⅓ or 45, it could not be played on the existing record players, geared to the traditional 78 rpm. A market for millions of new phonographs was thus being opened up. (In the end, inevitably, three-speed machines to accommodate all the varieties solved the problem.)

Almost from the start the Columbia entry took the lead. The outcome appeared clinched in the summer of 1949, when the National Association of Music Dealers came out in favor of the LP. Three of the four principal independents (Decca, London, and Mercury) thereupon adopted LP. In a last-ditch effort to salvage its 45 rpm, RCA threw an estimated $2 million into an advertising and publicity campaign. By the end of the year it capitulated. For all practical purposes, the 33⅓ rpm has monopolized the field ever since and all record makers, RCA Victor included, have prospered on its popularity.

In broadcasting the challenge was more serious, the penalties for the loser more lasting. For more than twenty years the National Broadcasting Company had ranked first in top-rated programs, advertising revenues, and profit. Suddenly, in 1948, CBS moved to close the gap and within a year succeeded in pre-empting first place. More and more of the shows drawing the largest audiences, and advertising income to match, were on the CBS list. To make the reversal more bitter, these were in many cases shows pioneered and nurtured by NBC.

Paley achieved this success by the simple stratagem of "raiding" enemy talent and abducting favorite shows. One after another top comedy headliners —Jack Benny, Amos 'n' Andy, Edgar Bergen, Red Skelton, Burns and Allen—were lured from NBC to CBS. The bait was a capital-gains deal. Each of the entertainers was set up as a corporation, putting him in a lower tax bracket. It was a device long familiar to Hollywood, suited to its star system, which broadcasting had hitherto resisted.

Presumably NBC could have offered the same deals and held on to the lucrative shows. With few exceptions its program executives were inclined to do so; the extra money it would have cost, they thought, was well worth it. But General Sarnoff objected as a matter of principle. He believed that encouragement of the star system in the long run would prove deleterious, by giving performers the upper hand over the broadcasting organizations. Instead he tried to compensate for the raids by generating new programs. A million and a half went into these innovations—and not one of them developed audience appeal to match what was lost to the competition.

Alluding to this lost round at the next stockholders' meeting, Sarnoff said: "Leadership built over the years on a foundation of solid service cannot be snatched overnight by buying a few high-priced comedians. Leadership is not a laughing matter."

In simple dollars-and-cents terms, it turned out, he was wrong. An NBC official said privately, "The General, I think, got himself involved emotionally in what was a problem in cold business. He resented the attitude of the performers whom, after all, we had helped build up into stars. He felt, I think, that they were being 'disloyal,' and that kind of thing. Some of us thought of talent simply as a marketable commodity, that's all. In the final analysis we have had to accept the star system and live with it anyhow."

The point of the story is that David Sarnoff sustained substantial defeats along with the splendid victories. Of course, in an industry so constantly in flux and so fiercely competitive, both victory and defeat have frequently been tentative. Conquered positions had to be continually shored up and defended.

A case in point is the RCA patent structure. Sarnoff had been the prime mover in its building in the 1920's, and it was widely regarded as the very foundation not only of his corporation's strength but of the vitality of the whole industry. Royalties paid by licensees—an average of less than 2 percent on their gross production—came to millions of dollars. In the first ten RCA years, when it was struggling to establish itself under heavy handicaps of divided corporate authority, there were times when income from licenses made the difference between red and black ink on the balance sheets.

Resentments against RCA control of patents had been audible from the beginning. But in the postwar years dangerous cracks appeared in the edifice. They were to multiply and widen.

The first substantial fissure came in 1946, at the very time when RCA was introducing television. That was when Zenith repudiated RCA licenses on which it had in large part built its prosperity. It ceased to pay royalties on the patent package and brought triple-damage suits against RCA as well as against original patentees like GE and Western Electric. The package, incidentally, was by then an accumulation of about 10,000 assorted patents and rights—not as great as it sounds, if we recall that some 50,000 patents on radio and related devices have been issued from 1895, when Marconi obtained his first one, to date.

The Zenith revolt was only the beginning. A few other manufacturers followed its lead. RCA and its codefendants filed countersuits. There was a jungle growth of litigation: antitrust, infringement, restraint of trade, in all conceivable combinations, with the Justice Department joining the melee. By the mid-fifties, according to one RCA official, legal affairs "were taking 40 percent of the time of our chief executives." Out-of-court settlements and a consent decree with the government were compacted in most cases. Often the litigation dragged along for five or ten years. Though battalions of lawyers were kept busy, the final arbiter of RCA strategy and terms of settlement was General Sarnoff.

The Zenith suits, involving claims for more than $62 million and counterclaims in proportion, were finally wound up in 1957. Technically it was a defeat for RCA, which agreed to pay Zenith $1 million a year for ten years, with GE and Westinghouse paying a substantial part of this sum. The settlement was reported in the press as "the biggest antitrust recovery in history." But there were certain far-reaching benefits flowing to RCA that took the edge off the defeat.

Howard Armstrong's claims on FM resulted in protracted and unhappy litigation. The inventor brought suits for infringement against RCA and NBC in July, 1948. The pretrial hearings which began the following February and continued for five years grew into the kind of endurance contest familiar in patent battles. Volume of testimony was piled upon volume to make the usual tower of contradictions, with the inventor growing increasingly bitter as time went on.

In a long and strikingly perceptive article in *Harper's* (April, 1958), titled "E. H. Armstrong: the Hero as Inventor," Carl Dreher remarked: "Beyond a certain point devotion to a cause, however admirable, enters the realm of pathology." Armstrong had apparently passed that point. He was tired, frustrated, his nervous stability eroded by crowding misfortunes. The condition was made worse by notification in 1953 that Zenith, which had been his staunchest supporter in the industry and through the years had paid him more than a million dollars in royalties, would pay no more.

Armstrong's wife, his lawyers, his closest friends begged him to reduce his load of work and especially to find an exit with honor from the nightmare of the lawsuit. On January 31, 1954, in the midst of the continuing hearings on the case, he committed suicide. So far as RCA itself was concerned, the suit was settled with a payment of $1 million to his estate; others in the industry continued the litigation with the estate.

In the sense that the patent structure still stands, Sarnoff has won the over-all war. But the company has lost a few important battles, besides the major engagement with Zenith.

In an inventory of Sarnoff's setbacks one could include, by stretching definitions a bit, his unsuccessful campaign of at least thirty years for the merging of American communications in their international dimension. In competition for global business, he recognized as far back as the 1930's, American companies were at a serious disadvantage vis-à-vis foreign communications monopolies, whether government-owned, private cartels, or a mixture of the two. Ever since he has argued that the American principle of unlimited competition, in this unique field, should be suspended at the nation's frontiers. He pressed this view during the war and returned to it repeatedly afterwards.

In an address to the American Bar Association in San Francisco in August, 1962, he identified the handicaps under which international telegraphy was working by reason of competition amoung ten American outfits engaged in the traffic. "Based on long experience in this field," General Sarnoff said, his own belief was that "the most practical solution would be the creation of a single privately owned American company, uniting the facilities and operations of the present U.S. carriers in the international communications field." In this way, he contended, the country's worldwide services could become "more flexible, more convenient, and more economical to the public—at home and abroad. And our unified American company would be able, for the first time, to deal with foreign government monopolies on an equal basis of strength." The independent company, he said, should be separate from the Communications Satellite Corporation.

His vision of an across-the-board merger of radio, voice, and cable interests in the foreign trade has been largely ignored by the other organizations competing in international communications. But he has not been finally defeated, since he regards it as unfinished business. He is convinced that the march of technology, dramatized in the communications satellites, will force acceptance of his viewpoint.

He raised the subject again in May, 1965, in a talk to the Armed Forces Communications and Electronics Association, in Washington. The success, only weeks earlier, of the Early Bird, poised at a height of 22,300 miles over the equator, gave powerful emphasis to his words. Regulations carried over from the past, making distinctions between voice and nonvoice types of transmission to other countries, have become an anachronism now that all kinds of signals could be relayed by the same switchboard in the skies. "The fragmentation of service," he said, "has simply been extended into space."

While the vast majority of other countries "speak as a single unit through state-controlled monopolies," the United States still "speaks with a multiplicity of voices because of the historic competitive nature of our internal communication structure," he pointed out. We can no longer "maintain a competitive pattern at the American end of international circuits," he declared. "We require a fundamental change in the policies and the regulations under which we now operate."

2

The most startling and most publicized setback for Sarnoff came in connection with the struggle for television in color.

In October, 1946, having delivered an address at the Princeton University Bicentennial celebration, David Sarnoff dropped in at his company's Research Center nearby. He wanted, in particular, to check on the continuing project that even then was keeping more men and more dollars engaged than any other: color television.

The engineers were in optimistic spirits. They showed him pictures of a ball game in progress, of bathing beauties cavorting, of girls in colorful dresses. The pictures were received simultaneously on two sets standing side by side. On one they came through clearly in ordinary black-and-white, on the other in color—still unstable, flickering, now and then running into blotches, but color notwithstanding.

Despite the defects, Sarnoff suggested an almost immediate press demonstration. The scientists protested that the apparatus was not ready, that they could make a more impressive showing a few months hence. To which Sarnoff retorted: "You wouldn't want to wake up some morning and discover that someone else had announced all-electronic color, would you?"

The demonstration took place in the laboratories on October 30. No apologies were offered for the shortcomings of the color—they were all curable, given time and perseverance. The big news, the reporters were told, was that two great principles had been established: (1) All-electronic color television—no rotating discs, no moving parts, nothing mechanical—was entirely feasible. (2) This system was "compatible"—the color images, that is, could be received simultaneously and perfectly by existing black-and-white sets.

"Compatibility" was the key word and concept around which the whole struggle on color would revolve. What made a system compatible was that a program in color could be viewed—not in color, to be sure, but in monochrome—on regular noncolor sets. No adapter or converter was required, as in the mechanical and incompatible systems, to make this possible.

A simple enough concept, yet explaining it proved difficult. Part of the public, certainly in the earlier stages of the controversy, clung to the mistaken idea that by the magic of compatibility black-and-white receivers would be able to pick up color broadcasts. In time it was more generally grasped that, whatever the method of broadcasting, compatible or not, a special color set was needed to bring in pictures in color.

General Sarnoff, asked for a definition in the course of an interview by *U.S. News & World Report,* put it this way:

"A compatible system in television is more or less the same as a compatible marriage, where the husband and wife see the same thing at the same time and don't get into a lot of wavy motions. A compatible color-television system must be one that uses the same number of lines and the same number of fields that are now used in the existing receiver in order to receive color pictures in black-and-white."

Like other major electronics companies, RCA had experimented since 1932 with the old mechanical processes of sending color images. After the perfection of monochrome TV, however, Sarnoff and his research chiefs had decided to concentrate on electronic techniques, precisely because these offered the prospect of compatibility. Meanwhile Columbia Broadcasting had made the opposite choice, and proceeded to focus its brains and capital on the incompatible mechanical system. There we have the makings of the monumental contest.

Few in the industry denied the claim that a compatible instrument was desirable. The advantages seemed self-evident. The system could be introduced without obsoleting the public's immense investment in black-and-white sets. Advertisers, in sponsoring a color show or presenting commercials in color, would be able to reach the total television audience, some in color and the rest in monochrome. Bill Paley knew this as well as David Sarnoff.

Why, then, did CBS executives opt for a system that was not compatible or that at best could be made compatible only by adding gadgets to existing TV sets? The answer, as nearly as one can adduce from company statements, was twofold. First, they believed that a satisfactory all-electronic system, if possible at all, was in the far, far future; second, they saw great prestige advantage in being first with a color TV system.

Without doubt, even as late as 1950, mechanical color transmission was further advanced than the alternative system. The deficiencies in RCA color were visible to the naked eye. But Sarnoff and his partisans argued that, while the "spinning wheel" techniques had already reached the limits of development, the all-electronic method had boundless room for improvement.

Superficially this looked like a case of cold-blooded self-interest: a determination to block the competing device for a number of years at least until RCA had perfected its chosen system. Such was the interpretation made not alone by the opposition but by some neutral observers. In the perspective of events, however, it became evident that Sarnoff's strictures on the incompatible process were fully justified. The clinching proof is that CBS itself—though it had three years of right-of-way to introduce its incompatible version—discarded it in favor of the all-electronic method when that became available.

The self-interest was plainly there: by 1950 RCA had already sunk about $20 million into its color research and field testing. But the assumption that a company's self-interest is necessarily against public interest is a figment of latter-day propaganda. In refusing to settle for what he judged to be second-best, Sarnoff was defending the industry and the public against what did prove to be a mistake. If the mistake did not mushroom into financial calamity, it was only because the inherent faults of incompatible mechanical color were so glaring that no genuine effort to market it was ever made by CBS or anyone else.

So much for the general background. The contest was so protracted and complex that arbitrary abbreviation of the story is unavoidable. A blow-by-blow account, even if space permitted, would be pretty dull to anyone but specialists in the field.

In a reversal of the usual form, General Sarnoff was *not* the first to press for commercial release of an important new electronic service. With respect to color television, his was for some years the unaccustomed and incongenial role of appearing to hold back a major innovation. The RCA electronic system was a long way from ready and the CBS mechanical system, he sincerely believed, was undesirable even if it were technically ready.

The initial petition for approval of standards, amounting to government authority to put color television on the market, came from Columbia Broadcasting, in 1946. Two months of testimony and tests, from December that year to February, 1947, convinced the Federal Communications Commission that no available system was good enough to approve. The rival companies then had about two and a half years for further research on their respective color technologies. By its own admission, CBS "curtailed" research in 1948, whereas RCA stepped up its work in this field.

3

The next set of hearings, once more on the initiative of CBS, opened on September 28, 1949, and continued until May 26, 1950—a stretch of eight months. Probably it was the longest such proceeding in the annals of the radio industry and it churned up emotional heat on a scale to match. Ten thousand pages of transcript were produced. Before it was over, and particularly after the Commission's decision was promulgated, the entire industry, most of the press, and both Houses of Congress were in the act; and the chairman of the Commission, Wayne Coy, dropped all semblance of juridical neutrality to become an ardent advocate of the CBS side.

Early in the hearings the commissioners and their technical staff witnessed demonstrations of the two systems. As compared with 1947, CBS could show very little, and NBC a great deal, of progress. Nevertheless, reception from the disc-scanning transmissions still seemed superior. In the greater candor of retrospect, Sarnoff would concede that in RCA color "the monkeys were green, the bananas were blue, and everyone had a good laugh."

On the basis of these initial comparisons, he could scarcely have hoped for FCC approval. Witnesses supporting RCA, however, contended that the faults of the all-electronic apparatus were temporary, those of the competing system inherent and incurable. They sought to prove that with whirling-disc color the size of the screen would remain limited to 12½ inches, whereas RCA could look ahead to a 21-inch screen, then standard in monochrome sets. They made the most, also, of the fact that in the all-electronic system the three primary colors were overlaid or "simultaneous," and not "sequential"— produced in rapid sequence—as in disc scanning.

But RCA rested its case, in the first place, on compatibility. Acceptable all-electronic color was inevitable and so close to realization that it saw no excuse for authorizing an incompatible substitute, even if its color was better *at this time*.

Many industry leaders, besides the main contenders, took the stand. Ostensibly, at least, nobody was opposed in principle to adding color to sight, although in their hearts there were doubtless those who prayed that this boon might be long postponed. Monochrome television was booming—so why kill the goose that laid the golden eggs? Sarnoff had one advantage. The RCA process did not require that the goose be killed: it would continue compatibly to lay the golden black-and-white eggs while others received colored eggs.

The president of the Radio Manufacturers Association said in his testimony that any system accredited for the public should "include the requirement of compatibility." The radio and electronic journals for the most part agreed on this. Dr. Elmer W. Engstrom, top man at RCA's Princeton Center, pleaded with the Commission to "specify compatibility as a requirement for any approved system." Even Frank Stanton, president of CBS, admitted under questioning that compatibility was "desirable" and that his system did "not fully satisfy this feature." But CBS spokesmen—and there is no reason for doubting their sincerity—simply did not believe that compatible all-electronic color could be perfected. Dr. Peter Goldmark, who headed the developmental work on CBS apparatus, said: "I think that the possibility of the RCA system ever becoming a practical broadcast service is extremely doubtful." This was the sum and substance of their presentation.

The high point of the seemingly interminable business, judging by the public attention it attracted, was the appearance of General Sarnoff on May 3, 1950. In what the leading trade publication called a "marathon performance," he testified for two full days and one evening session. Even his adversaries conceded that he acquitted himself brilliantly.

It had been said that Sarnoff was one of the few American industrialists who did not need an "interpreter" in talking to scientists or on scientific issues. Moreover, he was his own best counsel, being a veteran of some thirty years' experience as a witness before courts of law, official agencies, Congressional committees. Now he faced relays of exceptionally adroit lawyers— CBS, for example, was represented by former Judge Samuel Rosenman, famous as chief speech-writer for the late President Roosevelt—and interrogation by the commissioners themselves.

Sarnoff in 1950 was not, as his friends liked to believe, the hero of the electronics world. Within the industry, a tally of admirers and detractors would probably have balanced out. But both categories would have agreed that he was the "outstanding figure" in their world. His views, his mere appearance in a controversial context, spelled authority; they made "news" and usually made drama as well.

Characteristically, he found opportunity during the questioning to touch on his philosophy of business. He had, he said at one point, "never seen any protection in standing still." He accepted the challenge when the questioning went far afield into exploration of the whole RCA patent structure—germane to the examination because color television involved hundreds of old and new patents. Rosenman as well as counsel for the Commission attempted to read implications of "monopoly" into the licensing system, which Sarnoff of course denied. There was exciting semantic fencing on whether the "leadership" RCA claimed was not a species of "domination."

But the nub of his testimony was on the problem of compatibility. "You are being urged," Sarnoff warned, "to build a highway to accommodate the horse and buggy when already the self-propelled vehicle is in existence." CBS itself, he predicted—quite accurately, as it turned out—"would shelve its mechanical system in favor of an all-electronic system." The RCA color which the commissioners had viewed, he said, was not "the finished product." Development was so intense that already there had been significant improvements since the demonstrations earlier in these hearings.

At one point Sarnoff was asked what RCA would do if the FCC ruled for CBS standards. That, he replied, was "like asking a prizefighter who, after nine and a half rounds, is way ahead on points and has been steadily gaining throughout the fight, what he would do after the fight is over if he is felled by an unexpected blow in the last half of the last round. The only answer he can give is that while he may be felled, he will retain a fighting heart and will do the best he can under the circumstances."

After the adjournment of hearings all participants were instructed to file briefs in summation before June 26, 1950. On September 1, the Commission in an unusual and perhaps unprecedented procedure, issued an interim or tentative report which unmistakably foreshadowed a decision favoring the mechanical, sequential CBS system.

The reader will recall that in the years when specifications for "ordinary" television were in hot dispute the Radio Manufacturers Association formed a National Television Systems Committee (NTSC). Now, alarmed by the pro-CBS trend in Washington, a second such organization was set up to advise on color standards. This in turn selected a five-man *ad hoc* panel of top technicians, with the Philco representative as chairman; the other members were drawn from RCA (Dr. Engstrom), General Electric, Sylvania Electronics, and Hazeltine Electronics Corporation. The findings of this panel did not come through until June, 1951, long after the Commission had made its choice, but they played a weighty part in the final fate of colorcasting.

Commenting on the federal agency's preliminary judgment, the magazine *Broadcasting* wrote on September 11, in ringside style:

"The color battle is still on. CBS is way out in front on points. But there's a round to go. Two of the seven FCC judges wanted to stop the fight with an immediate CBS decision. One wanted to postpone it. The other four decreed it should continue, with a decision upcoming unless there was a surprise knockout."

There was no surprise knockout. On October 10, 1950, the FCC approved the noncompatible set of standards. The Commission sharply criticized the quality of RCA color, slurred over the matter of compatibility, and ruled that the CBS system could be marketed at once. Expected though it had been, the decision sent tremors of shock and apprehension through the electronics industry.

General Sarnoff issued a statement for his company: "We regard this decision as scientifically unsound and against the public interest. . . . The hundreds of millions of dollars the present set owners would have to pay to obtain a degraded picture with an incompatible system reduces today's order to an absurdity. Regardless of what anyone else may feel called upon to do, RCA will continue its effort to advance the bedrock principles on which the sound future of color television can be built and will be built."

The blow was more painfully abrasive than he could acknowledge publicly. He had taken a beating—not too familiar an experience in his case. Under his outward composure was the knowledge that the setback must be explained to shareholders and that his board of directors must be imbued with his own confidence in ultimate vindication. This would not be simple. Already huge sums had been siphoned off from profits and dividends into color. Thus far they had bought only the privilege of pouring in more and more, with no end in sight.

Far from allowing the blow to brake color research, Sarnoff ordered a crash effort—eighteen hours a day, seven days a week—for the color brigades. It is not often that the public at large becomes aware of a struggle in the world of business. This time, because television had become so large a part of daily life, popular interest ran high. Sarnoff planned to take advantage of this fact. By means of well-publicized periodic demonstrations of all-electronic color progress, he would in effect appeal to public and industry opinion and thus place the FCC on the defensive.

At the same time he appealed to the law. Within days after the decision was announced, RCA brought suit in a Federal District Court in Chicago asking it to "enjoin, set aside, annul, and suspend" the Commission's order. The decision, it charged, contravened the testimony; moreover, RCA color on which the judgment was based was an early model already outmoded by engineering progress. The ironic truth was that many if not most of the defects cited in the official ruling had been cured by the time it was issued.

The suit, *inter alia,* drew attention to the startling dimensions of the new industry now allegedly endangered. At the beginning of 1947 there had been about 5,000 TV sets in use; now, in October, 1950, there were 8 million, with a viewing audience of 30 million. Annual sales by all manufacturers came to $1.5 billion—of which RCA garnered $400 million, or nearly one quarter—and were going higher all the time.

While the case was being argued, RCA put on a showing of its updated color in Washington for the press and such officials and legislators as could be induced to attend. The prevailing judgment was probably voiced by the radio-television editor of the *New York Times,* Jack Gould, who wrote on December 10: "Last week's demonstration of the improved color system of the Radio Corporation of America materially changes the whole outlook on the dispute over video in natural hues. The success of the demonstration, which is a feather in the cap of Brigadier General Sarnoff, puts the Federal Communications Commission on a spot which appears certain to become controversial and embarrassing. Technically, it ultimately may be proved that the FCC committed a classic 'boner.' "

The Federal District Court ruled against RCA on December 20. An appeal was carried to the U.S. Supreme Court, which on May 28, 1951, sustained the lower court. The last legal resort was thus ended, the discomfiture of Sarnoff seemingly total. But there was a *Dubitant* comment by Justice Felix Frankfurter that would stand the test of unfolding events better than the majority verdict.

"From the point of view of the public interest it is highly desirable to have a color system that is compatible," the Justice commented. "The Commission's order sanctioning an incompatible system is based not on scientific unattainability of a compatible system, nor even on forecasts that its feasibility is remote. It rests on the determination that inasmuch as compatibility has not yet been achieved, while a workable incompatible system has proven itself, such a system, however intrinsically unsatisfactory, ought no longer to be withheld from the public." In sum he was asking: Why the unholy rush?

Sarnoff discerned a deeper, more generic significance in the outcome of the case. Neither the lower nor the highest Court had considered the substance of the FCC decision but had ruled only on its legality. Speaking to the Harvard Law School Association in New York in April, 1952, he raised a question which was causing apprehension among students and practitioners of government. If the judicial branch refused to examine the validity of actions by administrative agencies, what recourse did individuals and the public have against erroneous or harmful orders? Did it not invest those agencies—provided they abided by the legal forms—with arbitrary, autocratic authority?

"The growing tide of judicial unwillingness to review decisions of administrative bodies," Sarnoff warned, "has many serious implications for business and the public. It may result in drastic change in our system of courts and law. . . . One of the bulwarks of our form of government—the right of every person to have his day in court—would be swept away."

The verdict on the RCA case, he pointed out, meant that "according to the Supreme Court, an administrative agency—which often determines economic, scientific, and other questions vitally affecting the public interest—now has the power to speak with finality not only on matters of fact but also on questions of public policy." If federal commissions, boards, and other agencies are to be held to the principle of checks and balances, he concluded, "there ought to be some place to go where a judicial review of the substance and not merely the form of a case can be secured."

The issue he raised was destined to become increasingly acute in the coming years, as appointive agencies and their powers multiplied. It is at the heart of the continuing debate on Big Government.

Stung by growing criticism, the FCC chairman, Wayne Coy, took to the hustings to defend the ruling on color. He identified himself completely with the CBS cause, making speeches and haranguing the press. Its propriety aside, this conduct was scarcely wise. Should it develop that the Commission had, indeed, pulled a "boner," he was merely making it more osseous.

The *ad hoc* panel representing the TV set manufacturers released its report in June, 1951. It validated the basic standards embodied in RCA color and declared that compatibility was indispensable. And soon thereafter, on June 25, as if to reassert its primacy, Columbia Broadcasting staged a "gala première" of its officially crowned system.

From its New York studios an hour of assorted color, served with appropriate oratory, was networked to small invited audiences in Philadelphia, Baltimore, Washington, and Boston. Chairman Coy, hailing this "day of fulfillment" and "this hour of triumph," praised Paley and his associates who "had the vision, the faith, and the courage to fight the long uphill battle to develop the system and secure its adoption as the only system authorized." U.S. Senator E. C. Johnson, who had also made the CBS cause his own, greeted the première in a telegram as a "historic day in the progress of man."

The fatal flaw in the première, of course, was that neither the program nor the congratulatory rhetoric was accessible to the public. The *New York Times* put its editorial finger on the sore spot when it wrote that "the event was meaningless for owners of black sets, which require adapters to receive the color signals even in black-and-white."

The *Times,* besides, pointed out that, eight months after its hard-won go-ahead signal, CBS was not producing color sets. The implication was that the network was not really exploiting its "hour of triumph." The handful of manufacturers who had obtained licenses to make CBS type sets and the gadgetry for receiving colorcasts in monochrome failed to follow up. Available programs in color were, in any case, too few and too trivial to justify a sales campaign.

"The manufacturing industry," said the Washington *Evening Star,* anent the première, "is understandably reluctant to go ahead with CBS color in view of the imminent perfection of a compatible system." Sarnoff's showmanship was beginning to register. The *Wall Street Journal* rose above the battle to declare:

"With due respect to both the FCC and the Supreme Court we are here to say that they are deciding things in which they cannot possibly have the last word. The people who pay and watch television will finally decide, just as they decided what kind of automobile they wanted."

The crash program in Princeton was producing results. Close on the heels of the Columbia première, RCA unveiled the latest all-electronic developments at the Radio City Exhibition Hall in New York. Some two hundred reporters and industry observers, treated to a twenty-minute selection of color shorts, exclaimed audibly over its high quality. By simultaneously broadcasting the program on its regular channel, set owners in the metropolitan area were given direct proof that the system was compatible.

One of the industry leaders who had been skeptical, Allen B. Du Mont, now asserted that "the RCA picture was good enough to start commercial programs immediately." General Sarnoff demurred. Full commercial use, he thought, was still two to five years away. One of the elements of delay was in the fact that the war in Korea, unhappily, was then pre-empting the raw materials and productive capacity that a new service would require. This war, by the way, provided CBS with a plausible reason for not introducing commercially the officially authorized color system it had developed and defended.

In its issue of July 23, 1951, *Time* observed that Sarnoff, having "lost a round to CBS last year . . . did not stay down." The new color tube he had just shown to the industry "receives clear true color," and "it looked as if radio's miracle man had not run out of miracles."

After the verdict for CBS, the article went on, "old radiomen kept their eyes on Sarnoff. He is the man who put radio in the home—and never forgot it for a waking moment. He is the boss of RCA with its 52,000 employees (including those of the NBC radio and television network), thirteen manufacturing plants which turn out millions of radios, TV sets and hundreds of different electronic gadgets, of a research staff which year-in and year-out develops new wonders. Would Sarnoff, who boasts that he was born about the same time that the electron was discovered (as if they were somehow twins), allow himself to be bested in the next great advance of the industry that he had led for two decades? Those who know Sarnoff's vast ability and his vast pride—thought not. They listened when, coldly eyeing the FCC decision, he said: 'We may have lost the battle, but we will win the war.' "

So soon after a great defeat, while he was fighting to undo its damage, the reputation of Sarnoff thus seemed neither diminished nor tarnished. On the contrary, his qualities—both real and legendary—seemed somehow heightened in the public mind by the tests of trouble.

"Sarnoff was fighting his way out of a tough spot. For more than fifty of his sixty years Sarnoff has been doing just that. Driving through obstacles is his habit, his joy, his bitter necessity." This eloquent summation by *Time* mirrored the general feeling that here was a man who couldn't be kept down. Even Wall Street, traditionally skeptical of exorbitantly costly "miracles," seemed to agree. RCA stock, expected to decline in the aftermath of the pro-CBS color decision, rose impressively by mid-1951.

22

Triumph for Color

و‍ When David Sarnoff was completing forty-five years of his association with radio, in September, 1951, the all-absorbing industry problem was color television, and the solution was being hammered out in the Princeton, New Jersey, laboratories. Appropriately, therefore, the celebration of the unique "birthday" took place in the auditorium of that institution.

Except for top-echelon company officials and a few personal friends, the audience that afternoon was composed of the people employed on the premises. Reporters and photographers, it hardly needs saying, were on hand, knowing from past experience that any gathering built around Sarnoff was likely to produce news. The head of the laboratories, Dr. Elmer Engstrom—small, neat, bespectacled, and professorial—introduced Dr. Charles E. Jolliffe, one of the corporation's chief scientists, who presided over the proceedings.

To mark the happy occasion, the name of the institution was changed to the David Sarnoff Research Center. To justify the rechristening, Dr. Jolliffe and other staff members who made speeches had no need to depart from the known facts of Sarnoff's devotion to research, which he had defined as "the distance between an idea and its realization." They rehearsed the much-told tale of his loyalty to research in depression weathers, his initiative in bringing their work under one roof in Princeton, his genuine excitement over actual or potential scientific breakthroughs.

The ardor of speakers and audience went far beyond conventional flattery of the boss. Clearly these scientists and engineers counted him as one of their own guild, a layman who comprehended their special problems, trials, disappointments. Dr. Gano Dunn, who had worked closely with the company both as a member of its board and as president of the J. G. White Engineering Corporation, was one of the speakers. He touched on certain facets of Sarnoff's character which naturally would impress men whose discipline rated organization and precision highly.

"Everything he does has a finish to it," Dr. Dunn said, for example. "He is never sloppy, he never leaves things undone. He delegates them to others, too, and we don't always live up to what he expects of us; but as far as his own work is concerned, he turns out a finished job."

After asserting that "his modesty is phenomenal," Dr. Dunn unveiled a bronze plaque—rather less than modest in its ceremonial rhetoric—dedicating the Center to Sarnoff. As usual, messages of greeting were read. President Truman's was generous. Having attested to Sarnoff's "forty-five years of great achievements in the field of radio, television and electronics," he said:

"Through your leadership in American industrial life and in science, you have contributed immensely to the growth of America and its pre-eminence in communications. It is most fitting that RCA Laboratories at Princeton be named the 'David Sarnoff Research Center,' and I extend to you and your staff of scientists my warm good wishes for continued progress."

Another of the "birthday" greetings which was especially welcome to Sarnoff came from Dr. Lee De Forest. Frankly saddened by the worsening relations with Howard Armstrong—the marathon lawsuit on FM was then in progress—Sarnoff attached that much more value to the consistent friendliness of this other great inventor. Rarely did De Forest let a Sarnoff celebration pass without adding his mead of admiration.

On this occasion he told Sarnoff that he has been "an inspiration to every engineer in the electronic field," adding: "You are well justified in looking back over your forty-five years of unflagging effort in that field with a feeling of deep satisfaction of what has been accomplished during that period, so much of which accomplishment is the result of your deep insight into the various problems, and your inspiring leadership of the army of brilliant engineers which you have built up through the past three decades."

When his turn came to speak, the General had a surprise for his hosts, one that took the headlines all over the country next morning. His wife, he said, smiling at Lizette, had taught him the tactic of hinting at a gift one wanted. Well, he would ask the Research Center now bearing his name not for one but for three gifts—to be delivered within five years, at the fiftieth anniversary. There were those, he knew, who might think his requests excessive, but had he not often in the past shown more faith in research than the scientists themselves?

He realized, Sarnoff said, that the "presents" he asked for did not as yet exist. "However, anything that the human mind can conceive can ultimately be produced." Besides, the tasks he was setting were less formidable than those his listeners had already performed—for example, worldwide communications, radio broadcasting, myriad electronic devices for industry, the kinescope and the image orthicon television tube, the electron microscope, ultrafax, black-and-white television and now the compatible color television system, pioneering that already has "opened up the ultrahigh frequencies to practical use."

Facing the men whose knowledge and ingenuity had yielded such a harvest, he therefore did not hesitate to ask for the gifts, nor did he doubt that he would receive them by September, 1956. What he asked for was:

1. A true amplifier of light: "I should like you to invent an electronic amplifier of light that will do for television what the amplifier of sound does for radio broadcasting. . . . We can, of course, enlarge pictures optically, but in the process light is lost and the pictures become dimmer instead of brighter. What is needed is a true amplifier of light itself." He already had a name for it: Magnalux.

2. A "videograph," recording both black-and-white and color on magnetic tape, just as sound was already being recorded:

"In contrast with present kinescope recordings on film, the instantaneous recording of actual television picture signals on tape would be more economical, would save time in processing, and would simplify certain problems of distribution. . . . After all is said and done, television is just a lot of 'electrical dots' coming through the air. The dots strike the antenna, start electric currents in it, and these go through the various circuits of the receiver until they appear as a picture on the face of the kinescope. . . . I would like to have you produce a recorder that would record the picture elements on a simple and inexpensive tape at the instant when the dots reach the antenna and before they go through a lot of complicated circuits and photographic equipment. . . . Will you please let me have this 'Videograph' before 1956?" (The device, when developed, came to be known more simply as "video tape.")

3. "An electronic air conditioner for the home that would operate with tubes, or possibly through the action of electrons on solids, and without moving parts. It should be small, noiseless, inexpensive, and should fit into any size room. I would name this device 'Electronair.' "

Such were the gifts he craved. "Naturally, I look to the scientists of RCA to be first in solving these problems," he concluded. "But it is in the American spirit of competition that I call attention, publicly, to the need for these inventions." Nor should pioneers of technology be intimidated by the risks of upsetting existing industries through invention of better substitutes. Let the officials of the company "worry about obsolescence. You keep on researching and inventing. Go on and research, discover, and invent to your heart's content. Pitch your mental tents in the field of imagination."

After the address one of the electronics experts was asked what he thought of the three assignments. He shrugged skeptically and whispered: "I wonder whether the General realizes the kind of impossible tasks he has set for us. Well, I shouldn't say 'impossible,' since we specialize in the impossible here."

Would the three inventions be forthcoming in the next five years? Many editorial writers in the following weeks asked the question, alluded to the daring of Sarnoff's imagination and, in the light of his past forecasts, declared themselves optimistic. Forty-five years after he had stumbled on the electron, they said, this man was still marking the road into the future.

The plaque recording the revision of its name was later mounted in the entrance hall of the main building of the Research Center. At the top was a medallion-like portrait of Sarnoff in bas-relief, and under it this inscription:

Commemorating the forty-fifth anniversary of David Sarnoff's entry into the field of radio on September 30, 1906, this plaque is dedicated by his associates in the Radio Corporation of America as a symbol of their esteem and admiration.

As a pioneer of wireless, he has contributed immeasurably to the development of radio, television and electronics as new services to the nation and to the American people.

A creative crusader of progress endowed with a penetrating vision, David Sarnoff has continually led the way across new frontiers in science, art and industry to make the universe vibrant with international communications.

These laboratories, the RCA Victor plants, the RCA worldwide radio circuits and the NBC Radio-Television Networks, symbolize his faith in science, his constructive planning and enduring achievements.

David Sarnoff's work, leadership and genius comprise radio's preeminent record of the past, television's brilliant performance of the present, and a rich legacy in communications for the future.

This laboratory of RCA is named the David Sarnoff Research Center.

2

Columbia Broadcasting had spent millions on developing a color system. It had fought for and won a franchise to launch the new industry. Then it failed to follow up the victory; it allowed its authorized color system to languish. Why? Because it learned the hard way what the opposition had foreseen—that the introduction of noncompatible color was an economic impossibility.

The lassitude of CBS and the palpable improvements in the all-electronic instrument were turning the tide in RCA's favor within a year after the FCC decision. But the inertia of officialdom is a thing of steel. Chairman Coy persevered in defending the mechanical and incompatible system. Senator Johnson, well into 1953, was still fulminating against "powerful interests" blocking Columbia color in order that they might saturate the market with "millions upon millions" of black-and-white sets.

The blockade, of course, was being imposed not by sinister business interests but by practical shortcomings in the approved system. "Who is going to spend money to put on a color show," the *New York Times* asked on March 15, 1953, "if it means the loss of virtually all the existing audience?" And, for that matter, who would buy an expensive color set, or an adapter for monochrome reception, when only a couple of hours of color a week were available?

The National Television Systems Committee, after the initial report by its panel, had continued its studies. It obtained an almost complete industry consensus on compatible specifications, based overwhelmingly on the work done at the David Sarnoff Research Center. CBS itself, facing up to the inevitable, in time associated itself with the NTSC in formulating all-electronic standards.

In late 1953 RCA and the industry committee jointly petitioned the Federal Communications Commission to authorize the marketing of the compatible color system. No prolonged hearings were now required. Time had done its job of education. On December 17, 1953—three years and one month after the previous decision—the FCC in a historic about-face approved the competing apparatus. Perhaps to cushion the blow to its self-esteem, the Commission extended its endorsement to the NTSC rather than to RCA. Since the two sets of specifications were virtually identical, this made no practical difference. It is a safe guess that the cancellation of their abortive franchise drew sighs of relief from Columbia executives. In a sense it took them off a conspicuous and bruising hook.

RCA immediately ran full-page advertisements in key newspapers and in the trade journals announcing its "great victory." The text, signed by General Sarnoff, linked the event to that distant day at the World's Fair in 1939: "At that time we added sight to sound. Now we add color to sight." In a signed column within the ads, president Folsom dealt with the commercial aspects of the news. Color sets and programs in full color would be offered to the public as soon as possible. "The opportunity to enrich the lives of people everywhere is a privilege of leadership," he declared.

The note of boastfulness understandably riled some competitors. Philco was outraged to the point of publishing counteradvertisements denying that the Washington action was "a victory for RCA." "These standards were developed by the leading scientists," it declared, referring to the NTSC. "They are NOT the work of any one company." Commander McDonald of Zenith dispatched an angry letter to the FCC accusing the Radio Corporation of misrepresentation in its advertising.

But the facts were not really in doubt. No complex piece of technology is ever wholly the product of one mind or one laboratory. Color television, too, embodied patents and insights contributed or duplicated by others. Conscientious testing by the industry committee certainly affected the final shape of the apparatus. Yet the decisive ingredients had been provided, constantly refined, demonstrated, and field-tested by RCA, which had put more money into the undertaking than all other researchers combined. The long campaign for FCC approval had been conducted primarily by RCA. The 1950 decision had been widely (and in some quarters gloatingly) billed as a defeat for Sarnoff—to deny that the reversal was a victory for Sarnoff consequently seemed, at the least, ungenerous.

In a direct answer to McDonald, Sarnoff pointed to the magnitude of his company's research in color and its unswerving adherence to all-electronic and compatible principles. RCA, he went on, "has consistently been first in every major color television development. RCA was the first to create, develop and demonstrate a tricolor tube. A color tube is the heart of every modern color television receiver. We know of no significant contribution of the Zenith Radio Corporation to the creation and development of compatible color television."

This minor squall died down. More than that, it took a rather comical turn, in that those who had clamored for a slice of the credit then—in the words of a *Fortune* article—"just sat back and jeered." They were saying, in effect: "We, too, helped make this color system—and it's no damned good!" Zenith, for instance, though it had been most vigorous in staking a claim for credit, called the RCA color tube "a Rube Goldberg contraption." Ralph Cordiner of General Electric was quoted as saying: "If you have a color set, you've almost got to have an engineer living in the house."

The impasse was paradoxical and, for Sarnoff, highly disagreeable. Having participated (through NTSC) in the successful fight for approval, TV manufacturers and broadcasters then undertook what came to a tacit boycott of color television. Sarnoff had achieved his miracle—and was stuck with it. His repeated calls upon competitors to make sets and broadcast color were cold-shouldered and at times openly scoffed at. Now and then he reminded them that he had advised the industry to go into the television business; that the advice had proved good; and that he was no less confident now in recommending color. The boycott continued.

From the vantage point of 1962, *Fortune* could say: "For five years after it marketed its first set in 1954, RCA found itself the solitary tenant of the new world." Said an executive vice-president of RCA, W. Walter Watts: "We thought the other manufacturers would join us, but they stayed away in droves." And Dr. Engstrom explained: "Our competitors were as eager as we to have the right route established for color. Once that was done, the whole industry simply relaxed. We always had our arms around color, and we couldn't let go as the others could."

In plainer words, they had too much invested in color to let go. Besides, General Sarnoff had no intention of letting go. He stood firm, on occasion in lonely isolation, against those in the corporation and in Wall Street who thought that RCA should "cut its losses" by putting color in deep-freeze until other leading firms were ready to share the burdens of its commercialization.

Once more, as in the case of monochrome TV, he was thus in the heroic but financially debilitating posture of championing a new service in defiance of those who would ultimately get rich on it. Only this time the costs and the risks, the howls of pain in his company and the shouts of derision outside, were dramatically greater. RCA investments reached an estimated $130 million before the first dollar of profit came through.

The development and validation of television in natural colors eventually was ranked among the outstanding accomplishments in American industry. Sarnoff's refusal to settle for the second best, his faith in science, and other virtues read into his conduct are frequently trotted out as examples of "business idealism." But it was the prelude to the most difficult and inclement period in Sarnoff's business life. This, moreover, in his middle sixties, at an age when supremely "successful" men are expected to rest on their oars and admire the seascape!

Profitable operations in all other divisions of the sprawling electronics enterprise, it is true, yielded enough capital for pouring into the seemingly bottomless pit of color. But it cut into profits and dividends and acted as a brake on RCA stock values even in bullish markets. Uncertainty within the corporation over the outlook for color became more pronounced and articulate. There was grumbling in Wall Street over the depleting effect on RCA earnings.

Where did the huge investment during these grim years go? Not primarily into research, although refinement of equipment continued. It went into a lot of color programing for which advertisers were not yet prepared to pay the extra production costs; into elaborate sales and promotion campaigns. Because demand was too limited to permit the economies of quantity production, the first sets—though retailed at $1,000—represented an over-all loss to the sole manufacturer. This was the weight that RCA and Sarnoff carried, the protracted trial of their patience, with no sign that the industry boycott was cracking.

He could scarcely be blamed for the acidulous tone in which he on occasion tongue-lashed the boycotteers. In the course of an address to broadcasters in Miami, in December, 1956, he referred to "the Johnny-come-latelies who stayed out of TV for years and let others do the pioneering"— until they saw "gold in the rainbow."

"Remember when black-and-white television arrived?" he went on. "There were those who called us Televisionaries. There were those who said they would never produce black-and-white sets because television broadcasting could never be self-sustaining, and that revenues from advertisers would be insufficient to maintain it. But when the wagon was pushed uphill, and began to roll, plenty of them jumped on the wagon. There will be plenty that will jump on the color wagon when the going gets easier."

That time was slow in coming but when it did come the color wagon filled rapidly. The first credible indication that Sarnoff's faith in the new medium was not misplaced did not show up until 1958, almost five years after the FCC about-face. A sharp decline in sales of ordinary TV sets—due simply to saturation of the market—operated to muffle competitive scoffing. Color might revive a flagging industry after all. More television stations acquired color equipment, just in case.

Only five thousand of the $1,000 receivers were distributed in 1954. The following year, with sharp price reductions, sales volume climbed to 120,000. The first full year of profitable color-set sales was 1959, and by the end of 1961 color television had become a $100 million business. The ice of public doubts and indifference, and with it the industry boycott, was now breaking fast and noisily. A few other manufacturers ventured into production; Zenith offered its line of color sets in 1961, built around what it previously derided as the "Rube Goldberg contraption."

In 1963, American families for the first time bought from the RCA as much color television, reckoned in cash values, as conventional sets. The new industry promised by Sarnoff had not merely arrived but was heading for the financial skies. In 1965 that industry—counting transmitting and receiving equipment, advertising revenues, and other elements—had acquired what an ecstatic trade reporter called "the elite billion-dollars-a-year status."

RCA, at this writing, decidedly is no longer the "solitary tenant" of the world it forced open. Over 80 percent of the country's television stations are equipped for some kind of color telecasting, with about 150 of them able to originate color programs locally. More than twenty companies are manufacturing color sets. Nearly all of them have shown a remarkable capacity for forgetting who was responsible for their new source of affluence, a skill amounting to amnesia. The combined manufacturing capacity is not yet able to meet "the crushing consumer demand for color sets," as Dennis Duggan reported in the New York *Herald Tribune*. The bottleneck is the color tube, which RCA is straining to provide in the vast numbers being ordered.

Color television, the president of General Electric, Fred J. Borch, told his annual meeting in April, 1965, "is the most rapidly rising segment of the consumer goods industry." A significant statement, Gene Smith remarked in his *New York Times* roundup, "since General Electric had dragged its feet in the twelve-year evolutionary struggle for color television." For RCA color television has become a principal source of income and improving profits, and the main support of the impressive rise in the value of its stocks.

I shall not strain to find new words for an old, oft-repeated biographical fact: David Sarnoff was again magnificently vindicated. The service others had disdained, derogated, and boycotted became the mainstay of the radio business. Some of the very men and companies that had attacked and at times ridiculed Sarnoff's persevering faith in the future of color now hailed it— usually without a word of remorse or an avowal of credit to the chairman of RCA—as the most promising development in their industry.

The $130 million invested by RCA suddenly seemed trivial as against the boom they nourished. As yet, most of the color sets being sold are of RCA manufacture. The company's percentual share will necessarily shrink as competitors go into stride, but in absolute terms the volume of its business is likely to keep growing. Besides, most manufacturers buy the RCA color tube, the most costly single ingredient. Of the estimated sale of 2,200,000 tubes in 1965, about 1,500,000 will come out of the RCA plants.

But long after the industry boycott had collapsed at the production end, it persisted at the broadcasting end. For years NBC had been compelled to be the main provider of color programs. The principal deterrent to sales of sets has been, understandably, the dearth of color shows. Before assuming the somewhat higher costs of such programs, other broadcasters preferred to wait for the color market to expand. "We'll go into color when there's enough audience or sponsor demand for it," an unnamed CBS official was saying quite candidly in September, 1962, as reported by *Television Digest.* It was a vicious circle: no color shows until enough sets are in homes and not enough sets in homes until more and better color shows are available. So here once more RCA, through its wholly owned network, was for years practically alone in absorbing the costs of color telecasting.

The hard core of resistance was CBS—"the color laggard," in Gene Smith's phrase. Jack Gould, the influential radio-television editor of the *New York Times,* took that network sharply to task for its color—or rather, no-color—policies. "The main barrier to greater color programing," he called it on November 29, 1964. The network contends that the audience for color is as yet too small, he wrote, then went on:

"This CBS argument is not overly persuasive. It seems to be saying that when General Sarnoff makes color TV sufficiently profitable then CBS will enter the color field. But public responsibility in broadcasting would seem to go a little further. An improved and extended TV service is a national consideration, not just a private one. As the most profitable network in TV the Columbia chain certainly can do as much as others to bring about the new medium more rapidly. The longer CBS holds out, the longer it can argue that color is not yet important. The time may be at hand when the Federal Communications Commission should move into the color situation."

But the broadcasting boycott, too, was crumbling at the edges. Whether touched by Mr. Gould's plea—and implied threat—or not, officials of CBS began hinting that eventually they would embrace color. The third ranking network, ABC, was steadily increasing the proportion of color on its schedules and individual stations were beginning to run old color movies more frequently. "People resist change," Sarnoff has said, "but change is inevitable."

Early in March, 1965, NBC announced that, come the following fall, 95 percent of its regularly scheduled evening shows would be televised in color, as compared with 70 percent in the current season. Only a few days later CBS let it be known that it would finally provide color on a modest scale; two of its major weekly programs and one of its nighttime movie features would switch to color. This small start was reported by Gould as a "capitulation." A few weeks later CBS upped the ante; one half of all its nighttime shows would go to color. General Sarnoff did not conceal his satisfaction. "I guess this may have been the toughest fight of my life," he said with a grin.

In this turgid, long-drawn history one fact is settled beyond doubt. Sarnoff, in the words of Dennis Duggan, is "the undisputed pioneer of color television." And Jack Gould said it earlier, in the above-quoted November 29 article: "The hero of color TV and its indefatigable champion is Brigadier General David Sarnoff. Almost alone he has brought the medium to what it is today."

23

Tribute in Gold

ᴆ In December, 1955, David Sarnoff announced the appointment of his eldest son, Robert, then thirty-seven, as president and chief executive of the National Broadcasting Company. Sylvester (Pat) Weaver, who had held the post during the preceding two years, when Bob Sarnoff was executive vice-president, was named chairman of the board.

The organization was then facing a serious management problem, and many within and outside the network believed that this was the right solution. All the same, the move when it was made had an edge of the sensational. It was known that the General was—as he remains—touchy on imputations of nepotism. Himself the self-made man par excellence, this was wholly in character. As he had expected, the elevation of his son stirred some criticism. There were snide allusions to the "Sarnoff dynasty" and his "crown prince." The decision had taken courage, or gall, depending on who told the story. But it had a solid base in terms of practical managerial considerations.

Bob Sarnoff, after graduation from Harvard and a year at Columbia Law School, had served for a time under General "Wild Bill" Donovan in the broadcasting section of the Coordinator of Information (later the OSS), then as a communications officer in the Navy. After his discharge he sought a place in advertising and found it in the Cowles publishing and broadcasting organization. First he worked in Des Moines on the Cowles newspaper, where he made a good record in the home office, and a year later he transferred to *Look* magazine in New York.

In the latter part of 1947 he concluded that the magazine business was not what he really wanted. Television was then on the threshold of its career and

Bob rightly judged that it was destined to become the nation's dominant entertainment, news, and advertising medium. His training and abilities, he felt, justified him in seeking a place in the new business. He therefore discussed the prospects, not with his father but with his friend Frank Mullen, then the executive vice-president of NBC. Mullen hired him as a time salesman at the beginning of 1948. Though the elder Sarnoff expressed some misgivings, he raised no objections.

After a period in network sales, Bob went into the TV network program operation, still in its rudimentary and experimental phase at that time. He grew in experience along with the unfolding medium, first as manager of TV program sales and then in charge of program production. In 1952 he became vice-president in charge of NBC Film Division and a year later executive vice-president of the company. Thus when he assumed the presidency of NBC at the end of 1955 he had been through the mill in the TV business, which by that time had become the heart of the whole NBC enterprise.

A year later, on his initiative, Robert E. Kintner was brought into the organization as an executive vice-president. Kintner, a former newspaperman, had just resigned as head of the American Broadcasting Company. About eighteen months after he joined NBC he was named president, with Bob Sarnoff moving up to chairman of the board. The two Bobs worked together harmoniously, with Kintner as the principal operating officer and Sarnoff as chief executive.

The junior Sarnoff, forty-seven at this writing, is a tallish man, good-looking, with a quiet manner and a certain elegance in dress and deportment. He is basically the down-to-earth businessman, primarily concerned with practical results, although he has inherited much of his father's interest in public affairs.

In November, 1956, a year after his son became president of NBC, General Sarnoff brought the issue of nepotism into the open. A two-day meeting in Miami celebrating the thirtieth anniversary of the network provided an appropriate occasion. Speaking extemporaneously, he said in part:

"I should like to say a word or two about Bob, with pardonable pride which I naturally feel at his fine job. I should like to tell you what he himself, I am sure, would not tell you. That is the fact that it is not always easy for the son of a father who is head of an organization to overcome all the roadblocks that attach to such a situation. I am not weeping for him, because I think that perhaps there is an advantage or two also, which might counterbalance these difficulties in a measure. . . .

"Sometimes fathers are criticized—particularly if they head public corporations as distinguished from private organizations—for having members of their own family in the same business in positions of responsibility. I have thought a good deal about this and have developed my own philosophy. Right or wrong, I should like to suggest it to you because some of you might have similar experiences."

The gist of that philosophy, as he explained it, was "that when a man stands in the way of his own son's progress, he is not thinking of the son, he is thinking of himself. He is apprehensive about criticism which might be leveled against him. Now if what you do or fail to do is done in behalf of your son, I applaud it. If, however, what you do or fail to do is done to save yourself from possible criticism by some uninformed person who refuses to recognize that your son's ability had better be used for your company's benefit than that of a competitor, then I don't think you merit any applause. . . .

"I suggest that fathers have no more right to stand in the way of their sons' progress than the sons have to stand in the way of progress of their fathers. I am proud of the job that Bob and his associates in the NBC are doing and I wish them continued success."

This was the first time he aired the subject publicly—and the last. He did not delude himself that the airing would silence critics. The charge of nepotism was much too handy a weapon to be abandoned by those who needed one.

Earlier in the talk General Sarnoff had said that NBC now had "the best and most complete organization we have had since the advent of television." Fortunately for both father and son, this statement could stand the test of financial statistics.

The network has prospered consistently since Robert Sarnoff assumed full responsibility, notwithstanding the handicap of heavy initial drains by color broadcasting. NBC profits have risen steadily, reducing and almost eliminating the margin of advantage in this respect until then enjoyed by CBS. In news programs NBC has set the pace for all competitors. In 1960 the network's radio business, as distinct from television, began to show substantial profits in the face of a contrary trend in the industry as a whole. In short, successful operation has provided the most effective answer to charges of nepotism. The young man's rise from time salesman to president in seven years seems to have been justified by the ten-year record. No one in a position to watch the operation from close quarters has questioned Bob's solid abilities.

What of the other sons?

Edward, after the war, bought into the RCA distributorship in Hartford, Connecticut. A few years later he sold his interest and acquired a distributing franchise in Fresno, California. Subsequently he returned to New York, where he bought from his uncle Lew a small but promising messenger service. It has since then grown into a large and lucrative business.

The youngest son, Thomas, returned to Princeton after a brief military service. Midway, however—against the counsel but with the consent of his father—he transferred to Stanford University. After graduating in engineering he took a postgraduate course in business administration. Having fallen in love with California, he decided to sink roots there. First he worked in the production and then in the sales departments of the American Broadcasting Company—a Sarnoff with a competing network!—then in the production department of Metro-Goldwyn-Mayer. In 1952 Tommy switched to NBC and after ten years' service in the production and business administration departments of the company, he became vice-president in charge of coordinating its West Coast activities.

Toward his youngest brother, Irving, David always had an especially close, almost paternal attitude—possibly because the boy had been so very young when they all lost their father. After several successful years as a salesman in the cotton goods business, Irving, in his early twenties, bought a one-third partnership in Bruno–New York, a wholesale distributor of RCA and other electronic and musical products in the metropolitan area; before long he was credited with being considerably richer than his eldest brother. His untimely death, in 1961, was a desolating blow from which the General has not yet recovered.

Brother Morris, after experiments in other fields, went into insurance. Later he sold his interest in that business and engaged in a variety of other enterprises, from manufacturing razor blades to real estate, until forced into premature retirement by illness. He now resides in Florida.

Not until relatively late in his life did Lew emulate his brothers in money-making. Once started, however, he caught up with and perhaps outdistanced them (as measured in dollars and cents) in a fairly short period. His first association was in a small company engaged in cleaning and maintaining large buildings. Soon, under his direction, the company ranked among the biggest in its field, and from there Lew moved into other profitable enterprises.

2

Exactly half a century after little David was hired by the old Marconi Company, a thousand friends, associates, and industry people filled the Grand Ballroom at the Waldorf-Astoria. They had assembled on September 30,

1956, to commemorate what the toastmaster, John T. Cahill, chief RCA counsel, called "his golden wedding to radio and electronics."

It has been a successful marriage. By pleasant coincidence 1955 was the corporation's first billion-dollar year. There was thus real, glittering gold in the Golden Anniversary—as if his career were being stage-managed by fate for maximum dramatic effects. It seemed somehow typical of the man's life, yet another case of "Sarnoff luck."

The scene was opulent, the guests in an exuberant mood, the eulogies properly extravagant. Letters and telegrams of congratulation, all well spiced with flattery, were so numerous that only a small part could be read from the dais, among them greetings from Winston Churchill, President Eisenhower, Vice-President Nixon, former President Hoover, Arturo Toscanini, Dr. Lee De Forest, Adlai Stevenson, Bernard Baruch, Mayor Robert Wagner.

There were plenty of testimonial awards and honors, of course. The board of directors presented its chairman with a large gold medal: a three-quarters profile portrait in bas-relief on one side and the encomium on the other; a small replica in burnished bronze was at every guest's plate as a memento of the evening.

An outsized crystal vase was presented in the name of the eighty thousand RCA employees. It was decorated with fine engravings of Sarnoff's military awards and insignia, grouped around a big star for his rank of brigadier general. Handsome plaques came from the National Electronics Distributors Association and the National Appliance and Radio-TV Dealers Association. An illuminated scroll, signed by president-emeritus H. V. Kaltenborn, was presented for the Radio Pioneers of America. And I must not overlook the rose handed to the beaming guest of honor by his beaming eldest granddaughter, the thirteen-year-old Rosita, since it rated a photograph, along with the other trophies, in the gold-covered booklet recording the proceedings for posterity.

Here, in a golden glow, was fulfillment of "the great American dream—the office boy who became head of a tremendous and powerful corporation." The quotation is from an anniversary editorial in the New York *World-Telegram & Sun*. Now well into his sixty-sixth year, when most men retire or are retired, Sarnoff "seemed ageless," according to another editorial. His hair, it is true, was sparser and grayer, but his round, cherubic countenance, still fresh and unlined, glowed with health, vigor, and pride.

Earlier that year, upon reaching the conventional age of retirement, RCA's board of directors asked him to serve another ten-year term and the contract was sweetened with a stock option. Long before the term was ended, the first billion-dollar year was moving rapidly toward the first two-billion-dollar year and RCA equities were booming. Exercising the option, Sarnoff was at last endowed with what was for Horatio Alger the sole evidence of success—he became, that is to say, a millionaire.

I have tried to spare the reader, as far as possible, the panegyric oratory usual at such functions in hotel ballrooms, when men say the kind of things they would blush to utter sitting down. But at the half-century mark a few samples are perhaps permissible, to suggest the flavor of the festivities.

President Folsom offered a "warm, affectionate pledge of continued devotion and loyalty." Adlai Stevenson credited Sarnoff with contributions to technological advances which "have profoundly changed our civilization." The National Commander of the American Legion hailed him as "one of our greatest Legionnaires and outstanding industrialists." Senator Lyndon B. Johnson wrote: "Your work has not only expanded human knowledge but has contributed to the well-being, the security, and the prosperity of all your fellow-Americans."

Since their first meeting in London on the eve of D day, Sarnoff's relations with General Eisenhower, now President of the United States, had evolved into genuine friendship. Among the teeming laudations from outside, therefore, the highlight of the evening for Sarnoff was the one from the White House. Addressing his letter to "Dear Dave," the President wrote in part:

"The Golden Anniversary, marking your fifty years in the field of radio, television and electronics is made brilliant by your leadership and great contributions in the science, art, and industry of communications. You have established an outstanding record of service to the American people and to the Nation. You have helped greatly to bulwark the pre-eminence of the United States in electronics and worldwide communications."

Five years before, the reader will recall, Sarnoff had asked for three "presents" on his Golden Anniversary: a magnetic tape recorder for both black-and-white and color television images; an electronic amplifier of light; and an all-electronic air conditioner. As everyone already knew, the gifts had been duly invented. Dr. Engstrom, as head of the Research Center, took to the lectern to deliver the goods. The actual physical equipment was at Princeton and would be demonstrated to the press and assorted guests the following day, but he confirmed their existence and described them through a series of slides.

The television tape recorder—both in black-and-white and in color—had, in fact, been invented and exhibited to the press in late 1953, two years ahead of the five-year deadline. But meanwhile another company, Ampex, had produced a similar device—in black-and-white only—and beat RCA to the punch in its commercialization of a video tape. For a time Ampex had the huge market to itself, counting even RCA and NBC among its customers. However, before long RCA tape, for both color and black-and-white, was released and won a large slice of the market. Today the magnetic recorder is perhaps the most indispensable single tool of television broadcasting, which speaks well for Sarnoff's instinct in asking for it back in 1951.

The electronic light amplifier developed at the Princeton laboratories, Dr. Engstrom reported, already made images a thousand times brighter. As an important by-product the apparatus was adapted for use in X-ray fluoroscopes, where it already multiplied brightness one-hundredfold.

The research on an air conditioner, too, yielded a by-product: an all-electronic refrigerator, noiseless and without moving parts. Although prototypes of both pieces of equipment were ready for the fifty-year celebration, neither of them became available to the public until the 1960's, primarily because they were still too expensive to compete with the existing electric products. RCA is not in the refrigerator business, but at this writing Sears, Roebuck has marketed a noiseless electronic refrigerator, manufactured for it by Whirlpool, to which RCA turned over further development of the product.

The successful invention of the three items within a specified time—prescribed almost arbitrarily by an administrator, not a scientist—was a significant achievement. It provided support, once more, for Sarnoff's oft-reiterated thesis that modern techniques of collective research can bring into being almost anything the human mind can visualize. There were engineers at the party that night who had been openly skeptical five years before, when "the boss" gave them those "impossible" assignments.

In the press reports and editorials, however, these inventions-to-order were overshadowed by General Sarnoff's speech in response to the tributes. He had come prepared with a long list of predictions—and apparently things to come are considered more newsworthy than things already arrived. His anniversary speech is dealt with here at some length because it contained, I think, many of the elements for which he was by then famous: the long technological look, a wide-focused interest in social-political matters, even flashes of humor.

3

"Fifty years!" David Sarnoff exclaimed at the outset. "One has to pause to savor the fact. Why, most of you in this hall—and that includes *all* the ladies—were not yet born when I began my career on the ground floor of the

Marconi Wireless Company in 1906. And I mean the ground floor—for sweeping that floor was one of my occasional chores.

"Fifty years! Teddy Roosevelt was President. Horsecars plied the streets of New York. You could get a schooner of beer for a nickel, and a free lunch at the bar. Gaslight was used in most homes. The horseless carriage was a novelty. Radio broadcasting was unheard, and television was unseen.

"I was only fifteen years old and life for me was a blank page—challenging and a bit frightening in its clean white emptiness. Well, I have done a good deal of scrawling over it in half a century. I'd gladly make some erasures and edit out some errors if I could. Yet on the whole I am content. For they have been endlessly fascinating years for me and for the world of science, business, and industry where fate has placed me."

He went on to thank the Princeton researchers for their presents: his "faith in their genius has been fully justified." And again, he said, he dared peer into the future:

"However impressive the events that have filled the last fifty years, or even the last century, I am convinced that they will be eclipsed by the events of the next twenty years. I take this arbitrary span of time because we can hope that, 'with a little bit of luck,' all those present—myself included—will still be around to check on the accuracy of our vision. In fact, I have already been promised an eighty-fifth birthday party and you are all cordially invited to attend."

General Sarnoff then proceeded with an inventory of "twenty major developments within the next twenty years," in "capsule summaries." Since each of them really covered a category of expectations, the actual number of his predictions was many times twenty. He knew that he was "sticking out his neck," he said, but those are the "hazards of prophecy." I must condense his capsules further, quoting some of the text and paraphrasing the rest:

1. *Nuclear Energy:* "We will have learned to extract atomic fuel from relatively inexpensive materials, thus making this power both plentiful and economical. . . . *Direct* conversion of atomic energy into electricity—a principle already demonstrated experimentally by RCA—will be a fact. Atomic batteries, based on low-cost waste products from nuclear reactors and operating for many years without recharging, will supply energy for industry and for homes."

2. *Solar Energy:* "The energy of sun rays will be effectively harnessed and in worldwide use." It will prove of special value to underdeveloped peoples in tropical and semitropical areas where sunlight is abundant but present-day fuels and power sources too costly.

3. *Communications:* "Television, in full colors, will be completely global, so that man will be able not only to speak and to hear all around this planet but to see the entire world in natural colors." And of course, the Sarnoff special: "Individuals will be able to hold private two-way conversations, and see each other as they talk, regardless of the distances separating them."

4. *Transportation:* "Jet-propulsion and rocket-type vehicles, using nuclear fuels, will travel at speeds as high as five thousand miles an hour with greater safety and comfort than today's aircraft. . . . Inexpensive personal planes, flivvers of the skies, will fill the air. . . . Guided missiles will transport mail and other freight over vast distances, including oceans."

5. *Automation:* This process, already far advanced, "will reach a crescendo under the impact of cheap and abundant power." Though the transition will pose problems of adjustment, "ultimately it will free millions of people from arduous and hazardous work" and "will increase employment, reduce hours of labor and increase leisure."

6. *Materials:* Chemistry will provide "a tremendous array of new plastics, ceramics, lubricants, and categories of substances that as yet have no name will become available for personal and industrial uses."

7. *Electronic Light:* "Electroluminescence or 'cold light,' now emerging from the research laboratories, will bring into being startling new types of illumination. It will change the appearance of our factories, streets, stores, highways, and homes. Providing light without heat and almost without shadow, its glow will be subject to easy control for volume and color nuances to suit any taste or decor. Being light without glare, it will eliminate many of the perils of night driving and flying. It will also give us brighter and bigger TV pictures, and ultimately replace the TV tube altogether with a thin, flat-surface screen that will be hung like a picture on the wall."

8. *Computers:* These electronic marvels "will reach fruition." The million Americans now engaged in clerical tasks will be replaced by robots, freeing them for other work. "New products will, for the most part, have their performance predicted by computers, removing the need for building actual working models."

9. *Food:* "Striking developments in irrigation and flood control, more efficient use of solar energy, the electronic acceleration of germination and growth, as well as new chemical and biological discoveries will greatly expand mankind's food resources. At the same time, the oceans will be efficiently 'farmed' for nutritive products." This will in time provide the true answer to the population explosion.

10. *Health:* Ever closer ties between biology, chemistry and physics—

"applying the new tools of electronics and atomics"—will bring "an avalanche of improvements in preventive medicine, diagnosis, and treatment of human ills. . . . Man's life-span will be further extended, probably within hailing distance of the century mark."

11. *The Home:* "The housewife's dream of an all-automatic home will be realized. The day's chores in the home will be prescheduled, with each of the tasks performed electronically. . . . Electronic appliances will do the cooking and the dishwashing and will dispose of waste. Fortunately, we shall continue to do our own eating."

12. *Climate:* "Not only will the prediction of weather for months and even years ahead be perfected, but major steps will have been taken to make and control weather as desired. Ports now icebound will be unfrozen and icebergs rapidly melted. Progress will have been made in dissipating storms even of hurricane intensity, or of diverting them from a destructive course."

A dozen prophecies and all technological—"an area where we can tread with some assurance," Sarnoff said. "I wish I had the same degree of assurance with respect to developments in the social and political areas, where the most unpredictable force of all—human conduct—tells the story." Nevertheless, he added eight nontechnical categories, "perhaps in an overly optimistic spirit, yet with faith in the ultimate good sense of the race of men."

"Within the next twenty years," he believed, "Soviet communism will collapse under the weight of its economic fallacies, its political follies, and the pressures of restive, discontented populations. . . . The Soviet empire will fall apart as one satellite after another attains its own liberation. The Communist hierarchy will destroy itself by internal struggles for power and will be displaced by a military dictatorship which in turn will give way to representative government."

He foresaw the decline of the prestige of Marxism generally, through an ever-wider realization "that centralized state economy is incompatible with human freedom." At the same time "the dynamics of a people's capitalism within a democratic framework will be intensified." Living standards would rise all over the world, he guessed: "Slowly but surely the waters of wretchedness now covering so much of the earth will recede, and levels of well-being without parallel will be attained all over the world."

Levels of education, too, would rise and "the intellectual climate will be favorable to development of special talents and individual genius." Highly geared technology "will put a premium on brains" and education will respond to "this mounting demand for mental competence." At the same time, because of unprecedented popular access to information, "public opinion will be a more decisive element in the political life of nations" and democratic processes will become more effective.

He went along with the hope, widely held at the time, that because of the advent of weapons of near-total destructiveness "war as an instrument of international policy will be outlawed." All nations would be forced to implement true, foolproof disarmament.

His final forecast, dealing with science and religion, was his most ambitious —less a prophecy than a verbalized groping for a personal faith in a world replete with troubles:

"As a reaction against current cynicism and materialism, there will be an upsurge of spiritual vitality. The gradual elimination of physical hungers will deepen the more elemental hungers for faith and salvation, for age-old values beyond the material and temporal that gnaw at the heart of man.

"Science begets humility. Its every discovery reveals more clearly the Divine design in nature, the remarkable harmony of all things, from the infinitesimal to the infinite, that surpasses mortal understanding. The physical processes and laws of the universe are logical, all-embracing, and wholly dependable. They imply a Supreme Architect, and the beauty and symmetry of His handiwork inspire reverence.

"It may be that the imperfection of man, too, is a part of that creative symphony. The seed of moral perfection has been planted in man, but it has been left to him to nurture it to full flower in the harsh soil of mortal existence. Thus man is given a positive role in carrying out a phase of the blueprint of the Supreme Architect."

At this writing, nearly half of the twenty-year span to which his preview was limited has gone by. Some of his specific predictions have not yet matured to the point where fulfillment by 1976 is likely. It would have been more prudent, possibly, to extend his sights to the end of the century. But none of them, at least in the scientific areas, is mere daydreaming. They are all technically feasible and for the most part already at differing stages of development.

A few of his "overly optimistic" political forecasts no longer seem quite as farfetched as they had in 1956. Auguries of the disintegration, if not yet the collapse, of Soviet communism have been multiplying. His vision of Red puppet states attaining their own liberation seem confirmed by the full-scale Hungarian revolt only a month after he risked the prediction. Though that country's heroism did not win liberation, it provided the proofs of explosive forces under the policed surfaces of communism that may yet confound those who accept the "finality" of Soviet dominion in Eastern and Central Europe.

The truth, all the same, is that with respect to political and sociological developments Sarnoff's picture of the future is as clouded by wishful thinking as the average man's. Disarmament and the outlawing of war seem, if anything, more remote today than they did in 1956. Marxism as a science has, in fact, lost ground in advanced nations; but despotic centralized state economies under "socialist" and other labels are proliferating in Africa, Asia, and even Latin America. And unfortunately there are as yet few credible symptoms of any "upsurge of spiritual values." Techniques for projecting physical facts into the future simply cannot be applied to human conduct.

In his sweeping exercise in scientific prognosis at the Golden Anniversary there was a curious omission. The Soviet Sputnik was only a year in the future. What was still referred to as an "artificial moon" was the stuff of science fiction and popular journalism. But Sarnoff made no mention and offered no hint of earth-orbiting vehicles. It is hard to believe that he was not aware of the sensational developments in that area; RCA itself was working on some of the equipment. The omission, it is likely, was not an oversight but imposed by official secrecy.

Almost twenty years earlier, writing in the *American Magazine* of April, 1948, he had alluded to the possibility of using heavenly bodies to "bounce" electronic signals from one part of the earth to another: "The moon, less than two seconds away, might serve as a sounding board to relay broadcasts or a mirror to reflect television pictures. We may even find future broadcasters staking claims to Jupiter or Saturn!" While thus anticipating the reality in theory, he apparently had as yet no intimation of man-made moons to come.

Then, in an article in *Popular Mechanics* (December, 1951), Sarnoff had blueprinted television networks not only linking all countries and continents but ultimately capable of disseminating a single program to the whole world. But it was an overland, not a spatial, system that he visualized.

Some ninety years earlier, work had actually been started on an ambitious overland system of telegraph lines on a global scale, adjusted to the geographical configurations of the earth's surface. Before it had got very far, Cyrus Field succeeded in laying a transatlantic cable which made the overland scheme unnecessary. Now Sarnoff, following substantially the same routes, suggested construction of a worldwide television web, using microwave relays on land.

An Amercian transcontinental system, he proposed, would branch off in

California, one line going down the Pacific coast to Patagonia, the other up the coast to Bering Strait, and thence across Siberia, China, India, Iran, and Iraq. From the Middle East coaxial cables or microwave relays or a combination of the two would convey the signals to the countries of continental Europe and Britain, while other spurs would extend into Africa.

What he described was a chain of relay towers which, in his words, would "march across the countries of the globe like rows of pins on a battle map, each picking up, boosting, and sending signals to the next." These repeater stations would be spaced between twenty and fifty miles apart. The global network could be supplemented by what he called a "radio airlift," using regular passenger planes in flight over the Atlantic to provide a constant transoceanic channel; sixteen planes properly deployed, he calculated, would suffice to link America and Europe.

Just as the original telegraph design was canceled out by the Cyrus Field cable, so its adaptation by Sarnoff has been canceled out by earth-orbiting communications satellites. But it stands on the record impressively as testimony to the sweep of the man's mind. Few more daring electronic proposals had ever been committed to paper.

Of the several alternatives for electronic switchboards in space, Sarnoff at an early stage championed the Early Bird type of satellite which is now displacing the low-level Telstar and Relay satellites. In the address to the American Bar Association cited in an earlier context he also said:

"In its advanced form, I believe, our space communications system will consist of three synchronous satellites, each positioned about 22,300 miles above the equator. Moving at a speed matching that of the earth's rotation, they will in effect hover over a fixed point on its surface. Three such satellites, one each over the Atlantic, Pacific and Indian Oceans, would cover the entire global area except the polar regions."

One such synchronous satellite, the one over the Atlantic, has since then become a functioning fact. The Comsat's Early Bird was successfully positioned, then successfully put into practical operation in May, 1965. It would appear to be the first step in the realization of the "advanced form" foreseen and advocated by David Sarnoff.

24

The Crusade That Failed

ᐒ David Sarnoff had firm opinions on many domestic and world problems and expressed them with his accustomed vigor in speeches and occasional writings. He brought to them, however, little of the ardor and systematic follow-up evident in his pursuit of specific electronic goals. Though he might sympathize with their objectives, he never threw himself into any of the movements for speeding up social change. Clearly he was not by temperament a reformer or a crusader for "causes."

The nearest he came to engaging in a long-term political crusade was in his fight against communism. But even here he could not be induced to join any of the teeming anti-Communist leagues and committees. He sought to alert the American people to the danger and, if possible, to influence official policies; but he stopped short of participating in organized action.

In the mid-thirties, as a reaction to the confusions and despairs of the depression, communism—not as it was but as the bewitched and bewildered imagined it to be—won adherents throughout American society. Artists, intellectuals, entertainers seemed especially vulnerable to its propaganda. Doubtless there were fellow travelers among Sarnoff's out-of-office friends. They engaged him in ideological polemics in those years when free economy was on the defensive. But they never succeeded in drawing him into their miasmic world. It was not fashionable at that time to include communism in any indictment of totalitarianism, but Sarnoff in his speeches denounced them all—Brown, Black or Red—as part of the identical evil.

Outspoken opponents of the totalitarian affliction usually came to it through political thought or experience. Sarnoff, uniquely, came to it through his involvement in communications. He was affronted by the misuse of science and technology to propagate antidemocratic movements like fascism or communism. Long before many Americans were conscious of the phenomenon, he was aware of the worldwide "struggle for the minds of men" and accordingly, as we have seen, began pressing for a strong Voice of America.

During the war, as an Army officer, he necessarily avoided frontal attacks on communism, with which we were then in history's strangest alliance. But he steered clear, too, of the modish but senseless glorification of Stalin and his works. With the cessation of hostilities, the Brown and Black variants having been beaten, only the Red remained. Our main prize of victory, the cold war, was under way. Sarnoff was among those who saw and proclaimed its mortal threat. With increasing frequency and sharpness he warned that unless the great democratic powers developed a will to win that conflict they could lose it by default.

A few statements in 1950: Before the Senate Committee on Foreign Affairs he said that our immediate goal "should be to ring the Iron Curtain countries with radio broadcasting" in order to mobilize their internal forces of resistance. "It is our task to penetrate the Iron Curtain," he told the Society of Naval Engineers, "to awaken the Soviet people . . . to give hope to the enslaved populations of the satellite states." Addressing an Encampment of the Veterans of Foreign Wars, he said that "the greatest threat ever faced by free men" was communism and that "the time has passed for treading softly in fear of offending the Politburo, for protocol and compromise."

During the presidential campaign of 1952, Sarnoff was asked by General Eisenhower for a confidential assessment of the cold war as he saw it. He came through with a 35-page document, dated September 19, presenting a strategy for what he called "psychological peacefare." In sum it proposed that the free world seize the initiative by making common cause with the restive peoples in the Communist-captive world. He recommended the formation of a High Command, headed by a Secretary with Cabinet rank, charged with "the prevention of a Hot War through victory in the Cold War." With regard to the Red satellite states, a lively issue in the campaign, he wrote:

"Let us not be thwarted from the path of victory by those who shy away from slogans of Liberation. For those already under the Kremlin's iron heel, there is only one gateway to freedom and it is Liberation. We cannot in good conscience exhort them to seek freedom without spelling it out in terms of ultimate liberation."

As a first step, he asked that the American government issue a Declaration of Peace: a clear-cut commitment to "a world under law," as uninhibited and uncompromising as the adversary's commitment to an all-Communist world. Once such a decision to attain victory is made, he believed, "the development of appropriate methods becomes possible."

The fact that he submitted this unpublished analysis to Eisenhower had no special political implications. He would quite as readily have given his views to the Democratic candidate had he been asked. It seemed to him that the cold war, like any "real" war, should not be treated as a partisan issue. He had reached the conclusion that, if we failed to muster the intellectual clarity and moral strength for a firm decision to win the political-psychological struggle, we would remain on the defensive, confused, easy prey for the enemy.

To mark its twenty-fifth anniversary, *Fortune* invited a number of prominent Americans to set forth their expectations for the country and the world in the next twenty-five years. It was an assignment cut to Sarnoff's measure. His was the first article in the series, published in the issue of January, 1955, under the title "The Fabulous Future."

In a many-faceted preview of 1980 he gave the major space to the stirring promises of the technological age. He described the many ways in which the electron, the atom, solar energy, and other new forces would transform and enrich man's life—provided freedom prevailed against "the continuing communist drive for world power." General Sarnoff therefore devoted a final section to this all-important proviso—captioned "The Challenge of Communism"—and expressed hope that "the free world has learned at last not to drop its guard under the spell of the Kremlin's tactical amiability." It drew more attention and provoked more comment than anything else in the whole magazine series.

The maintenance of military ascendancy was indispensable, he wrote, and in this connection "the most important immediate need" seemed to him "clear superiority in the development of the longest-range guided projectiles, the so-called ICBM Intercontinental Ballistic Missiles." He called for a "crash program" to achieve that superiority. However:

"The immediate danger is not a bombing contest but the debilitating, bankrupting, ruthless, and relentless communist offensive in a cold war that may continue throughout the coming quarter-century. . . . We do not shrink from appropriating fifty billion dollars or even more for armaments, but we are still reluctant to spend a few billions to meet the more urgent needs of the prevailing cold war. Because there is no sound of shooting, no thunder of exploding bombs, we do not as yet have the feeling of life-and-death urgency. But it *is* that urgent. Our defeat in the present non-military struggle would doom what remains of freedom on this planet as completely as defeat in a shooting war.

"The cold war is where the communists are determined to defeat *us*. And that, by the same token, is where we could defeat *them*, once we recognized the new state of affairs and decided to meet it resolutely, with the same concentration of effort, the same readiness for sacrifice and risk, the same dedication to victory as if it were an old-style military challenge.

"The West and its allies in Asia can capture the initiative only by a definite decision: to win the cold war, or at the very least to prevent the communists from winning it. In my view, this is the only real guarantee against a hot war. . . .

"The importance of winning the cold war cannot be glossed over in looking ahead to 1980," he concluded. "Unless we assure peace, unless we gain the initiative in the cold conflict—by means short of a hot war—the triumphs of science and technology that I have sketched in broad strokes will be emptied of meaning. If freedom is lost, if the dignity of man is destroyed, advances on the material plane will not be 'progress' but a foundation of a new savagery. . . . Our supreme commitment, as we look ahead to a crucial quarter-century, must be to win the peace—not a peace of totalitarian dominion but a genuine peace rooted in liberty."

2

Barely two months after the appearance of this article Sarnoff was at the White House for one of his frequent sessions with President Eisenhower. When their talk touched on recent cold-war events, Sarnoff plunged into a spirited restatement of the need for a full-scale counteroffensive to win the contest. In essence it was an elaboration of his campaign analysis several years earlier and of the recent *Life* article.

Apparently the President had not read the article and his recollection of the campaign document had presumably been dimmed by time and crowding crises. Perhaps, also, a face-to-face exposition is more effective than one in writing. In any event, Eisenhower reacted as if the ideas were new and exciting.

"Dave," he said in effect, "I'd like you to repeat what you've just told me to some of my associates here."

"Of course, Boss, I'd be glad to."

Right there and then, by telephone, the President arranged a meeting for Sarnoff that very afternoon with Allen Dulles, head of the CIA, Nelson Rockefeller, who was then on the presidential staff, and a number of others from the State and Defense Departments. Sarnoff went through that conference in some embarrassment. After all, his general thesis was neither original nor novel, being typical of the "hard" approach in the debate on cold-war policies. To the officials rounded up by the President, he assumed, it could scarcely be new or astonishing.

The upshot of the meeting was that Sarnoff agreed to prepare a detailed Memorandum embodying his concepts. This he submitted to President Eisenhower and the others on April 5, 1955. It was titled: "Program for a Political Offensive Against World Communism." On May 9, James Hagerty, the press secretary, released it to White House correspondents, with the implication at least of presidential blessings.

Basically the Memorandum was a sharply reasoned reiteration, in more detailed and concrete terms, of the policies its author had been plugging for many years. Yet its impact seemed tremendous. The Memorandum was well reported in the press and on the air and evoked favorable editorials across the nation. The full text was published by the weekly *U.S. News & World Report*. It was read into the Congressional Record by Senator Lyndon B. Johnson, with laudatory prefatory remarks. Made available as a pamphlet by Sarnoff's office, edition after edition was quickly exhausted in response to continuing demand. A paperback book on cold-war strategy included the Memorandum as a signed chapter. The Freedoms Foundation at Valley Forge awarded its George Washington Honor Medal that year to Sarnoff in recognition of the Memorandum. In due time the paramount award was made in Moscow, where *Pravda* denounced him as a warmonger in its best vituperative style.

Probably no more cogent and persuasive outline of a strategy for victory over communism had as yet appeared in the United States, certainly not in such succinct and nonacademic form. It remains one of the highlights of the historic debate on foreign policy in the 1950's. Its warning that we dare not settle for less than victory in the political-psychological war was summed up in a much-quoted line: "Whether we freeze to death or burn to death, our civilization would be equally finished." The document analyzed "how the communists wage cold war," then argued, item by item, that analogous techniques could be used with even greater effect by the free world.

Shortly after the release of the Sarnoff plan by the White House, Senator Lyndon B. Johnson traveled to New York to address a dinner in Sarnoff's honor at the Waldorf-Astoria, under the auspices of the Williamsburg Settlement. The senator praised the Sarnoff thesis and himself called for "the greatest political offensive in history . . . to win the cold war." But this view, though shared by millions of their countrymen, was largely washed out by tides of wishful hoping. In July, 1955, came the so-called Summit Conference in Geneva—and then disillusionment. Sarnoff was among those who steadfastly resisted the general euphoria.

I have before me a file of Sarnoff pronouncements in this subject area, year after year. In the nature of the case they are repetitive. He persevered in his demand for a cold-war counteroffensive to weaken and ultimately cancel out the Communist threat. Testifying before the Committee on Armed Services, with Senator Johnson presiding, he declared: "It is late, but not too late, to face up to the imperatives of the cold war. In the battle for men's minds, Soviet successes have been due less to the genius of the Kremlin than to the lethargy of the West. After all, we are not without opportunities for taking the initiative."

Another opportunity to press his viewpoint came when he was invited to make the principal address at the solemn Veterans Day ceremonies, on November 11, 1958, at the Tomb of the Unknowns. In summing up the lessons "especially pertinent to our time" inherent in the sacrifices of the three nameless patriots, General Sarnoff placed Courage at the head of the list, and went on to say:

"In this period of crisis we would do well to take their lesson of courage to heart. For only with unwavering courage can we face up to the Communist campaign of bluster and blackmail. Only with that sort of courage can we meet and defeat the Red strategy of nibbling and intimidation. Above all, only with supreme courage can we overcome the constant temptation to compromise on principles in the name of expediency. We must keep our eyes on the compass of principle to help us steer a true course. Without its fixed points of integrity, we are helpless in the winds of propaganda and the storms of abuse blowing from Moscow and Peiping."

But none of his oratory and writings, the 1955 Memorandum included, had any real effect on the course of national policy. The impulse toward "accommodation" with the Soviet Union gained the upper hand. Among its memorable expressions was Khrushchev's barnstorming across the United States as the guest of the American government.

Sarnoff was one of thirty-odd guests at a reception for the Soviet dictator at the New York home of Governor Harriman. The party was off-record but news of a brief and barbed interchange between the Russian leader and an eminent American of Russian origin leaked out. As reported by *Life,* General Sarnoff proposed to Khrushchev a "free exchange of information" in the interests of peace.

"We would like to communicate freely with the Russian people," he said.

"We do not prevent Russian programs in the United States. Why doesn't the Soviet government permit the same freedom?"

Khrushchev was angered, or pretended to be. "You want to propagandize us!" he exclaimed.

"All I want, Mr. Chairman, is a free interchange of information such as we are having in this room."

That was "a loaded question," Khrushchev fairly shouted. His government couldn't allow outsiders to interfere with the education of Soviet youth and "raising such questions could lead to no good."

He was right—it led to no good. The thirty-odd guests found the man dogmatic, inflexible, incapable of discussion on a rational level.

Around 1961 David Sarnoff ceased to talk publicly about communism. Tacitly he acknowledged that the "hard" line on the cold war, of which he had been so determined an exponent, no longer had much chance—that his crusade had failed. But an echo to his efforts came to him, rather unexpectedly, in a letter from President John F. Kennedy, dated June 22, 1962. The President wrote:

"Just a note to tell you that I have been aware of your activities in regard to the cold war situation including your speeches and magazine articles, and I commend you for your efforts in this area. It is always important to have those respected leaders in fields other than government speak out on our national problems. Americans—and citizens of other countries around the world—realize that they are not spoken with government self-interest, but from a patriotic citizen's most candid view. I urge you to keep up the good work and I would welcome hearing from you at any time if you have ideas that you would like to give me."

3

In the middle 1950's Sarnoff was also engaged in a campaign of persuasion closer to his own industrial terrain.

Electronics is a primary force in modern warfare. Massive research on weapons and weapons systems developed during the war, in partnership with the government, was not abandoned with the cessation of hostilities. In this enterprise RCA continued to play a leading role. Work for the Armed Forces and for NASA, the space agency, has been a growing segment of the company's business.

Sarnoff had witnessed the damage and the terror imposed on England by Hitler's V-1 and V-2 rockets. The impress on his mind and nerves was indelible. Under the deprecating name of "doodlebugs" he saw clearly the long-range monstrosities of tomorrow. He returned home convinced that missiles capable of delivering nuclear annihilation to any point of the globe from any other point were inevitable, simply a matter of time. In ten years, he said in 1945, rockets would attain speeds of five to ten thousand miles an hour.

He talked missiles to anyone who would listen—and to some who would not. The fact that the Soviets had lured or kidnaped the most important German scientists and engineers in the nuclear and electronic areas indicated that the Kremlin meant to be there first with the most in the missile race. The United States, by comparison, seemed to him scarcely aware that a life-and-death race was involved.

Long before most experts, even in the military community, seemed too worried by the looming threat, Sarnoff was therefore thinking in terms of detection of approaching missiles. Pending the development of true means of interception, the need to gain a little time for defensive action seemed to him all-important. Patent No. 2571386 issued to him in October, 1951, stands as a token of that concern. It was a blueprint for an early warning system that combined microwave relays, the best available methods of detection and direction finding, and a "fence" of airplanes equipped with the latest electronic techniques. The planes, his plan provided, would be airborne around the clock.

Our temporizing on the "ultimate missile" worried him deeply. In his *Fortune* article, as already noted, he asked for a "crash program" to provide "the longest-range guided projectiles." There was no point, he insisted, in waiting for proof that the Soviets were developing them; it might by then be too late. Some of his friends thought he was "obsessed" on the subject.

At the Forrestal Memorial Dinner in January, 1956, he cited a recent statement by the Secretary of Defense, Charles E. Wilson, that the ICBM "might be attained in five years." But this was no excuse for complacency, Sarnoff warned. By "brutal methods, supplemented by stealing information from free people," he argued, the Soviets could reduce the lead-time, even as they had done on nuclear explosives.

"It would be folly," he said, "for us to take too lightly the warning by Soviet Premier Bulganin, only a few weeks ago, that 'rocket missiles which have been developed, particularly over the past several years, are becoming intercontinental weapons.' . . . For the sake of our own security and the survival of our civilization, we dare not permit the Kremlin even a temporary monopoly of such horror weapons. . . . Not necessarily the use of these weapons but the mere *threat* of their use could serve the Soviets' purposes in the cold war they wage so relentlessly."

Certain organizational steps to speed up work on the ICBM had finally been ordered by President Eisenhower, but Sarnoff was far from mollified: "The critical factor is the *degree of acceleration* that can be brought to bear on this critical problem. The question is how quickly will the new organizational concept be translated into dynamic action at all working levels." The Manhattan Project that won the race against Germany for the atom bomb could not be duplicated for the missile race against Soviet Russia, Sarnoff agreed. The technical problems were of a different order. But "the lessons learned and the experience gained" in that project should be adapted at once to the new conditions. As an immediate step, he said, "this calls for the mobilization of men with the best brainpower, imagination, ingenuity, initiative, and drive that can be found and obtained."

Sarnoff, more and more perturbed, importuned influential friends to speak out on the issue, among them Bernard Baruch. At first the financier thought that he was being an alarmist; Sarnoff not only succeeded in converting him but induced him to talk to the President about the urgency of the matter. Then came the Soviet Sputnik and the complacency turned into panic. The consolations of Wilson's five-year timetable had been washed out in some ten months. The crash program was finally undertaken. Sarnoff's needling had been, on the surface, unavailing. Yet it had not been entirely without effect. His pressures, he had reason to believe, had been a factor in the organizational preparations and the mobilization of engineering talents that, in practice, helped this nation close the celebrated missile gap.

25

The "Public Figure"

⊘ In the early 1940's, at the request of Franklin D. Roosevelt, David Sarnoff became a member of the President's Committee on Fair Employment Practices (FEPC), set up to combat job discrimination against Negroes and other minorities.

In February, 1964, President Lyndon Johnson reached him by telephone in Hollywood, Florida, where he was spending his seventy-third birthday at the home of his brother Morris. He invited General Sarnoff to serve on a Presidential Commission on Heart Disease, Cancer and Stroke.

These assignments bracket a quarter of a century of public-service chores for every President since Roosevelt, as well as for the governors of his home state and the mayor of his home city. Congenitally unable to treat any job casually, impelled to surpass and get results, he put far more time and effort into these chores than people normally spare for such civic efforts. The assignments have been so many and diverse that only a bare listing of the more important ones follows.

Toward the end of his second term, President Truman named a Citizens' Advisory Committee on Manpower Utilization in the Armed Services and appointed Sarnoff as chairman. The Committee was directed by Congress to examine the operations of the Defense Department and recommend possible savings in men, money, and material. The following year Sarnoff was re-appointed to the post by President Eisenhower. After many months of intensive hearings and studies, General Sarnoff on February 17, 1953, presented the Committee's report. It recommended the elimination of half a million men and economies totaling $5 billion.

Shortly thereafter he served on the Rockefeller Committee on Department of Defense Organization, created by President Eisenhower. It was instructed to propose measures for improving organizational procedures in the department, in particular with respect to the Secretary's relationships with civilian and military officials. After its findings were transmitted, in April, 1953, Sarnoff was among those invited by the Senate Armed Forces Committee to testify on some aspects of the problems covered by the study.

Having observed Sarnoff's work in the European Theatre in connection with D day and its aftermath, it was natural that Eisenhower as President should turn to him for help to solve some of his pressing problems. The military reserve program had been faltering since the letdown that followed the truce in Korea. To meet this situation, the President formed a National Security Training Commission in November, 1955; he appointed Sarnoff as chairman and the appointment was unanimously confirmed by the Senate. The Commission functioned until June, 1957.

Its first task was to make proposals to Congress for the welfare of the Ready Reserve contingents undergoing six months of training. More important, in 1956 it undertook a campaign to stimulate enlistments in the Reserve. Himself a Reserve officer, General Sarnoff staged a drive with few precedents in such government projects.

In the space of a few months he sparked more than six thousand radio and television announcements and programs, estimated to be worth $2 million in air time. Dinah Shore, Perry Como, Garry Moore, Phil Silvers, Martha Raye, Ed Sullivan, and other stars were drawn in as "recruiting officers." Almost overnight the American people became Reserve-conscious, as reflected in sharply rising enlistment figures. At the end of the campaign Sarnoff turned back to the government $12,000 of the $50,000 appropriated for the Commission's work.

The Army Department conferred upon him a formal Commendation "for his services in behalf of the Reserve Forces of the Nation." The document, signed by General Maxwell D. Taylor as Chief of Staff and by the Secretary of the Army, Wilber M. Brucker, stated in part: "He has played a key role in marshalling public opinion and bringing about a better understanding of the Reserve Component program of the Army." The Commendation was followed, a month later, with an award of the Army's "Exceptional Service Medal."

In June, 1959, the Senate Committee on Appropriations brought into being a small Committee of Consultants on Medical Research, and Sarnoff was one of the few laymen in the group, the rest being physicians. The assignment of the Consultants was to appraise the scope of federal aid being provided for medical research and how the money was being used. Sarnoff took an active part in ten months of hearings and analyses. The resulting report, submitted in May, 1960, recommended larger appropriations.

On the urging of President Kennedy, Sarnoff in June, 1961, became vice-chairman of a Citizens' Committee for International Development. Its objective was to help generate public support for the Foreign Aid Program. An equivalent organization, in which Sarnoff served as a member of the board of directors, was constituted by President Johnson in February, 1965.

Sarnoff was only a rank-and-file member of the Presidential Commission on Heart Disease, Cancer and Stroke—moreover, one of the minority of laymen in a very large assemblage of medical specialists. Yet the imprint of his mind was on the final report to a degree not known to the press and the general public.

When the suggestions of its various subcommittees were collated and presented to the Commission, Sarnoff was astonished by the fact that none of them carried a "price tag." This seemed to him an almost fatal flaw. The program would be futile, he told his colleagues, unless its likely costs were set forth. Only in that way could a utopian blueprint be reduced to a fiscally manageable reality suitable for action by Congress. Despite considerable opposition, his view was finally adopted by the full Commission. After the report was made public, it was generally conceded that consideration of costs had been a decisive factor in weeding out secondary recommendations and in building a practical foundation under the program.

The simple fact is that with the passing of time Sarnoff emerged more visibly as what is called a public figure, though nobody has ever succeeded in defining the words. "The growing recognition that he is the elder statesman of the industry"—as Newsweek put the matter in December, 1951—was increasingly matched by recognition beyond the purlieus of business. In consequence he was called upon ever more frequently for services in government. This is one of the automatic rewards—and penalties—of eminence.

Actually, Sarnoff's zeal for the common weal was not excessive or obtrusive. He did not seek the many official appointments that came to him, and he declined some of them when it could be done gracefully. One of the more difficult to evade was the post of Assistant Secretary of Defense, pressed upon him by Secretary Wilson at the behest of President Eisenhower. He managed to talk his way out of it without impairing his relations with either man. But in many instances he took on work for which he had little time or appetite. Then, once he accepted a duty, his built-in diligence took over and he did a comprehensive job.

On the invitation of General George Marshall, in 1951, he acted as national chairman of the annual Red Cross fund drive. As noted at another point, he prepared an elaborate study of Civil Defense Planning for Governor Harriman in 1955; and in 1960 Governor Rockefeller drew him into the New York State Defense Council, to appraise problems of survival under nuclear attacks.

For some years Sarnoff was on the board of the Free Europe Committee. He was a trustee of the American Heritage Foundation as of 1953; elected chairman of the organization five years later, he served until 1963. On President Kennedy's invitation, he joined the Board of Trustees of an American Freedom from Hunger Foundation, the United States spearhead in a global attempt to deal with the causes of hunger and malnutrition. He was also a trustee, from 1959 to 1963, of the U.S. Commission for Refugees, concerned with the plight of displaced persons all over the world. And to descend from the lofty to the trivial, Sarnoff was even chosen "Father of the Year" for Father's Day in 1953.

Add to tasks of this order his many years as trustee or director of a remarkably varied array of organizations—some of them have been mentioned in an earlier chapter, but the list kept growing, as he was tapped by the World Rehabilitation Fund, the National Foundation for Infantile Paralysis, and his own synagogue, Temple Emanuel. Add, further, his active membership in a long list of radio, electronics, economic, journalistic, and military societies. And what we get is a portrait of the completely engaged American. The mystery is how he found slivers of time for his family and friends, and even for an occasional holiday.

2

A great radio-television organization must bend over backward to avoid suspicion of playing favorites in reporting the news. It is therefore simple prudence for its top officials to maintain a stance of political neutrality. Practical considerations aside, however, Sarnoff is not a man of intense political feeling or overmastering convictions outside his business-scientific preserves.

He is not at heart a "political animal." Except on technology, he did not develop a philosophy or fixed system of thought—the *Weltanschauung* that for some men predetermines their response to events and personalities. His running commentary on affairs has been at bottom pragmatic, guided by common sense rather than commitment to any political party or ideology. His mind, in general, is too empirical to embrace abstractions and his temper too rationalistic to tolerate fanaticism.

He cannot be tagged as a Democrat or a Republican, a "liberal" or a "conservative." On social and fundamental human issues, his natural reactions have been what are generally considered liberal. On issues of basic national economy, they have been just as naturally conservative.

He belonged to the Urban League, an organization promoting the welfare of Negroes, and he worked conscientiously, beyond the call of duty, as a member of the Committee on Fair Employment Practices. Movements for improved race relations, equal opportunities for minority groups, wider education, the curbing of bigotry, could count on his support. Our task, he said in accepting the first World Brotherhood Award from the Jewish Theological Seminary, in 1951, is to remove "the blindfolds of prejudice" so we can see that all men, "despite their differences in the color of their skin or the cast of their features or their language or religion, are of the same dust." His relations with the many trade unions represented in his industry were generally amicable, and labor leaders came to think of him as a sympathetic friend.

But this "liberalism" did not extend to latter-day tinkering with the free-enterprise system. Earlier than most industrial leaders—in 1930, for example —he urged upon business "the doctrine of social responsibility" as the best guarantee of the doctrine of free economy. Yet he has been profoundly worried by the rise of the welfare state, the growth of Big Government, and its overt intrusions on private enterprise. In time he came to regard these trends as inevitable and irreversible—but sadly, not in approval.

Whatever the question, he did not hide his opinions. Few business leaders of his stature have been as articulate as Sarnoff. For one thing, he has spent much more time in corporate and public life—he has been making speeches and writing articles for half a century. Many of his views have been quoted, in their sequential order, in the preceding pages. But the temptation to make a comprehensive analysis is defeated by the sheer bulk of his output of opinions, proposals, forecasts.

Principally these have dealt with his specialized field, whether talking to the industry or to the public. Very early in his career, as we know by now, he had adopted the role of interpreter of the thrusting forces of electronics. In time this became almost second nature. A typical Sarnoff speech was likely to combine straight exposition, some practical advice, and an estimate of coming developments.

Consider, to choose recent examples, two addresses in 1964 on computers, a term covering many varieties of data processing and other electronic "brains." The first was in July, before the National Automation Conference of the American Bankers Association, held at the New York World's Fair. In this he concentrated on "The Social Impacts of Computers."

"Over the next twenty years, I am convinced, computers will touch off an explosion in the social sciences comparable to that which we witnessed during the past half century in the physical sciences," he told the bankers. There would be a "progressive blending of computers and communications"—"a global link-up of computers accomplished through communication satellites, high-capacity transistorized cables, microwave conduits, as well as standard telephone and telegraph links." Then he described how these new tools are likely to be applied to increase leisure, accelerate education, help eradicate disease and expand the span of life. Also, "the computer will make it possible to restore a direct dialogue between the people and their political leaders, in the tradition of the Athenian assembly or a New England town meeting." The new devices would transfer voting from outside booths to the home, with immediate tabulation. It will become feasible to obtain a prompt expression of public opinion on important questions by the entire citizenry.

It is a safe guess that the assembled bankers, on returning to their offices, would look at the data-processing machines on their premises with new eyes.

Sarnoff's second talk on the same subject was made in October, in San Francisco, before a Joint Computer Conference, under the title "The Promise and Challenge of the Computer." This time he was addressing insiders, top-level technicians and industrial captains in the new electronic business. His presentation therefore covered more practical aspects.

He stressed the accelerating expansion of the field. Some $2 billion had been spent by industry and government on computer programs in the preceding year. But this was taking place, he said, in "a technological Tower of Babel." Men trained in one species of machine were not capable of functioning with any other. Because they spoke different technical languages, the electronic brains could not communicate with one another; they could not pool or exchange information. Recalling the history of television and color TV, Sarnoff showed that orderly growth could not begin until there had been industry-wide consensus on standards, symbols, vocabularies, procedures. Given this all-important basis for healthy progress, he saw for the "memory machine" a truly spectacular "tomorrow":

"Tomorrow's standard computers and their peripheral equipment will instantly recognize a handwritten note, a design or drawing which they will store and instantly retrieve in original form. The computer of the future will respond to commands from human voices in different languages and with different vocal inflections. Its vocabulary will extend to thousands of basic words in the language of its country of residence, and machines will automatically translate the speech of one country into the spoken words of another.

"The computer will become the hub of a vast network of remote data stations and information banks feeding into the machine at a transmission rate of a billion or more bits of information a second. Laser channels will vastly increase both data capacity and the speeds with which it is transmitted. Eventually, a global communications network handling voice, data, and facsimile will instantly link man to machine—or machine to machine—by land, air, underwater, and space circuits. We will see computer switchboards in space, similar to those presently in operation on the ground, routing in milliseconds any communication to and from virtually any point in the world."

And this was only his introduction to a broad panorama that held the audience enthralled. The computer, Sarnoff said, "will affect man's ways of thinking, his means of education, his relationships to his physical and social environment, and it will alter his ways of living. . . . The ultimate implication of the computer is that it provides a means of releasing the productive powers of the human brain to an almost limitless degree. Yet the computer imposes as a precondition the sternest discipline to which the mind has yet been subjected." Before the end of this century, he believed, the forces he was sketching "will coalesce into what unquestionably will become the greatest adventure of the human mind."

Those who heard him were all computer specialists, in the engineering or the business end of this new electronic field. But how many of them had ever grasped the possibilities of their own life's work in such sweeping, imaginative perspective? "I've thought of data-processing equipment as just another business," one of them said, "but when General Sarnoff got through I felt I was part of a wonderful adventure."

Another major address deserves to be summarized not alone because it is his most recent (delivered shortly before this book went to press) but because it dealt, in Sarnoff's words, "with the most dynamic element in the communications revolution."

The occasion and the setting were most impressive. Some 3,000 delegates from more than one hundred nations met in Washington for an entire week in mid-September, 1965, at a privately sponsored World Conference on Peace Through Law. Many of the world's most shining luminaries of jurisprudence, including scores of high-court judges and ministers of justice, took part. At the American end, Chief Justice Earl Warren served as honorary chairman, with former Presidents Truman and Eisenhower as his co-chairmen, and President Johnson was among the speakers.

The legal and political problems posed by communications through orbited satellites were high on the agenda, and Sarnoff was the principal speaker on the subject. By general consensus of the audience his presentation, on September 17, was a tour de force, marked once more by his special skills in delineating future developments.

As he saw it, that future was almost upon us, charged with terrific power for good or ill. Its implications must be understood and confronted at once, he declared: "The rate of change in the art of communications is so great that if we delay even five years in coming to grips with its problems, they may pass beyond our control. . . . Already the Soviet Union is operating a proto-type satellite communications system of its own."

Only a few years ago it was assumed that cost and technical complexity would prevent proliferation of the systems. But progress has been so rapid that the costs will soon be within the means of a score or more nations. At present, signals from Early Bird and other satellites have to be picked up for rebroadcast by a specially equipped ground station. This enables any country to exclude unwanted television from the skies. That margin of protection, however, will be erased when the signals can be received directly on any television or radio set—just as short-wave radio broadcasts from distant points are received today.

"Within five or ten years," Sarnoff said, "I believe that we will develop high-power broadcasting satellites capable of transmitting television and radio *directly into the home.* These would be nuclear-powered synchronized satellites radiating up to thirty kilowatts of power, sufficient to transmit simultaneously on three television and three radio channels to home receivers within an area of one million square miles. . . .

"When many nations possess the capability for transmission through space to any place on earth, they must agree to a new pattern of global regulation. Otherwise, the prospect of social and economic gains will be thwarted by the ensuing chaos in the world's airwaves. . . . When, for example, a Russian satellite can broadcast directly to a Kansas farm, or an American satellite can broadcast directly to a Hungarian collective, what will be the reaction in both countries? When we can reach the homes of the world with instantaneous sight and sound, what rules of conduct are to apply, and who is to establish them?"

In short, Sarnoff warned that unless basic controls under law are imposed—

for which the International Telecommunications Union founded exactly a century ago provides a useful precedent—direct satellite communications will become "propaganda instruments used primarily for heating up the cold war, for stimulating subversion, for promoting conflict and confusion on a world-wide scale."

Action "prior to the orbiting of the first direct broadcast satellite" is therefore the compelling need. Otherwise, "a universal instrument for communicating education and knowledge on a scale that can advance all of humanity to higher levels of understanding and improved standards of living" could become a rampaging Frankenstein. Agreement might begin in various areas where the ideological element is relatively less acute—he listed cultural and instructional programs, certain types of news events, the deliberations of the United Nations—and then be extended on that foundation.

"The adjustment of law to technology, and of technology to law, may be the enduring task of this generation," General Sarnoff concluded. "It is a challenge to our combined wisdom and leadership. We can meet it by joining all mankind in a brotherhood of sight and sound through global communications."

3

Taken together, Sarnoff's half century of speeches and papers in this vein—his blend of hard facts and creative clairvoyance—comprises a history of the electronic age. It is a history recorded not only as it happened but before it happened, and has the character of a three-dimensional motion picture.

As if viewing the landscape of events from an airplane in flight, he described the hard terrain of the present visible directly below: what was known and accomplished and in use. But he also focused his camera on the dimmer distances ahead to a far horizon and described the emerging terrain. In time, as the plane covered the intervening time-space, what were hazy, faraway shapes—short-wave telegraphy, broadcasting, television, color television—became in their turn part of the solid present. But by then new shapes loomed on the horizon to intrigue his attention.

Today those emerging realities are, for Sarnoff, as exciting as any he foresaw in the past. They include the unborn powers inherent in memory machines, new varieties of communications satellites, electroluminescence, the potentials of the laser beam, electronic diagnosis in medicine and electronic replacements for human organs, microscopy providing unprecedented magnification and telescopy piercing unprecedented distances, new reaches in

miniaturization, the unexplored frequencies above microwaves—into submilli-
meter, infrared, and light waves. Nor is this a complete inventory. As Sarnoff
often assured students majoring in science and engineering, "No youth of
today or tomorrow need sigh with Alexander for more worlds to conquer."

Quite naturally, much of his thinking revolved around science—its promises and problems, its impacts on society, its implications for morals and
faith. Though not himself a scientist, Sarnoff had a profound appreciation of
the scientific mind and vocation. "In my years of association with scientists
and engineers," he once said, "I have acquired a deep respect for their
creative faculties, their constant search for knowledge and facts, and for their
integrity of purpose. I have tried in my small way to stimulate and encourage
them in their work, to share with them their dreams and disappointments, and
to rejoice in their triumphs."

A notable Sarnoff statement on the practice of science was made in a
Commencement Address at the Drexel Institute of Technology, in Philadelphia, in June, 1953. He was awarded the degree of Doctor of Engineering.
What made his address especially significant was that he tried to convey to an
upcoming generation, the graduates, his own mature feelings about their
calling—to infect them, if he could, with his own spirit of adventure and
dedication. A few excerpts must suffice:

"Always and everywhere freedom and science flourish best in the same
climate"—he was referring to the climate of freedom—"each fortifying the
other. They draw their vitamins for healthy growth from the same political
soil. . . . Behind the Iron Curtain, truth has been outlawed. It leads a secret
and stunted existence in the underground of men's minds. But science cannot
prosper under such conditions, for it needs the invigorating sunshine of
liberty.

"The essence of science is the search for truth about the natural laws which
govern life. The principles it uncovers are then taken over by engineers who
proceed to fashion them into instrumentalities for mankind to enrich our
everyday life. This, basically, is the task that will be assigned to you who are
graduating today in engineering."

He did not make light of economic motivations; a man must make a living.
But these were not enough:

"For some it will remain merely a trade, like any other trade. But for
others, the more imaginative and courageous, it can be a noble and satisfying
dedication. They will face the challenge and the opportunities of engineering
with the same proud sense of fulfilling a vital public function that the best
men feel in the fields of medicine, or law, or the arts. They will assume its

responsibilities in a spirit of mission, in the awareness that they are starting out upon a great adventure.

"It is this difference of approach, believe me, that will determine for each of you whether engineering will be just a treadmill—or a fascinating highway to knowledge and achievement. In this, even more than in other areas of effort, the more you put into it—in terms of work and devotion—the more you will get out of it. . . . This consciousness of worlds to conquer, it seems to me, is as important a part of your equipment as the things you have already learned from books and laboratories. Both the electron and the atom, as tools of mankind, are young like yourselves. Whether they will be developed beneficently for life, or channeled largely for destruction and death, will depend primarily upon your generation."

Science, he went on to emphasize, "is not an end in itself but only the means to an end." It "is meaningless except as an instrument of human decency and human happiness":

"The scientist, however, must not paralyze his capacity for good by brooding on his capacity for evil. The fact that science has sometimes been diverted for the purposes of war is not a reflection on science but on man. . . . You will be the men who pull the levers and push the buttons and harness the forces in the whole process. You have every right to enter upon your dedication with a sense of pride, tempered by a sense of responsibility."

Variations on this theme show up whenever one reads a Sarnoff speech or article addressed to younger people and their teachers. "Whatever course you have chosen for yourself," he told another class, "it will not be a chore but an adventure if you bring to it a sense of the glory of striving—if your sights are set far above the merely secure and mediocre. In one's personal life, as in world affairs, appeasement can be the shortest road to failure."

On another academic occasion he declared:

"In recent years, there has been such obsessive emphasis on security, that I fear it has obscured older and more real values. Some young people have adopted Ferdinand the Bull, smelling flowers from dawn to dusk, as the symbol of the good life. I have been disappointed, at times, to find boys in their twenties, or even in their teens, worrying about pensions and old-age security when they will have reached sixty-five. There seems to me something unhealthy where youth is so lacking in confidence. Maybe we have to relearn the meaning of ambition and of struggle. When has anything worthwhile been attained except by overcoming obstacles? And the thrill, believe me, is as much in the battle as in the victory."

He frequently underlined the need to encourage—and to back financially—

"basic research" as distinct from "applied research." He saw danger in the fact that "practice tended to get priority over theory." Scientific works, he said, should be judged "by what they added to the treasure-house of knowledge and understanding," and not simply "by what they added to industry and everyday life." In the summer of 1952, during his one visit to Israel, the Weizmann Institute of Science conferred upon him its first Honorary Fellowship. In his address of acceptance he commended the institution for its support of pure science. It seemed to him vital, he said, "that we cultivate 'science appreciation' much as we do 'music appreciation' "—for its intrinsic worth rather than its immediate utility.

The Soviet Sputnik, it will be recalled, alarmed and alerted the country on the shortcomings of technical education in the United States. There was talk of a lack of inspiring teachers and a consequent reluctance by bright students to prepare for careers in science and related fields. Sarnoff not only shared these apprehensions but his mind reached out for practical remedies. Nearly two years before the advent of the Sputnik, he had proposed "the establishment of a National Educational Reserve made up of qualified teachers of mathematics and the sciences drawn from the ranks of industry." In January, 1958, some months after the Russians had administered the shock, he revived the idea in testifying before a subcommittee of the U.S. Senate Committee on Armed Forces.

"I propose," he said, "that industrial concerns release—with full pay for at least one year—a reasonable number of men and women for teaching assignments in nearby high schools. It is obviously impractical for any one company, or even a small group of companies, to carry out this plan. If it is to realize its full potential, it must have national sponsorship and a large number of companies behind it. It must also have the backing of state education authorities who would have to certify members of this Reserve to teach in their schools."

Although neither the Senate nor industry responded to the call, he persisted in propagating the idea for years. Finally, to test it, he set up a very small pilot project under a very large title: the Industry-Science Teaching Program. In 1962, with the cooperation of the New York school authorities, RCA assigned fifteen outstanding engineers and researchers from its own ranks to lecture to science classes in four Brooklyn high schools.

Announcement of the teaching project brought Sarnoff a cordial letter of encouragement from President Kennedy. "I want to congratulate you on the idea," the President wrote him on October 19, 1962, "and offer my best wishes for its success. . . . I would hope that other industries follow your pilot program and, benefitting from its experience, voluntarily do likewise in their own local areas."

At the end of the first year school officials who had been evaluating the effort declared that it had been highly successful. Direct contact with "real" scientists, it was established, had raised the pupils' interest in a scientific and engineering career. During the second year Bell Laboratories, International Business Machines, U.S. Steel, Pfizer Pharmaceutical, and a number of other companies joined the experiment. The project is still under way. There has been a good deal of favorable publicity but so far the undertaking has not attained dimensions to make a real dent on the national problem. But Sarnoff remains hopeful and, as always when under the spell of a new idea, continues to advocate it.

"There are more than 1,350,000 physical scientists and engineers in the United States," he explained to a large gathering in June, 1964. "If only 5 percent of them would devote a fraction of each year to education, our high school students would have direct access to nearly seventy thousand of the finest technical brains available anywhere."

Notwithstanding this concern for attracting more young people to the scientific disciplines, Sarnoff did not underrate the humanities. Our tasks were different from Moscow's, he said, reflecting the contrasts in our over-all philosophies. "Soviet schooling," he declared in December, 1958, at a dinner given by Brandeis University, "is not concerned with the happiness and preferences and creative drives of the individual man or woman, but solely with fortifying the might of a faceless state."

Certainly we must provide ever larger and more competent specialists for the needs of this technological era, he went on. "But we would be killing the goose that laid the golden eggs of our civilization if, in the preoccupation with material progress and power, our institutions of learning retreated from the humanities and all they connote. . . . Our rapid conquest of outer space will be an empty victory if it leads to neglect of inner space—of man himself, his gifts for contemplation, his passion for freedom and justice, and his hunger for salvation."

4

"Salvation" is a telltale word in any attempt, however cursory, to sum up David Sarnoff's public pronouncements. The metaphysical import seems, at first blush, out of place in a man concerned with the forces and hardware of physics. But Sarnoff saw no contradiction. He denied repeatedly that science and morality, science and soul-searching, are somehow in conflict.

"Let us not lose the sense of the awe and mystery of life," he said. "The claim that there is an inherent conflict between science and our immortal souls—that science is the natural enemy of the soul—does not stand up under examination. The man in an airplane is not necessarily less devoted to truth, justice, and charity than his forefathers in an oxcart. Virtue does not necessarily go along with primitive plumbing, and human dignity can be nurtured in a skyscraper no less than in a log cabin."

The ethical precepts implanted in his earliest years, inherent in his whole background, pervaded his thinking. Running through many of his public utterances there has been an awareness of spiritual dimensions and moral absolutes beyond the compass of intellect; an awareness of the infinitude of the unexplained and unexplainable, of the great mysteries of the universe and man's place in it.

We have already heard him assert, at his Golden Anniversary in 1956, that "a hunger for faith and salvation, for age-old values beyond the material and the temporal, gnaws at the mind and spirit of man." Science, he added, tends to deflate man's pretensions of omniscience, for "its every victory reveals more clearly a Divine design in nature, a remarkable conformity of all things, from the infinitesimal to the infinite, that surpasses mortal understanding."

"In studying the lives of scientists," he once explained, "we find that their love of nature was generally linked with a devout spirit. Everywhere in science, whether in electronics or aerodynamics, in chemistry or physics, scientists throughout the ages have beheld the handiwork of the Supreme Architect of the Universe.

"Hans Christian Oersted, the Danish scientist who liberated a mighty force in discovering the relations between electricity and magnetism, exclaimed: 'The Universe is a manifestation of an infinite reason, and the laws of Nature are the thoughts of God.' Faraday, the Columbus of the Electrical Age, watched the sunsets as one of his favorite pastimes, and one day as a rainbow arched the sky he said: 'He hath set His testimony in the heavens.' " Sarnoff never forgot Marconi's statement that science can tell us *what* happens but not *why* it happens. His rationalist disposition did not rule out a Force or Supreme Intelligence beyond the grasp of mortal reason. There is, in short, a strong strain of the spiritual—or, more precisely, the ethical—in his makeup. In a public address in New York in November, 1959, he said at one point:

"Because more and more of the chores of living are turned over to machines, there is danger that thinking and feeling may also be mechanized and standardized, which is to say dehumanized. We may forget that there can be no electronic computers for setting standards of human probity, for measuring the great inherited truths, for differentiating between Good and Evil—that there can be no mechanical substitutes for conscience and compassion."

To guard against these dangers, he urged that education—not only in schools but in the homes and in houses of worship—take "indispensable measures of defense." One of these was "to cultivate man's appreciation of his own importance and uniqueness as a child of God." The vastness of the space being opened up by science seems to dwarf man, but "the center of the universe remains man himself." Another was "to help our children, in this time of great flux in human affairs, to find fixed points of faith and confidence." They should be taught "the fundamental truth that under the turbulence of change there is a bedrock of unchanging values. . . . The things that we most cherish—or at any rate that we *should* most cherish—cannot be displaced by machines. Freedom and justice, love and conscience, are not subject to automation."

It would be misleading, however, if the reader supposed that Sarnoff's speeches were constantly, or even often, pitched on these rarefied heights. For the most part he dealt with mundane affairs, with topical problems in the news, with the surge of electronic progress. And whatever the subject, he related it always to the business or scientific facts to which he wished to draw attention—he was tending to his knitting.

Outside the special areas of his interests and direct experience, his opinions on the whole have been temperate and even conventional. He might give them a higher gloss by his powers of imagination and diction, but they never offended, let alone scandalized, public opinion. His natural disposition was against "extremism," and he did not knowingly trespass beyond the boundaries of prudence. Even his crusade against communism was substantially in line with grass-roots American sentiment. The moral values he preached on occasion were, after all, of the copybook variety—what other varieties are there? And he never for a moment forgot his obligations of leadership: to stockholders, to his company, to the industry.

26

In the Eighth Decade

➛ According to the *New York Times* dispatch from Washington, dated August 30, 1961, several participants "said they could not recall an occasion when so many legislators had come together to honor a private citizen." There were, in fact, more than thirty senators at the luncheon, and Vice-President Johnson dropped in for a while. The private citizen was David Sarnoff and the occasion was the fifty-fifth anniversary of his association with communications and electronics.

This was a new twist in the observances of that odd "birthday"—the hiring of an office boy in 1906—celebrated at five-year intervals. Because Congress was preparing to adjourn, the ceremony was staged a month sooner, and because of an unexpected live roll call in the Upper House, the festivities were a bit hurried.

Senator George D. Aiken of Vermont, in introducing the guest of honor, recalled that twenty-one years before he had been at the World's Fair in New York when "something new" was demonstrated—something "called television." What he remembered best was "that the receiving set was upstairs and the transmitting equipment downstairs, with a floor between us. That seemed a whale of a distance in those days to transmit a picture." He was now proud, therefore, to greet "the man responsible for that promising innovation." He would not go into Sarnoff's background, the senator said, because it "is known not only to everybody here but all over the world." But, he added, "I do want to call attention to one thing. He was first educated in a public school, but thereafter he attended the Sarnoff school—the best in the world, scientifically speaking."

348

Obviously moved by the warmth and the unique nature of the gathering on Capitol Hill, General Sarnoff made an extemporaneous response. It amounted to a frank accounting of his debt to the adopted fatherland.

"There are times in one's life when the tongue is a little dry and the mind a little overwhelmed," he said. "In the language of my profession, that makes for a poor transmitter—and that describes this moment. However, I am comforted by the knowledge that your receivers are unimpaired and in good tune. Therefore I would like, Mr. Chairman, to transmit for a few minutes on the frequency that originates in the heart, without interference from that of the mind."

What he chose to transmit were high moments in the sixty-one-year odyssey that began in an immigrant ship in 1900. In his extensive travels through the world thereafter, he said, a number of trips stood out in his memory. He recalled his second crossing of the Atlantic, only seven years after the first, as the Marconi wireless operator on a passenger ship; and another in 1929, with the American Reparations Commission, when his traveling companions included Owen D. Young, J. P. Morgan, Thomas Lamont, and Nelson Perkins.

"The impressive and human part of that trip to me," he explained, "was not only the companionship of these important men, who were much older and wiser than I, but the fact that I was a member of that group, and that we were met at Cherbourg by high officials of the French government. . . . I shall never forget the moment, during this third trip, when I stood on the deck of the tender, reflecting on this novel experience. The picture that flashed through my mind then was my first crossing of the Atlantic in the steerage. I thought of the contrast between the two crossings—and the fact that this could happen only in America. For it is as true today as it was then that no other country in the world provides such vast opportunities to develop and to express whatever talents an individual may possess.

"On that occasion, I remember saying to myself, 'God bless America.' Surely I am no exception, for there are many, many others in the United States who have also developed, advanced, and prospered. I have tried to convey this message to the rising generation of Americans and to point out to them that in my view there are more opportunities in our country today than there were when I arrived in New York in 1900. There are more people in the world, more wants to satisfy, and more resources and tools to employ than there were then."

Sarnoff then addressed himself to what was symbolically the crowning trip "that has occurred only today":

"From New York I have come to the capital of this nation to be received and honored by the distinguished members of the United States Senate—the greatest deliberative body in the world. I am not sure that any man deserves so great an honor as you are bestowing upon me, but I do want to express to you how deeply moved and profoundly grateful I am for the friendship you have shown me, for this handsome tribute and this wonderful reception."

To complete the ceremony, Senator Aiken read and presented a formal citation: *"Fifty-Fifth Anniversary Testimonial to David Sarnoff,* in commemoration of his dedicated services and outstanding contributions to the advancement of communications and electronics in the United States of America." Inscribed on a beautifully illuminated scroll, it was signed by the Vice-President and thirty-five senators.

In the afternoon the two senators from his own state and three from other states eulogized him on the floor of the Senate. Senator Jacob Javits guessed that the word "sarnoff," lower case, would one day be added to the dictionary, to signify the qualities he personified. "The ambition of many young men," he said, "will be to grow up to be a 'sarnoff,' " and therefore he saluted the original and "foremost 'sarnoff' in the world."

As Sarnoff, hale and hearty, crossed the biblical line of three-score-ten, requests for his appearance at public-service and educational functions in all parts of the country continued to increase. They grew not only more numerous but more insistent. However sincere the impulse to hand him yet another diploma or medal, it was usually heightened, we may surmise, by the knowledge that his name would draw a bigger audience. He had become "good box office." A few of the invitations he accepted, the great majority he rejected.

One of those he accepted was from Yeshiva University, which had designated him as the first recipient of its newly established Distinguished Science Award. The Wardorf-Astoria ballroom was jampacked for the gala dinner. Among the notables flanking Sarnoff on the dais was Commander Scott Carpenter, the astronaut. The peak event of the evening was a memorable experience of all those in attendance: on a large screen they saw and heard the President of the United States, filmed in the White House for this occasion.

"I am delighted to be able in this way to join you in the tribute to my friend General Sarnoff," Mr. Johnson began.

"It has been said that the greatest use of a lifetime is to spend it on something that outlasts it. By that standard, General Sarnoff has already more than earned the award that you present to him tonight. Few people have contributed more to our beloved America. He is responsible for major expansions on the horizons of knowledge. He has brought the benefits of science and technology to all the people. He has devoted himself with a singleness of purpose to the advancement of scientific thought and the advancement of scientific talent to national problems.

"No one better illustrates the genius of America. His life, from immigrant boy to industrial statesman, is an inspiring record. The establishment of a new science center for Yeshiva University is a fitting occasion for the presentation of the Distinguished Science Award to General Sarnoff. . . .

"I understand that Scott Carpenter is with you this evening. On this, the second anniversary of Scott's flight, it is particularly appropriate, I think, that General Sarnoff be honored for refusing to be bound by existing frontiers of science, that a new science center be established to enlarge our scientific resources, and that we be rededicated to the principles of courage in scientific inquiry represented by Scott Carpenter's flight two years ago and General Sarnoff's record of a lifetime.

"As a holder of a degree from Yeshiva, it gives me great pride and satisfaction to participate in this tribute to my old and dear friend David Sarnoff."

Nine months later, on March 1, 1965, it was the turn of the American Legion to pay tribute, in the words of the Citation cast in bronze, to "the achievement of one of its most illustrious members." The Legion, assembled in Washington for its annual Conference, had selected Sarnoff to receive its National Commander's Award. It was bestowed, the plaque specified, "in recognition of nearly sixty years of creative service to the electronic communications industry which has served America's military and civilian needs so well in times of war and peace." The current National Commander, Donald E. Johnson, in introducing the recipient of his award, allowed himself a spice of levity: "We recognize the genius of a man who, perhaps as much as any living individual, has helped to convince the world that radio and television are here to stay."

Sarnoff not only confirmed that they were here to stay but proceeded, in his characteristic style, to show that they were merely precursors of ever-greater wonders to come. Within a decade or so, he promised, the audience of television will be global and "may run to a billion." By that time "we will see several operational satellite systems in space—performing distinct functions of communications, sensing, and surveillance. Equipped with their own special computers and message switchboard, and linked to computers on the ground, they will bring into instant reach any information that is available on earth and in space beyond—by sight, sound, or facsimile."

Referring to his long years of association with electronics, he told the Legionnaires: "The principal lesson these years have taught me is that the power to communicate is the power to lead. The nation which achieves the greatest mastery of this power is equipped for leadership in many other areas of national and international endeavor."

Clearly Sarnoff's faith in science and his consciousness of its awesome powers had not been eroded by the passage of time.

2

In 1966 there will presumably be a commemoration of the sixtieth anniversary. But the object of these tributes is no longer as impressed as he used to be; he may be, one suspects, a bit bored by the stock phrases and sentiments and the sound of his own voice over a microphone. What can prefabricated "occasions" add to his stature? Already, at seventy-five, he stands tall on the national scene.

The company that is his main handiwork holds acknowledged world primacy in its field. The normal competitive pressures upon him are immense, of course, and significant projects are under way in the David Sarnoff Research Center. For the first time in his long career, however, he is not embroiled in an all-absorbing industry "war." There is, at long last, surcease from struggle. If it were in his nature to do so, he could rest cozily on his laurels.

In September, 1965, he proposed to the board of directors a realignment of RCA management which, in theory at least, should lighten his load of responsibilities. Effective on January 1, 1966, Dr. Engstrom became chief executive officer and chairman of the executive committee and thus occupied the top executive spot. Robert W. Sarnoff, the General's son, in line with Dr. Engstrom's recommendation, succeeded him as president of RCA. At NBC, the younger Sarnoff's place as board chairman was taken over by its president, Robert E. Kintner. While relinquishing the duties of chief executive, David Sarnoff continued to serve as an active chairman of the board, under a five-year contract, that is to say, until he would be eighty. However titles may be reshuffled, whatever the intention in theory, it is a safe guess that the elder Sarnoff's influence will be strong.

Bob Sarnoff's promotion to the presidency had been generally foreseen within the company and in the industry. If there is any lingering prejudice against a son succeeding his father, it was not manifest either in the press comments or in the heavy and favorable mail drawn by the announcement. As for the General, he did not conceal a father's natural gratification that his own son will carry on his life's work—and that the son has what it takes to do it.

The plain fact is that in a decade at the helm of NBC the younger man acquitted himself brilliantly. "Under Robert Sarnoff's direction," said Dr. Engstrom in proposing his nomination before the board, "NBC enjoyed its most successful years in terms of service, prestige, and profits. He demonstrated at NBC, as well as in many important assignments for RCA, those qualities of business and administrative judgment and leadership that make him thoroughly qualified to administer the operations of RCA."

The measure of the elder Sarnoff's success as an industrialist and business executive is, in the final analysis, in the statistics of growth of his company.

In 1920, its first full year of operations, total RCA business volume was $2 million, on which no profits were earned and no taxes were paid. The corporation employed 457 persons and its total assets amounted to $25 million. For the first seventeen years of its existence the earnings were not paid out in dividends but plowed back into research, development, and expansion. Thereafter dividends were declared every year, with increases as earnings warranted.

In 1964 Sarnoff could declare that "sustained profit momentum places the RCA on the firmest footing since its founding forty-five years ago." In 1965 RCA business volume for the first time reached the $2 billion annual level. Operating profits after taxes were approximately $100 million, an all-time record for the corporation. The company's employees totaled 100,000 and its assets were appraised at more than $1.1 billion. RCA shareholders reached a new high of 248,000. The total cash dividends declared on common stock exceeded $40 million.

Many of Sarnoff's technological prophecies have yet to be fulfilled. But the most important predictions, those that he backed with millions, have all come true. Without exception, the spectacular gambles on which he staked all have paid off munificently, for his own company, the industry, and the country at large. Though their contributions have been of quite different character, it would be as impossible to write a history of electronics without featuring Sarnoff as it would be to write a history of the electrical industry without featuring Edison.

Most important for a man of his dynamic temperament, he continues to be thoroughly engaged in all the newest manifestations of electronic magic. RCA has a hand in virtually every space project going or planned. Space vehicles designed and built by his company—a flock of the weather-monitoring Tiros, the Relay I and Relay II communications satellites—are orbiting the earth. The television systems which provided thousands of close-up photographs of the moon in the several Ranger shots in 1965 were of RCA manufacture, and RCA provided the cameras for the Nimbus satellite.

Against this background of achievement it seems carping to ask the question posed in the introductory chapter: Is David Sarnoff, in the simplest dollars-and-cents meaning of the words, a great businessman? Yet it has long been asked and argued. Those who took the negative conceded the boldness of his vision and his steady nerves in following through on it. At bottom their doubts were related to the defects of these very virtues. His mind and heart, they said, are oriented to creative "leaps," rather than the humdrum marketplace. Was a potential service needed, was its development an obligation of leadership—these have been his instinctive criteria in making the great decisions.

"I don't mean that the General is not interested in the profit element," a friendly critic told me. "His theory is simply that if a thing is needed, it must eventually pay off."

The fact that Sarnoff's thinking was geared to the future has not always been reassuring to investors. The hope, even the certainty, of profits five or ten years hence seemed to them cold solace. Critics went along with his dictum that "the high cost of trail-blazing is the price of leadership," but wished aloud that he would let others blaze a few of the costlier trails. A journalistic analysis in 1951 labeled "Sarnoff's lack of interest in some of the commercial aspects of radio" as "his major weakness." This, it said, "may account for the fact the RCA's brilliant record in research and financing has not been equaled by its sales record—until recently."

In leafing through a batch of Wall Street analyses of RCA for the guidance of investors, in the final months of 1964, I found repeated references to that "high cost of trail-blazing." The financial experts were uniformly optimistic, but mainly on the ground that the company was *not* just then opening any new trails. Sarnoff had magnificent courage, they said in chorus, but fortunately for the investor he was *not* applying it just then! However, RCA earnings of 62 cents a share in 1961 increased to approximately $1.70 in 1965—thanks to commercial translation of products yielded by his previous expenditures on research and development.

The company, one brokerage house declared, has been "a long-suffering victim of its own creative ingenuity," but "finally is profiting handsomely in its role as a leading technological innovator." Another recommended purchase of RCA securities on the ground that "there are no major pioneering programs on the horizon to penalize profits."

The General himself has always scoffed at such views. Of the thousands of RCA products and services, he retorted in one instance, about 80 percent did not exist at the war's end. They had been made possible by research. Network broadcasting, which he initiated, has been all-important in keeping the RCA balance sheet in the black. Television and then its acquisition of color, though slow in yielding financial returns, have become the most lucrative activities. Admittedly there are companies with comparable resources which make a lot more money, but the explanation for this he finds in the nature of their respective businesses, not in the relative competence of their management.

He emphatically entertains no doubts of his own business acumen. In the most trying formative period, which included many years when his authority was limited, Sarnoff maneuvered the steady expansion and diversification of RCA business by trading his confidence in the future for the companies, plants, and rights called for by his ambitious blueprint for growth. He met the additional cash requirements for the expanding program through long-term borrowing from insurance companies at favorable rates of interest and a sale of debentures in 1955. Except for this debenture issue, the securities reached the market indirectly, through distribution by General Electric, Westinghouse, Victor Talking Machine, and others. RCA equities were the medium of exchange he employed in bargaining for what he wanted, with the potential growth of the company, in the final analysis, as the main collateral.

He was able to inform the FCC under oath in 1939 that "no single stockholder, whether an individual, a corporation or a financial institution, owns more than one-half of one percent of RCA stock." This guaranteed the kind of independence from outside controls—and the kind of managerial power for the chief executive—rarely enjoyed by a publicly owned corporation.

True, the company paid no dividends until 1937, eighteen years after its birth. Never since then, however, has it been obliged to skip a dividend or experienced a deficit year. It was his strategy to plow earnings back into growth: a strategy dictated by the character of the business and fully justified by time. This is the other side of the debate, the side that regards Sarnoff's business abilities as a match for his other transcendent talents.

Can pioneering and money-making be combined? Sarnoff not only believed that they could but that a pace-setting organization in a brand-new field had no real alternative. He remains convinced, as are most historians of electronics, that had he skimped on development—waiting for others to introduce network broadcasting, television, color and other services—the Radio Corporation would have shrunk to a minor company.

3

A documentary on the Sarnoff story prepared by *Life,* in slidefilms and text, was presented in September, 1955, at a dinner of the Hundred Year Association of New York. It referred to him as "the incarnation of the

American Dream." His name, it said, "is synonymous with the extraordinary advances in communications which bring the whole world within hearing and seeing distance of Twentieth Century man."

In the intervening decade this verdict has been powerfully reinforced. Today it is all but unanimous. If we limit ourselves to externals, to the visible and computable facts of his career, we may affirm with certainty that David Sarnoff has attained and surpassed his hopes and ambitions. Every radio and television in the land, by its mere existence, blares forth his fame. His career is integral with the great science explosion of our century. Few of his contemporaries have been as fulsomely admired, applauded, rewarded.

In his seventy-fifth year, Sarnoff's manner is brisk and his energies seem unimpaired. Having weathered his one dangerous illness several years ago—a gall-bladder operation in the nick of time—he appears in good health, although he remains under orders to resist the seductions of a robust appetite. His mental powers seem at their peak, his relish for work as keen as ever. He and Lizette take pride in their sons and daughters-in-law and delight in their eight grandchildren. Mrs. Sarnoff continues to be busy with hospital work; in June, 1965, Mundelein College awarded her an honorary degree of Doctor of Humane Letters in recognition of her welfare services. But in recent years she has given more and more time to sculpture, a hobby she took on late in life and in which she has developed astonishing skill.

Sarnoff, a journalist once wrote, has "a well-developed sense of destiny." The truth is that he has never quite got over the wonder and the drama of his own transformation. Now and then he stands back and looks, with as much detachment as he can, at his own life. He looks at it through the eyes of a scared little boy in the slums, or of a fifteen-year-old sacrificing sleep to practice the Morse Code. And he finds the spectacle quite as phenomenal, as great a strain on credulity, as so many others do.

Self-denigration assuredly is not in his nature. Nevertheless, he attributes much of his success to plain luck. The luck, as he has often said, of having been brought to America when he was young enough to take full advantage of its freedoms and opportunities. The luck of having found a foothold in an industry as young as himself. The luck, too, of having been afforded so much time to work out his destiny.

In any assessment of his qualities, Sarnoff's overflowing vitality rates high. Always he worked harder and longer, yet returned to his work more refreshed, than anyone around him. Even today he probably reads and digests more technical papers and assorted reports pertinent to his trade than any other person in his organization. Whatever the problem or the negotiation, he has come to it with more detailed knowledge of the facts.

That vitality is manifest not alone in physical energy but in enthusiasm, in a genuine involvement in the problem at hand that transmutes a mere job into a challenge. Within his personal electromagnetic field, according to those who have felt its vibrations, the seemingly routine and humdrum somehow begins to glow with excitement. "Part of it," one of them said to me, "is his will to win. Even in small things, D. S. starts by ruling out defeat."

Sustaining his other gifts there is plain competence in many directions. Lawyers, not only on his own but on the opposing side of confrontations, have said repeatedly that he would have made an outstanding lawyer. One of the country's leading electronic scientists once explained, as I have recorded earlier, that "a great scientist was lost in Sarnoff." *Time* called him "one of the most imaginative strategists of the cold war." General Harbord, who knew both war and Sarnoff at close quarters, declared that "Sarnoff would have made a damn good strategist on the battlefield. He's at his best when the roadway seems beset by entanglements."

Every chief executive, from a President of the United States down, is given personal credit for the accomplishments of his subordinates and, by the same token, must assume personal blame for blunders and failures not of his own making. Sarnoff is no exception. Without doubt he has been extolled for achievements by his scientists and other associates, as he has himself frequently pointed out; but the score is balanced by responsibility he has shouldered for mistakes and bad breaks beyond his personal control. What matters, in the sum-total, is that his leadership, intelligence, and imagination have been decisive in producing the final score.

The late Elmer E. Bucher was close to Sarnoff from the earliest Marconi Company days. He devoted the last two decades of his life to writing a documented history of the Radio Corporation that runs to fifty-six manuscript volumes. In the last of these he wrote of Sarnoff:

"It fell to his lot to shape the very course of electronic progress in the United States, to chart new paths for its growth, to develop communications services—in a word, to make plain wireless telegraphy only a footstep to increased communications and services. . . . He did more to elevate space radio to the status of a powerful industry than any other individual in the world."

This is the summary estimate, true, of a man whose admiration of Sarnoff amounted to hero worship. But Bucher also had a strong allegiance to historical truth, and he knew the science and business of electronics in all their dimensions from the inside. In the light of what the reader now knows—after all allowances are made for error and mythology, Bucher's judgment seems fundamentally justified. In an incredibly intricate, rapidly changing industry, David Sarnoff assumed and fulfilled the self-imposed obligations of clarifying events and trends; of separating the enduring from the ephemeral, and setting the course for further development.

In speaking to young people, as he has done so often, Sarnoff has been too sensible to offer his own career as an inspiration to new generations. It has been implicit, however, in his consistent calls to self-reliance and valor, in his assurances that there is no lack of stirring opportunities for the able and the ambitious, and above all, in his ability to translate career into the language of adventure. These were not theories but a distillation of his own experience, exemplified in his own struggles and triumphs. Sarnoff's lifelong awareness of frontiers and horizons to be pushed forward usually came through to youthful listeners, and so did the cleavage he saw so clearly between the drudge and the creator.

Nowadays success stories are no longer in vogue, regarded condescendingly at best. Ambition and diligence are old-fashioned, "square." Security is something legislated, not achieved. Precisely now, therefore, the saga of David Sarnoff, more underprivileged and handicapped than any Horatio Alger boy, seems a wholesome and useful object of attention. His life's story, one hopes, will long stand as an inspiration to young Americans.

It is appropriate, I think, to close this biography with his own words. I have chosen to quote what follows because his origins do invest the man's life with special significance. One June 28, 1956, General Sarnoff spoke from the steps of the Statue of Liberty in New York harbor in an observance of National Unity Day under the aegis of the American Museum of Immigration. He said in part:

"No American can stand at the feet of the Goddess of Liberty without a surge of patriotic emotion. The Beautiful Lady, as she has often been called, sums up so much of our nation's history and destiny. More than any other physical object on earth, this Statue has become for all mankind a symbol of freedom and promise, justice and compassion. These are the American ideals. And today, when a fateful contest is under way between liberty and slavery, they are more important and more binding than ever before. . . .

"Those who, like myself, are themselves immigrants or the first offspring of immigrants should realize at last that their immigrant forebears not only *took* something from America but *gave* something to America. . . . They brought with them the hungers for human freedom, individual dignity and self-improvement that are at the heart of the American Dream. . . .

"America is less an amalgam than an integrated mosaic. Yet again and again, in time of danger or crises, we have demonstrated a unity that has amazed the world. Enemies who have counted on divisive influences because of our history of mass immigration have always been disappointed.

"The temptation in proving that the immigrant has served America well is to cite celebrated names and spectacular careers. But I prefer to cite humble names by the million:

"Recently I paused before a war memorial in a small town in Westchester County. I glanced down the list of its sons who died in two world wars. The names in the roster were Anglo-Saxon and Latin, Slavic and Jewish, Scandinavian and Oriental. Yet all were true Americans! The same amazing unity and allegiance are revealed on the Rolls of Honor in every city, town, and hamlet of our beloved America. Each of these memorials is a portrait in miniature of this nation of immigrants, welded by common loyalty to high ideals to make and preserve a mighty country."

INDEX

ᔰ

Date Due